ASCENT®
CENTER FOR TECHNICAL KNOWLEDGE

Autodesk® Civil 3D® 2025
Beyond the Basics
for General Civil Design

Learning Guide

Imperial Units - Edition 1.0

ASCENT - Center for Technical Knowledge®
Autodesk® Civil 3D® 2025
Beyond the Basics for General Civil Design
Imperial Units - Edition 1.0

Prepared and produced by:

ASCENT Center for Technical Knowledge
630 Peter Jefferson Parkway, Suite 175
Charlottesville, VA 22911

866-527-2368
www.ASCENTed.com

Lead Contributor: Jeff Morris

ASCENT - Center for Technical Knowledge (a division of Rand Worldwide Inc.) is a leading developer of professional learning materials and knowledge products for engineering software applications. ASCENT specializes in designing targeted content that facilitates application-based learning with hands-on software experience. For over 25 years, ASCENT has helped users become more productive through tailored custom learning solutions.

We welcome any comments you may have regarding this guide, or any of our products. To contact us please email: feedback@ASCENTed.com.

AS-C3D2501-BTB1IM-SG   //   IS-C3D2501-BTB1IM-SG

Contents

Preface

The *Autodesk® Civil 3D® 2025: Beyond the Basics for General Civil Design* guide is designed for civil engineering professionals who want to continue exploring the Autodesk Civil 3D software's interactive, dynamic design functionality. It continues on from the topics covered in the *Autodesk Civil 3D 2025: Essentials* guide and includes more sophisticated techniques that extend your mastery of the software. This guide covers configuring the software, Civil 3D's styles and settings, alternative ways to create surfaces, and creating parcels. It also goes beyond the basics for more advanced corridor and pipe network design. Finally, it covers customizing sheet set properties, performing quantity takeoffs, and visualization.

Topics Covered

- Create a Civil 3D template drawing.

- Create and manage styles and label styles.

- Create data shortcuts.

- Create and edit parcels and print parcel reports.

- Create, edit, view, and analyze surfaces.

- Create assemblies, corridors, and roundabouts.

- Add appurtenances to pressure pipe networks.

- Customize sheet set properties.

- Perform quantity takeoff and volume calculations.

* For professionals looking to learn only the survey functionality, consider the *Civil 3D Essentials for Surveyors* guide.

Prerequisites

- Access to the 2025.0 version of the software, to ensure compatibility with this guide. Future software updates that are released by Autodesk may include changes that are not reflected in this guide. The practices and files included with this guide might not be compatible with prior versions (e.g., 2024).

- Knowledge of Civil 3D basics as taught in *Autodesk Civil 3D: Essentials*, or equivalent experience.

- Experience with AutoCAD® or AutoCAD-based products and a sound understanding and knowledge of civil engineering terminology.

Note on Learning Guide Content

ASCENT's learning guides are intended to teach the technical aspects of using the software and do not focus on professional design principles and standards. The practices aim to demonstrate the capabilities and flexibility of the software rather than following specific design codes or standards.

Note on Software Setup

This guide assumes a standard installation of the software using the default preferences during installation. Lectures and practices use the standard software templates and default options for the Content Libraries.

Configuration Changes

The following configuration changes need to be made to ensure the practices run smoothly. For more information on making these configuration changes, consult the Civil 3D help documentation.

- Set the *Template* file location to **C:\Civil 3D Beyond\Ascent-Config**, as shown below.

- Set the *Pipe Catalog* location to ***C:\Civil 3D Beyond\Ascent-Config\Pipes Catalog***, as shown below.

- Set the *Pressure Pipe Catalog* location to ***C:\Civil 3D Beyond\ Ascent-Config\Pressure Pipes Catalog\Imperial***, as shown below.

Set the Survey Settings

Importing survey user settings will have no effect on a drawing template. You import the survey user settings now to establish the path to where the Figure Prefix Database resides.

1. In *TOOLSPACE*, select the *Survey* tab. Click ![icon] (Survey User Settings), as shown below.

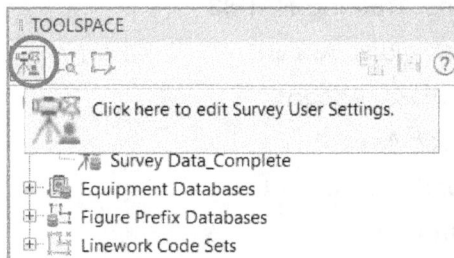

2. Click ![icon] (Import User Settings), as shown below.

3. Browse to *C:\Civil 3D Beyond\Ascent-Config\Survey Settings* and select **ASCENT-Settings.usr_set**, then click **Open**.

4. Importing the user settings causes all branches to contract. You can expand each branch by clicking the **+** icon. Note how the paths have changed for the various entries.

   - A simple way of expanding all branches is to close the Survey User Settings window by clicking **OK** and reopening the file as you did in the first step of these instructions.

5. Set the *Survey User Settings* drop-down lists as follows:

   - *Survey Database Setting*: **Training-NAD83**

   - *Extended properties definitions:* **Ascent**

   - *Current equipment database*: **Ascent**

   - *Current linework code set*: **Ascent**

   - *Current figure prefix database*: **Ascent**

   - *Figure Style*: **ASC_Standard**

6. Click **OK** to exit the Survey User Settings.

Lead Contributor: Jeff Morris

Specializing in the civil engineering industry, Jeff authors training guides and provides instruction, support, and implementation on all Autodesk infrastructure solutions.

Jeff brings to bear over 20 years of diverse work experience in the civil engineering industry. He has played multiple roles, including Sales, Trainer, Application Specialist, Implementation and Customization Consultant, CAD Coordinator, and CAD/BIM Manager, in civil engineering and architecture firms, and Autodesk reseller organizations. He has worked for government organizations and private firms, small companies and large multinational corporations, and in multiple geographies across the globe. Through his extensive experience in Building and Infrastructure design, Jeff has acquired a thorough understanding of CAD Standards and Procedures and an in-depth knowledge of CAD and BIM.

Jeff studied Architecture and a diploma in Systems Analysis and Programming. He is an Autodesk Certified Instructor (ACI) and holds the Autodesk Certified Professional certification for Civil 3D and Revit.

Jeff Morris is the Lead Contributor for *Autodesk Civil 3D: Beyond the Basics for General Civil Design*. This title was formerly part of *Autodesk Civil 3D: Fundamentals*, for which he was the lead contributor since 2019.

In This Guide

The following highlights the key features of this guide.

Feature	Description
Practice Files	The Practice Files page includes a link to the practice files and instructions on how to download and install them. The practice files are required to complete the practices in this guide.
Chapters	A chapter consists of the following: Learning Objectives, Instructional Content, Practices, Chapter Review Questions, and Command Summary.
	• **Learning Objectives** define the skills you can acquire by learning the content provided in the chapter.
	• **Instructional Content**, which begins right after Learning Objectives, refers to the descriptive and procedural information related to various topics. Each main topic introduces a product feature, discusses various aspects of that feature, and provides step-by-step procedures on how to use that feature. Where relevant, examples, figures, helpful hints, and notes are provided.
	• **Practice** for a topic follows the instructional content. Practices enable you to use the software to perform a hands-on review of a topic. It is required that you download the practice files (using the link found on the Practice Files page) prior to starting the first practice.
	• **Chapter Review Questions**, located close to the end of a chapter, enable you to test your knowledge of the key concepts discussed in the chapter.
	• **Command Summary** concludes a chapter. It contains a list of the software commands that are used throughout the chapter and provides information on where the command can be found in the software.

Practice Files

1. Type the URL *exactly as shown below* into the address bar of your Internet browser to access the Course File Download page.

   Note: If you are using the ebook, you do not have to type the URL. Instead, you can access the page by clicking the URL below.

   Download #1:

   https://www.ascented.com/getfile/id/liparisPF

   Download #2 (for the optional practice in Chapter 4):

   https://www.ascented.com/getfile/id/listrostachysPF

2. On the Course File Download page, click the **DOWNLOAD NOW** button, as shown below, to download the .ZIP file that contains the practice files.

   DOWNLOAD NOW ▶

3. Once the download is complete, unzip the file and extract its contents.

   The recommended practice files folder location is:
   C:\Civil 3D Beyond

   Note: It is recommended that you do not change the location of the practice files folder. Doing so may cause errors when completing the practices.

   Stay Informed!
   To receive information about upcoming events, promotional offers, and complimentary webcasts, visit:
   www.ASCENTed.com/updates

Autodesk Civil 3D Styles and Settings

In this chapter, you will learn about Autodesk® Civil 3D® drawing templates and how to change the settings within the program to conform to specific standards. You will create settings and styles and incorporate them into a unique Civil 3D template. You will also learn how to use online maps and apply it to the template.

Learning Objectives

- Examine a Civil 3D drawing template.
- Control and distribute Civil 3D styles and settings.
- Use online maps.
- Create a Civil 3D template.

1.1 Autodesk Civil 3D Templates and Settings

A drawing template (.DWT extension) contains all blocks, Paper Space title sheets, settings, and layers for a new drawing. As with the AutoCAD software, a template (.DWT) file in the Autodesk Civil 3D software is the source file from which new drawings acquire their settings, units, layers, blocks, text styles, etc., which enforces standardization. With the Autodesk Civil 3D software, in addition to the AutoCAD components noted, the drawing template is also the source for specific Autodesk Civil 3D styles and settings.

As you will learn, Autodesk Civil 3D styles and settings (feature and command) have a profound impact on the appearance of objects, labels, and tables. These styles and settings also act as the primary mechanism that controls the behavior and default actions. Selecting the correct template for your intended design and standards needs is a significant component of fully using the benefits that the Autodesk Civil 3D software offers. Therefore, it is highly recommended that all styles and settings be set up in the template file before you use the Autodesk Civil 3D software in a project.

To use the Autodesk Civil 3D software efficiently and effectively, you need to understand the nature of the AEC object styles and configure styles and settings to control the object display. All of these styles and settings affect the final delivered product and enable you to deliver a product with consistent quality.

Drawing Settings in Detail

The values in the drawing settings influence every aspect of the drafting environment. Each tab has values affecting a specific drawing area, for example, layer naming properties, coordinate systems, default precisions, input and output conventions, abbreviations for alignment, volume units, etc. After implementing the Autodesk Civil 3D software, most of the time you will only need to access the first two tabs. The other tabs are used for tweaking your current drawing environment, when needed.

To access the drawing settings, in the *TOOLSPACE>Settings* tab, select the drawing name (at the top), right-click, and select **Edit Drawing Settings**.

Units and Zone

In the *Drawing Settings* dialog box, the *Units and Zone* tab (as shown in Figure 1−1) sets the Model Space plotting scale and coordinate zone for the drawing. The scale can be a custom value or selected from a drop-down list. A zone is selected from a drop-down list of worldwide categories and coordinate systems.

A drawing that has been assigned a coordinate system enables points to report their grid coordinates and/or their longitude and latitude. Conversely, when assigning a coordinate system, grid coordinates and longitude and latitude data can create points in a drawing.

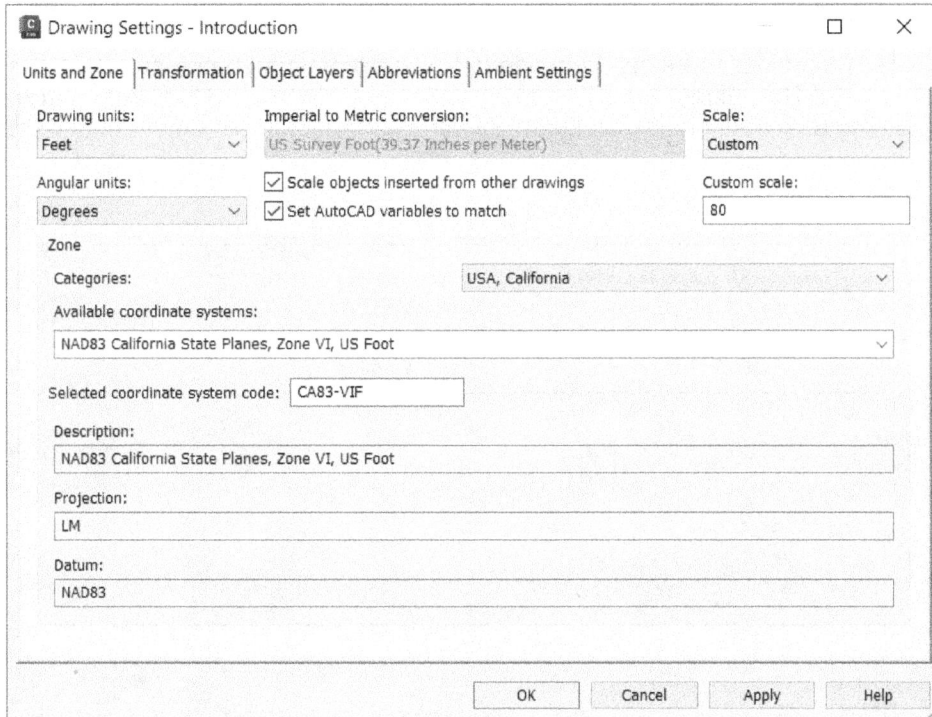

Figure 1–1

When plotting from the *Model* tab, the drawing scale in the upper right corner is the scale at which you would prefer the drawing to be printed. When in the *Model* tab, changing this scale automatically updates all Autodesk Civil 3D annotations that are scale-dependent. (Autodesk Civil 3D annotations are automatically resized for correct plotting in each viewport that displays them based on that viewport's scale.)

Changing the drawing scale does not automatically change the **ltscale** variable. It is recommended that you set **ltscale to 1** and ensure that **msltscale** and **psltscale** are also set to **1**. If this is not the case, you need to assign this variable manually. Refer to the AutoCAD help documentation if you need more information on variables, such as **ltscale**, **msltscale**, and **psltscale**.

You can also set the drawing scale by assigning a different annotation scale in the *Status Bar*, as shown in Figure 1–2. In layouts, you can change either the VP scale or annotation scale and have both update.

Figure 1–2

Transformation

During the life of a project, there can be reasons to change assumed point coordinates to a coordinate system. The values in the *Transformation* tab (as shown in Figure 1-3) transform local coordinates to a state plane coordinate system, UTM system, or other defined planar system.

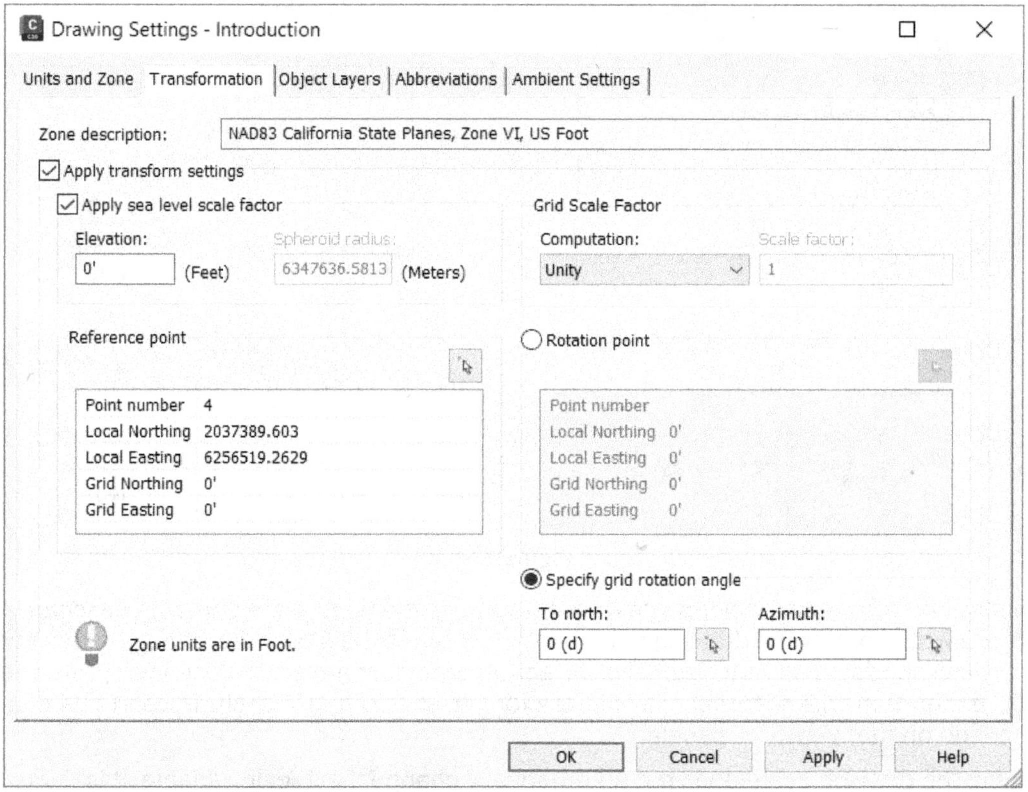

Figure 1-3

Object Layers

The *Object Layers* tab (shown in Figure 1–4) assigns layer names to Autodesk Civil 3D objects. A modifier, which can be a prefix or a suffix, is associated with each layer's name. The value of the modifier can be anything that is typed into its *Value* field. Traditionally, the value is an * (asterisk) with a separator (a dash or underscore). The Autodesk Civil 3D software replaces the asterisk with the name of the object of the same type. For example, the base surface layer name is **C-TOPO** with a suffix modifier of -* (a dash followed by an asterisk). When a surface named **Existing** is created, it is placed on the layer **C-TOPO-EXISTING**, and when a surface named **Base** is created, it is placed on the layer **C-TOPO-BASE**.

The last column of the *Object Layers* tab enables you to lock the values. When a value is locked at this level, the Autodesk Civil 3D software does not permit it to be changed by any lower style or setting.

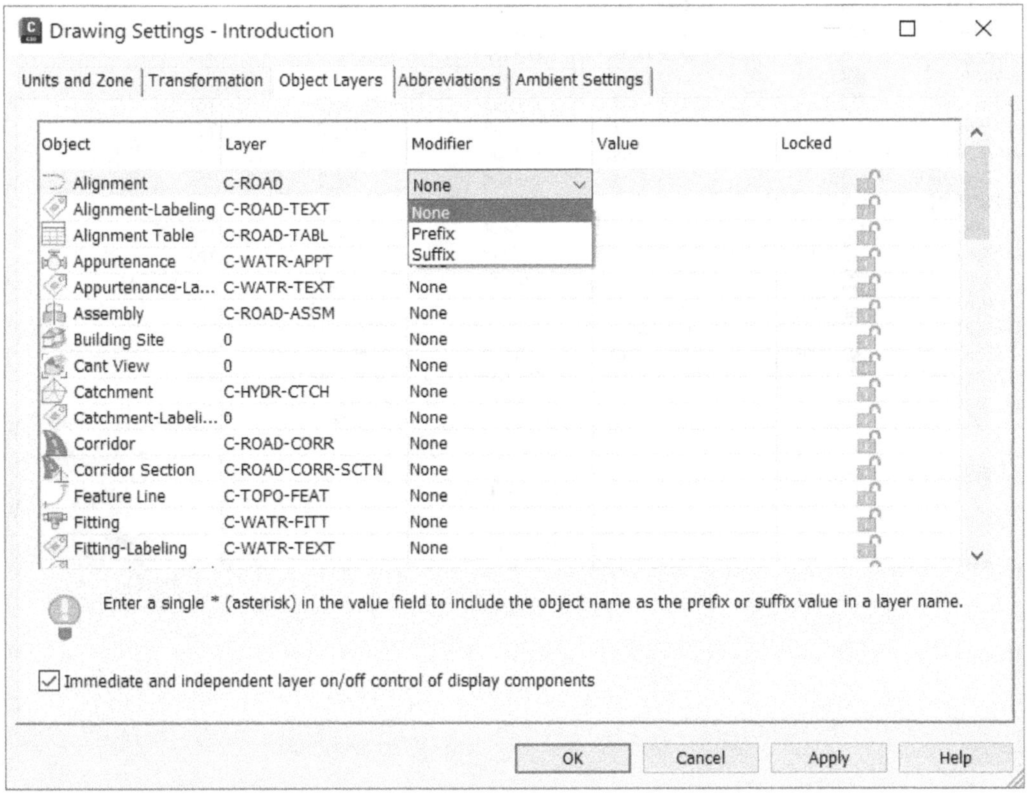

Figure 1–4

To change the listed object layers, double-click on a layer name. In the *Layer Selection* dialog box (shown in Figure 1–5), select the layer from the list. If the layer does not exist, click **New** in the *Layer Selection* dialog box. This opens a second dialog box, in which you can define a new layer for the object type.

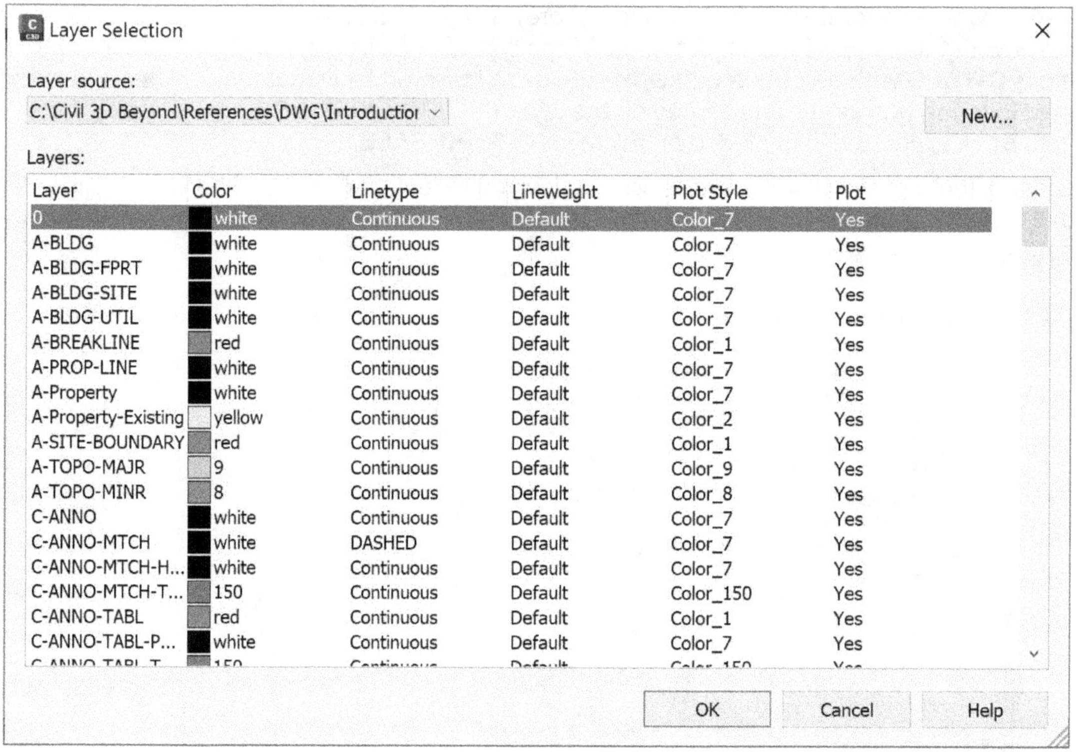

Layer	Color	Linetype	Lineweight	Plot Style	Plot
0	white	Continuous	Default	Color_7	Yes
A-BLDG	white	Continuous	Default	Color_7	Yes
A-BLDG-FPRT	white	Continuous	Default	Color_7	Yes
A-BLDG-SITE	white	Continuous	Default	Color_7	Yes
A-BLDG-UTIL	white	Continuous	Default	Color_7	Yes
A-BREAKLINE	red	Continuous	Default	Color_1	Yes
A-PROP-LINE	white	Continuous	Default	Color_7	Yes
A-Property	white	Continuous	Default	Color_7	Yes
A-Property-Existing	yellow	Continuous	Default	Color_2	Yes
A-SITE-BOUNDARY	red	Continuous	Default	Color_1	Yes
A-TOPO-MAJR	9	Continuous	Default	Color_9	Yes
A-TOPO-MINR	8	Continuous	Default	Color_8	Yes
C-ANNO	white	Continuous	Default	Color_7	Yes
C-ANNO-MTCH	white	DASHED	Default	Color_7	Yes
C-ANNO-MTCH-H...	white	Continuous	Default	Color_7	Yes
C-ANNO-MTCH-T...	150	Continuous	Default	Color_150	Yes
C-ANNO-TABL	red	Continuous	Default	Color_1	Yes
C-ANNO-TABL-P...	white	Continuous	Default	Color_7	Yes
C-ANNO-TABL-T...	150	Continuous	Default	Color_150	Yes

Figure 1–5

Abbreviations

The *Abbreviations* tab (shown in Figure 1–6) sets standard values for reports referencing alignment or profile data. Some entries in this panel have text format strings that define how the values associated with the abbreviation display in a label.

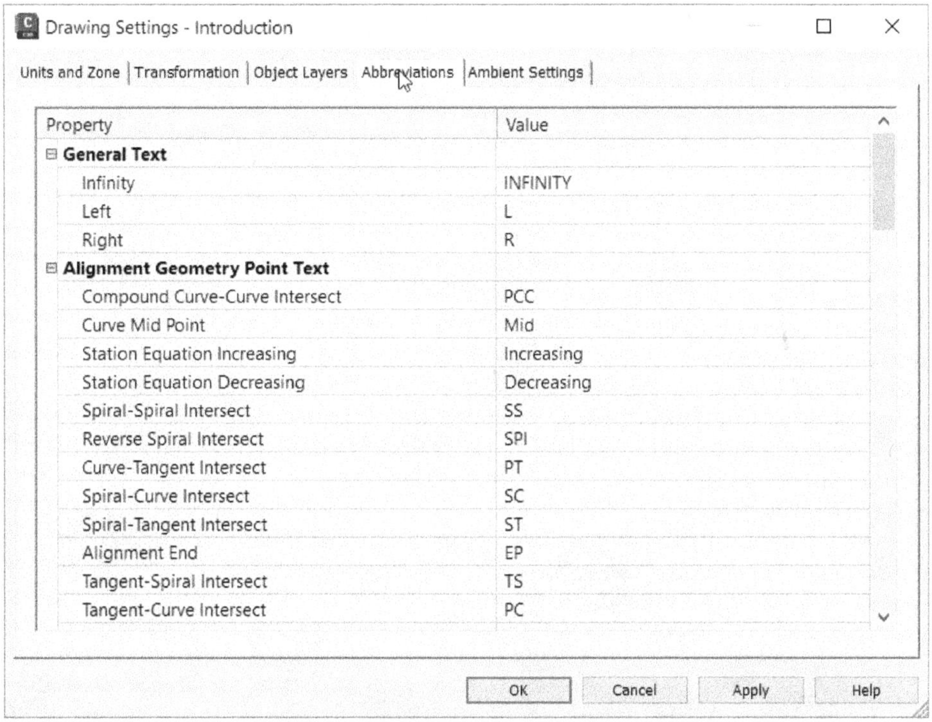

Figure 1–6

Ambient Settings

In the *Ambient Settings* tab (shown in Figure 1–7), the values influence prompting and reports. For example, the *Direction* area affects the prompting for direction input: **Decimal Degrees**, **Degrees Minutes and Seconds** (with or without spaces), or **Decimal Degrees Minutes and Seconds**. Any value set at this level affects everything (labels and commands) in the drawing.

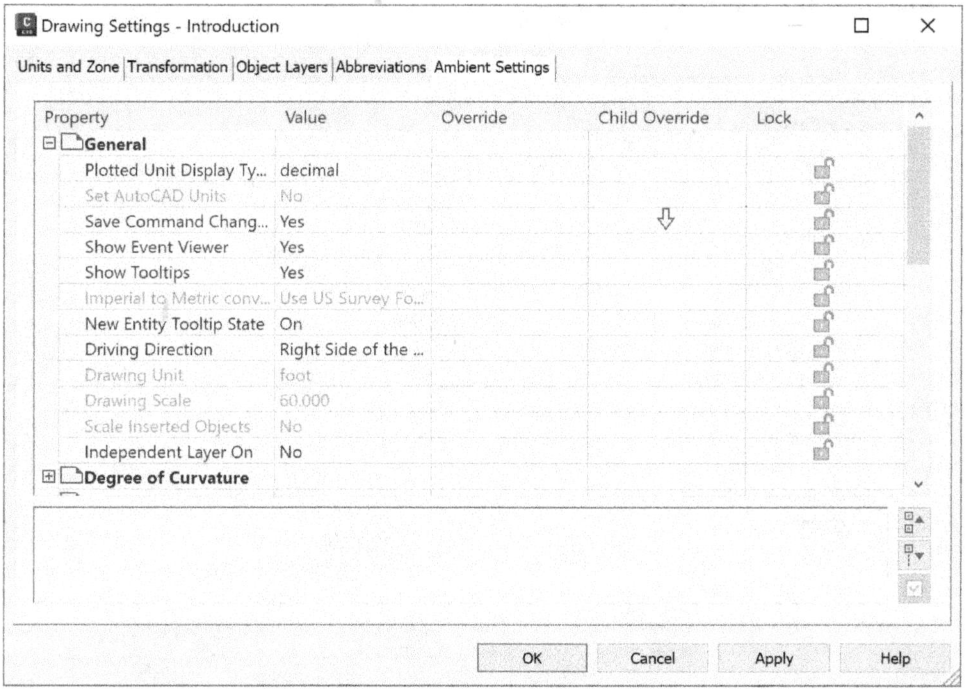

Figure 1–7

The values assigned in the *Edit Label Style Defaults* dialog box (shown in Figure 1–8) control text style, plan orientation, and the basic behavior of label styles. Similar to feature settings, this dialog box is available at the drawing level and at the individual object's level. Editing label style defaults at the drawing level affects all label styles in the drawing. Editing them at the object level (such as surfaces) only affects that object's labels.

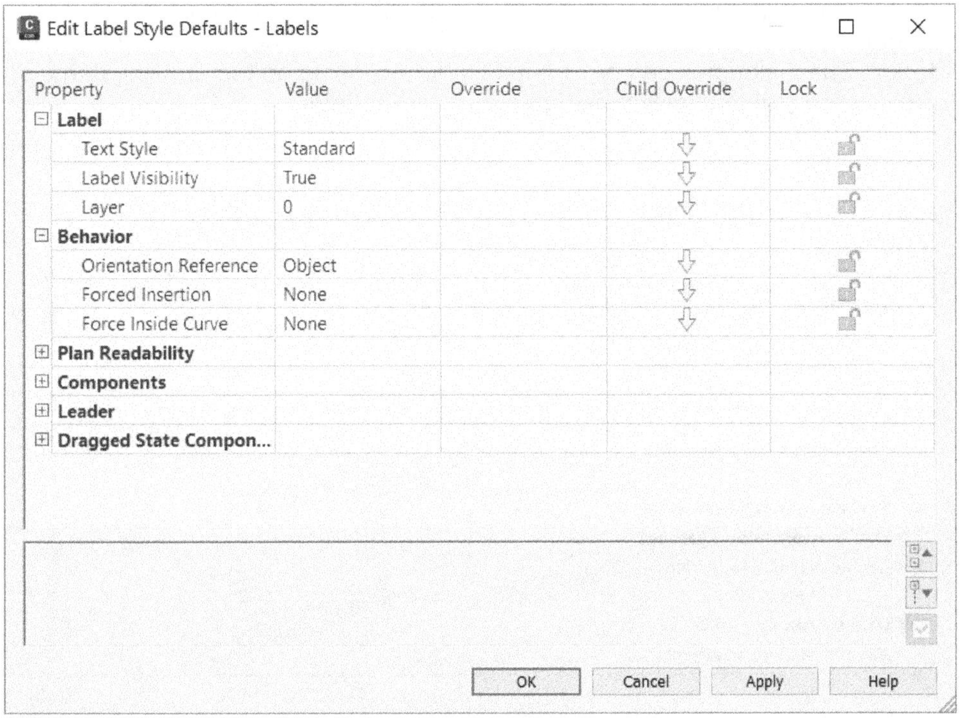

Figure 1–8

In the *Label, Behavior,* and *Plan Readability* areas, the values affect the overall visibility of labels, their default text style, label orientation, and the rotation angle that affects plan readability.

The values in the *Components, Leader,* and *Dragged State Components* areas affect the default text height for the label, colors for the text, leader, and surrounding box, and type of leader. There are also several settings defining what happens to a label when you drag it from its original position.

Edit Autodesk LandXML Settings

The *LandXML Settings* dialog box (shown in Figure 1–9) provides settings that control how Autodesk LandXML data is imported and exported from the Autodesk Civil 3D software. Autodesk LandXML is a universal format for storing surveying and civil engineering data that enables you to transfer points, terrain models, alignments, etc., between different software platforms. For more information, refer to www.landxml.org and the Autodesk Civil 3D help documentation. The dialog box can be opened by right-clicking on the drawing name in the *TOOLSPACE>Settings* tab and selecting **Edit LandXMLSettings**.

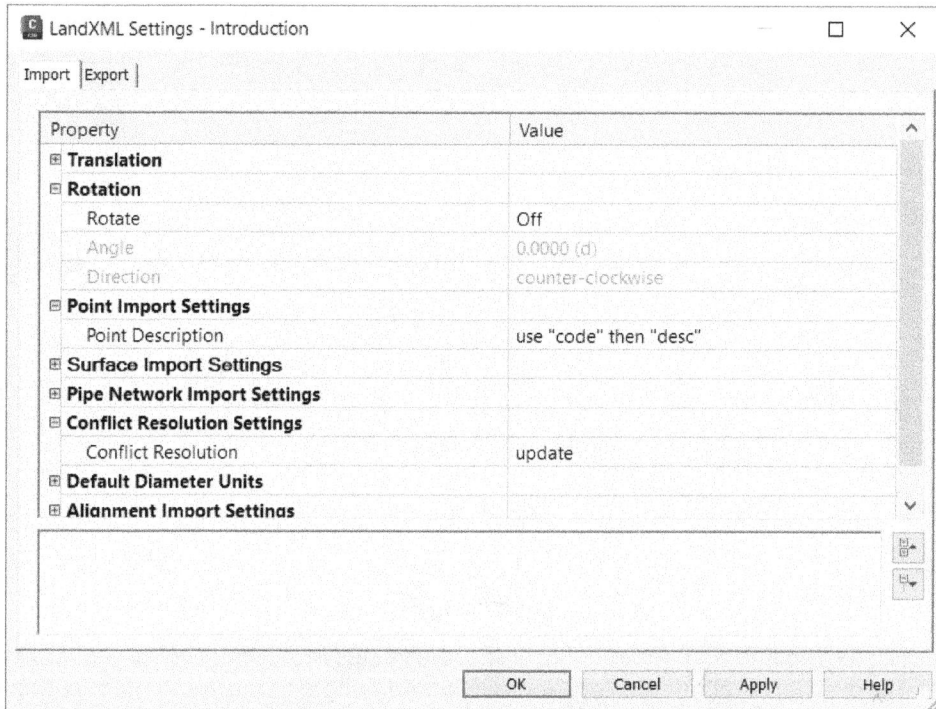

Figure 1–9

Feature Settings

In the *TOOLSPACE>Settings* tab, each object type collection has an *Edit Feature Settings* dialog box, as shown for Surface in Figure 1–10. Its main function is to assign default naming values and initial object and label styles, and override the default values found in the drawing settings for that object type. You can access the feature settings by right-clicking on the object tree in the *TOOLSPACE>Settings* tab and selecting **Edit Feature Settings**.

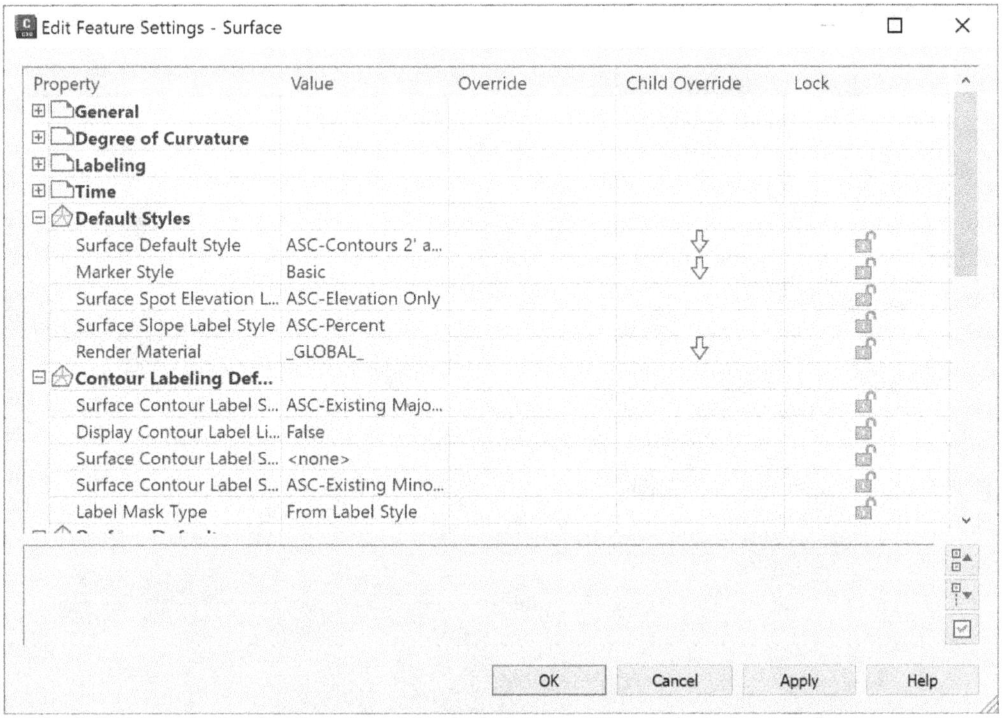

Property	Value	Override	Child Override	Lock
⊞ ☐General				
⊞ ☐Degree of Curvature				
⊞ ☐Labeling				
⊞ ☐Time				
⊟ ⌂Default Styles				
Surface Default Style	ASC-Contours 2' a...		⇩	🔓
Marker Style	Basic		⇩	🔓
Surface Spot Elevation L...	ASC-Elevation Only			🔓
Surface Slope Label Style	ASC-Percent			🔓
Render Material	_GLOBAL_		⇩	🔓
⊟ ⌂**Contour Labeling Def...**				
Surface Contour Label S...	ASC-Existing Majo...			🔓
Display Contour Label Li...	False			🔓
Surface Contour Label S...	<none>			🔓
Surface Contour Label S...	ASC-Existing Mino...			🔓
Label Mask Type	From Label Style			🔓

Figure 1–10

Command Settings

Similar to feature settings, in the *Edit Command Settings* dialog box (shown in Figure 1–11), you can set the default object and label styles used when creating objects with a specific command. Each object type contains a unique set of commands. Typical values in these dialog boxes include the name format (e.g., surface 1, parcel 1), design criteria (e.g., minimum area, frontage, length of vertical curve, and minimum horizontal curve), etc. To open the dialog box, expand a collection in the *TOOLSPACE>Settings* tab until the commands display. Right-click on the command to which you want to assign default settings and select **Edit Command Settings**.

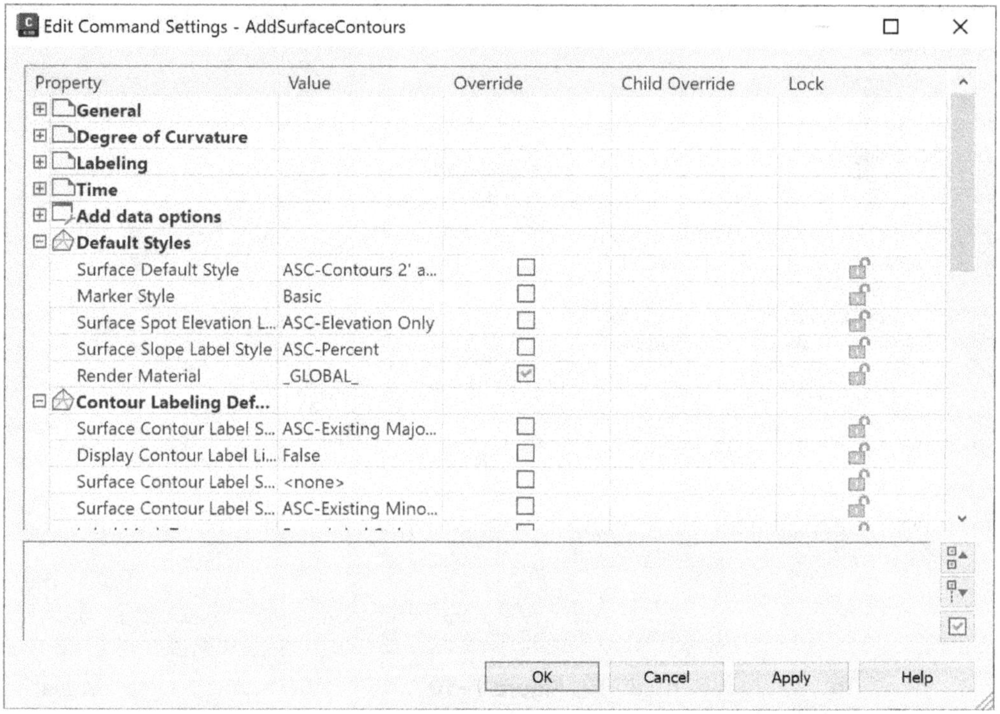

Figure 1–11

💡 Hint: Style and Setting Overrides

In the E*dit Label Style Defaults*, *Feature Settings*, and similar dialog boxes, a downward pointing arrow in the *Child Override* column indicates that a setting or style lower in the settings tree has a different value than the one displayed. Selecting the arrow (which creates a red **x** over the icon) and clicking **OK** removes the variant settings and makes all lower setting's dialog boxes and styles match those assigned in the dialog box. This can be a quick way of standardizing multiple settings and styles at the same time.

For example, in the *Edit Label Style Defaults* dialog box shown in Figure 1–12, an arrow is present in the *Child Override* column for *Label Visibility* and *Layer*, indicating that some surface label styles are assigned a layer other than **0** and a visibility of **False**. Since an arrow is not shown for the *Text Style* property, all surface label styles are using a text style of **Standard**.

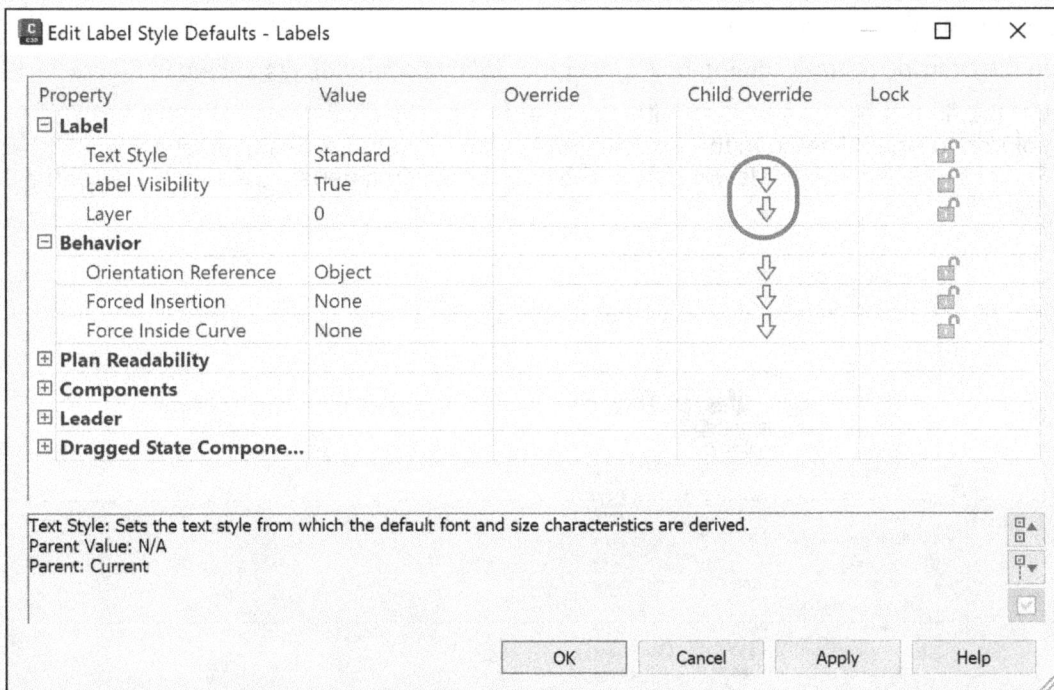

Figure 1–12

The *Override* column indicates whether a value in this window is overriding a higher settings dialog box. Clicking the **Lock** icon prevents you from changing that value in a lower setting's dialog box or style.

Styles and label styles are covered throughout the guide as required.

Practice 1a
Autodesk Civil 3D Settings

Practice Objective

- Modify Civil 3D settings.

In this practice, you will modify Autodesk Civil 3D settings.

1. Open **Introduction.dwg** from the *C:\Civil 3D Beyond\ References\DWG* folder.

2. Select the *TOOLSPACE>Settings* tab to make it active. The tabs are listed vertically along the right side of the Toolspace.

3. In *TOOLSPACE>Settings* tab, right-click on the drawing's name (**Introduction**, at the top) and select **Edit Drawing Settings**.

4. In the *Drawing Settings* dialog box, select the *Object Layers* tab, as shown in Figure 1–13.

5. For the first three rows dealing with alignments, use the drop-down list in the *Modifier* column to select **Prefix**. In the *Value* column, type *- (asterisk dash), as shown in Figure 1–13. Note in the lower part of the notice that an asterisk is a substitute for the object's name.

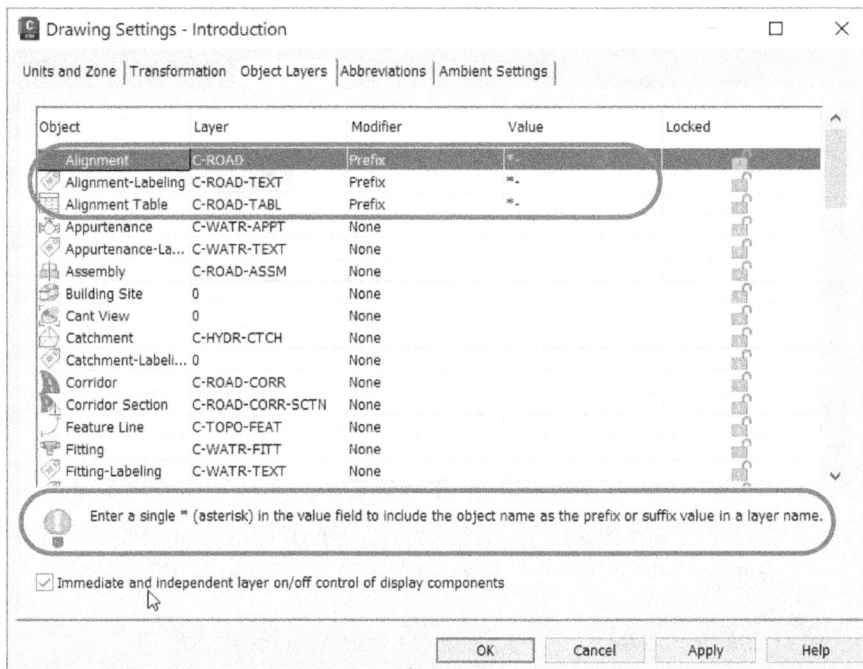

Figure 1–13

6. Select the *Abbreviations* tab.

7. In the *Alignment Geometry Point Text* section, for the *Curve Mid Point*, change the existing **Mid** text to **MD**, as shown in Figure 1-14.

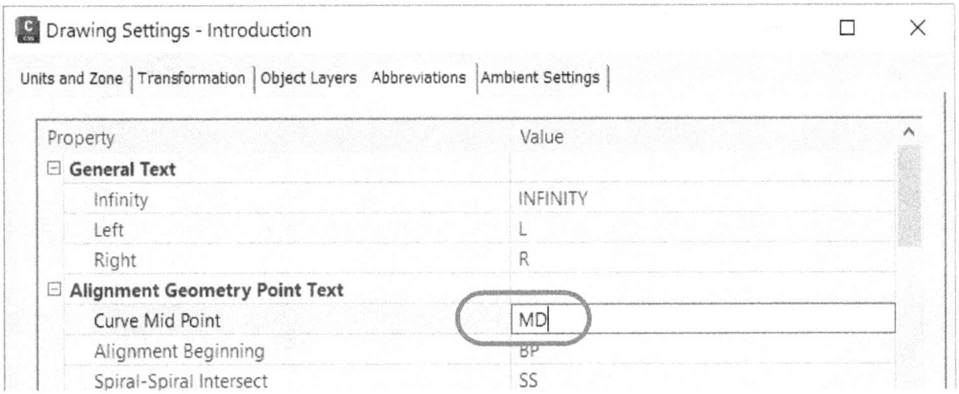

Figure 1-14

8. Select the *Ambient Settings* tab.

9. Under *Elevation>Unit*, use the drop-down list to select **meter**, as shown in Figure 1-15.

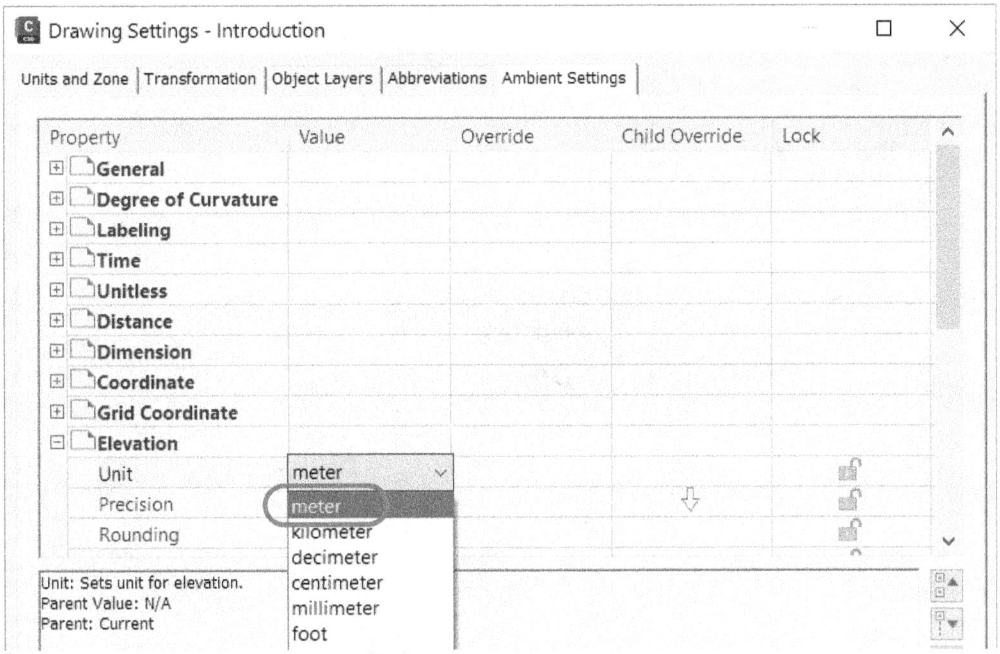

Figure 1-15

10. Click **OK** to close the *Drawing Settings* dialog box.

11. Zoom in to the knuckle bend of the *Ascent Place* alignment.

12. Hover the cursor over an empty space until the tooltip appears displaying the surface elevation information. Note that the surface elevation is shown in meters, whereas the distance of the station offsets (SO) of the alignments remain in feet, as shown in Figure 1–16.

    Note: This change in settings is for demonstration purposes only. It is highly unlikely that this would ever be done in real-world application.

13. Notice that the curve midpoint text still shows as **Mid**. Type **RE** (for Regen) at the command line. The drawing regenerates and now the curve midpoint text displays as **MD**, as shown in Figure 1–16. The elevations in the tooltip are displayed in units.

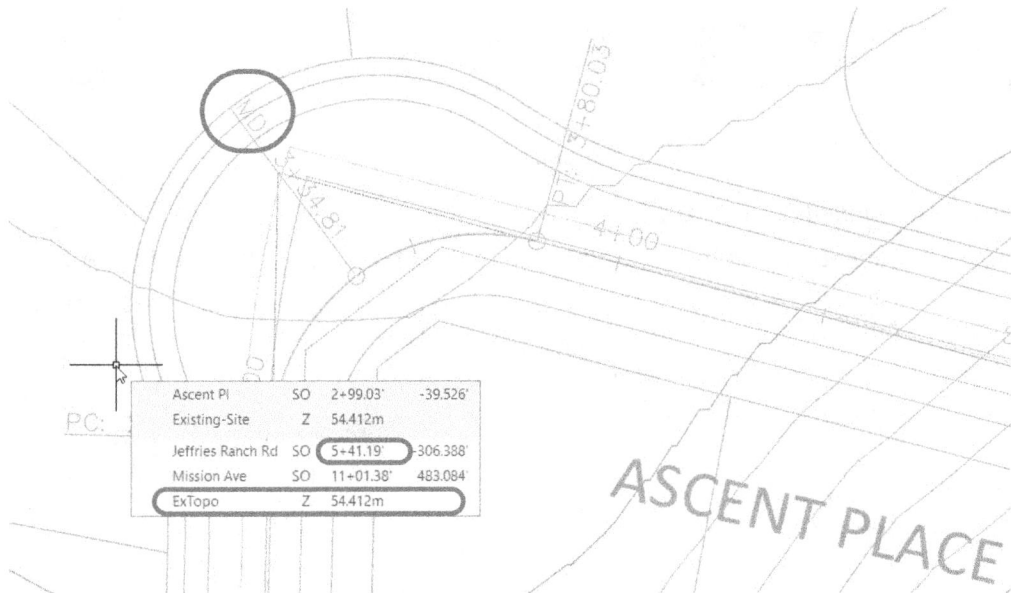

Figure 1–16

14. Pan southward to the intersection of **Jeffries Ranch Rd** and **Ascent Place**.

15. To the right of the existing *Alignment Station* Offset label, create another label. A convenient way of doing this is to select the **Jeffries Ranch Rd** alignment (the green line running east to west) and in the contextual ribbon, expand the *Add Labels* drop-down list and select **Station/Offset - Fixed Point**, as shown in Figure 1–17.

Figure 1–17

16. Select a point to the west of the existing label.

17. Click on the existing label, right-click, and select **Properties**. Note that the layer of the label is **C-ROAD-TEXT**, as shown on the top in Figure 1–18.

18. Press <Esc> to deselect the first label, then repeat the procedure for the label you just added. Its layer is **Jeffries Ranch Rd-C-ROAD-TEXT**, as shown on the bottom in Figure 1–18. This is because you set the alignment labels (and other alignment objects) to have a prefix of the alignment name and a dash.

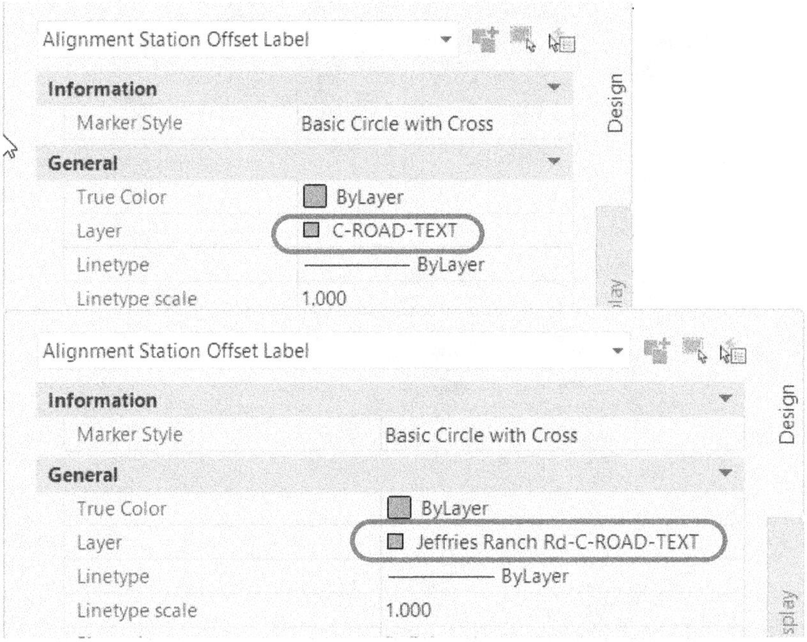

Figure 1–18

19. Save and close the drawing.

End of practice

1.2 Styles

Styles are preconfigured groups of settings (specific to an individual object type or label) that make the objects display and print the way you want them to. For example, in the list of surface styles shown in Figure 1–19, each surface style is configured differently to display different features, such as contours at different intervals and on the correct layers. The display of a terrain model could be changed by swapping one surface style for another. Styles enable an organization to standardize the look of their graphics by providing preconfigured groupings of display settings.

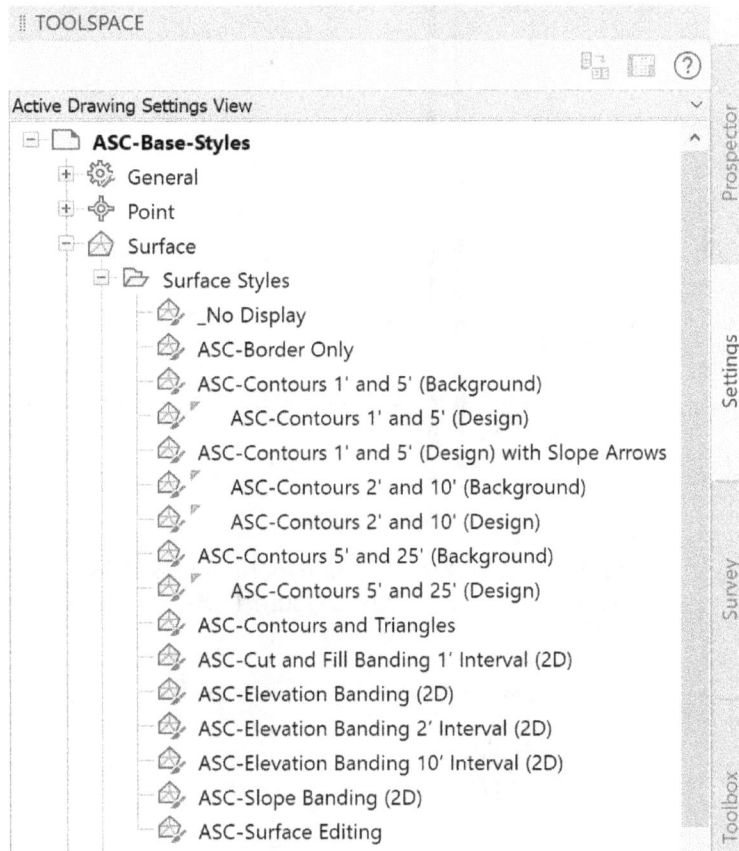

Figure 1–19

Styles are central to the Autodesk Civil 3D software. Their flexibility enables an office or company to create a unique look for their drawings. By changing the assigned style, you can change the composition of a profile view, as shown in Figure 1–20.

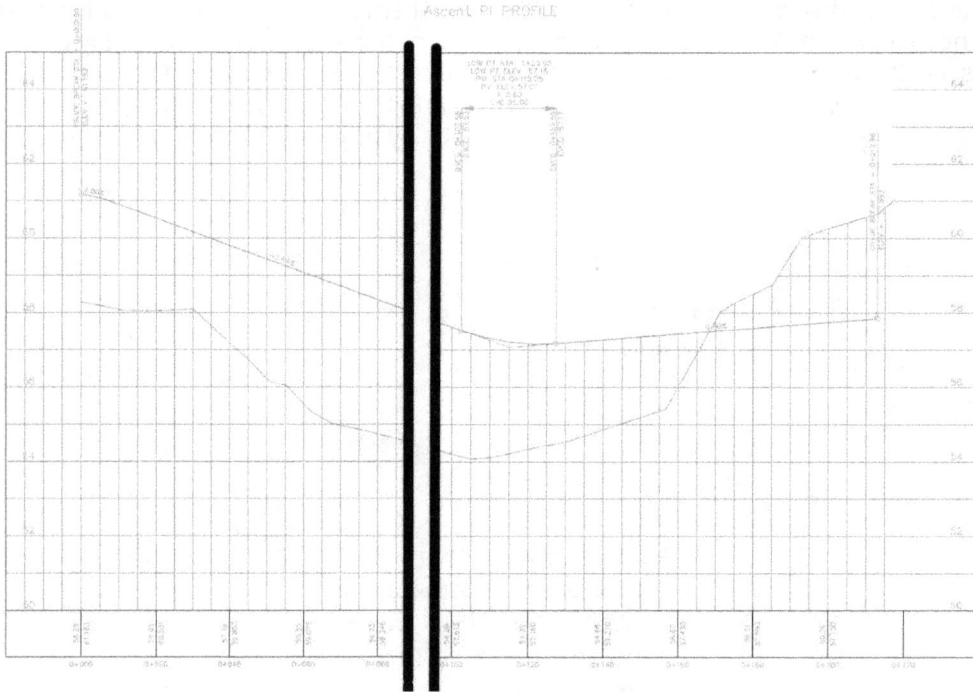

Figure 1–20

In the *TOOLSPACE>Settings* tab, an object type branch identifies each style type and lists its styles below each heading. An example is shown in Figure 1–21.

Figure 1–21

Two Categories of Styles

The two categories of styles you work with most often are **object styles** and **label styles**. Some objects have table styles as well. Object styles control how Autodesk Civil 3D objects (points, surfaces, alignments, etc.) display, what combination of components the object displays, which layers they display on, and many other settings. Label styles are similar except that they control the text and other annotations associated with the objects.

For example, an alignment object style specifies many settings, including the layers on which to draw tangents and curve segments (which might be different) and the symbols to add at certain points as required (such as a triangle at the PI point). Alignment label styles include major and minor station labels, the display of station equations, design speeds, and similar annotations. By separating object and label styles, you can mix and match the right combination for a specific object.

Styles are the lowest items in the *TOOLSPACE>Settings* tree and are typically dependent on other settings above them. If a style is given a unique setting different from feature settings or label style defaults (such as a different text height), then that style is considered to have an override.

Object Styles

Object styles stylize an object's data for display and print. To edit a style, in the *TOOLSPACE>Settings* tab, right-click on the style and select **Edit**. Much of the work for the object styles is done in the *Display* tab. For certain objects, other tabs might need to be modified.

For example, in the *Surface Style* dialog box, the *Display* tab enables you to toggle on or off triangles, borders, contours, and other items, as well as define the layer, color, linetype, etc. that are assigned, as shown in Figure 1−22.

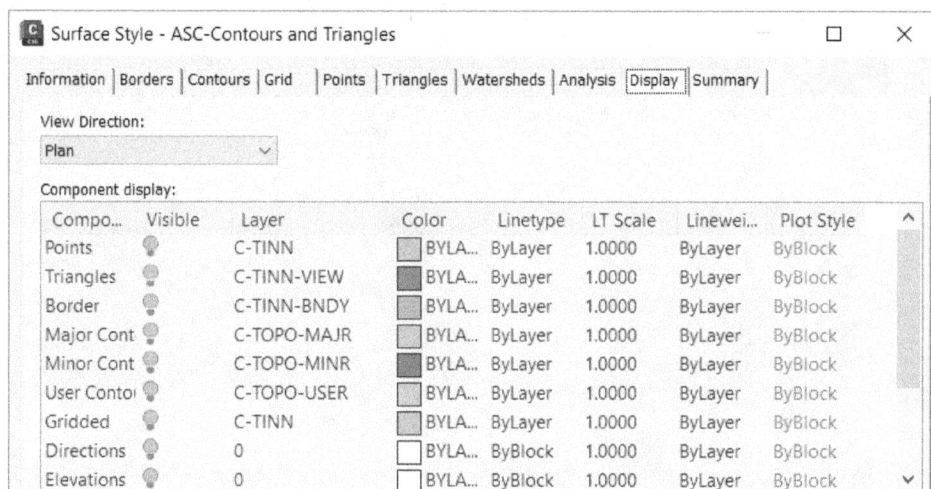

Figure 1−22

The *Contours* tab sets the contour interval, smoothing, and other settings, as shown in Figure 1–23.

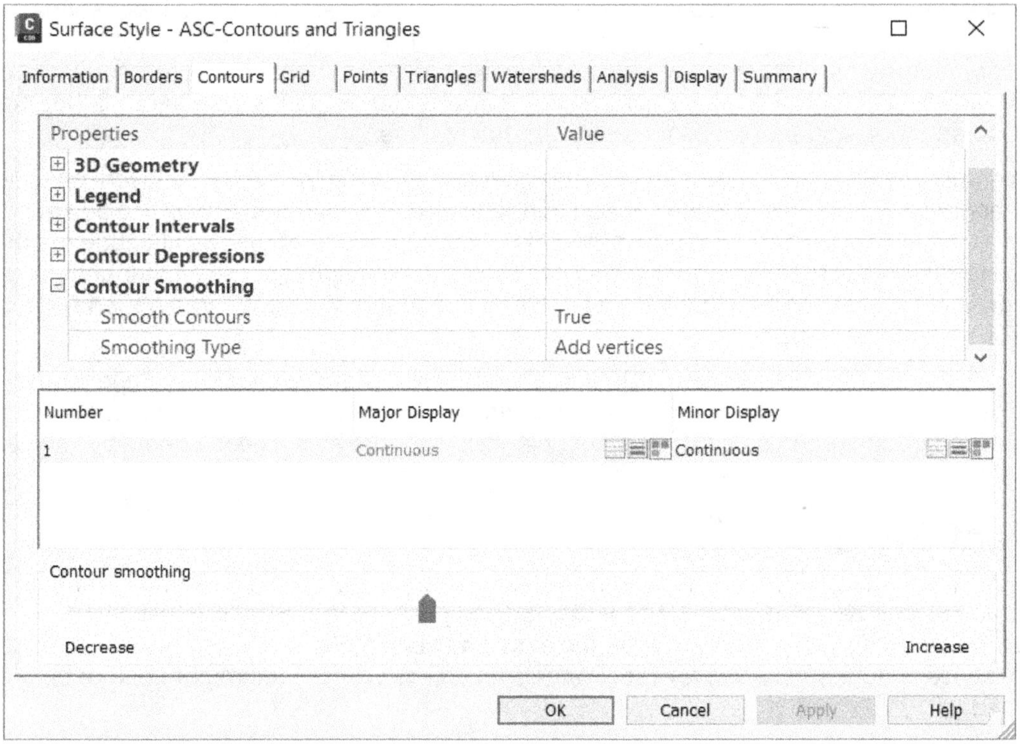

Figure 1–23

From the default Autodesk Civil 3D template, the respective *Parcel Style* dialog box for Open Space, Road, or Single Family, (as shown in Figure 1–24) define how each displays their segments and hatching by assigning different layers for the components. The other tabs are rarely used for the parcel styles.

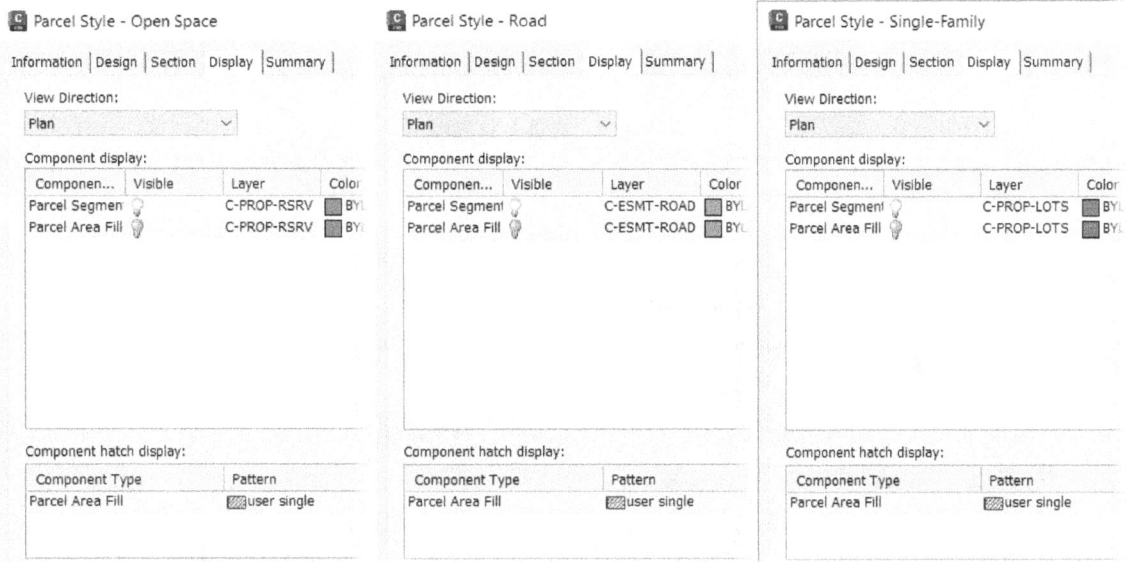

Figure 1–24

An object style represents a specific task, view, type, or stage in a process, for example, a surface style for developing a surface, reviewing surface properties, or documenting surface elevations as contours for a submission. For parcels, styles represent a type such as open space, commercial, easement, single family, etc. One style can cause an object to look different in various views. For instance, you might want to display both the point and the label in the plan view but only the point marker in a model (3D view).

As shown in Figure 1–25, there are four view directions to consider when creating an object style:

- Plan
- Model (3D view)
- Profile
- Section

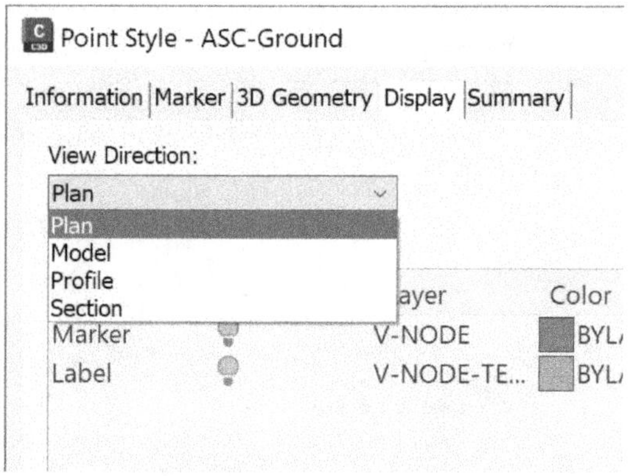

Figure 1–25

Label Styles

Label styles produce annotations of values from existing conditions or a design solution. A label annotates a contour's elevations, a parcel's number and area, a horizontal geometry point's station on an alignment, etc.

A label style can have text, vectors, AutoCAD blocks, and reference text. The content of a label depends on the selected object's components or properties. For instance, a line label can annotate bearing, distance, and coordinates, and use a direction arrow. A parcel area label can contain a parcel's area, perimeter, address, and other pertinent values. A surface label can include a spot elevation, reference for an alignment's station and offset, or other pertinent surface information.

- To access the values of a label style, in the *TOOLSPACE>Settings* tab, select the style, right-click on its name, and select **Edit**.

- A style's initial values come from *Edit Label Style Defaults* dialog box and the style's definition.

- All labels use the same interface.

- The object properties available for each label vary by object type.

Each label style uses the same tabbed dialog box. The *Information* tab describes the style as well as who defined and last modified its contents. The values of the *General* tab affect all occurrences of the label in a drawing. For example, if *Visibility* is set to **False**, all labels of this style are hidden in the drawing. Other settings affect the label's text style, initial orientation, and reaction to a rotated view.

The *Layout* tab (shown in Figure 1–26) lists all of a label's components. A label component can be text, line, block, or tick. The *Component name* drop-down list contains all of the defined components for the style. When selecting a component name in the drop-down list, the panel displays information about the component's anchoring, justification, format, and border.

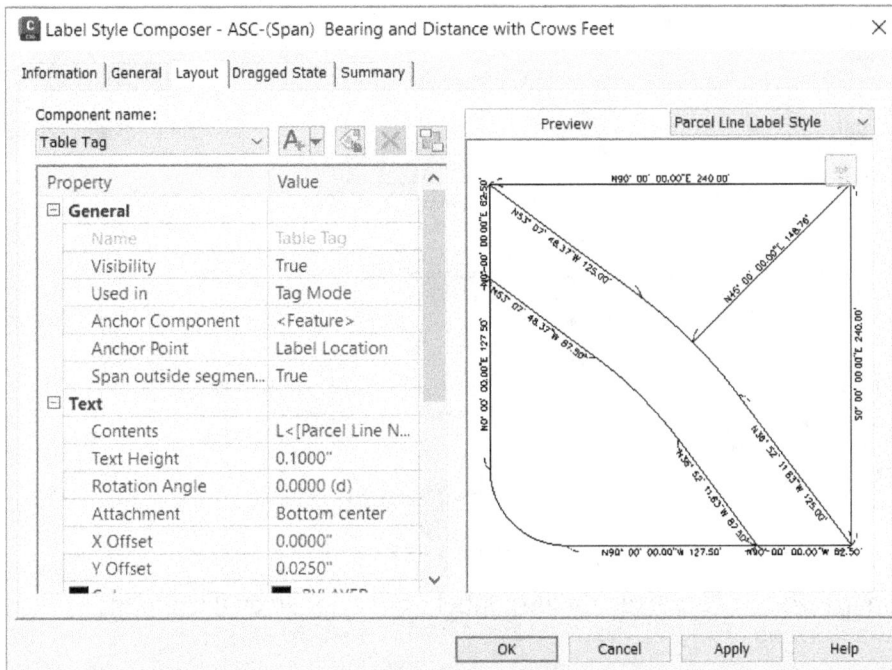

Figure 1–26

When defining a new text component, you assign it an object property by clicking ⬚ (Browse) for *Contents*. This opens the *Text Component Editor* dialog box, as shown in Figure 1–27. The *Properties* drop-down list displays the available object properties. The number and types of properties varies by object type. For example, a parcel area label has more and different properties than a line label does. Once a property has been selected, the *Unit*, *Precision*, and other settings can be set to display the property correctly in the label. Click ⬆ next to the *Properties* drop-down list to place the property in the label layout area to the right.

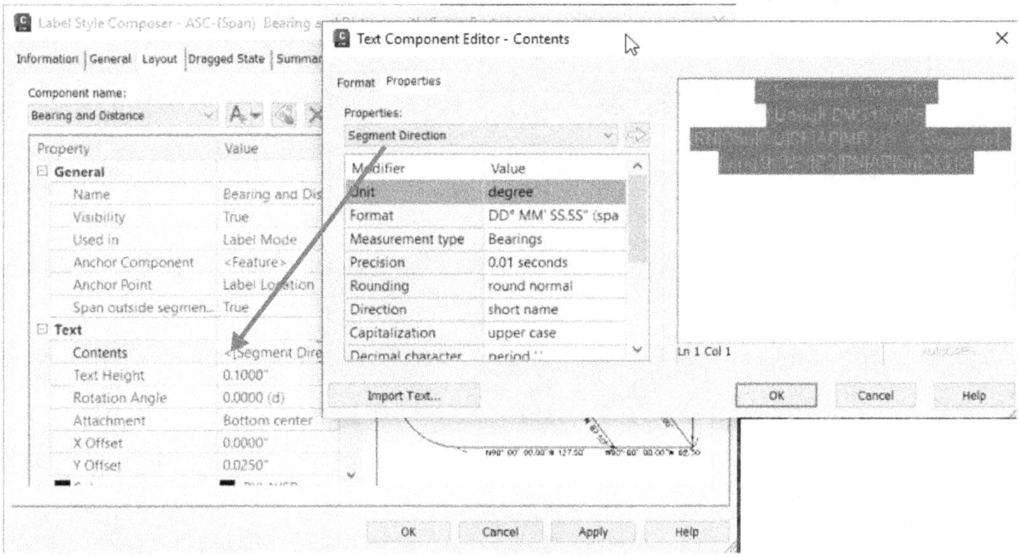

Figure 1–27

The values in the *Dragged State* tab define a label's behavior when it is dragged to a new location in the drawing.

The key to having the label display correctly when it is not in the dragged state is to line up the anchor point of the component with the attachment option for the text. Each has nine options from which to select. The options are shown in Figure 1–28.

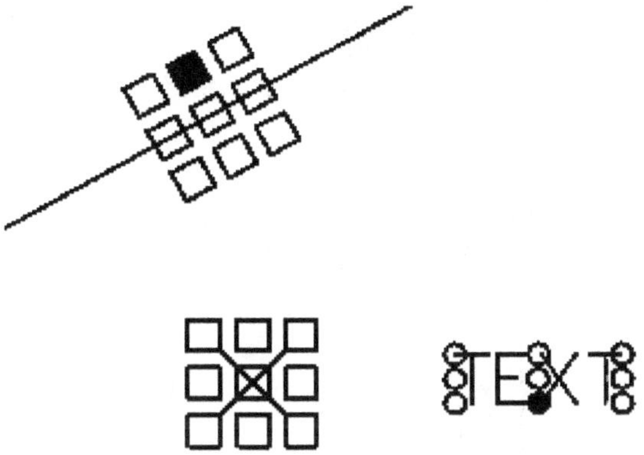

Figure 1–28

Lining up the square hatched anchor point with the circular hatched attachment option results in the text centered above the object, similar to the bearing distance label shown in Figure 1–29.

Figure 1–29

Customizing styles needs to be managed carefully. Consult with your BIM manager as to the standards and procedures for such customization. If you do modify an existing style or create a new one, be sure to put your name or initials in the *Created by:* field for easy identification, as shown Figure 1–30.

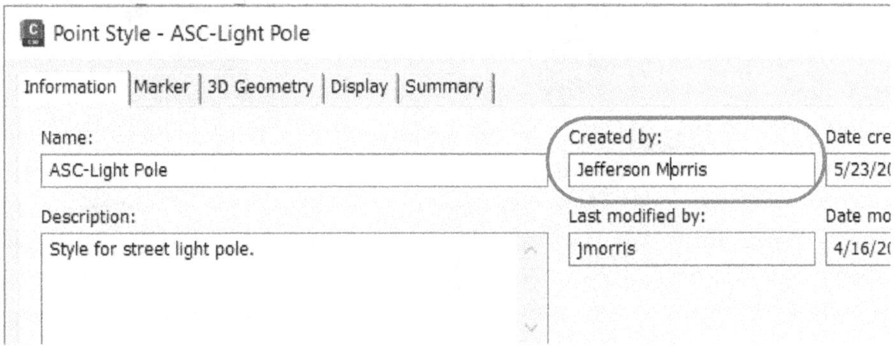

Figure 1–30

When installing the Autodesk Civil 3D software, the first thing you should do is set the standard Imperial or Metric Civil 3D template as your default template. Alternatively, your BIM manager can develop styles to be used in your organization's drawing template file.

Point Style

A point style defines a point's display, its 3D elevation, and its coordinate marker size. In the example shown in Figure 1–31, the point style is an X for a ground shot.

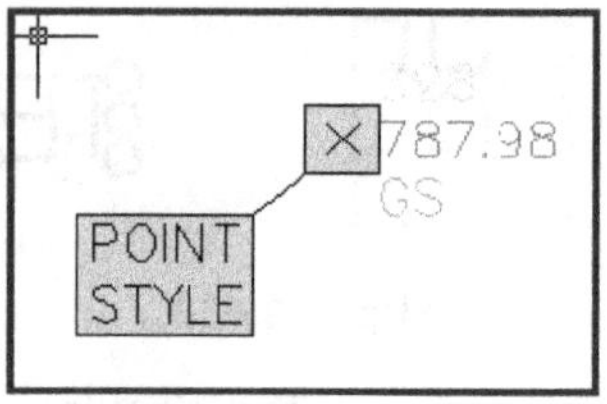

Figure 1–31

The *Point Style* dialog box has five tabs: *Information*, *Marker*, *3D Geometry*, *Display*, and *Summary*.

The *Information* tab sets the point style's name and description, as shown in Figure 1–32.

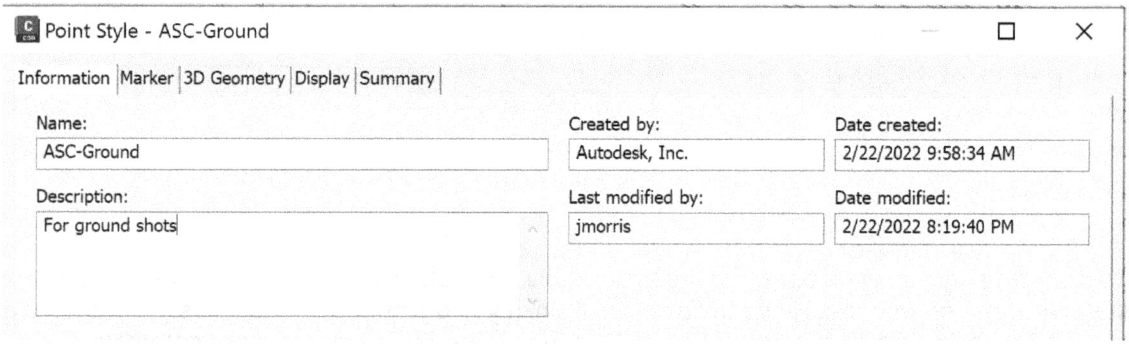

Figure 1–32

The *Marker* tab supports three marker definition methods, as shown in Figure 1–33.

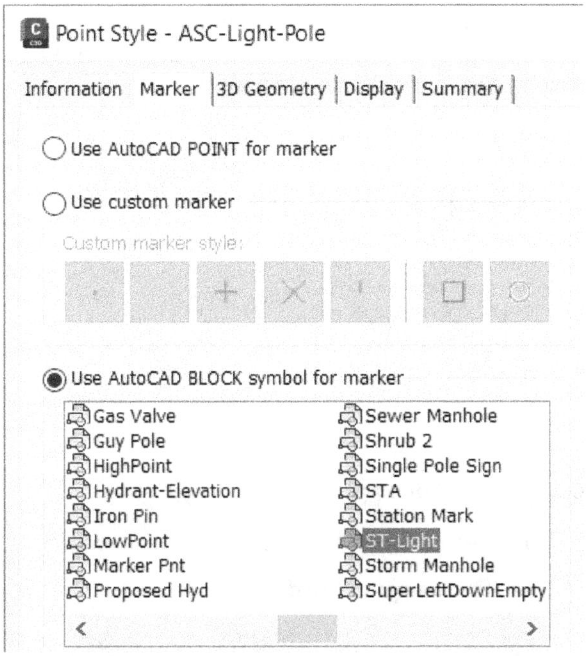

Figure 1–33

- **Use AutoCAD POINT for marker:** All points (nodes) in the drawing follow AutoCAD's **PDMODE** and **PDSIZE** system variables. You do not have independent control over points using this option. (This option is seldom used.)

- **Use custom marker:** This option creates markers similar to an AutoCAD point (node). However, the marker is under the Autodesk Civil 3D software's control, and each point style can display a different combination of marker styles. When using this option, select the components of the style from the list of custom marker style shapes. A custom marker can have shapes from the left and right sides. The first comes from one of the five icons on the style's left side, and you can optionally add none, one, or both shapes from the right.

- **Use AutoCAD BLOCK symbol for marker:** This option defines the marker using a block (symbol). The blocks listed represent definitions in the drawing. When the cursor is in this area and you right-click, you can browse to a location containing drawings that you want to include as point markers.

Options for scaling the marker display in the marker panel's top right corner. The most common option is **Use drawing scale** (as shown in Figure 1–34), which takes the marker size (0.1000") and multiplies it by the current drawing's annotation scale, resulting in the final marker size. When the annotation scale changes, the Autodesk Civil 3D software automatically resizes the markers and their labels to be the appropriate size for the scale.

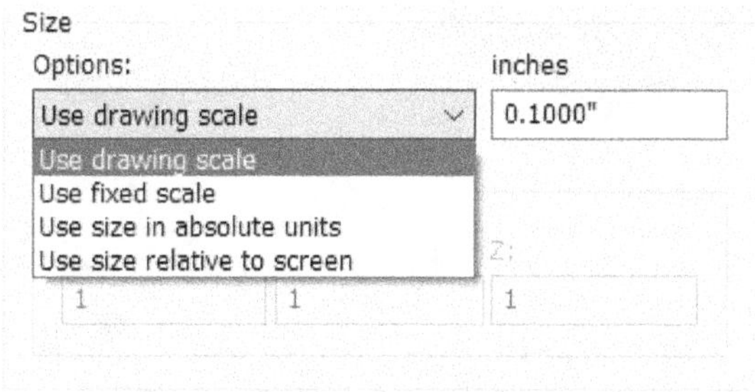

Figure 1–34

The other options are described as follows:

Use fixed scale	Specifies user-defined X, Y, and Z scale values.
Use size in absolute units	Specifies a user-defined size.
Use size relative to screen	Specifies a user-defined percentage of the screen.

The *3D Geometry* tab affects the point's elevation. The default option is **Use Point Elevation** (as shown in Figure 1–35), which displays the point at its actual elevation value.

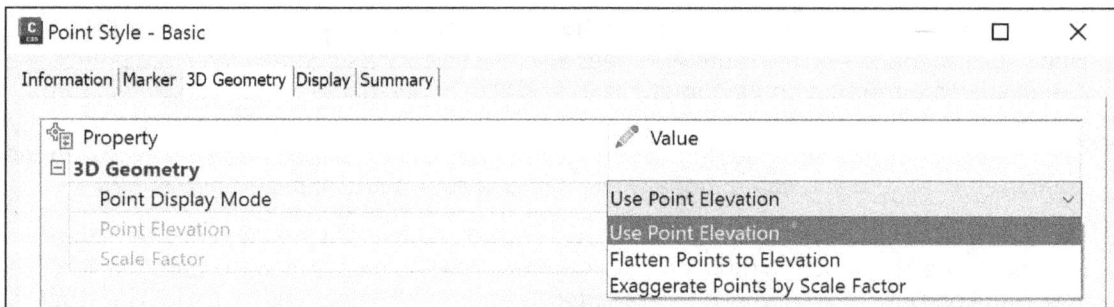

Figure 1–35

The other options are described as follows:

Flatten Points to Elevation	Specifies the elevation to which the point is projected (flattened). The *Point Elevation* cell highlights if this option is selected and is 0 elevation by default. When using an AutoCAD object snap to select a marker using this option, the resulting entity's elevation is the default elevation of 0. If selecting by point number or point object, the resulting entity is the point's actual elevation.
Exaggerate Points by Scale Factor	Exaggerates the point's elevation by a specified scale factor. When selecting this option, the *Scale Factor* cell highlights.

The *Display* tab assigns the marker and label layers and sets their visibility and properties. Setting the property to **ByLayer** uses the layer's properties. Alternatively, you can override the original layer properties by setting a specific color, linetype, or lineweight.

A style's view direction value affects how the point and label components display in the plan, model, profile, and section views, as shown in Figure 1–36.

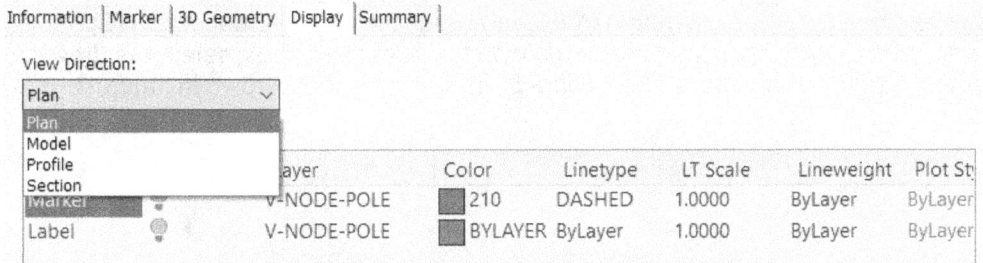

Figure 1–36

The *Summary* tab is a report of all of the style's settings. Controlling a leader arrow from a label in the dragged state points to the boundary of the marker (yes) or the center of the marker (no). It is also changed under **Marker>Leader** and stops at marker. You can also edit style variables in this tab.

Point Label Style

The Autodesk Civil 3D point label style annotates point properties beyond the typical point number, elevation, and description. A typical point label style is shown in Figure 1–37.

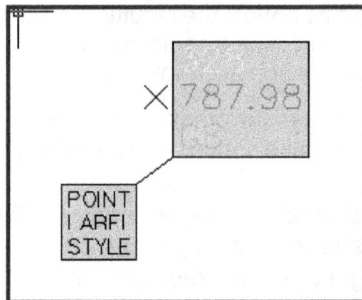

Figure 1–37

In the *TOOLSPACE>Settings* tab, the drawing name and object collections control these values for the entire drawing (at the drawing name level) or for the selected collection (*Surface*, *Alignment*, *Point*, etc.) To open the *Edit Label Style Defaults* dialog box, select the drawing name or a heading, right-click, and select **Edit Label Style Defaults...**, as shown in Figure 1–38.

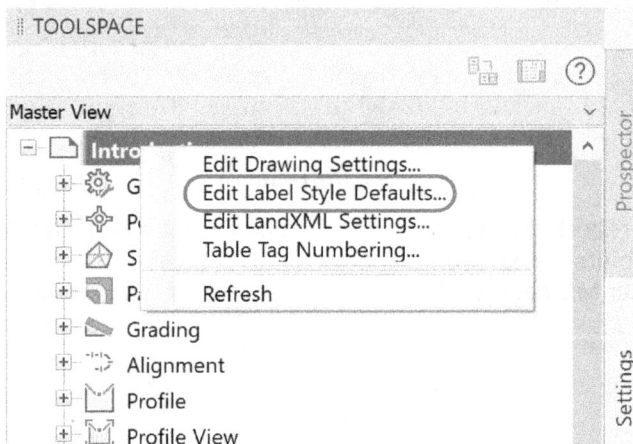

Figure 1–38

All Autodesk Civil 3D label style dialog boxes are the same. The basic behaviors for a label are in the settings in the *Edit Label Style Defaults* dialog box. The values in this dialog box define the label layer, text style, orientation, plan readability, size, dragged state behaviors, etc.

The *Label Style Composer* dialog box contains five tabs, each defining specific label behaviors: *Information*, *General*, *Layout*, *Dragged State*, and *Summary*. The *Information* tab names the style, as shown in Figure 1–39.

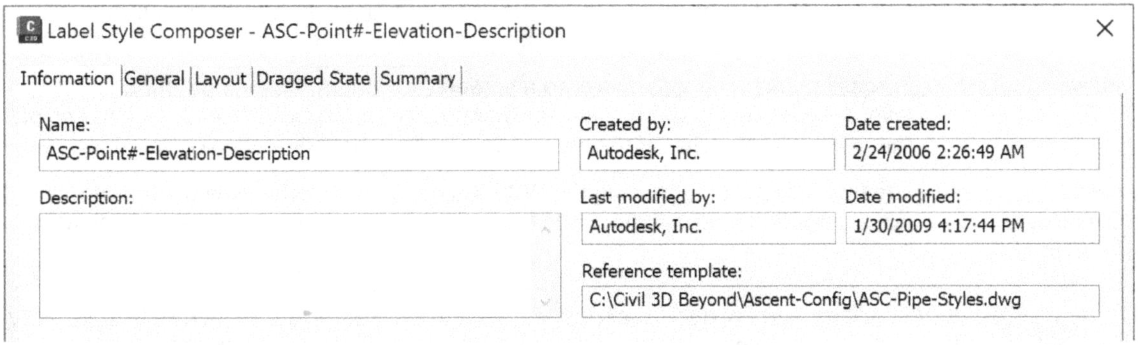

Figure 1–39

The *General* tab contains three properties: *Label* (text style and layer), *Behavior* (orientation), and *Plan Readability* (amount of view rotation before flipping text to read from the bottom or the right side of the sheet), as shown in Figure 1–40.

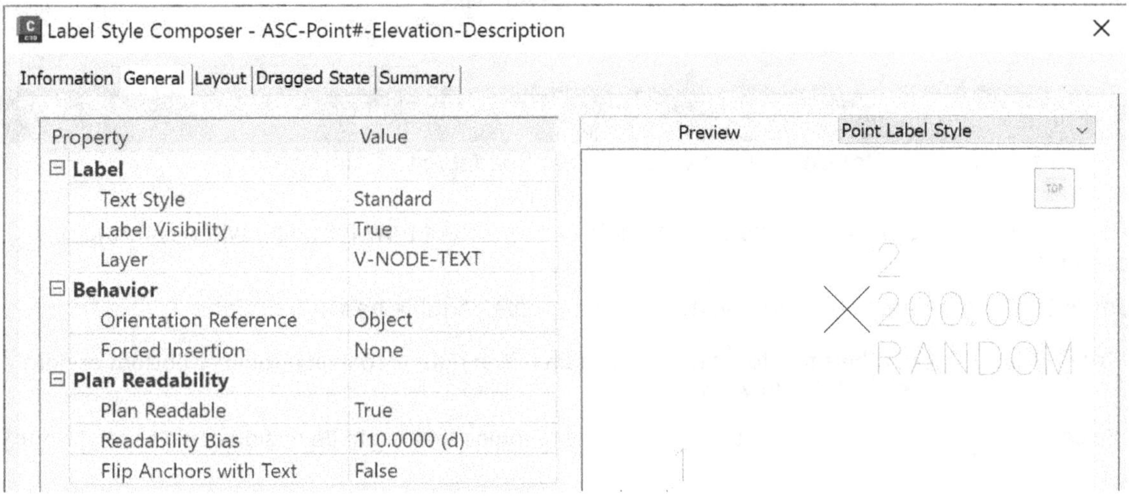

Figure 1–40

The *Label* property sets the *Text Style*, *Label Visibility*, and *Layer*. Select the *Value* cell next to the *Text Style* and *Layer* to open browsers and change their values. Selecting the *Label Visibility* cell displays a drop-down list containing the options **true** and **false**.

The *Behavior* property sets two variables that control the label's location. The *Orientation Reference* variable contains the following three label orientation options:

Object	Rotates labels relative to the object's zero direction. The object's zero direction is based on its start to end vector. If the vector changes at the label's anchor point, the orientation updates automatically. This is the default setting.
View	Forces labels to realign relative to a screen-view orientation in both model and layout views. This method assumes that the zero angle is horizontal, regardless of the UCS or Dview twist. If the view changes, the label orientation updates as well.
World Coordinate System	Labels read left to right using the WCS X-axis. Changing the view or current UCS does not affect label rotation. The label always references the world coordinate system.

Under the *Behavior* property, the **Forced Insertion** variable has three optional values that specify the label's position relative to an object. This setting only applies when the *Orientation Reference* is set to **Object** and the objects are lines, arcs, or spline segments.

None	Maintains label position as composed relative to the object.
Top	Adjusts label position to be above an object.
Bottom	Adjusts label position to be below an object.

💡 Hint: Plan Readability

If you select **Top** or **Bottom**, set the value of *Plan Readable* to **True**.

The *Plan Readability* property has three variables that affect how text flips when rotating a drawing view.

Under the *Plan Readability* property, the *Plan Readable* variable has two options.

True	Enables text to rotate to maintain left-to-right readability from the bottom or right side of the drawing.
False	Does not permit text to flip. The resulting text might be upside down or read from right to left.

The *Readability Bias* variable is the amount of rotation required to flip a label to become left-to-right readable. The angle is measured counter-clockwise from the WCS 0 (zero) direction.

The *Flip Anchors with Text* variable has two options:

True	If the text flips, the text anchor point also flips.
False	The label flips, but maintains the original anchor point. The behavior is similar to mirroring the original text.

The *Layout* tab defines the label contents, as shown in Figure 1–41. A label component is an object property that it labels. Point properties include northing, easting, raw description, etc. If user-defined properties are in use, they will also be available. A label might have one component with several properties or several components each containing an object property, as well as regular text (such as *Northing:*).

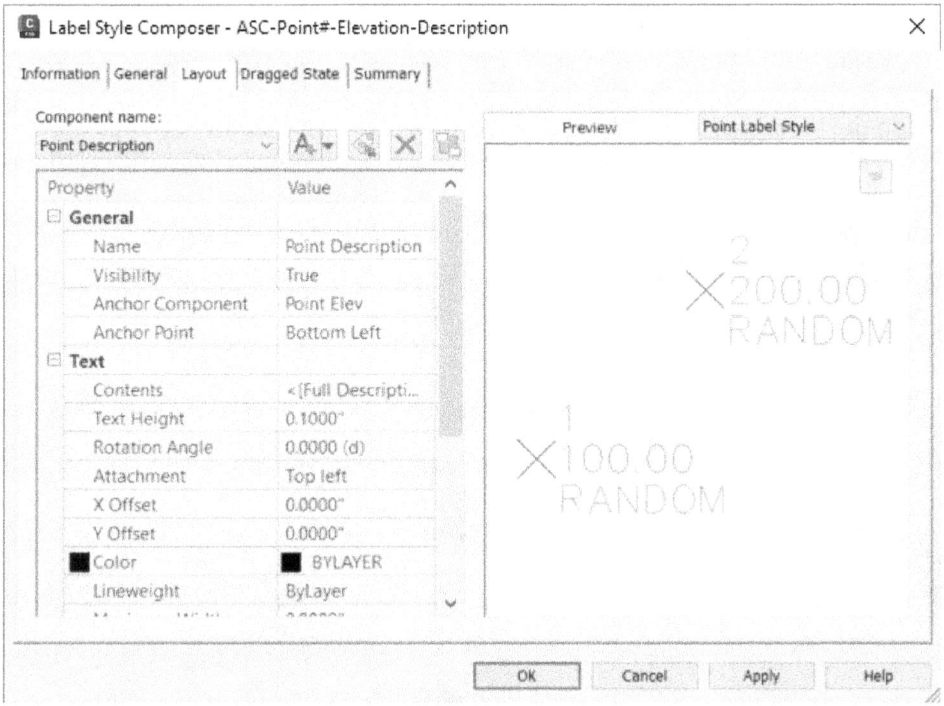

Figure 1–41

A point style label component can be text, lines, or blocks. Other object type label styles can include additional components, such as reference text, ticks, directional arrows, etc. To add a component, expand the drop-down list (as shown in Figure 1–42) and select the component type.

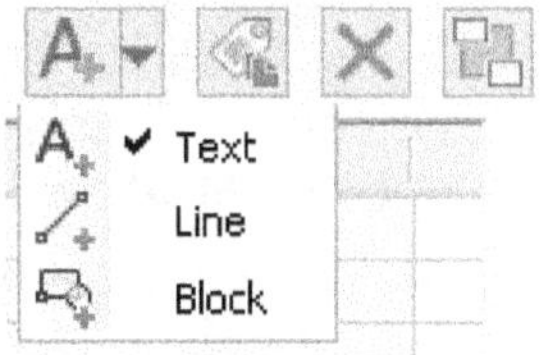

Figure 1–42

The remaining icons in the *Layout* tab are described as follows:

	Copies the current component and its properties.
	Deletes the current component.
	Changes the display order of a label's components. For example, use this icon to change the draw order of the label's component, such as text above a mask.

Depending on the label component type, it might have any combination of three areas: *General*, *Text*, and *Border*. *General* defines how the label attaches to the object or other label components, its visibility, and its anchor point.

If the label component is text, the *Text* property values affect how it displays its object property. To set or modify a label's text value, select the cell next to *Contents* to display ⚏ (as shown in Figure 1–43). Click ⚏ to open the *Text Component Editor* dialog box.

Property	Value	∧
⊟ **General**		
Name	Point Description	
Visibility	True	
Anchor Component	Point Elev	
Anchor Point	Bottom Left	
⊟ **Text**		
Contents	<[Full Description ⚏	
Text Height	0.1000"	
Rotation Angle	0.0000 (d)	
Attachment	Top left	
X Offset	0.0000"	
Y Offset	0.0000"	
■ Color	■ BYLAYER	
Lineweight	ByLayer	
Maximum Width	0.0000"	∨
⊟ **Border**		

Figure 1–43

The *Text Component Editor* dialog box (shown in Figure 1–44) defines the properties that the label annotates. When creating a label component, double-click on the text in the right pane to highlight it. In the left pane, select the property that you want to add, set the property's format values, and then click ⬒ to add the new property to the label component.

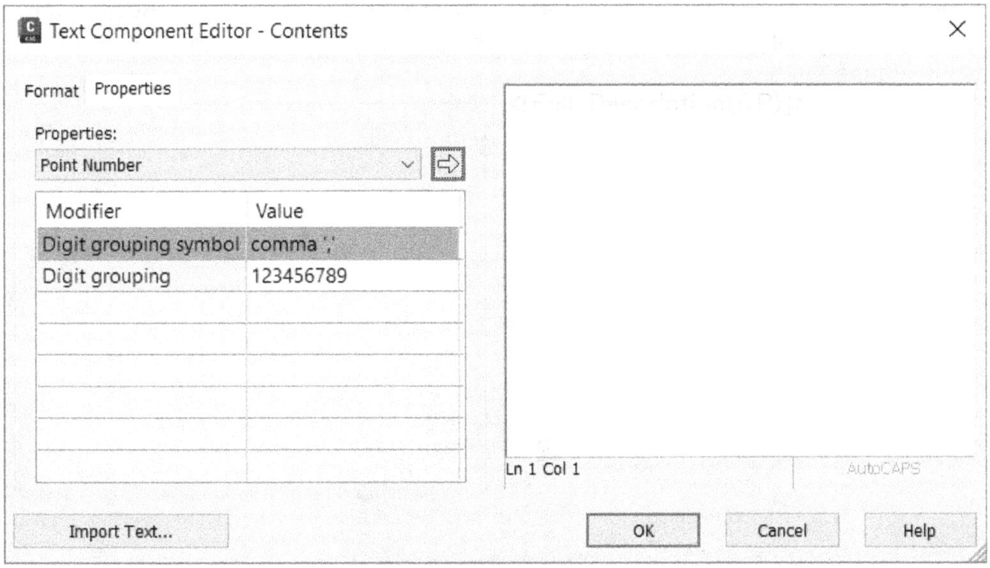

Figure 1–44

It is important to maintain the process order and to remember that the text on the right in brackets needs to be highlighted before you can revise its format values on the left.

The *Dragged State* tab has two properties: *Leader* and *Dragged State Components*. This tab defines how a label behaves when you are dragging a label from its original insertion point.

The *Leader* property defines whether a leader displays and what properties it displays. You can use the label's layer properties in the *General* tab (**ByLayer**) or override them by specifying a color, as shown in Figure 1–45.

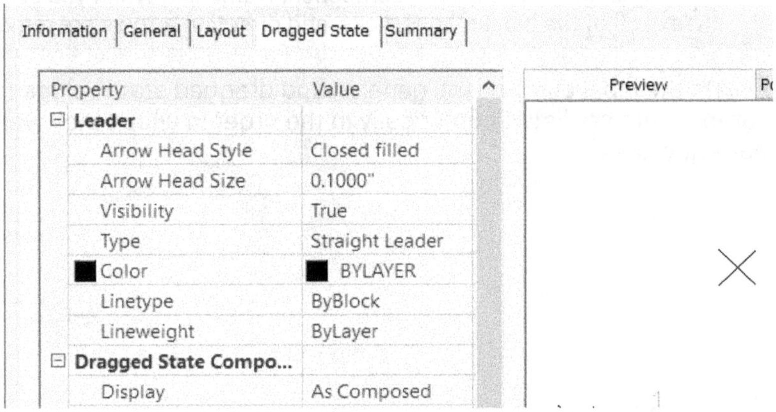

Figure 1–45

The *Dragged State Components* property defines the label component's display after it has been dragged from its original position. Select the cell next to *Display* to view the two display options, as shown in Figure 1–46.

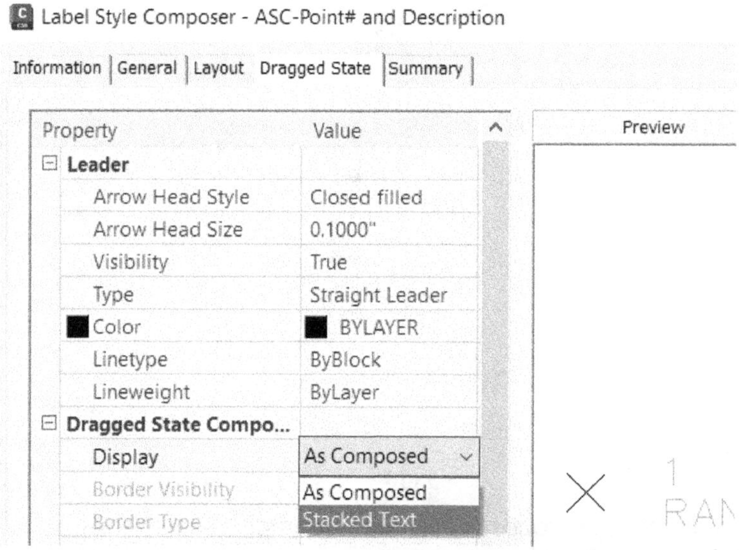

Figure 1–46

As Composed	The label maintains its original definition and orientation from the settings in the *Layout* panel. When you select **As Composed**, all of the other values become unavailable for editing.
Stacked Text	The label text becomes left justified and label components are stacked in the order listed in the *Layout's Component Name* list. When you select **Stacked Text**, all of the blocks, lines, ticks, and direction arrows are removed.

The *Summary* tab lists the label component, general, and dragged state values for the label style. The label components are listed numerically in the order in which they were defined and report all of the current values.

Practice 1b
Point Marker Styles

Practice Objectives

- Create a point marker and label style to ensure that the correct symbol is assigned to specific points.
- Create an appropriate label style for the point marker.

In this practice, you will create a marker style so a street light is displayed properly. Then you will modify a copy of an existing label style to include more information in the label.

1. **Add a block symbol.** Open **SUV-A1.dwg** from the *C:\Civil 3D Beyond\Working\Survey* folder.

2. In the *TOOLSPACE>Settings* tab, expand the *Point* collection until *Point Styles* displays. Expand the *Point Styles* collection. Review the *Point Styles* list and note that there is no light pole style.

3. In the *Point Styles* list, select the **ASC-Guy Pole** style, right-click, and select **Copy....**

4. In the *Point Style* dialog box, in the *Information* tab, change the point style's name to **ASC-Light Pole** and enter your name or initials in the *Created by:* field.

5. Select the *Marker* tab. Select the **Use AutoCAD BLOCK symbol for marker** option. In the block list, scroll across as required and select the AutoCAD block **ST-Light**, as shown in Figure 1–47.

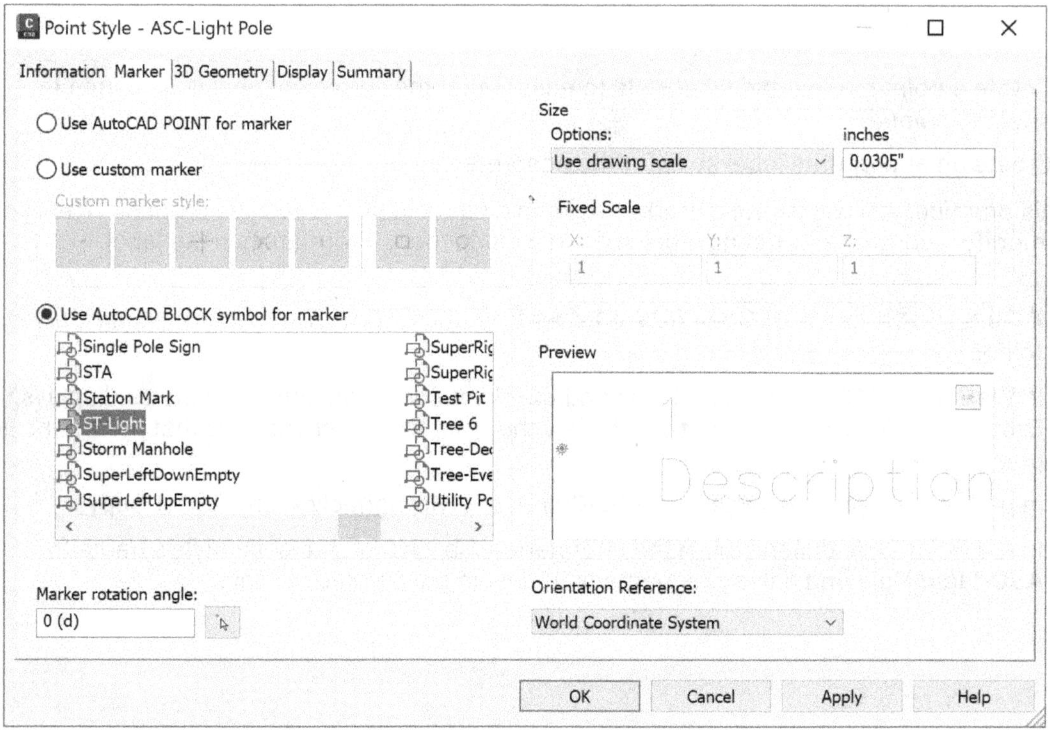

Figure 1–47

6. Select the *Display* tab and note that the layer settings are from the *Guy Pole* point style (**V-NODE-POLE**). You will reassign both the marker and label layer.

7. Selecting the **Marker** component, then hold <Shift> or <Ctrl> and select the **Label** component, as shown in Figure 1–48.

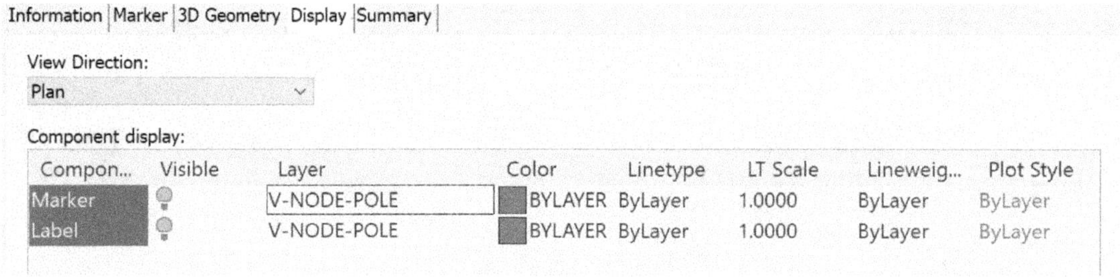

Figure 1–48

8. With both components selected, click on the *Layer* name for either component to display the drawing layer list in the *Layer Selection* dialog box.

9. Click **New** in the top right corner of the *Layer Selection* dialog box. The *Create Layer* dialog box opens (as shown in Figure 1–49), enabling you to create new layers without having to use *Layer Manager*.

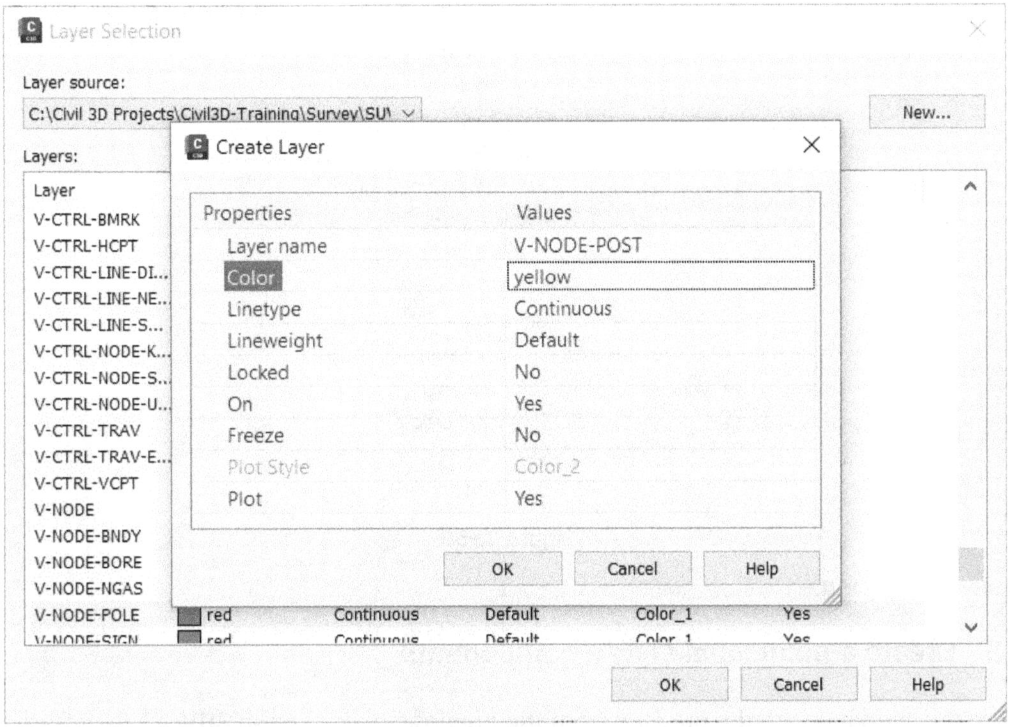

Figure 1–49

10. For the *Layer name*, type **V-NODE-POST**, and set the *Color* to **yellow**, as shown above in Figure 1–49. Click **OK** to exit the *Create Layer* dialog box, then click **OK** to exit the *Layer Selection* dialog box.

11. Click **OK** to create the point style.

12. Review the *Point Styles* list and note that **ASC-Light Pole** is now a point style, as shown in Figure 1–50.

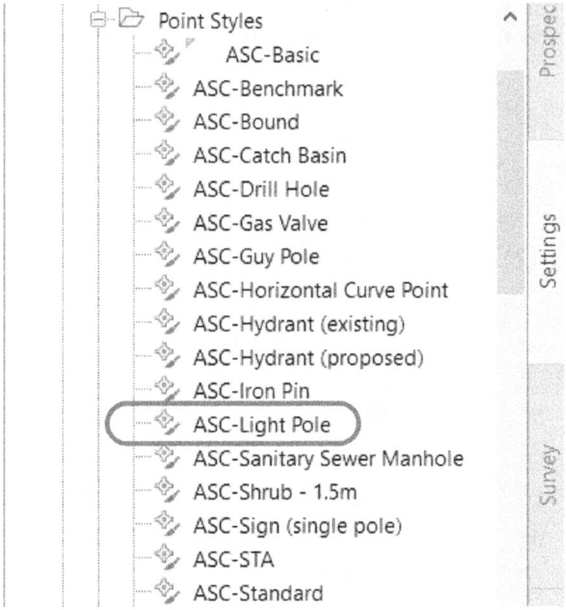

Figure 1–50

13. Save the drawing.

Task 1: Create a point label style's components.

1. Continue working with the drawing from the previous task or open **SUV-A2.dwg** from the *C:\Civil 3D Beyond\Working\Survey* folder.

2. In the *TOOLSPACE>Settings* tab, expand the *Point* collection until the *Label Styles* list displays.

3. From the list of label styles, select **ASC-Point#-Elevation- Description**, right-click, and select **Copy**.

4. In the *Label Style Composer* dialog box, in the *Information* tab, change the name to **ASC-Point#-Description-N-E** and enter your name or initials in the *Created by:* field.

5. Select the *Layout* tab and do the following (as shown in Figure 1–51):

- Expand the *Component name* drop-down list and select **Point Number**.
- Set the *Anchor Component* to **<Feature>**.
- Set the *Anchor Point* to **Top Right.**
- Set the *Attachment* to **Bottom left.**

Note: These settings attach the bottom left of the label to the top right of the point object.

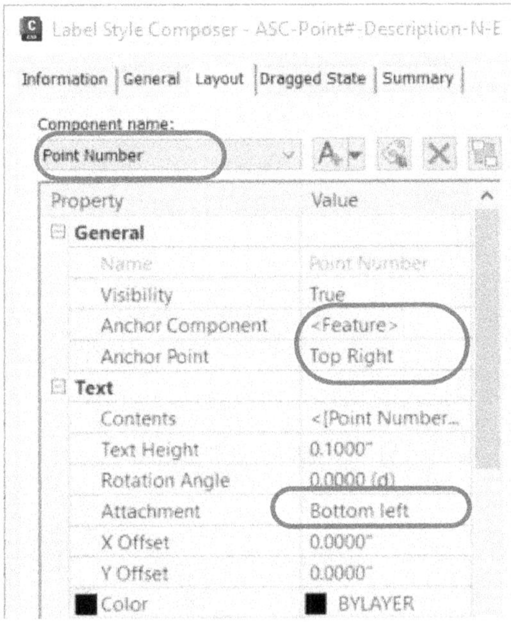

Figure 1–51

6. Since the elevation label is not required, you can delete it. Expand the *Component* name drop-down list, select **Point Elev** and click ✕, as shown in Figure 1–52. At the *Do you want to delete it?* prompt, click **Yes**.

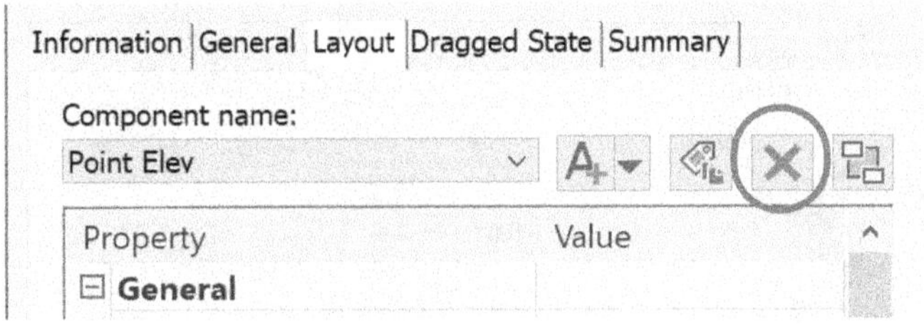

Figure 1–52

7. Expand the *Component* name drop-down list, select **Point Description** and set the following (as shown in Figure 1–53):

- *Anchor Component*: **Point Number**
- *Anchor Point:* **Bottom Left**
- *Attachment:* **Top left**

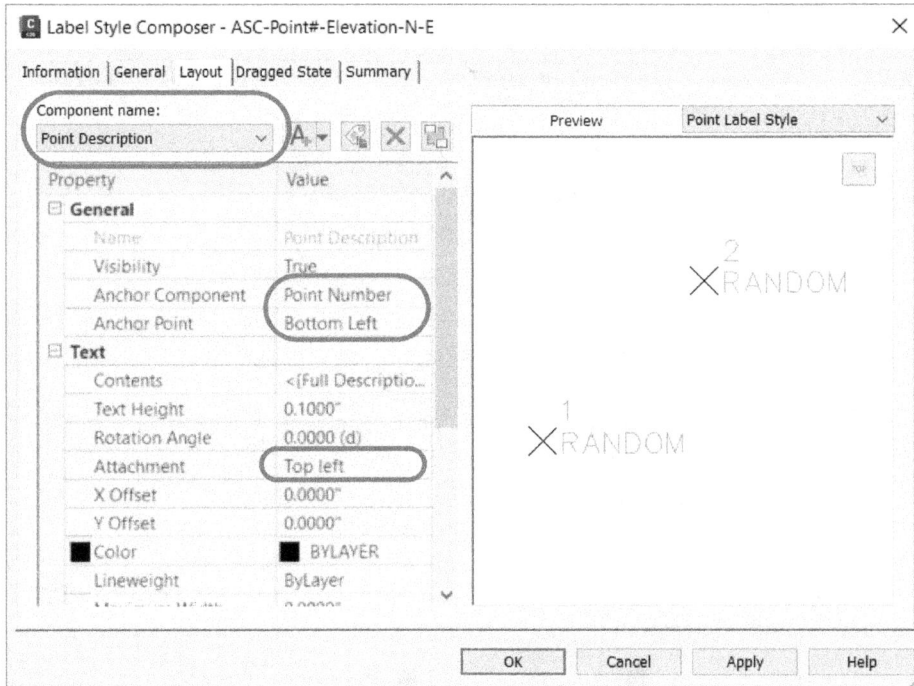

Figure 1–53

You will now add a new text component to display the northing and easting.

8. Expand the **Create Text Component** flyout (as shown in Figure 1–54) and select **Text** to create a text component.

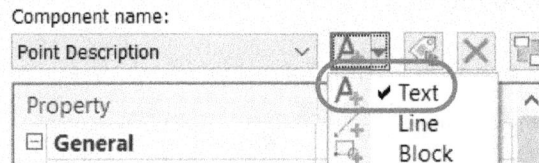

Figure 1–54

9. Change the default *Name* **text.1** to **Coordinates**, and then set the following:
   - *Anchor Component:* **Point Description**
   - *Anchor Point:* **Bottom Left**
   - *Attachment:* **Top left**

10. You will now change the contents from the default label set by the Autodesk Civil 3D software to display the coordinates. Click ⋯ next to *Label Text* in the *Contents* row, as shown in Figure 1−55.

Figure 1−55

11. In the *Text Component Editor* dialog box, double-click on the text in the right side panel to highlight it and type **N:**.

12. Expand the *Properties* drop-down list and select **Northing**. Change the *Precision* to **0.001** and click ⬅, as shown in Figure 1–56, to add the code to display the northing.

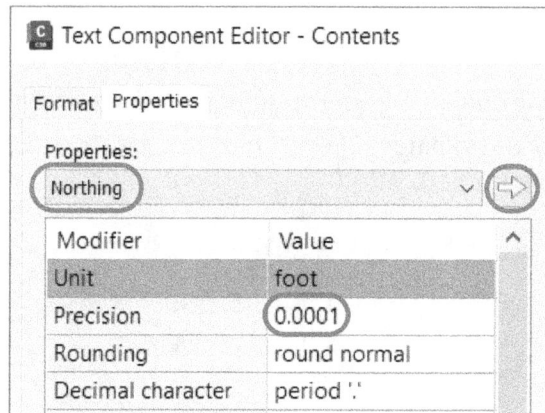

Figure 1–56

13. Click at the end of the code. Press <Enter> to insert a new line, then type **E:**. Select **Easting** in the *Properties* drop-down list and add it to post the code in the right side panel. The following should be displayed:

- N:<[Northing(Uft|P3|RN|AP|GC|UN|Sn|OF)]>
- E:<[Easting(Uft|P4|RN|AP|GC|UN|Sn|OF)]>

14. Select all of the code for the easting. Change the *Precision* to **0.001** and click ⬅ to revise the easting code.

15. Select the *Format* tab and verify that *Justification* is set to **Left**. Click **OK** to accept the changes in the *Text Component Editor* dialog box, and click **OK** again to accept the changes in the *Label Style Composer*.

16. Save the drawing.

Task 2: Apply style components.

1. Continue working with the drawing from the previous task or open **SUV-A3.dwg** from the C:\Civil 3D Beyond\Working\Survey folder.

2. In the *TOOLSPACE>Prospector* tab, expand the *Point Groups* collection until the *StreetLights* point group displays. Select the **StreetLights** group, right-click, and select **Properties**.

3. In the *Point Group Properties* dialog box, in the *Information* tab, expand the *Point style* drop-down list and select **ASC-Light Pole**. Then expand the *Point label style* drop-down list and select **ASC-Point#-Description-N-E**, as shown in Figure 1-57.

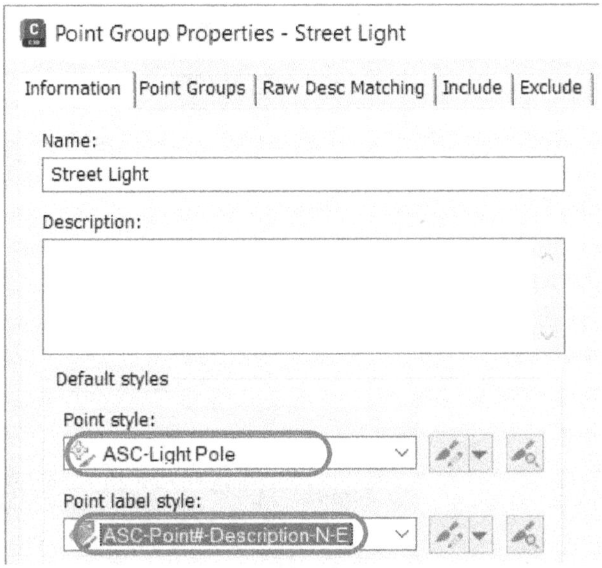

Figure 1-57

4. Click **OK** to accept the changes and close the dialog box. If the symbol and label do not change, in the *TOOLSPACE>Prospector* tab, right-click on the *StreetLights* point group and select **Update**.

5. The symbols for the light pole points have now been changed. Additionally, both the point symbols and point labels are annotative. In the *Status Bar*, expand the *Annotation Scale* drop-down list and change the scale of the drawing to **1" = 40'**, as shown in Figure 1-58. The size of the labels and point symbols change.

Figure 1-58

6. Save and close the drawing.

Task 3: Work with a label style.

1. Open **Introduction.dwg from** the *C:\Civil 3D Beyond\ References\DWG* folder.

2. Verify that the *TOOLSPACE>Settings* tab is still active.

3. View the label style default. In the *View* tab>*Named Views* panel, expand the *Named Views* drop-down list and select **Contour label**. It will zoom to a preset view of the contour labels, as shown in Figure 1–59.

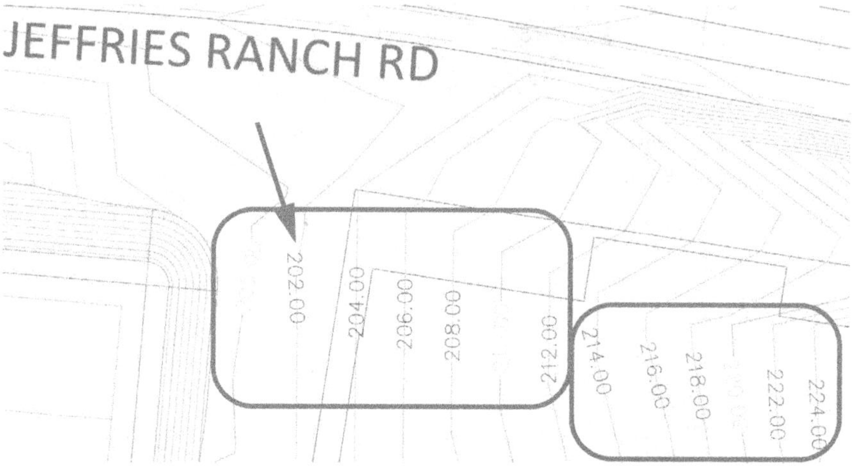

Figure 1–59

Note: The labels are not rotated to the correct drafting standards. The contour label style being used is rotating the text so that it remains plan readable (so they do not display upside down). The highlighted labels are rotated more than 90° from horizontal. This is caused by the Readability Bias setting being larger than 90°. This setting controls the viewing angle at which the contour text should be flipped.

You can change the setting in this specific contour label style only or for all surface labels in the drawing. In this task, you will assign a new value to all of the surface label styles.

4. In the *TOOLSPACE>Settings* tab, right-click on the *Surface* collection and select **Edit Label Style Defaults**, as shown in Figure 1–60.

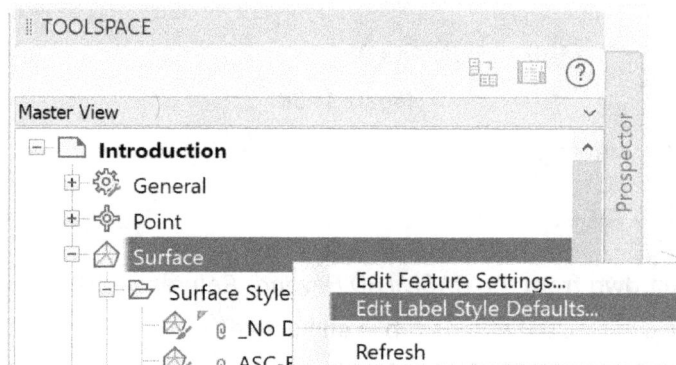

Figure 1–60

5. Under the *Plan Readability* property, note that the current value for the *Readability Bias* is 91° and that it is an override for the project settings. Uncheck the *Override* box for *Readability Bias*, which restores the default value of **110**, as shown in Figure 1–61, and click **Apply**.

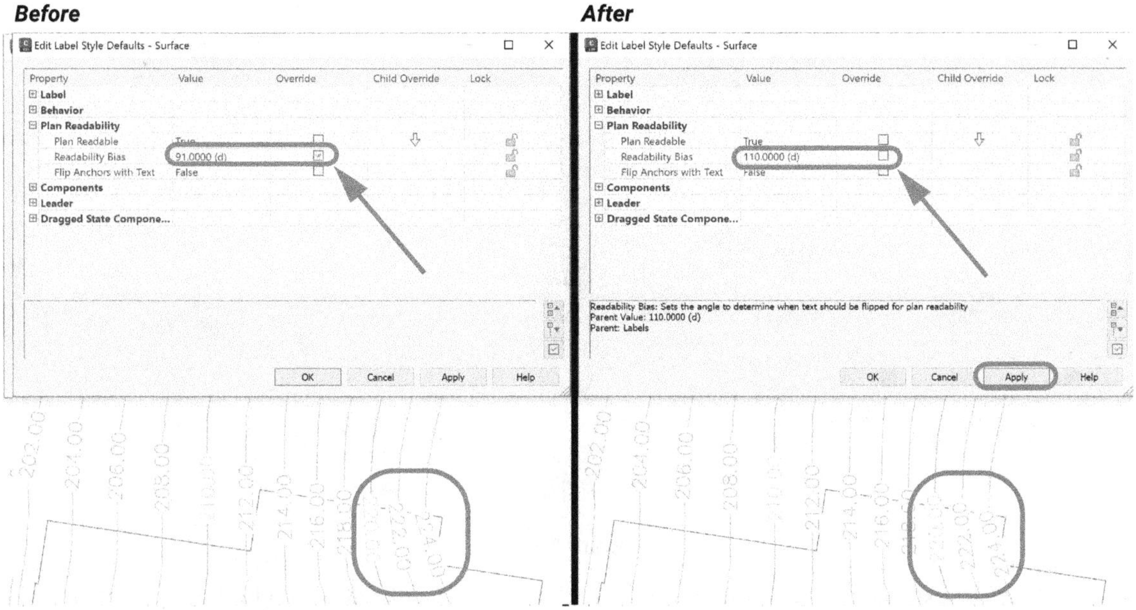

Before   **After**

Figure 1–61

6. Review the changes to the contour labels, then click **OK** to close the *Edit Label Style Defaults* dialog box.

7. In the *TOOLSPACE>Settings* tab, click **+** next to *Surface*, and then click **+** next to *Label Styles and Contour*.

8. Right-click on **ASC-Existing Major Labels** and select **Edit**.

9. In the *Label Style Composer* dialog box, in the *Layout* tab, click ⬚ (Browse) next to *Contents* to open the *Text Component Editor*. Delete all of the information in the content area to the right.

10. In the *Properties* drop-down list, select **Surface Elevation**. Change the *Precision* to **1**, and click ⇨ to place the text component in the content area, as shown in Figure 1–62.

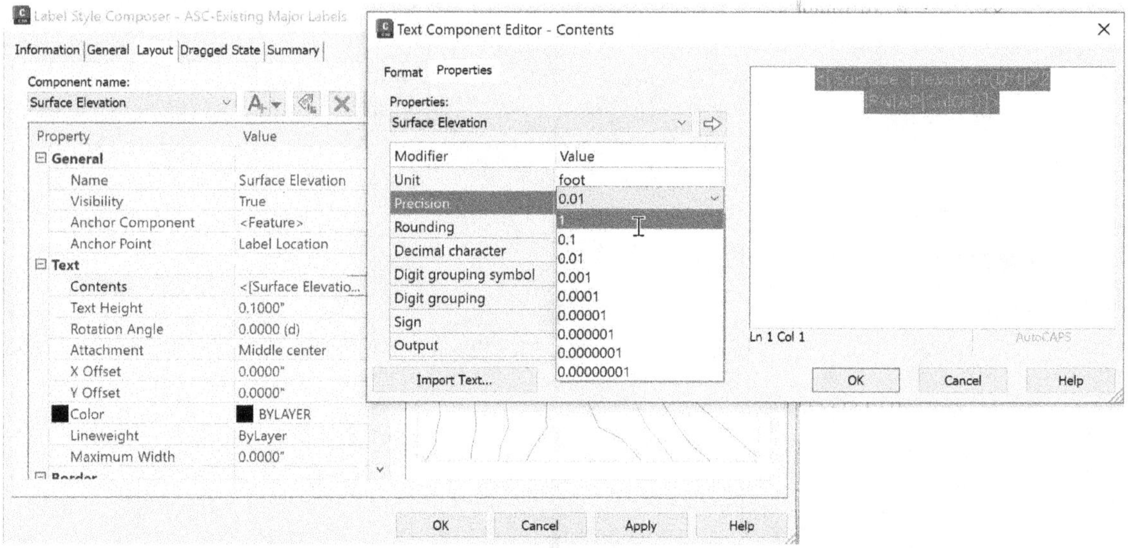

Figure 1–62

11. Click **OK** to exit the *Text Component Editor* dialog box. Click **OK** again to exit the *Label Style Composer* dialog box.

12. Repeat Steps 8 to 11 to change the **ASC-Existing Minor Labels** style in the same way.

13. Save the drawing.

End of practice

1.3 Description Key Sets

Description keys categorize points by their field descriptions (raw description). If a point matches a description key entry, the point is assigned a point and label style and a full description (a translation of the raw description). Description key sets can also scale and rotate points.

The description key's first five columns are the commonly used entries, as shown in Figure 1–63.

Code	Style	Point Label Style	Format	Layer	Scale Parameter	Fixed Scale Fact...	Use drawing sc...	
STA*	☑ STA	☑ Point#-Elevati	$*	☑ V-CT	☑ Parameter 1	☐ 1.000	☐ No	
SWMH*	☑ Storm Se	☑ Point#-Elevati	$*	☑ V-NC	☑ Parameter 1	☐ 1.000	☐ No	
TR*	☑ Tree	☑ Point#-Elevati	$*	☑ V-NC	☑ Parameter 1	☐ 1.000	☐ No	

Figure 1–63

*   To create a new description key row, select an existing code, right-click, and select **New**. To edit a code, double-click in the cell.

Code, Point, and Label Style

Description code is a significant part of data collection. Codes assigned to a raw description trigger action by the description key set. Each entry in the set represents all of the possible descriptions that a field crew would use while surveying a job. When a raw description matches a code entry, the key set assigns all of the row's values to the matching point, including point style, label style, translation of the raw description, and possibly a layer. Codes are case-sensitive and must match the field collector's entered raw description.

A code might contain wild cards to match raw descriptions that contain numbering or additional material beyond the point's description. For example, MH? would match MH1, MH2, etc., but not MH12, since the ? (question mark) symbol matches only single characters, whereas UP* would match UP 2245 14.4Kv POWER, since the * (asterisk) matches any string characters. Common wild keys are as follows:

# (pound)	Matches any single numeric digit (e.g., T# matches T1 through T9).
@ (at)	Matches any alphabetic character (e.g., 1@ matches 1A through 1Z).
. (period)	Matches any non-alphanumeric character (e.g., T. matches T- or T+).
* (asterisk)	Matches any string of characters (e.g., T* matches TREE, TR-Aspen, Topo, or Trench).
? (question mark)	Matches any single character (e.g., ?BC matches TBC or 3BC).

Matching a key set entry for the code assigns a point style at the point's coordinates. If the *Point Style* is set to **Default**, the *Settings* tab's Point feature's *Point Style* is used (which is set in the *Edit Feature Settings* dialog box, as shown in Figure 1–64).

Matching a key set entry for the code assigns a point label style to annotate important point values. This is usually a number, elevation, and description. If the *Point Label Style* is set to **Default**, the *Settings* tab's Point feature's *Point Label Style* is used (which is set in the *Edit Feature Settings* dialog box, as shown in Figure 1–64).

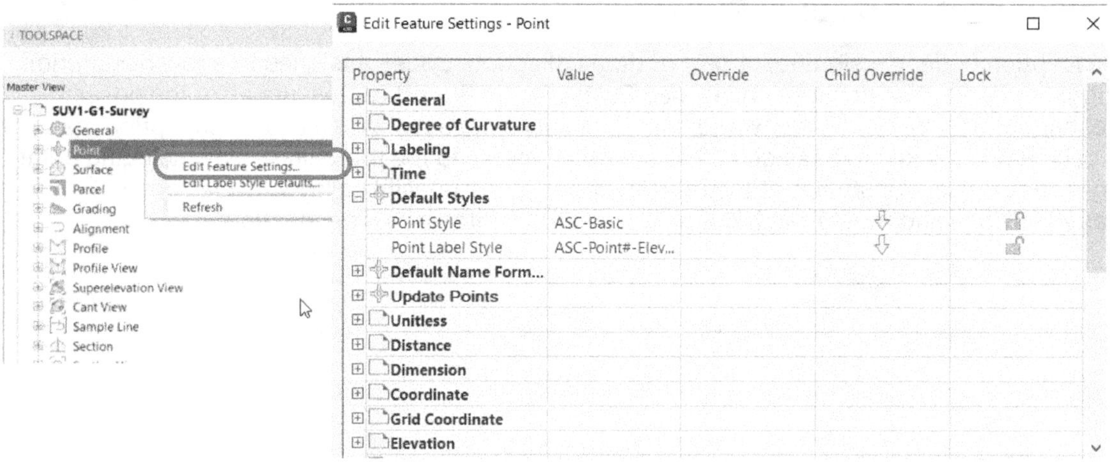

Figure 1–64

Format

The *Format* column for the description key set translates the raw description (what the surveyor typed) into a full description (what you want it to read). When spaces are included in a raw description, the Autodesk Civil 3D software assigns parameter numbers to each description element. Parameters are represented by a $ sign followed by a number. For example, the description *PINE 6* has two elements: PINE and 6, with PINE as parameter 0 ($0) and 6 as parameter 1 ($1). When the *Format* column contains $*, it indicates that the software should use the raw description as the full description. The *Format* column can reorder the parameters and add characters to create a full description. For example, the raw description *PINE 6* can be translated to 6' PINE by entering **$1' $0**.

A complex raw description is as follows:

> TREE D MAPLE 9

For the raw description to match the description key set entry, the entry **TREE** must have an asterisk (*) after TREE (as shown in Figure 1–65). The raw description elements and their parameters are TREE ($0), D ($1), MAPLE ($2), and 9 ($3). The *Format* column entry of **$3' $2 $0** creates a full description of **9' MAPLE TREE**.

Code	Style	Point Label Style	Format	Layer	Scale Parameter	Fixed Scale Fact...	Use drawing sc...	
☑ STA*	☑ STA	☑ Point#-Elevati	$*	☑ V-CT	☑ Parameter 1	☐ 1.000	☐ No	
☑ SWMH*	☑ Storm Se	☑ Point#-Elevati	$*	☑ V-N(	☑ Parameter 1	☐ 1.000	☐ No	
☑ TR*	☑ Tree	☑ Point#-Elevati	$*	☑ V-N(	☑ Parameter 1	☐ 1.000	☐ No	

Figure 1–65

If a point does not match any description key set entry, it receives the default styles assigned by the _All Points group.

The *Layer* column assigns a layer to the matching point. If the point style already has a marker and label layer, this entry should be toggled off. The description key set also contains the *Scale Parameter* and *Rotate Parameter* columns. In the example in Figure 1–65, the 3 for the trunk diameter can also be a tree symbol scaling factor when applied to the symbol's X-Y.

The most common parameter is the **Scale** parameter. With this parameter, a surveyor will enter the size of a tree as part of the description and the description key file will insert a symbol scaled to the value provided by the surveyor.

The **Rotate** parameter is used less frequently, but it can be useful. For example, you can edit the point file in the office (not in the field) once you have determined the bearing of a roadside curb. Then, you can append that rotation value as a parameter to the description of each hydrant, street sign, light standard, etc. along the road to have them inserted with the proper rotation so the symbols will be inserted with the proper angle to be perpendicular to the curb.

1.4 Figure Styles

Figure styles (found in the *TOOLSPACE>Settings* tab, under *Survey>Figures>Figure Styles*) affect how the survey linework displays in a drawing. They should be part of your template file. These styles are not critical. However, to make figures work more efficiently, you should define the layers they use in the drawing.

- Figure styles are tied to the *Figure Prefix* database. The *Figure Prefix* database assigns a figure style to a figure that is imported into a drawing.

- A figure style includes the layers for its linework and markers.

- A marker is a symbol placed on the figure's segment midpoints and end points. They call attention to the figure's geometry. Although a figure style includes marker definitions, they typically do not display.

- In the *Figure Style* dialog box, the *Information* tab assigns a name to a style. The *Profile*, and *Section* tabs define how the marker displays in various views.

- The *Display* tab defines which figure's components display and which layers they use for plan, model, profile, and section views, as shown in Figure 1−66.

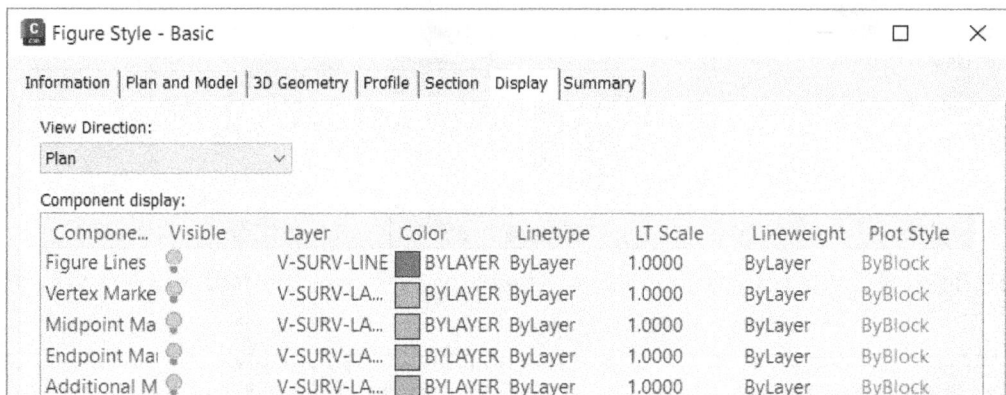

Figure 1−66

Figure Prefix Database

The *Figure Prefix* database (found in the *TOOLSPACE>Survey* tab) assigns the figure a style and a layer, and defines whether the figure is a surface breakline and/or lot line (parcel segment). If you did not define any figure styles, you should at least assign a layer to correctly place the figure in the drawing. Toggling on the *Breakline* property, as shown in Figure 1–67, enables you to select all of the tagged survey figures and assign them to a surface without having to insert or select from a drawing. Toggling on the *Lot Line* property creates a parcel segment from the figure in the drawing and, if there is a closed polygon or intersecting lines to form an enclosure, assigns a parcel label and creates a parcel in the designated site.

Name	Breakline	Lot Line	Layer	Style	Site
Trail	✓ Yes	☐ No	0	ASC-Road Cent ⌄	Survey Site
Building	☐ No	☐ No	0	ASC-Bldg-Foot ⌄	Survey Site
CL	✓ Yes	☐ No	0	ASC-Road Cent ⌄	Survey Site
EOS	✓ Yes	☐ No	V-ROAD-SHLD ⌄	Standard ⌄	Survey Site
EOP	✓ Yes	☐ No	0	ASC-Curb ⌄	Survey Site
DITCH	✓ Yes	☐ No	V-ROAD-DTCH ⌄	ASC-Standard ⌄	Survey Site

Figure Prefix Database Manager - ASCENT

OK   Cancel   Help

Figure 1–67

If the *Name* is **EOP** (as shown above in Figure 1–67), any figure starting with EOP uses these settings. This is similar to using a description key set, except that the entry in the Figure Prefix database does not need an asterisk (*). The entry *Name* matches EOP-R or EOP-West or EOP-Main-East. When inserting survey figures in the drawing, Survey checks the Figure Prefix database for style or layer values.

Practice 1c
Create Figure Prefixes and a Description Key Set

Practice Objectives

- Create a figure database for automatically stylizing linework when importing field book or ASCII files.

- Assign point symbols, labels, layers, etc. on import by setting up description key sets.

In this practice, you will learn to create figure prefixes to assist in automatic linework creation. You will also create a new description key set entry and apply it to an existing point. In addition, you will update the description key set to use parameters.

> 💡 **Hint: Software Configuration**
>
> For the practices in this chapter to work properly, the configuration changes as noted in the preface of this course must be made.

Task 1: Create a new description key set entry.

1. Open **SUV-B.dwg** from the *C:\Civil 3D Beyond\Working\Survey* folder.

2. In the *TOOLSPACE>Settings* tab, expand the *Point* collection to the *Description Key Set* collection.

3. Select **Civil 3D**, right-click, and select **Edit Keys...**.

4. In the *DescKey Editor*, right-click in any *Code* cell and select **New...**, as shown in Figure 1–68.

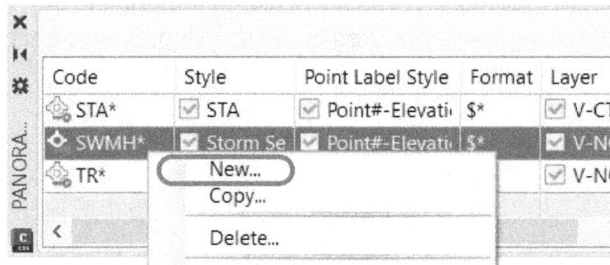

Figure 1–68

5. Double-click in the *Code* cell in the newly created row and type **HYD**, as shown in Figure 1–69.

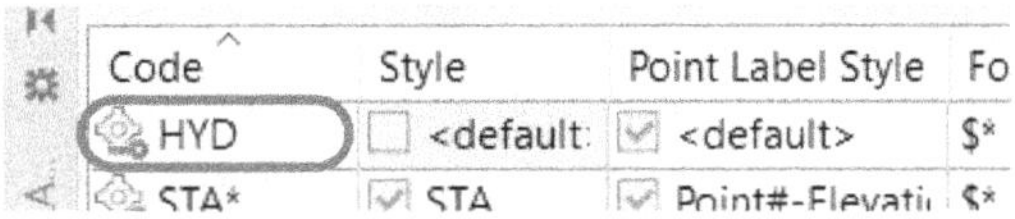

Figure 1–69

6. In the *Style* cell, toggle on the point style and select the **Style** cell to open the *Point Style* dialog box, as shown in Figure 1–70. Select **ASC-Hydrant (existing)** in the drop-down list and click **OK** to assign the style to the code.

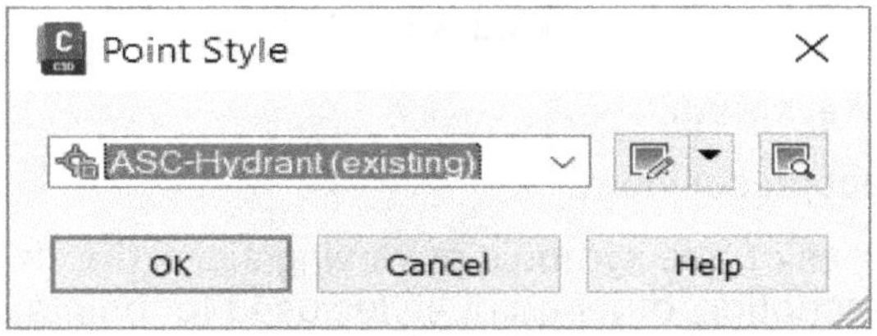

Figure 1–70

7. Leave **<default>** selected as the *Point Label Style* and **$*** as the *Format*. This means the label will be the same as the one entered by the surveyor.

8. Leave the checkbox toggled off in the *Layer* column.

9. Select the **Yes** option in the *Use drawing scale* column and clear the checkbox for the *Scale Parameter*, as shown in Figure 1–71. You do not have a scale parameter and will not be using a fixed scale.

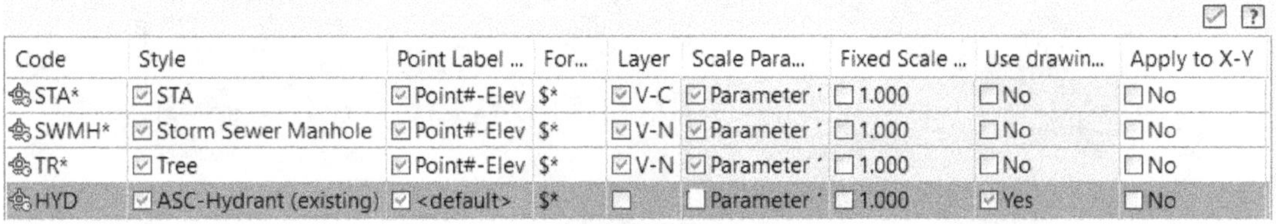

Code	Style	Point Label ...	For...	Layer	Scale Para...	Fixed Scale ...	Use drawin...	Apply to X-Y
☑ STA*	☑ STA	☑ Point#-Elev	$*	☑ V-C	☑ Parameter '	☐ 1.000	☐ No	☐ No
☑ SWMH*	☑ Storm Sewer Manhole	☑ Point#-Elev	$*	☑ V-N	☑ Parameter '	☐ 1.000	☐ No	☐ No
☑ TR*	☑ Tree	☑ Point#-Elev	$*	☑ V-N	☑ Parameter '	☐ 1.000	☐ No	☐ No
☑ HYD	☑ ASC-Hydrant (existing)	☑ <default>	$*	☐	☐ Parameter '	☐ 1.000	☑ Yes	☐ No

Figure 1–71

10. Close the *DescKey Editor* vista by clicking ☑ in the top right corner of the palette.

11. Open **SUV-Complete.dwg** from the *C:\Civil 3D Beyond\Working\Survey* folder.

12. In the *TOOLSPACE>Settings* tab, go to the *Point\Description Key Set* branch.

13. Select **Ascent**, right-click, and select **Edit Keys....**to see an example of a robust description key set, as shown in Figure 1–72.

Code	Style	Point Label Style	Format	Layer	Scale Parameter	Fixed Scale Factor	Use drawing scale	App
☐ BRUSH*	☑ Tree Brusl	☑ ASC-Point#-El	$2' $1 (1	☑ V-NC	☑ Parameter 2	☑ 3.100	☐ No	☑ `
☐ CTREE*	☑ Tree C	☑ ASC-Point#-El	$2' $1 (1	☑ V-NC	☑ Parameter 2	☑ 3.100	☐ No	☑ `
☐ DTREE*	☑ Tree D	☑ ASC-Point#-El	$2' $1 (1	☑ V-NC	☑ Parameter 2	☑ 3.100	☐ No	☑ `
↻ GS	☑ ASC-Grou	☑ <default>	GROUN	☑ V-NC	☑ Parameter 1	☐ 1.000	☐ No	☐ I
HYD*	☑ ASC-Hydr	☑ <default>	Hydrant	☐	☑ Parameter 1	☐ 1.000	☐ No	☐ I
STA*	☑ ASC-STA	☑ ASC-Point#-El	$*	☑ V-CT	☑ Parameter 1	☐ 1.000	☐ No	☐ I
SWMH*	☑ ASC-Storr	☑ ASC-Point#-El	$*	☑ V-NC	☑ Parameter 1	☐ 1.000	☐ No	☐ I

Figure 1–72

14. Close the *Description Keys* vista.

15. Select the **Point Inspect** preset view.

16. Notice the different types of tree symbols at varying sizes, the size and type of trees documented in the description, other point styles used for points of the same description, as shown in Figure 1–73.

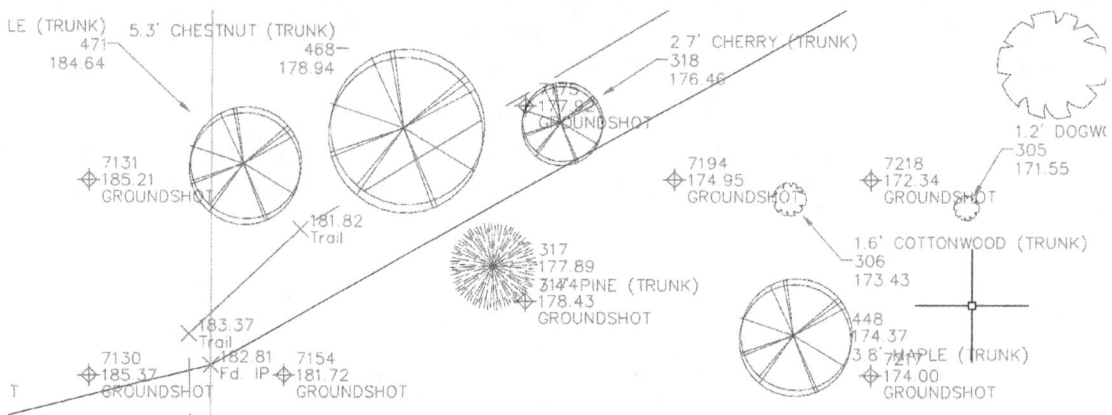

Figure 1–73

Task 2: Apply the new description key set to an existing point.

1. In **SUV-B.dwg** in the *Transparent* tab, click ⊕ (Zoom to Point), and then type **260** and press <Enter>.

2. In the *TOOLSPACE>Prospector* tab, select the **_All Points** group, right-click, and select **Apply Description Keys**, as shown in Figure 1–74.

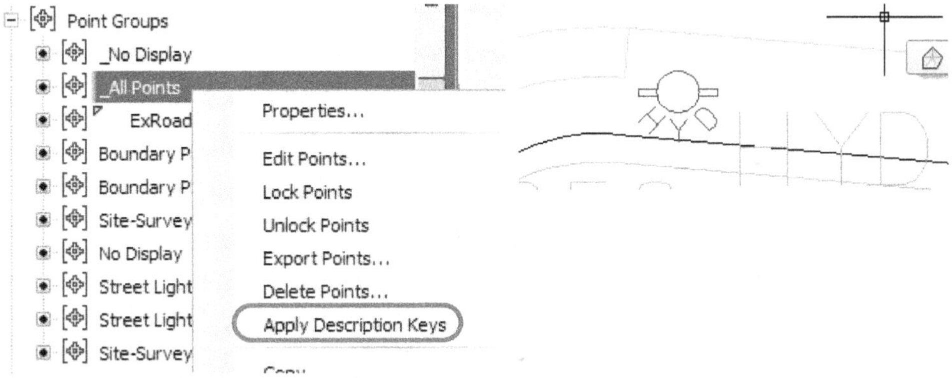

Figure 1–74

- The point updates to display the Hydrant symbol and its new description.

3. Save the drawing.

Task 3: Update the description key set to use parameters.

In this task, you will use the **Parameters** feature to control the display properties of symbols in your drawings.

In this case, you will use the **Rotate** parameter, so that the pumpers on the hydrant display correctly (i.e., running parallel to the road).

1. In the *TOOLSPACE>Settings* tab, expand *Point>Description Key Sets*. Select **Civil 3D**, right-click, and select **Edit Keys...**, as shown in Figure 1–75.

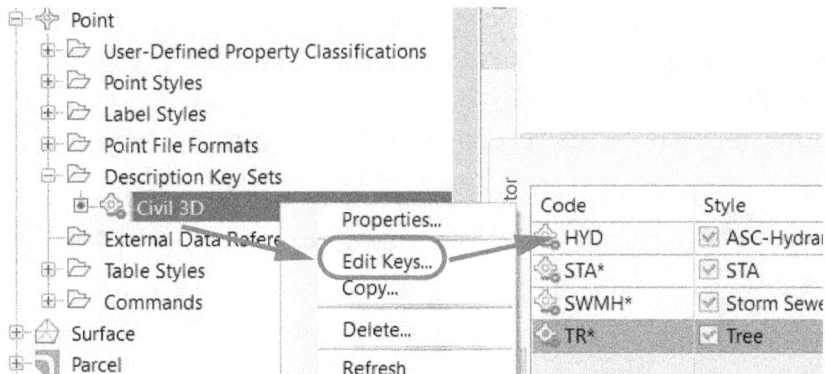

Figure 1–75

2. In the *HYD* row, in the *Code* column, type **HYD***. The asterisk symbolizes a wildcard (i.e., any character after the letters HYD).

3. In the *HYD* row, select the checkbox in the *Marker Rotate* column (as shown in Figure 1–76), select the cell, and select **Parameter 1** in the drop-down list.

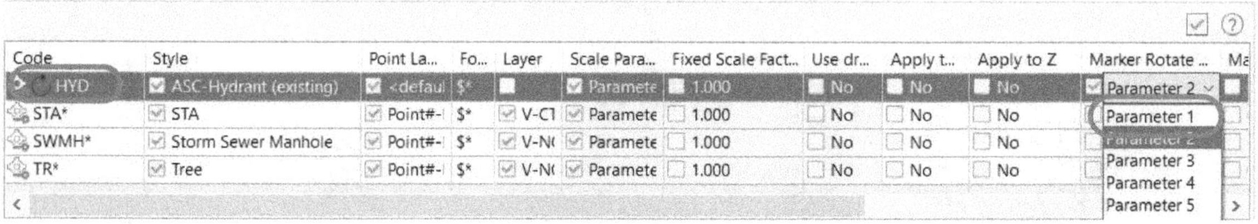

Code	Style	Point La...	Fo...	Layer	Scale Para...	Fixed Scale Fact...	Use dr...	Apply t...	Apply to Z	Marker Rotate ...	Ma
> HYD	☑ ASC-Hydrant (existing)	☑ <defaul	$*	■	☑ Paramete	■ 1.000	■ No	■ No	■ No	☑ Parameter 2 ∨	☐
STA*	☑ STA	☑ Point#-|	$*	☑ V-C1	☑ Paramete	☐ 1.000	☐ No	☐ No	☐ No	Parameter 1	
SWMH*	☑ Storm Sewer Manhole	☑ Point#-|	$*	☑ V-N(	☑ Paramete	☐ 1.000	☐ No	☐ No	☐ No	Parameter 2	
TR*	☑ Tree	☑ Point#-|	$*	☑ V-N(	☑ Paramete	☐ 1.000	☐ No	☐ No	☐ No	Parameter 3	
										Parameter 4	
										Parameter 5	>

Figure 1–76

4. Click ☑ in the top right corner of the dialog box to close the *Panorama* view.

5. Using the AutoCAD **Distance** inquiry, you will note that the bearing of the curb is 5° clockwise, as shown in Figure 1–77.

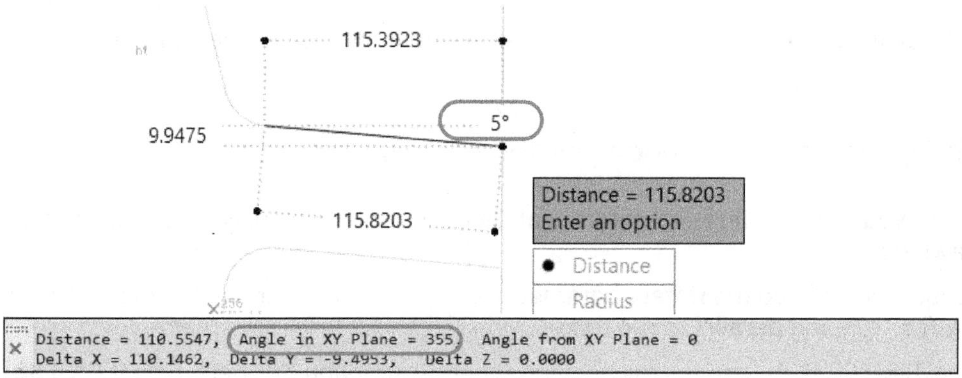

Figure 1–77

6. In *Model Space*, select the *Hydrant point* object, right-click, and select **Edit Points**.

7. Set the *Raw Description* from *HYD* to **HYD -5**. Ensure that you put a space after **HYD**. The **-5** indicates the required rotation.

8. Select the row, right-click, and select **Apply Description Keys**, as shown in Figure 1–78.

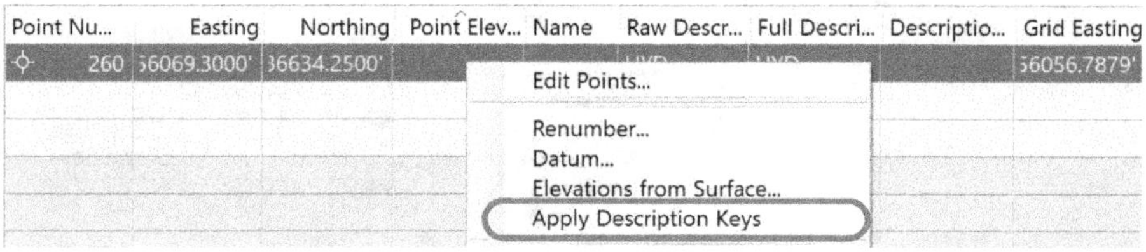

Figure 1–78

9. Click ☑ in the top right corner of the dialog box to close the *Panorama* view.

- The hydrant has now been rotated to display the hydrant pumpers following the bearing of the curb, as shown in Figure 1–79. The curb line is accentuated in the figure for clarity. The rotation is slight and may be difficult to discern.

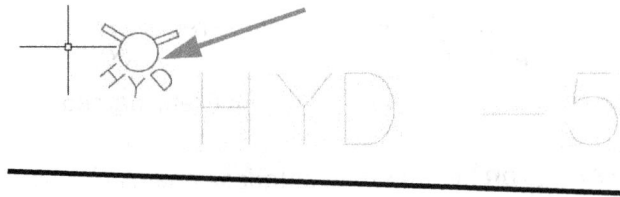

Figure 1–79

10. The label also displays the rotation angle text **-5**, which you do not want. In the *TOOLSPACE>Settings* tab, expand the *Point* and *Description Key Sets* collections. Select **Civil 3D**, right-click, and select **Edit Keys...**.

11. In the HYD row, change the *Format* from $* to **Hydrant**, as shown in Figure 1–80.

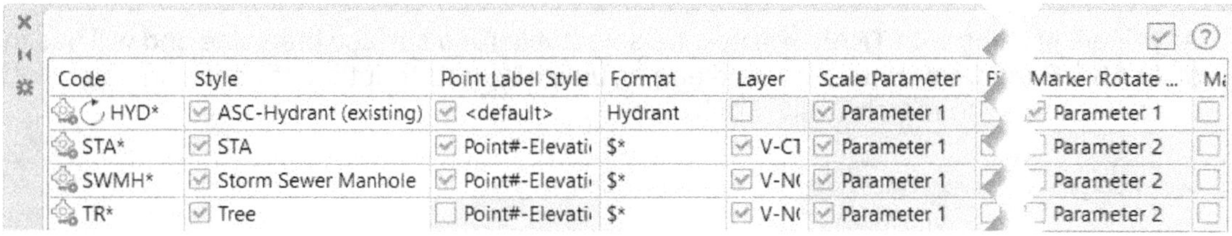

Code	Style	Point Label Style	Format	Layer	Scale Parameter	Fi	Marker Rotate ...	Mi
⊙ HYD*	☑ ASC-Hydrant (existing)	☑ <default>	Hydrant	☐	☑ Parameter 1	☐	☑ Parameter 1	☐
STA*	☑ STA	☑ Point#-Elevati	$*	☑ V-C1	☑ Parameter 1	☐	Parameter 2	☐
SWMH*	☑ Storm Sewer Manhole	☑ Point#-Elevati	$*	☑ V-N(	☑ Parameter 1	☐	Parameter 2	☐
TR*	☑ Tree	☐ Point#-Elevati	$*	☑ V-N(	☑ Parameter 1	☐	Parameter 2	☐

Figure 1–80

12. Click ☑ in the top right corner of the dialog box to close the *Panorama* view.

13. In *Model Space*, select the Hydrant point object, right-click, and select **Apply Description Keys**. The changes are now applied, as shown in Figure 1–81.

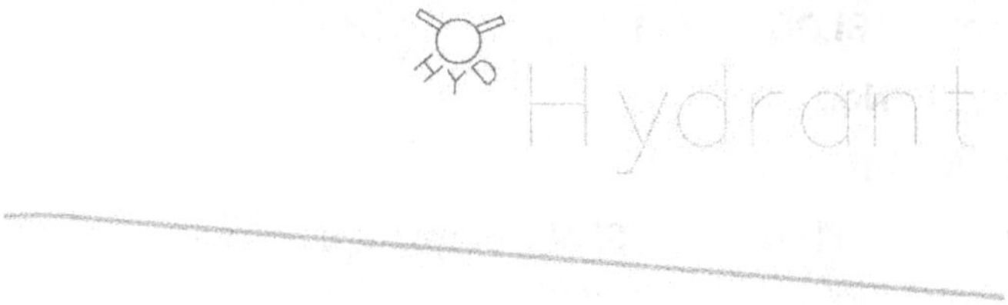

Figure 1–81

14. Save and close the drawing.

Task 4: Create Figure Prefixes

1. Open **SUV-C.dwg** from the *C:\Civil 3D Beyond\Working\Survey* folder.

2. In the *TOOLSPACE>Survey* tab, right-click on *Figure Prefix Databases* and select **New...**. Type **XXX-Fig-DB** for the name (substitute your initials for XXX).

3. Right-click on the newly created **XXX-Fig-DB** Figure Prefix database and select **Make Current**.

4. Right-click on the **XXX-Fig-DB** Figure Prefix database again and select **Manage Figure Prefix Database...**.

5. In the *Figure Prefix Database Manager*, click to create a new figure definition, then do the following, as shown in Figure 1–82:

   - Change the *Name* to **TRAIL**.
   - Select *Breakline*.
   - Set *Style* to **ASC-Road Centerline**.

   Any figure starting with **TRAIL** will now be selectable for a surface breakline and will use the style **ASC-Road Centerline**. As noted earlier, unlike with description key sets, an asterisk (*) is not necessary to match Trail1, Trail2, etc.

Name	Breakline	Lot Line	Layer	Style	Site
TRAIL	✓ Yes	☐ No	0	ASC-Road Cent	Survey Site

Figure 1–82

6. Click to create a new figure definition.

   - Change the *Name* to **BLDG**.
   - Set the *Breakline* to **No.**
   - Set the *Style* to **ASC-Buildings**.

7. Click **OK** to exit the dialog box. Open **SUV-Complete.dwg** from the *C:\Civil 3D Beyond\Working\Survey* folder if not already opened.

8. In the *TOOLSPACE>Survey* tab, expand the *Figure Prefix Databases* branch.

9. Right-click on the **ASCENT** Figure Prefix database and select **Manage Figure Prefix Database...** This display a robust figure prefix database, as shown in Figure 1–83.

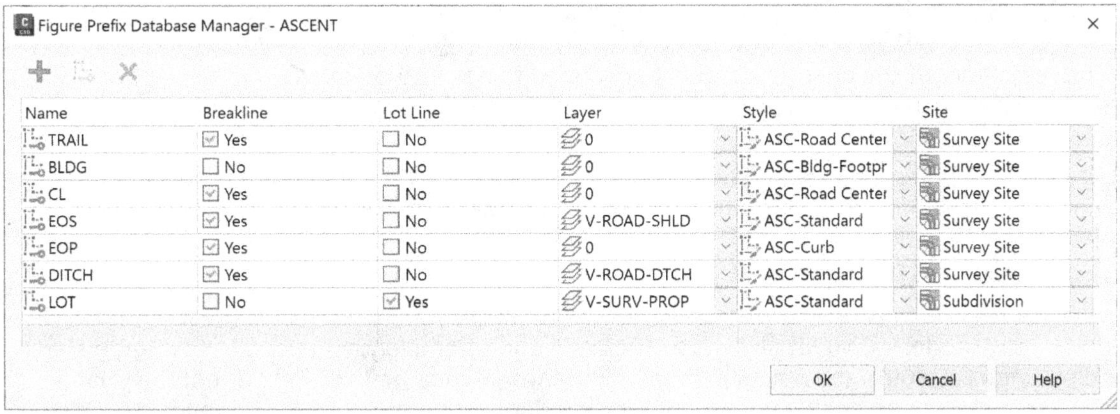

Figure 1–83

10. Close the *Figure Prefix Database Manager* panel.

11. Select the **Figure Inspect** preset view.

12. Notice the different types of lines for **Mission Avenue** for the daylighting, center line, edge of pavement, etc, as well as the trial, as shown in Figure 1–84. These are all controlled through the Figure Prefix database.

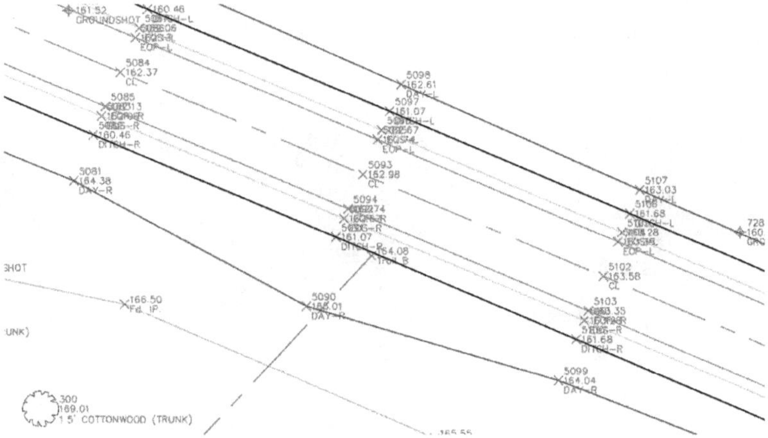

Figure 1–84

13. Close the drawings, saving them if prompted.

End of practice

1.5 Templates

Hint: Advanced Topics (Optional)

The remainder of the chapter contains advanced topics and practices and these may be skipped if the topics don't apply to you or if you have time constraints.

A drawing template (.DWT extension) contains all blocks, Paper Space title sheets, settings, layers, Autodesk Civil 3D styles, and content-specific settings for a new drawing.

Creating Template Files

To use the Autodesk Civil 3D software efficiently and effectively, you need to configure styles and settings to control the object display. All of these styles and settings affect the final delivered product and enable you to deliver a product with consistent CAD standards. Once all of the styles required for a set of drawings have been created, saving the file as a template enables you to use the same styles over and over in various projects. To create a template file, use the **Save As** command and in the *Save As* dialog box, change the *File of Type* to **DWT**. After giving the template a name, the *Template Options* dialog box opens, as shown in Figure 1–85. It enables you to enter a description, set the measurement units, and save new layers as reconciled or unreconciled.

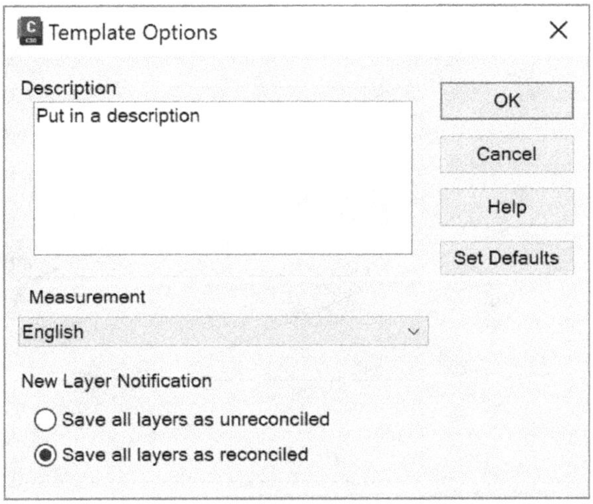

Figure 1–85

Hint: Default Coordinate System

If you work primarily within one coordinate system, set that coordinate system as your default template to ensure that all drawings will be set up with the same coordinate system. Enter a message in the template to this effect.

1.6 Managing Styles

There are three methods of managing styles in a drawing: **Import**, **Purge**, and **Reference**. These commands are located in the *Manage* tab>*Styles* panel.

Import

The **Import** styles command ( ) enables you to import the styles from a source drawing into the current drawing. The *Import Civil 3D Styles* dialog box opens, as shown in Figure 1–86. It lists the styles that are available for import and also displays the style differences between the source and the current drawing. Each style collection lists three subcategories: styles to be added, styles to be deleted, and styles to be updated. When you use the **Import** command, the styles in the design file are overwritten. However, if the styles change in the DWG or DWT source file that you imported, the styles in the design file do not automatically update.

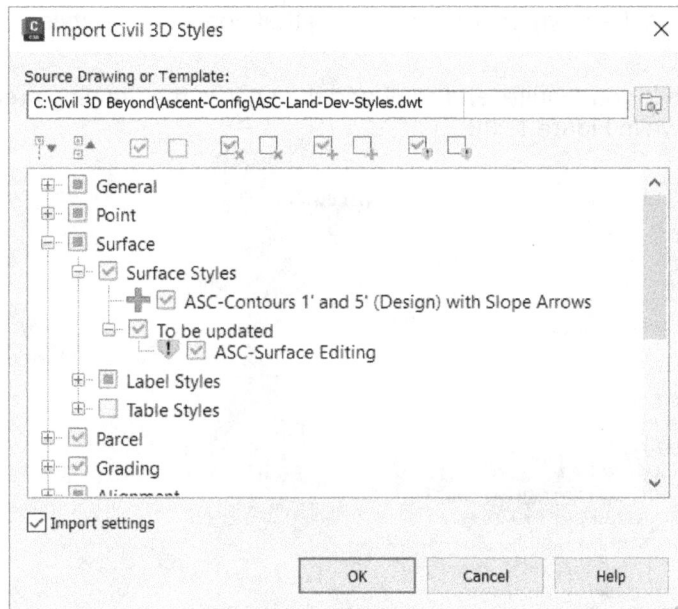

Figure 1–86

Drag-and-Drop Method

Another method for importing styles is by the drag-and-drop method. This is the preferred method when only a few specific styles need to be imported into your current drawing. The steps are as follows:

1. Ensure that both the source drawing (where the style resides) and the destination drawing (where you want to import the style into) are open in Civil 3D.

2. In the Toolspace of the destination drawing, go to the *Settings* tab and set your display option to **Master View,** as shown in Figure 1–87.

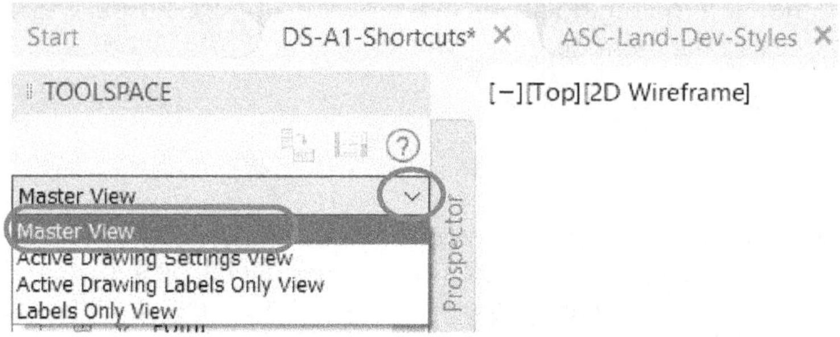

Figure 1–87

3. On the *Settings* tab, note that your current drawing is in bold. Click on the - symbol next to the drawing name to collapse its branch, revealing the other drawing you have open.

4. If required, click on the **+** symbol of the drawing that contains the styles you need to expand the branch.

5. Browse to the style you require, and click and drag it into the drawing area of your current drawing, as shown in Figure 1–88.

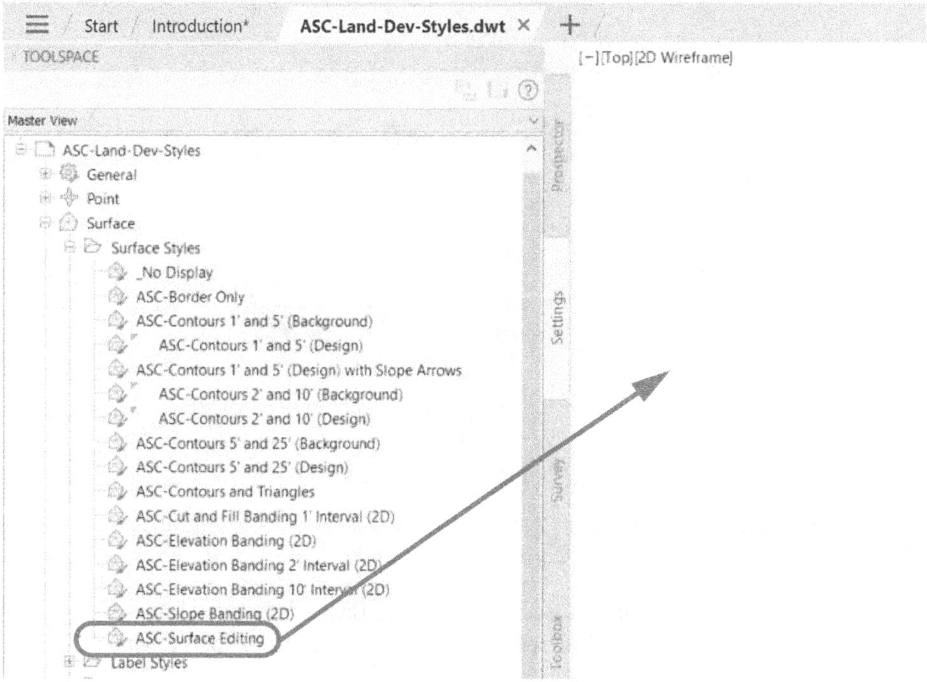

Figure 1–88

6. Repeat these steps for other styles you wish to import on an individual basis.

Purge

The **Purge** styles command (✏️) enables you to purge all of the selected unused styles in a drawing. Typically, you will need to run this command more than once as there are some styles that are used as parents to other styles. The purging information displays in the *Style Purge Confirmation* dialog box, as shown in Figure 1–89. The Command Line prompts you when there are no unused styles in the drawing.

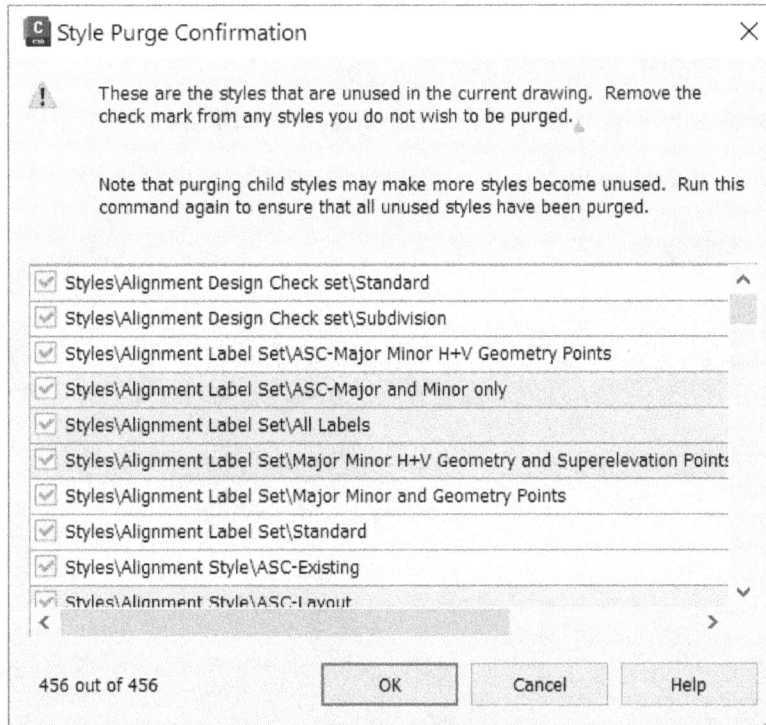

Figure 1–89

Reference

The **Reference** styles command (✎) enables you to attach one or more DWG or DWT files to your design file. Styles that are in the attached files override styles with the same name in the design drawing. If the styles in the attached DWG or DWT file change, the styles in the design file also change. Using the **Reference** styles command enables you to maintain a consistent style across multiple drawings, and it can be used to implement and maintain a company-wide CAD standard. Figure 1–90 shows the *Attach Referenced Template* dialog box.

- When multiple style templates are attached, you can set the priority using the arrows on the right of the *Attach Referenced Template* dialog box.

- You can choose which objects are to be referenced from the attached template by clicking the double down arrow symbol (⩔) in the lower right corner, as shown in Figure 1–90.

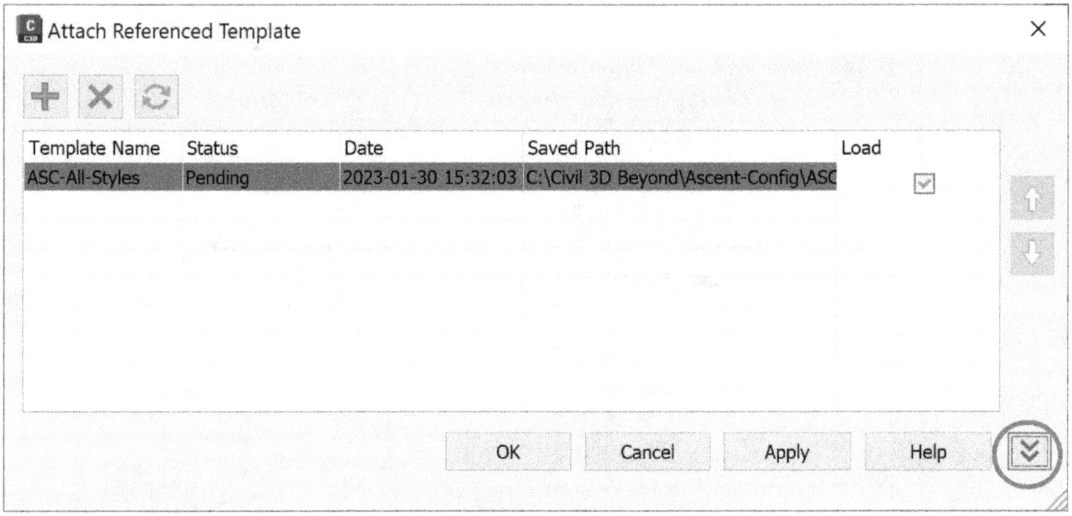

Template Name	Status	Date	Saved Path	Load
ASC-All-Styles	Pending	2023-01-30 15:32:03	C:\Civil 3D Beyond\Ascent-Config\ASC	☑

Figure 1–90

- In the expanded window are multiple tabs where you can drill down to the various components within the reference template and check on or off which ones are to be loaded. If you select an individual component, its settings are displayed in the right panel in read-only mode, as shown in Figure 1–91.

Figure 1–91

💡 Hint: Reference Template Default

If you are creating a reference template in the DWT format, you can pre-configure these settings for each time the reference template is loaded. This is done by clicking on the **Set Reference Template Defaults** icon in the *Manage* tab>*Styles* panel, as shown in Figure 1–92. The icon is only available when you are working in the drawing template file (*.DWT).

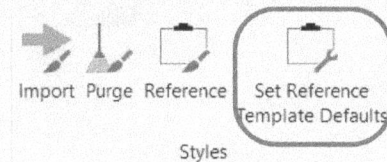

Figure 1–92

1.7 Online Map Service

Once a coordinate zone is assigned to a drawing, a new *Geolocation* tab appears in the ribbon to the far right, as shown in Figure 1–93. If a drawing template is already set up with a coordinate zone, the *Geolocation* tab will show up when using that template.

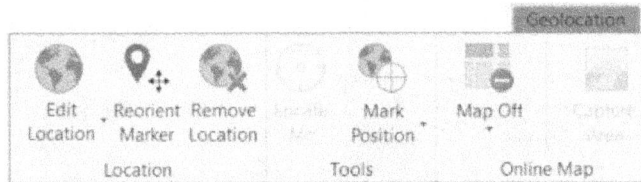

Figure 1–93

This service is only available if you have an Autodesk account and you are signed in. To sign in, go to the upper right area of the Civil 3D application, as shown in Figure 1–94.

Figure 1–94

The online maps are geolocated – meaning they have coordinates and therefore they "know where they belong." Since the Civil 3D drawing is set up with a coordinate zone, it too knows where it belongs. The Online Map Service will access maps in various styles and dynamically reference them in your drawing. They have the following characteristics:

- The map is temporary (there are options to "capture" a map).

- The map displays behind all other objects in the drawing, thus no need for changing display orders.

- The map covers a large area (in fact, it covers the extents of the coordinate zone assigned to the drawing).

- Since the map is temporary, you cannot plot the map.

The first time you access the online maps, you are greeted with a splash screen outlining the "fine print" along with a link to the **Terms of Service**, as shown in Figure 1–95. You need to accept these by clicking **Yes** in order to use this service.

- Select the **Remember my choice** option to avoid seeing this splash screen in the future.

  Note: If you did check the box and selected the Remember my choice option, the way to restore the splash screen is through the Systems tab in the Options dialog box, where you can change the Hidden Messages setting.

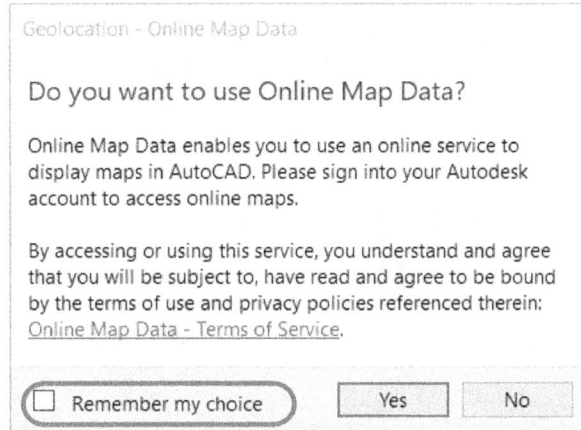

Figure 1–95

Map Styles

In the *Map* drop-down list in the *Online Map* panel, there are two groups of four choices each for map styles, as shown in Figure 1–96.

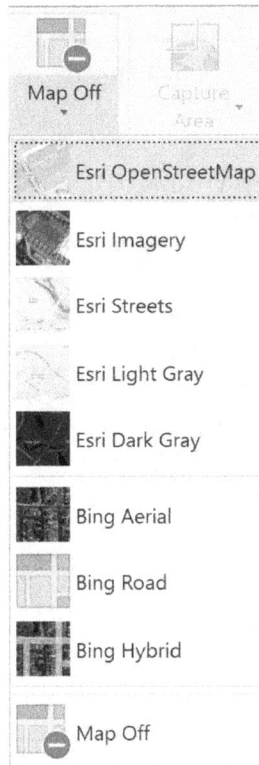

Figure 1–96

- **ESRI Imagery** displays Aerial Maps based on ESRI sources.

- **ESRI Streets** displays Street Maps based on ESRI sources.

- **ESRI Light Gray** displays Maps based on ESRI sources in a light tone.

- **ESRI Dark Gray** displays Maps based on ESRI sources in a darker tone.

- **Bing Aerial** displays the map as a satellite image.

- **Bing Road** displays the map as a vector image similar to road maps.

- **Bing Hybrid** displays the map as a satellite image with the vector data draped over.

- **Map Off** displays no map. If the maps are displayed in multiple viewports, each viewport can have a different map style.

Practice 1d
Autodesk Civil 3D Template

Practice Objectives

- Examine a drawing template.
- Import object and label styles to be used in the drawing and purge any styles not being used.

In this practice, you will create Autodesk Civil 3D styles, import styles, and purge styles for both objects and labels.

Task 1: Examine a drawing template.

1. Open the **ASC-C3D (CA83-VIF) NCS.dwt** template file from the *C:\Civil 3D Beyond\Ascent-Config* folder. Change the Files of type to Drawing Template (*.DWT) to be able to select the template files. You will then need to browse to the appropriate folder again.

2. Note the message explaining the coordinate system the template is set to.

3. Check that the *Geolocation* tab (highlighted in blue) on the far right is available, as shown in Figure 1–97, since there is a coordinate system assigned.

   Note: You need an Autodesk account and you need to be signed in to use online maps. To sign in, go to the upper right area of the Civil 3D application.

| Add-ins | Express Tools | Featured Apps | Geolocation |

Figure 1–97

4. In the *Geolocation* tab>*Online Map* panel, select **Bing Road** as the map style from the *Map* drop-down list, as shown in Figure 1–98.

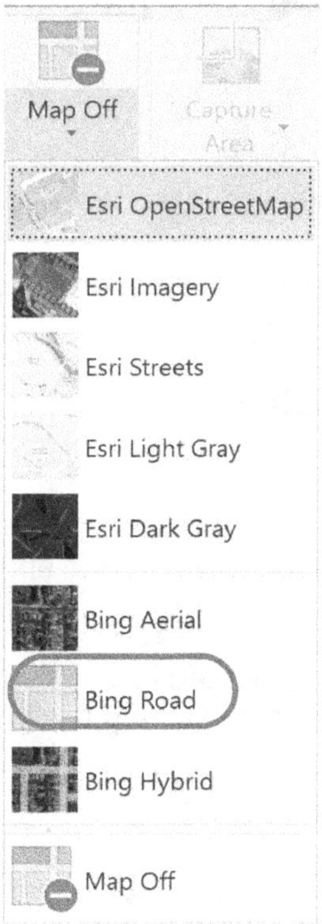

Figure 1–98

5. If the *Geolocation - Online Map Data* alert box opens, click **Yes** to accept the terms and proceed. Note that you can prevent this message from appearing by checking the **Remember my choice** checkbox.

6. Note that the map is not limited to your drawing area. As you zoom out, the image resamples itself. As you zoom in, more detail becomes available.

7. Select the *Manage* tab. In the *Styles* panel (shown in Figure 1–99), note that the **Set Reference Template Defaults** icon is only available when you are working in the drawing template file (*.DWT). Do not invoke this command.

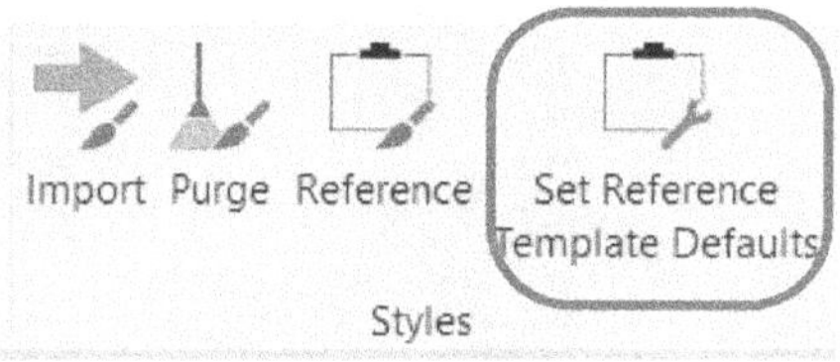

Figure 1–99

8. In the *Manage* tab>*Styles* panel, click (Reference), as shown in Figure 1-100.

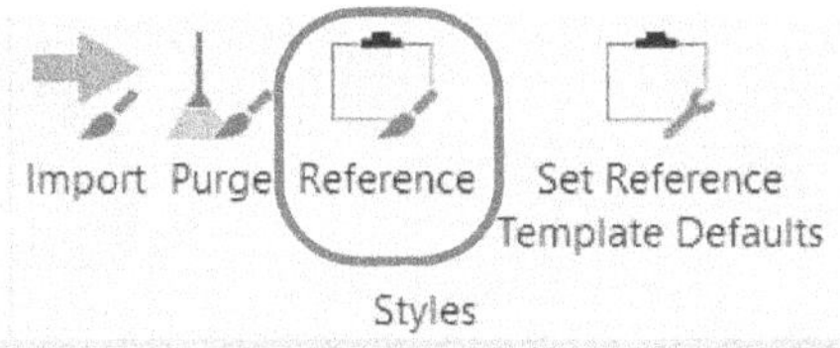

Figure 1-100

9. In the *Attach Referenced Template* dialog box, select the **ASC-Base Styles** template, then

    click the double down arrow symbol () in the lower right corner to examine which styles and settings will be used for new drawings. When you drill down through the tree in the lower left panel, you can inspect each style and choose to load it or not by checking the checkbox, as shown in Figure 1-101.This is the same as picking the *Set Reference Template Defaults* in the previous step.

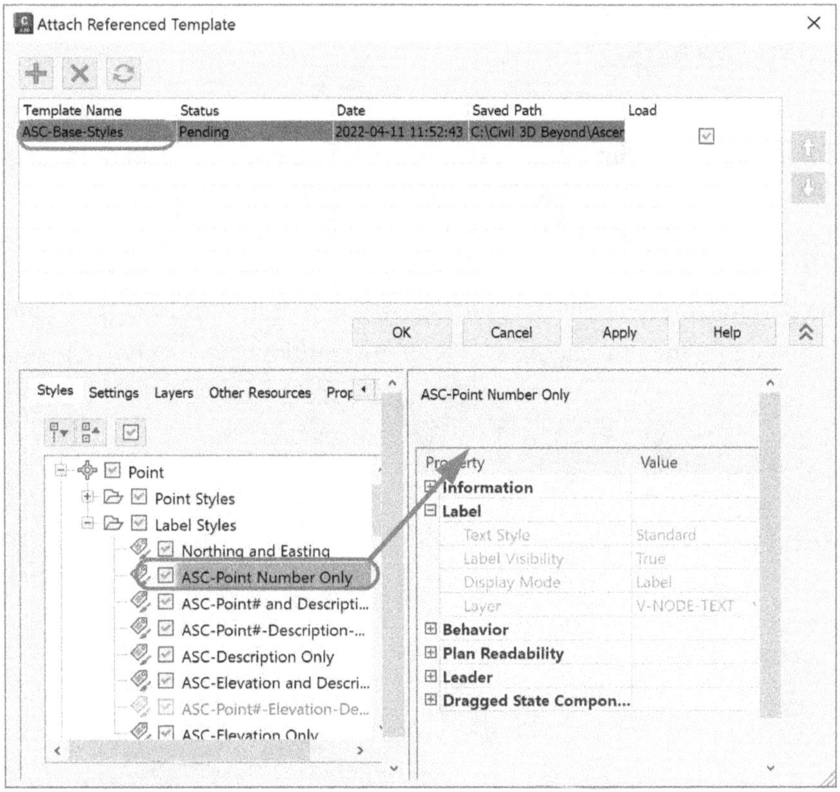

Figure 1-101

10. Close the file without saving it.

Task 2: Drag and drop styles.

1. Open **ASC-Land-Dev-Styles.dwt from** the *C:\Civil 3D Beyond\Ascent-Config* folder. Change the *Files of Type* to **Drawing** (*.DWG) to be able to select the drawing files. You will then need to browse to the appropriate folder.

2. Open **Introduction.dwg** from the *C:\Civil 3D Beyond\ References\DWG* folder.

3. Note the tabs across the top of the drawing area, one for each file you have open.

4. Go to the *TOOLSPACE>Settings* tab and set your display option to **Master View**, as shown in Figure 1–102.

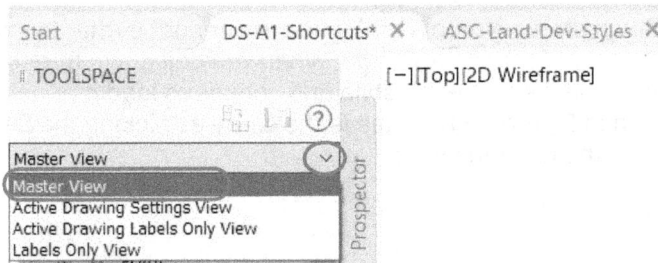

Figure 1–102

5. On the *Settings* tab, note that **Introduction** (your active drawing) is in bold. Click on the - symbol next to the drawing name to collapse its branch.

6. If required, click on the **+** symbol next to the **ASC-Land-Dev-Styles** drawing to expand the branch.

7. Expand the *Surface>Surface Styles* collection and select the **ASC-Surface Editing** style.

8. Click and drag it into the drawing area of your current drawing, as shown in Figure 1–103.

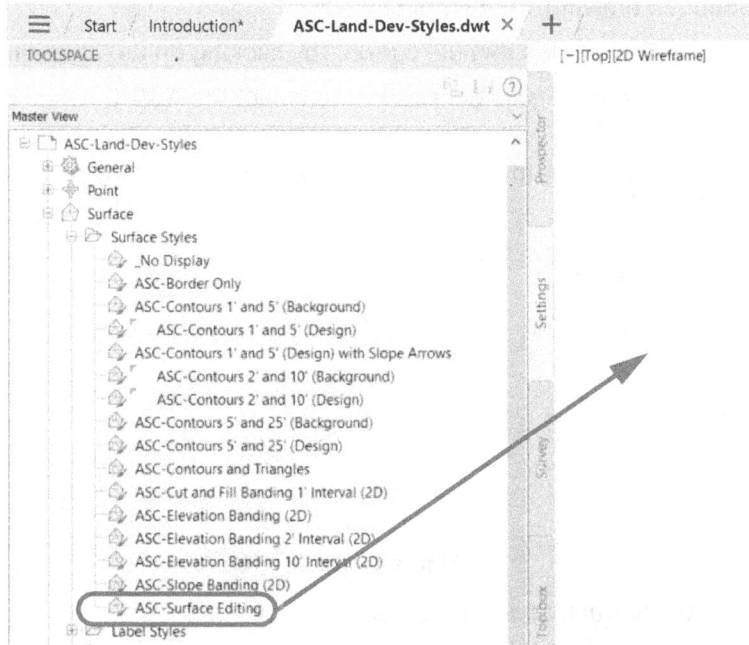

Figure 1–103

9. Expand the branch of the **Introduction** drawing and verify that the new **ASC-Surface Editing** style is listed under *Surface>Surface Styles*.

10. Change the surface style to the **ASC-Surface Editing** style by changing the surface properties. Note the point markers, triangles, and slope arrows shown in Figure 1–104.

Figure 1–104

11. Save the **Introduction** drawing, but do not close it.

12. Make the **ASC-Land-Dev-Styles.dwt** file current (by clicking on its tab at the top).

13. Expand the *Surface>Surface Styles* collection and select the **ASC-Surface Editing** style. Right-click and select **Edit**.

14. In the *Surface Style* dialog box, in the *Information* tab, put your name under **Created by:**, as shown in Figure 1–105.

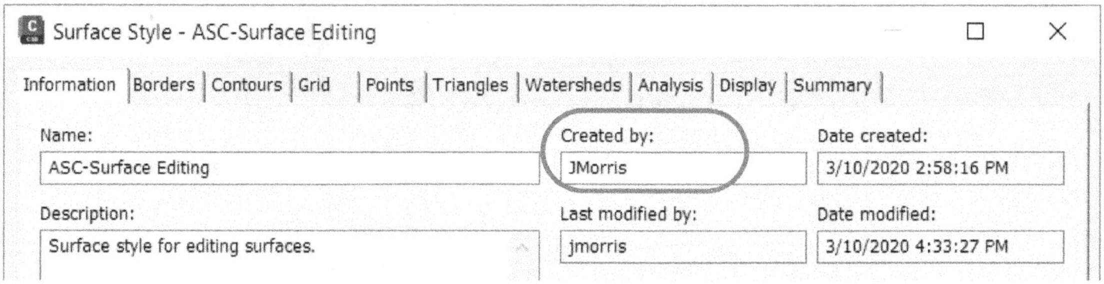

Figure 1–105

15. Click **OK** to close the *Surface Style* dialog box.

16. Save and close the **ASC-Land-Dev-Styles.dwt file.** Note that this file has now been updated *after* you imported the styles in the previous steps.

Task 3: Import styles.

1. Continue working in the **Introduction** drawing.

2. In the *Manage* tab>*Styles* panel, click (Import).

3. Select and open the **ASC-Land-Dev-Styles.dwt** file from the *C:\Civil 3D Beyond\Ascent-Config* folder.

4. In the *Import Civil 3D Styles* dialog box, expand *Surface Styles* and note that **ASC-Contours 1' and 5' (Design) with Slope Arrows** must be added and **ASC-Surface Editing** must be updated, as shown in Figure 1–106.

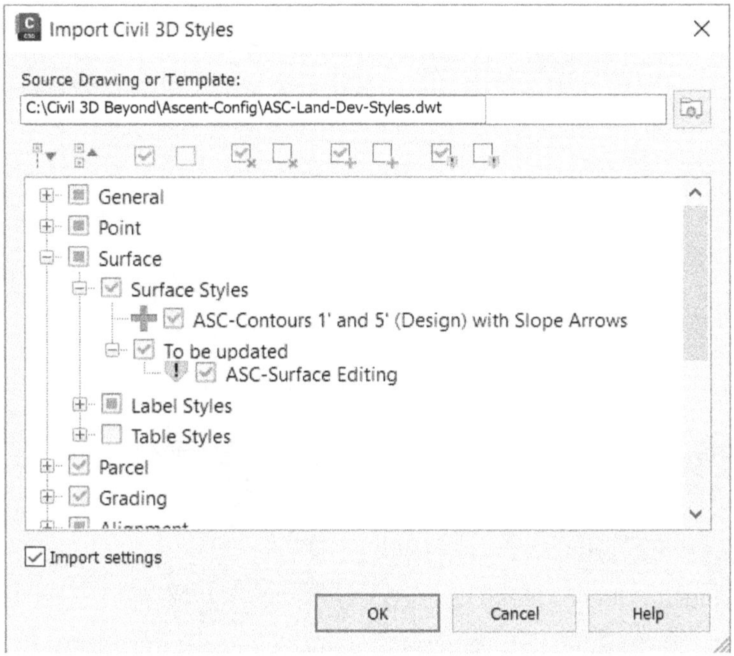

Figure 1–106

- **ASC-Surface Editing** displays in the list because you edited this style after you imported it.

5. Click **OK** in the *Warning* dialog box regarding overwriting duplicate styles. Click **OK** in the *Message* dialog box.

6. Change the surface style of the **Existing-Site** surface to the newly imported **ASC-Contours 1' and 5' (Design) with Slope Arrows** style by changing the surface properties. Note the slope arrows shown in Figure 1-107.

Figure 1-107

7. Save the drawing, but do not close it.

Task 4: Purge styles.

1. In the *Manage* tab>*Styles* panel, click ⚒ (Purge).

2. In the *Style Purge Confirmation* dialog box, browse up and down to see all the styles that are marked for purging. Also, note the total in the lower left corner. Leave all checked and click **OK**.

3. You will need to repeat this command since there are nested styles. The simplest way to do that is simply press <Enter> to repeat the last command, and press <Enter> again to proceed with the purge.

4. Keep repeating the **Purge** command until all is purged. Keep an eye on the total count in the lower left corner as you proceed.

5. Save the drawing.

Task 5: Attach a styles template.

1. In the *Manage* tab>*Styles* panel, click ▭ (Reference).

2. In the *Attach Referenced Template* dialog box, click ➕ (Attach New Template).

3. In the *C:\Civil 3D Beyond\Ascent-Config* folder, select the **ASC-Land-Dev-Styles.dwt** file and click **Open**.

4. Note that the template is added to the top of the list. You could change the priority by using the arrow keys on the right. Also note the yellow alert symbols when you expand the dialog box, which indicate all the impending changes when the template is applied, as shown in Figure 1–108.

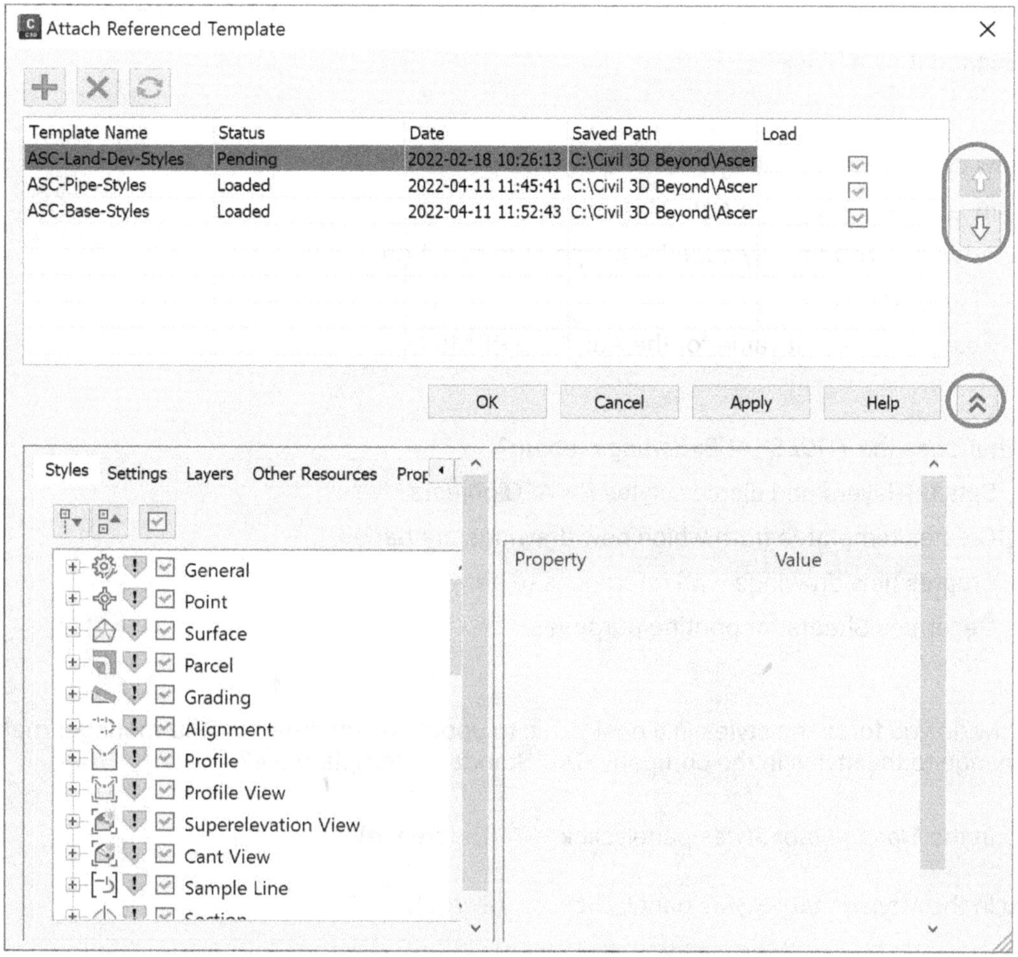

Figure 1–108

5. Click **OK** to apply the changes and close the dialog box.

6. Save and close the drawing.

End of practice

Chapter Review Questions

1. How can you plot the online map?

    a. You cannot because it is copyrighted.

    b. Explode the online map.

    c. Capture the online map.

    d. Insert it as a block.

2. How do you change the symbol of a Civil 3D point?

    a. Insert the appropriate AutoCAD block.

    b. Add a description key code for the point description.

    c. Change the point style.

    d. Assign a different value for the AutoCAD PDMode.

3. What does the *TOOLSPACE>Settings* tab do?

    a. Sets the layers and display styles for AEC objects.

    b. Creates templates from which new drawings are based.

    c. Creates new drawings with references to data.

    d. Generates Sheets for printing purposes.

4. How do you force the styles in a design file to update every time the CAD manager makes a change to the styles in the company CAD Standards template file?

    a. In the *Manage* tab>*Styles* panel, click (Reference).

    b. In the *Manage* tab>*Styles* panel, click (Purge).

    c. In the *Manage* tab>*Styles* panel, click (Import).

    d. You have to create a new style manually because there is no way to force an update to styles in an existing drawing.

Command Summary

Button	Command	Location
	Prospector	• **Ribbon:** *Home* tab>*Palettes* panel • **Command Prompt:** prospector
	Settings	• **Ribbon:** *Home* tab>*Palettes* panel • **Command Prompt:** settings
	Surface Properties	• **Contextual Ribbon:** *Surface* tab>*Modify* panel • **Command Prompt:** editsurfaceproperties
	Style Purge	• **Ribbon:** *Manage* tab>*Styles* panel • **Command Prompt:** purgestyles
	Import Styles	• **Ribbon:** *Manage* tab>*Styles* panel • **Command Prompt:** importstylesandsettings
	Survey	• **Ribbon:** *Home* tab>*Palettes* panel • **Command Prompt:** survey
	Toolbox	• **Ribbon:** *Home* tab>*Palettes* panel • **Command Prompt:** toolbox
	Toolspace	• **Ribbon:** *Home* tab>*Palettes* panel • **Command Prompt:** toolspace

Project Management

In this chapter, you will learn about the various project structures that can be used inside of an Autodesk® Civil 3D® project. Then, you will create a new project and learn how to switch between different projects. Using data shortcuts, you will practice creating references to AEC objects to share design data, which ensures that you always have the most up-to-date design data in the current model.

Learning Objectives

- List the three different ways in which Autodesk Civil 3D project drawings can be organized.
- Examine ways in which teams can collaborate with each other and share design information in the Autodesk Civil 3D software.
- Share design information with other members of the design team using data shortcuts.

2.1 Autodesk Civil 3D Projects

There are multiple ways of organizing Autodesk Civil 3D project drawings.

Single-Design Drawing Projects

Since Autodesk Civil 3D surfaces, alignments, and other AEC objects can be entirely drawing-based, you can have a single drawing file act as the repository for all design data. Realistically, this might only be feasible for smaller projects and/or those worked on by only one person. The only external data might be survey databases and externally referenced (XREF) drawings.

Multiple Drawings Sharing Data Using Shortcuts

This approach permits multiple existing conditions and design drawings to share data. For example, a surface could exist in one drawing and an alignment in another. A third could contain a surface profile based on the alignment and terrain model, and all could be kept in sync with each other using data shortcuts. This approach is usually preferable to the single-drawing approach, because it permits more than one user to work on the project at the same time (in the different design drawings) and keeps the drawings at more manageable sizes. Using data shortcuts is essential in larger projects to ensure that the regeneration time for drawings is at an acceptable speed. This approach does not create any external project data other than survey databases and XML data files that are used to share data between drawings.

Once an object has been referenced into the drawing and the drawing has been saved, the object is saved in the drawing. Therefore, it only needs access to the source drawing for validation and synchronization purposes if the source object changes. This makes it easy to share drawings with others because it ensures that the referenced objects display even if the source drawings are not available.

Shortcuts tend to be efficient for projects with a small number of drawings and project team members. Since the XML data files that connect drawings must be managed manually, keeping a large number of drawings and/or people in sync with shortcuts can be cumbersome. It is recommended that your BIM manager establishes procedures to ensure that data is not unintentionally deleted or changed. These procedures need to be properly documented.

Autodesk Docs Design Collaboration

The Autodesk Docs cloud software enables Civil 3D to share external reference files (XREFs) and data shortcuts (DREFs) to be stored and shared within a project in a Autodesk Docs Hub. This enables you to collaborate your Civil 3D design through these references in the cloud with anyone anywhere.

Autodesk Docs makes extensive use of the Autodesk Desktop Connector, which serves as a traffic director between the Autodesk Docs project files in the cloud and the local caches on your hard drive.

When opening an Autodesk Docs-based drawing for the first time (or after a long interlude), the Desktop Connector checks the local cache of the drawings and reference files to see if they are up to date. If not, the Desktop Connector downloads a fresh copy of the files. This can take some time, depending on the file sizes, your download speeds, and the traffic in the Autodesk Docs cloud.

Multiple Drawings Sharing Data with Autodesk Vault

The Autodesk Vault software is a data and document management system (ADMS). It is used in conjunction with other Autodesk applications in different industries. When working with the Autodesk Vault software, all project drawings, survey databases, and references are managed and stored inside an SQL-managed database. Autodesk Vault includes user-level access permissions, drawing check-in/out, project templates, automated backups, data versioning, etc. These benefits are offset by the additional time required to manage and administer the database and, in some cases, needing to purchase additional hardware and software. If you work on large projects with multiple design drawings or have many team members (more than ten), you might find that Autodesk Vault is the best way to keep those projects organized.

2.2 Sharing Data

In the Autodesk Civil 3D workflow, you can use two methods of project collaboration to share Autodesk Civil 3D design data: data shortcuts (local based or through Autodesk Docs) and Vault references.

Autodesk Vault and data shortcuts can be used to share design data between drawing files in the same project, such as alignment definitions, profiles, corridors, surfaces, pipe networks, pressure networks, sample line groups, and view frame groups. They do not permit the sharing of profile views, assemblies, or other Autodesk Civil 3D objects. Drawing sets using shortcuts typically use XREFs and reference other line work and annotations between drawings. Whether using Vault shortcuts or data shortcuts, the process is similar.

The example in Figure 2–1 shows the sharing of data in a project collaboration environment. The data is divided into three distinctive levels. Using either data shortcuts or Autodesk Vault, these levels can be accessed and contributed to on a local or remote server or across a wide area network (WAN).

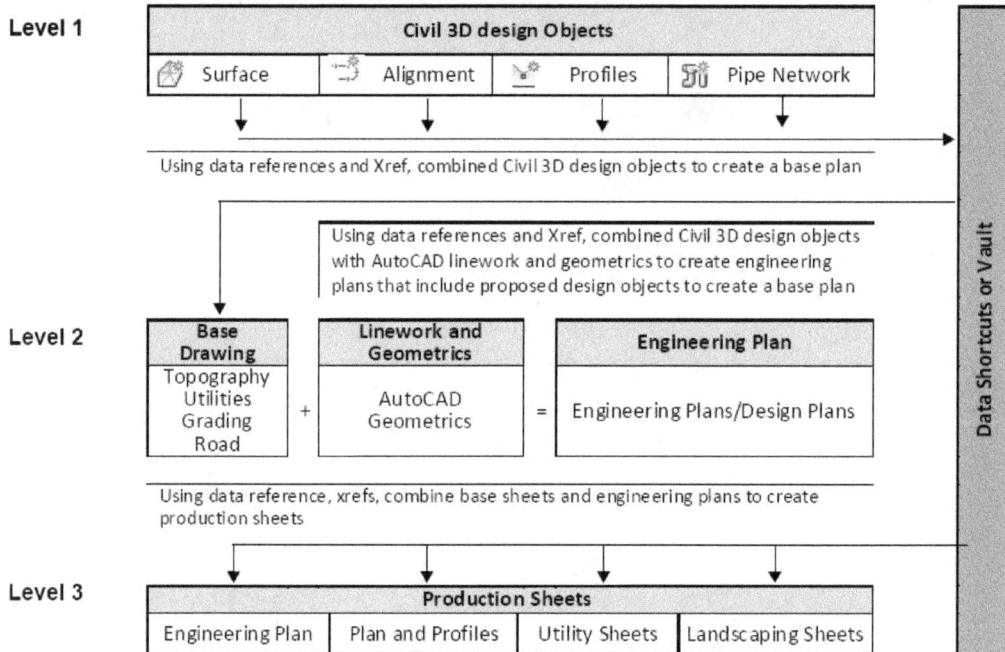

Figure 2–1

2.3 Using Data Shortcuts for Project Management

Data shortcuts can be used to share design data between drawing files through the use of XML files. Using data shortcuts is similar to using the Autodesk Vault software, but does not provide the protection of your data or the tracking of versions the way the Autodesk Vault software does.

Data shortcuts are managed using the *TOOLSPACE>Prospector* tab, under the *Data Shortcuts* collection, or in the *Manage* tab>*Data Shortcuts* panel, as shown in Figure 2–2. The shortcuts are stored in XML files in one or more working folders that you create. They can use the same folder structure as the Autodesk Vault software. This method simplifies the transition to using the Autodesk Vault software at a future time.

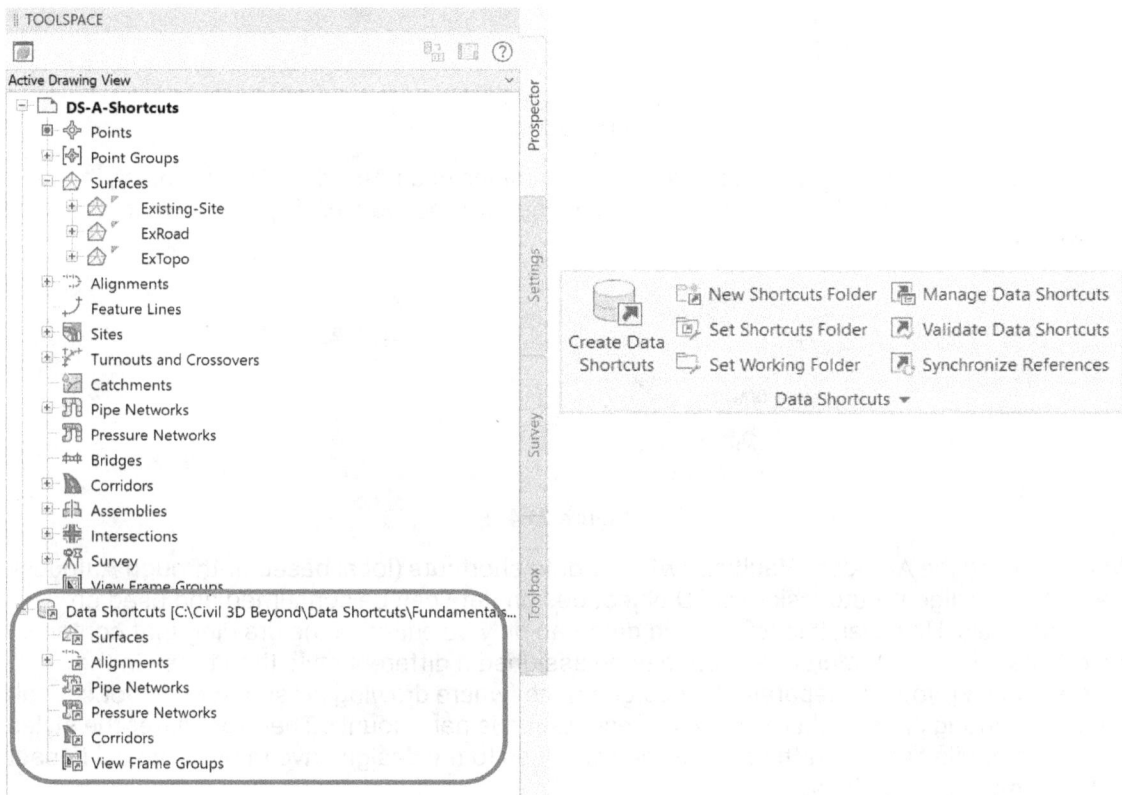

Figure 2–2

When the data shortcuts reside in an Autodesk Docs project in the cloud, it is designated as such in the *TOOLSPACE>Prospector* tab with a small cloud symbol and a path pointing to the Autodesk Docs project, as shown in Figure 2–3.

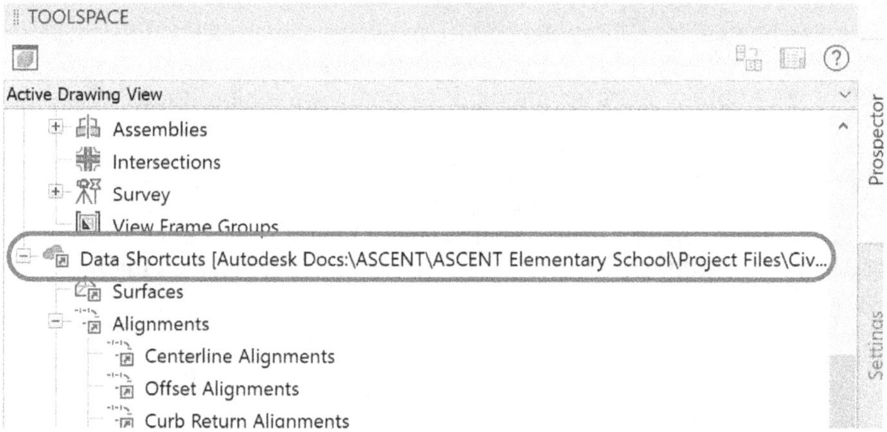

Figure 2–3

Similarly, when you are working in a drawing that resides in an Autodesk Docs project, in the *TOOLSPACE>Prospector* tab, the drawing has a cloud symbol as a prefix, as shown in Figure 2–4.

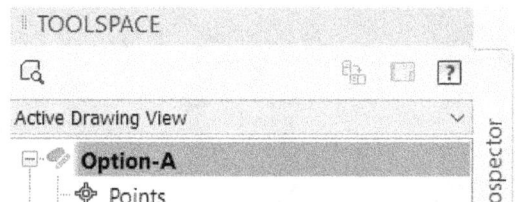

Figure 2–4

Whether using the Autodesk Vault software or data shortcuts (local based or through Autodesk Docs), the intelligent Autodesk Civil 3D object design data can be consumed and used on different levels. However, this referenced data can only be edited in the drawing that contains the original object. As referenced data can be assigned a different style than those in the source drawing, you can separate the design phase (where drawing presentation is not critical) from the drafting phase (where drawing presentation is paramount). Therefore, after the styles have been applied at the drafting phase, any changes to the design have minimal visual impact on the completed drawings.

Changing the name of a drawing file that provides data shortcuts or the shortcut XML file itself invalidates the shortcut. In the *Manage* tab, there is a Data Shortcut Manager that is used to correct such issues. It is used to repair references broken through renamed drawings or re-pathing drawings containing the Civil 3D objects.

Update Notification

If the shortcut objects are modified and the source drawing is saved, any drawings that reference those objects are updated when opened. If the drawings consuming the data referenced in the shortcuts are open at the time of the edit, a message displays to warn you of the changes, as shown in Figure 2–5.

> **Note:** This message does not necessarily means that the data shortcut definitions have changed. Civil 3D recognizes that the timestamp of the source drawing is newer than that of the current drawing, but it cannot determine what has changed (if anything).

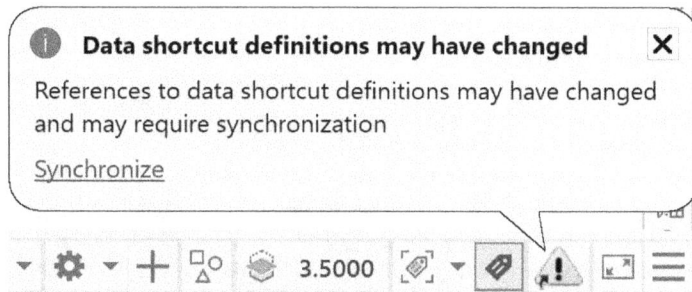

Figure 2–5

The following modifier icons help you to determine the state of many Autodesk Civil 3D objects.

	The object is referenced by another object. In the *TOOLSPACE>Settings* tab, this also indicates that a style is in use in the current drawing.
	The object is being referenced from another drawing file (such as through a shortcut or Autodesk Vault reference).
	The object is out of date and needs to be rebuilt, or is violating specified design constraints.
	A Vault project object (such as a point or surface) has been modified since it was included in the current drawing.
	You have modified a Vault project object in your current drawing and those modifications have not yet been updated to the project.

Figure 2–6 shows how the modifier icons are used with an Autodesk Civil 3D object as it displays in the *TOOLSPACE>Prospector* tab.

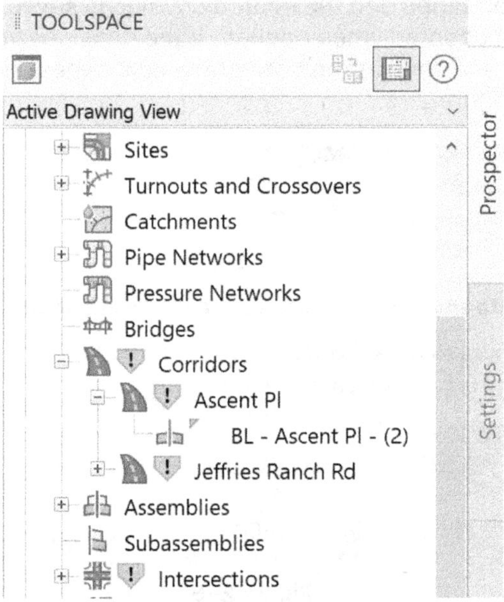

Figure 2–6

To update the shortcut data, click **Synchronize** in the balloon message or right-click on the object in the *TOOLSPACE>Prospector* tab and select **Synchronize**.

Autodesk Docs Notification

In the current release of Autodesk Docs, there is no standard Civil 3D notification indicating that the data shortcuts have changed. For that, you need to go to the *Collaborate* tab and click

 (Check Reference Status). It will examine if any of the referenced data items have changed and need updating.

Removing and Promoting Shortcuts

Shortcut data can be removed from the Shortcut tree in the *TOOLSPACE>Prospector* tab by right-clicking on it and selecting **Remove**; however, this does not remove the data from the drawing. To do so, right--click on the object in the *TOOLSPACE>Prospector* tab and select **Delete**. This removes the shortcut data from the current list so that the item is not included if a data shortcut XML file is exported from the current drawing.

You can also promote shortcuts, which converts the referenced shortcut into a local copy without any further connection to the original. You can promote objects by right-clicking on them in the *TOOLSPACE>Prospector* tab and selecting **Promote**.

Data Shortcut Workflow

1. In the *TOOLSPACE>Prospector* tab, right-click on **Data Shortcuts** and select **Set the Working Folder...**.

2. In the *TOOLSPACE>Prospector* tab, right-click on **Data Shortcuts** and select **New Data Shortcuts Folder...** to create a new project folder for all of your drawings.

   Note: Whenever Civil 3D is searching for folders, you can use the Autodesk Desktop Connector to browse to the local cache folders of files that reside in an Autodesk Docs project.

3. Create or import the data that you want to share in the source drawing and save it in the current working folder under the correct project folder.

4. In the *TOOLSPACE>Prospector* tab, right-click on **Data Shortcuts** and select **Associate Project to Current Drawing**.

5. In the *TOOLSPACE>Prospector* tab, right-click on **Data Shortcuts** and select **Create Data Shortcuts**.

6. Select all of the items that you want to share, such as surfaces, alignments, profiles, etc., and click **OK**.

7. Save the source drawing (and close, as required).

8. Create and save a new drawing or open an existing drawing to receive the shortcut data. Expand the *Data Shortcuts* collection and the relevant object trees (*Surfaces*, *Alignments*, *Pipe Networks*, *View Frame Groups*, etc.).

9. Highlight an item to be referenced, right-click, and select **Create Reference...**. Repeat for all of the objects, as required. You are prompted for the styles and other settings that are required to display the object in the current drawing.

10. (Optional) Add an XREF to the source drawing if there is additional AutoCAD® objects that you want to display in the downstream drawing.

    Note: The Autodesk Civil 3D tools for data shortcuts are located in the Manage tab>Data Shortcuts panel (as shown in Figure 2–7) and in the TOOLSPACE>Prospector tab.

Figure 2–7

Workflow Details

- **Set Working Folder** sets a new working folder as the location in which to store the data shortcut project. The default working folder for data shortcut projects is *C:\Users\Public\Documents\Autodesk\Civil 3D Beyond*.

  - In a shared working environment, the working folder needs to be accessible by all project team members. Often working folders are named for the year of the project, or perhaps the major clients for the project.

  - For project team members who reside outside of your firewall, consider setting up an Autodesk Docs project for design collaboration and file referencing.

  - The default working folder is also used for Autodesk Vault projects and local (non-Vault) Survey projects. If you work with the Autodesk Vault software, local Survey, and Data Shortcut projects, you should have separate working folders for each project type for ease of management.

- **New Shortcuts Folder** creates a new folder for storing a set of related project drawings and data shortcuts.

- **Create Data Shortcuts** creates data shortcuts from the active drawing.

Data shortcuts are stored in the *_Shortcuts* folder for the active project and used to create data references to source objects in other drawings. Each data shortcut is stored in a separate XML file.

Advantages of Data Shortcuts

- Data shortcuts provide a simple mechanism for sharing object data, without the added system administration needs of the Autodesk Vault software.

- Data shortcuts offer access to an object's intelligent data while ensuring that this referenced data can only be changed in the source drawing.

- Referenced objects can have styles and labels that differ from the source drawing.

- When you open a drawing containing revised referenced data, the referenced objects are updated automatically.

- During a drawing session, if the referenced data has been revised, you are notified in the Communication Center and in the *TOOLSPACE>Prospector* tab.

- When data shortcuts reside in an Autodesk Docs project, design collaboration and file referencing can be done beyond the firewall of your organization.

Limitations of Data Shortcuts

- Data shortcuts cannot provide data versioning.

- Data shortcuts do not provide security or data integrity controls.

- Unlike the Autodesk Vault software, data shortcuts do not provide a secure mechanism for sharing point data or survey data.

- Maintaining links between references and their source objects requires fairly stable names. However, most broken references can be repaired using the tools in the Autodesk Civil 3D software.

Practice 2a
Starting a Data Shortcuts Project

Practice Objective

* Create a new data shortcuts project with the correct working folder for the project being worked on.

In this practice, you will walk through the steps of creating project-based data shortcuts folders.

Task 1: Set the working folder.

In this task, you will set up a new working folder as the location in which to store data shortcuts projects. The default working folder for data shortcuts projects is *C:\Users\Public\Documents\ Autodesk\Civil 3D Beyond*.

1. Open **DS-A-Shortcuts.dwg** from the *C:\Civil 3D Beyond\ Data Shortcuts\Practice* folder.

2. Configure Civil 3D to reduce the fading of XREF files. Type *Options* at the command line. In the *Options* dialog box, go to the *Display* tab and use the slider in the lower left corner to change the *Fade control* from the default value of 50% to **6%** for the *Xref display*, as shown in Figure 2–8. Click **OK**.

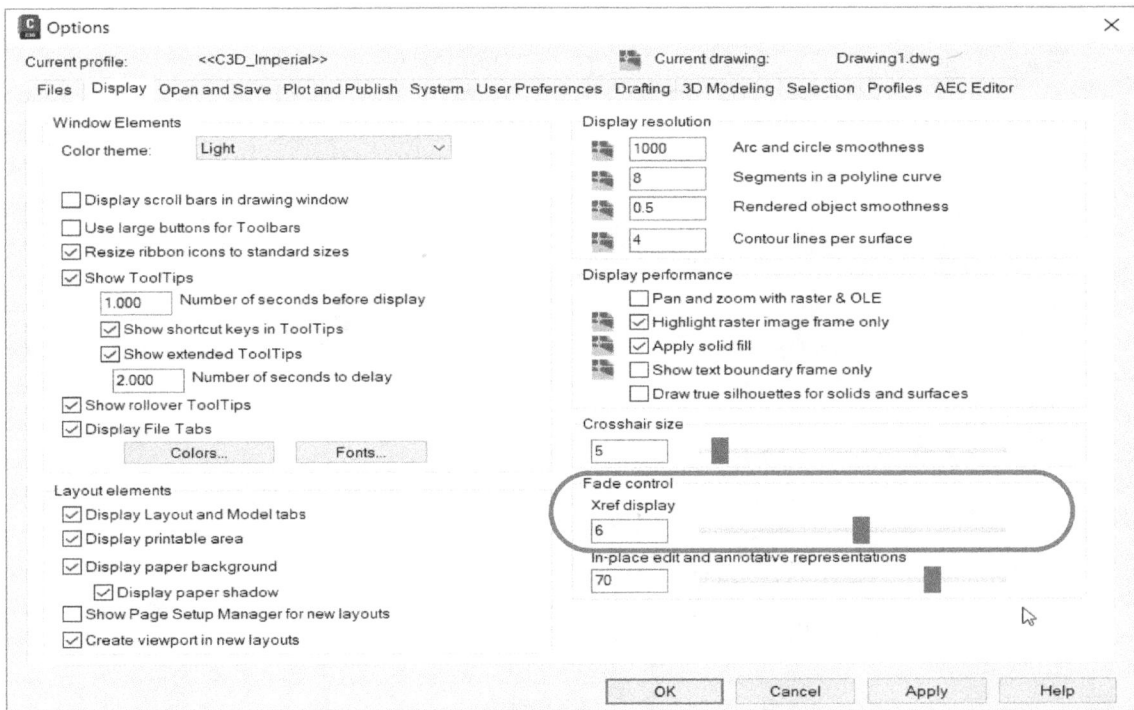

Figure 2–8

3. In the *Manage* tab>*Data Shortcuts* panel, click ☐ (Set Working Folder), as shown in Figure 2–9.

Figure 2–9

4. In the *Set Working Folder* dialog box, select the *C:\Civil 3D Beyond\Data Shortcuts* folder, right-click to create a new folder, and name it **Lesson**.

5. Select the newly created folder and click **Select Folder**.

Task 2: Create new shortcuts folders.

In this task, you will create a new folder for storing a set of related project drawings and data shortcuts. A second project folder is created to help you understand how to change the project in which you are working.

1. Continue working with the drawing from the previous task.

2. In the *Manage* tab>*Data Shortcuts* panel, click 🗔 (New Shortcuts Folder), as shown in Figure 2–10.

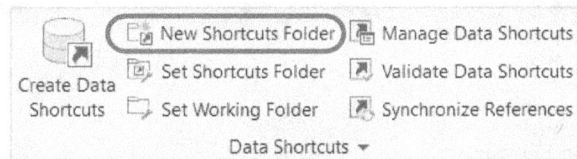

Figure 2–10

3. Templates are normally found in the default folder *C:\Civil 3D Templates*; however, you will be using customized project templates for this task. In the *New Data Shortcut Folder* dialog box, type **Ascent Phase 1** for the name and select the **Use project template** option. Click the ellipses, as shown in Figure 2–11, and browse to *C:\Civil 3D Beyond\Ascent-Config\ Ascent Project Templates*. From the project templates available, select *Base Project* and click **OK**.

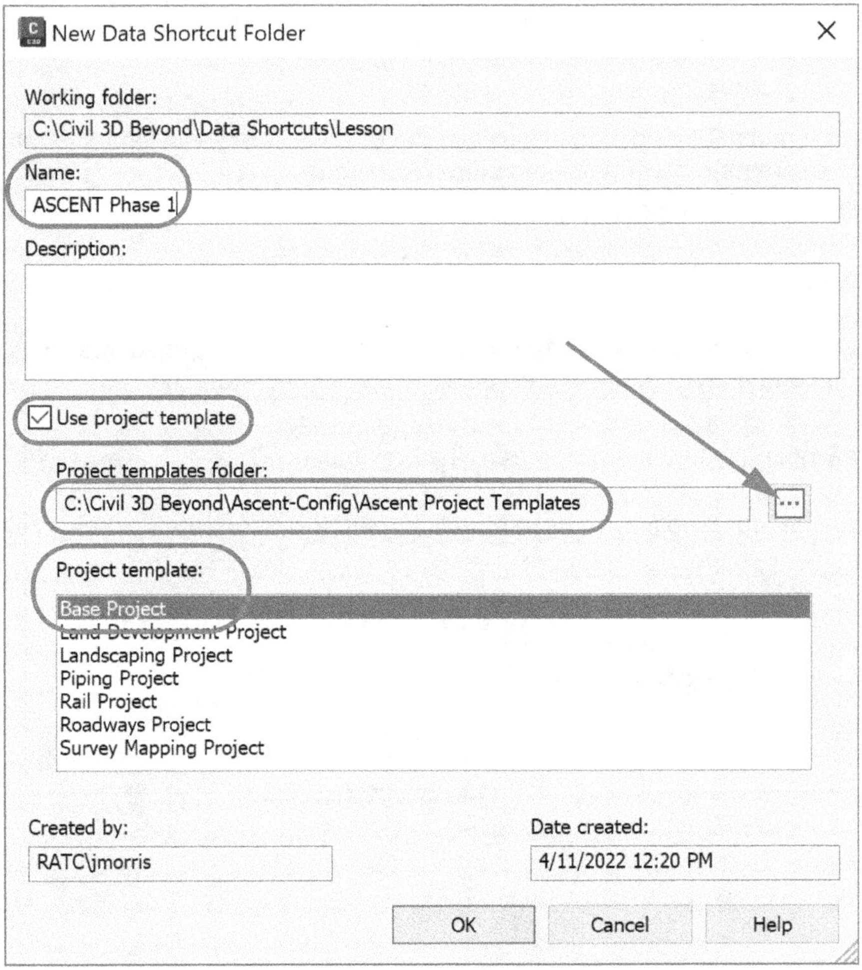

Figure 2–11

Note: The Autodesk Civil 3D software will replicate this template folder structure and all included forms and documents in the Ascent Phase 1 project folder.

4. In the *TOOLSPACE>Prospector* tab, a *Data Shortcut* folder is displayed in *C:\Civil 3D Beyond\ Data Shortcuts\Lesson\ Ascent Phase 1*, as shown on the left in Figure 2-12. In Windows Explorer, verify that the *Civil 3D* folder structure is created for this project, as shown on the right in Figure 2-12.

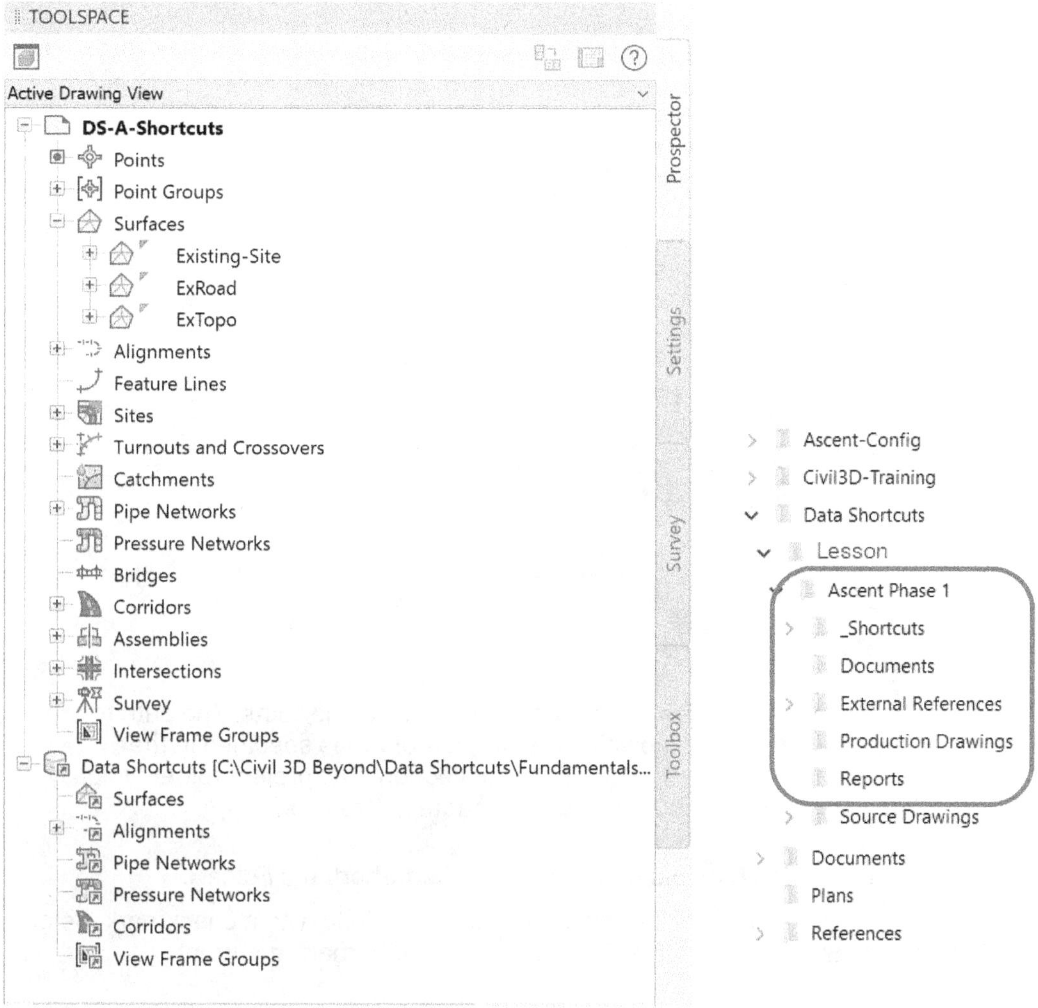

Figure 2-12

5. Create another new shortcuts folder. In the *Manage* tab>*Data Shortcuts* panel, click

   (New Shortcuts Folder).

6. In the *New Data Shortcut Folder* dialog box, type **Ascent Phase 2** for the name and uncheck the **Use project template** option. Click **OK** to close the dialog box.

You now have two projects in the working folder: *Ascent Phase 1* and *Ascent Phase 2*, as shown in Figure 2–13. Note the additional folders in *Ascent Phase 1*. These have been copied from the *Base Project* project template.

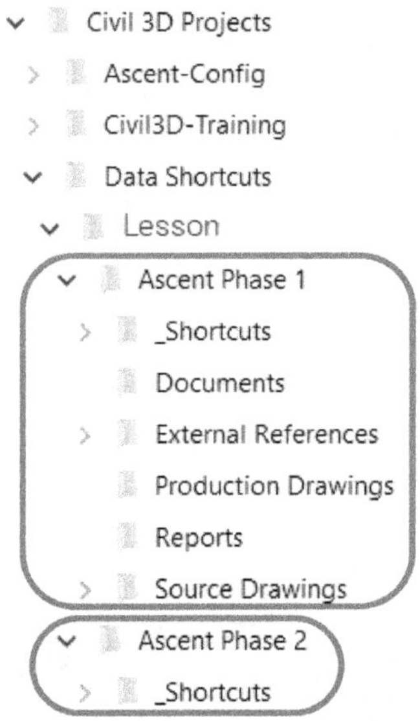

Figure 2–13

Task 3: Set up the shortcuts folder.

Setting the shortcuts folder specifies the project path for data shortcuts. The path to the current *Data Shortcuts* folder (also known as the project folder) is specified in the *TOOLSPACE>Prospector* tab, in the *Data Shortcuts* collection. The project folder typically contains both data shortcuts and source objects for data references.

1. In the *Manage* tab>*Data Shortcuts* panel, click 🗔 (Set Shortcuts Folder).
2. The current *Data Shortcut* folder is indicated by a green circle with a checkmark. Select **Ascent Phase 1**, as shown in Figure 2–14, and click **OK** to make it current.

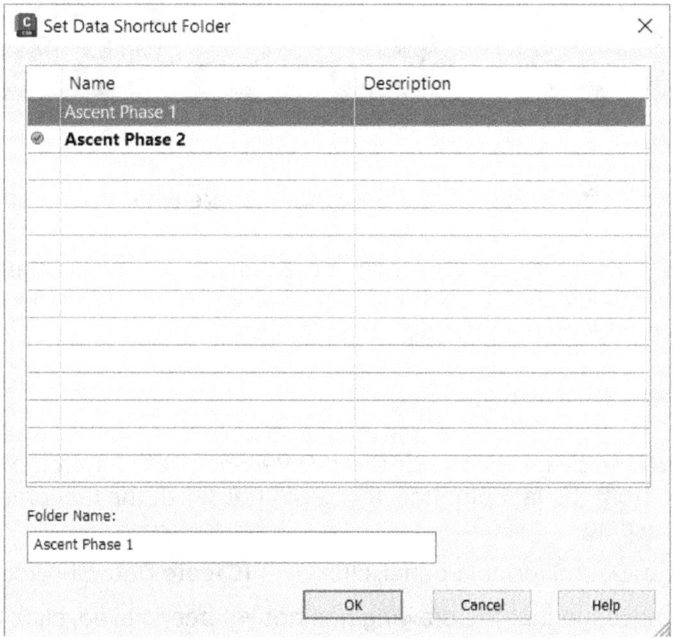

Figure 2–14

3. In the *TOOLSPACE>Prospector* tab, right-click on **Data Shortcuts** and select **Associate Project to Current Drawing...**, as shown in Figure 2–15.

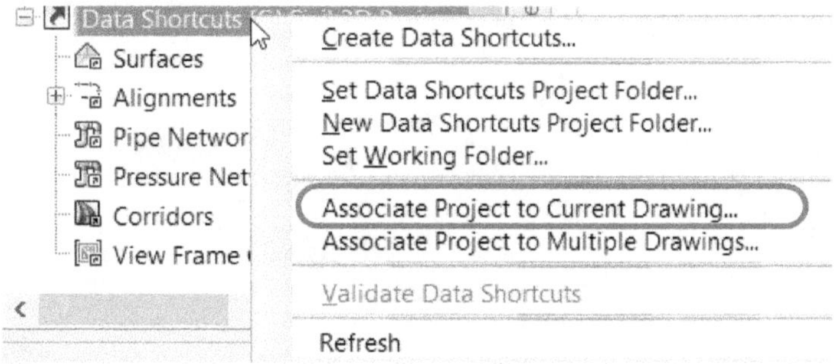

Figure 2–15

4. Verify that **Ascent Phase 1** is the selected project and click **OK**.

5. Note that in the center of the title bar of Civil 3D (top of the Civil 3D window), the project name appears in parentheses after the drawing name: **DS-A-Shortcuts.dwg (Ascent Phase 1)**.

6. Save the drawing.

End of practice

Practice 2b
Manage File Sizes with Data Shortcuts

Practice Objective

- Create data shortcuts from objects in a drawing to share with other team members.

In this practice, you will walk through the steps of creating project-based *Data Shortcuts* folders. It simulates a situation in which the existing conditions and/or design work has been done and you now need to share elements of the design with team members.

Task 1: Create data shortcuts.

1. Open **DS-A-Shortcuts.dwg** from the *C:\Civil 3D Beyond\ Data Shortcuts\Practice* folder if not already open from the last practice. If you did not finish the last practice, please do so now before proceeding.

2. In the *Manage* tab>*Data Shortcuts* panel, click (Create Data Shortcuts).

3. If you receive a message that the drawing has not yet been saved, click **OK**. Save the drawing and start the **Create Data Shortcuts** command again.

4. In the *Create Data Shortcuts* dialog box, a list of all of the available objects for use in shortcuts displays. Select **Surfaces**, **Alignments**, and **Corridors** (as shown in Figure 2–16) and click **OK**.

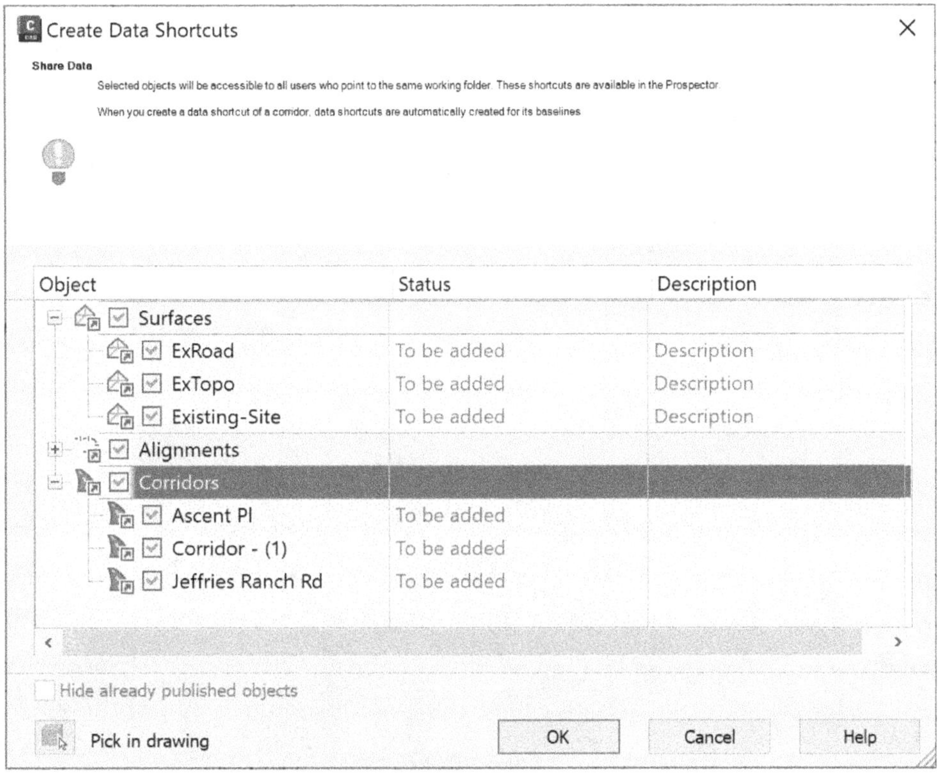

Figure 2–16

5. You have now created shortcuts for the surfaces, alignments, and corridors. This means that if the shortcuts and drawings are in a shared network folder, anyone on the network has access to these Autodesk Civil 3D objects.

Note that in the *TOOLSPACE>Prospector* tab, under the *Data Shortcuts* and *Surfaces* collections, you can now access all of the surfaces. In the list view, the source filename and source path display, as shown in Figure 2–17.

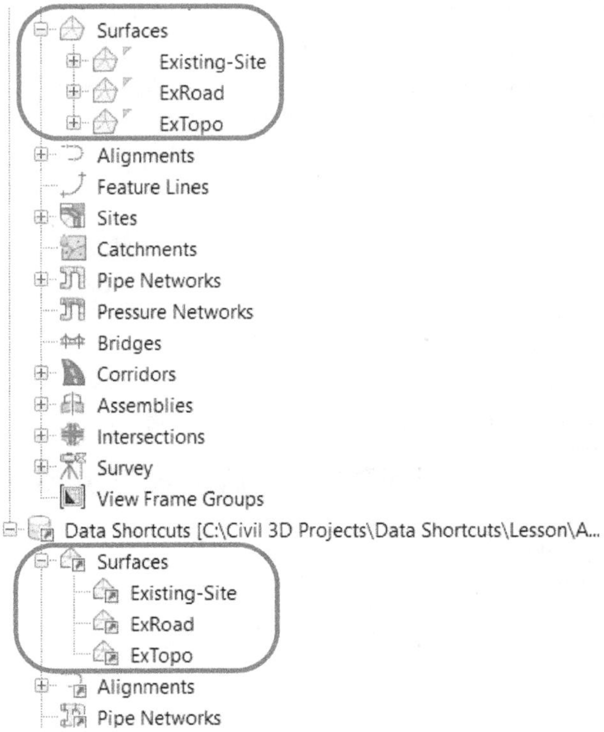

Figure 2–17

6. Save the drawing, but do not close it.

Task 2: Data-reference data shortcuts.

1. Start a new drawing using the **ASC-C3D (CA83-VIF) NCS.dwt** file from the *C:\Civil 3D Beyond\Ascent-Config* folder.

2. Save the file in *C:\Civil 3D Beyond\Data Shortcuts\Practice* as **Reference File.dwg**.

3. Erase the text in the middle of the screen regarding the coordinate settings.

4. In the *TOOLSPACE>Prospector* tab, ensure that *Data Shortcuts* points to the *C:\Civil 3D Beyond\Data Shortcuts\Lesson\ Ascent Phase 1* folder by hovering over the *Data Shortcuts* heading. The full path gets revealed in the tooltip, as shown in Figure 2–18. If it is not set to *Ascent Phase 1*, repeat the steps from the previous practice.

Figure 2–18

5. In the *TOOLSPACE>Prospector* tab, right-click on **Data Shortcuts** and select **Associate Project to Current Drawing...**, as shown in Figure 2–19.

Figure 2–19

6. In the *TOOLSPACE>Prospector* tab, verify that the *Data Shortcuts* points to the correct folder, as shown in Figure 2–20, and click **OK**.

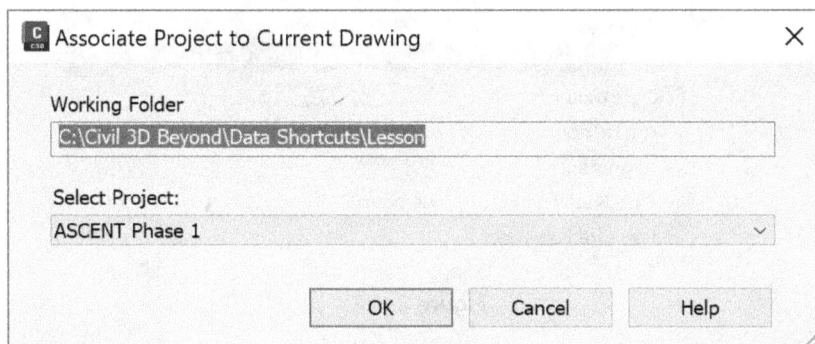

Figure 2–20

7. Save the drawing.

8. In the *TOOLSPACE>Prospector* tab, under the *Data Shortcuts* collection, expand the *Surfaces* collection (if not already expanded) and the *Alignments>Centerline Alignments* collection, as shown in Figure 2–21.

Figure 2–21

9. Under the *Surfaces* collection, select the surface **Existing-Site**, right-click, and select **Create Reference...**, as shown in Figure 2–22.

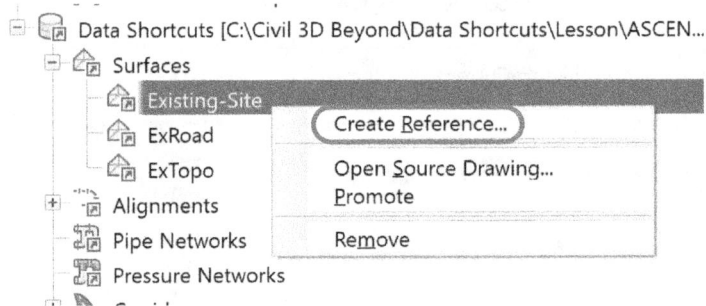

Figure 2–22

10. In the *Create Surface Reference* dialog box, do the following (as shown in Figure 2–23):

- Type **ExSurface** for the *Name*.
- Type **Data referenced surface** for the *Description*. The reference name and description do not need to be the same as the source name and description.
- Select **Contours 2' and 10' (Background)** for the *Style*.
- Click **OK** to close the dialog box.

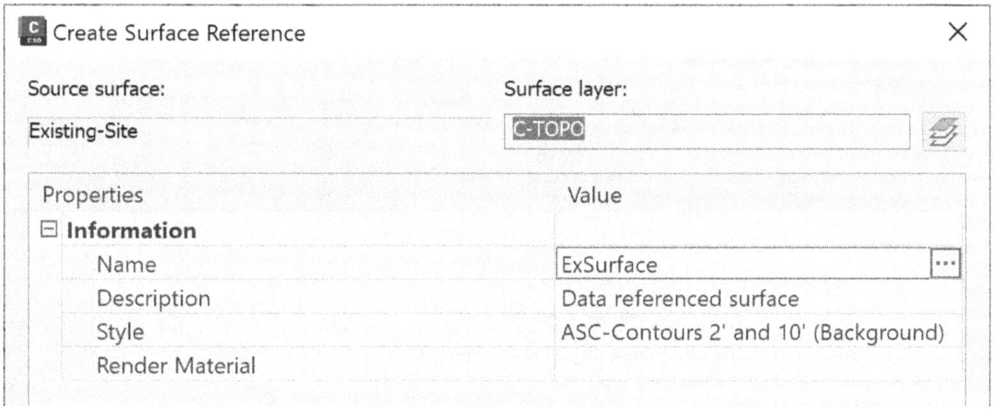

Figure 2–23

11. Type **ZE** and press <Enter> to display the surface reference.

12. You will now create a data reference to the alignment. In the *Alignments>Centerline Alignments* collection, right-click on **Ascent PI** and select **Create Reference...**.

13. In the *Create Alignment Reference* dialog box, accept the default for the *Name* and type **Data referenced alignment** for the *Description*. Set the *Alignment style* to **ASC-Layout** and set the *Alignment label set* to **ASC-Major and Minor only,** as shown in Figure 2–24. Click **OK** when done.

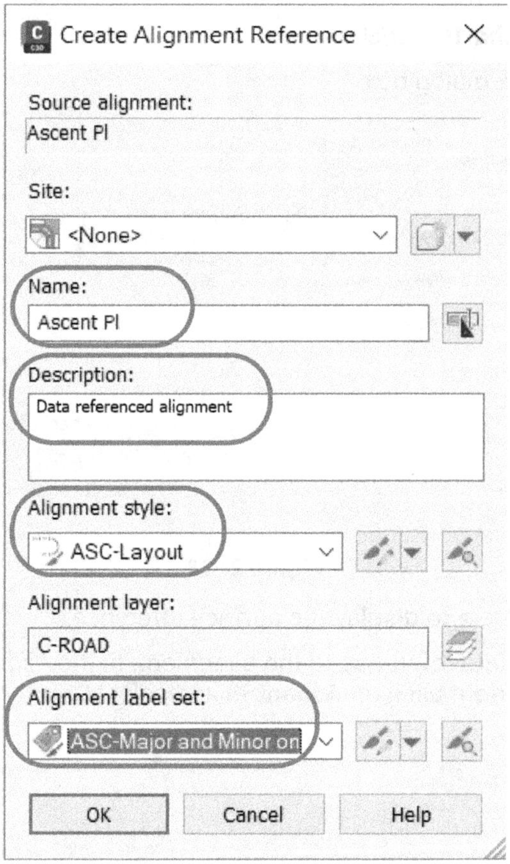

Figure 2–24

14. Zoom in to the end of the **Ascent PI** alignment, as shown in Figure 2–25.

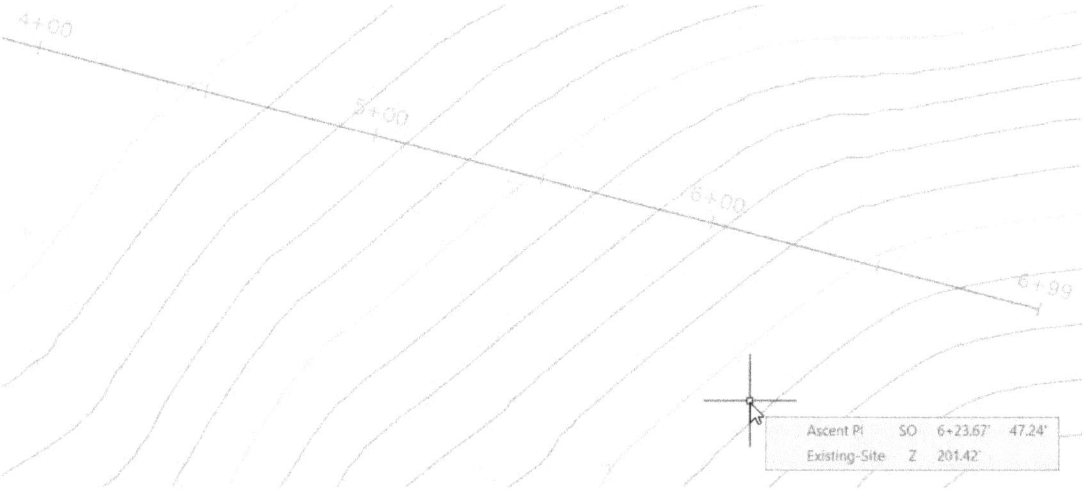

Figure 2–25

15. Create a data reference to the corridor: In the *Corridors* collection, right-click on **Ascent PI** and select **Create Reference...**. Accept all of the defaults and click **OK**.

16. In Model Space, select the **Ascent PI** referenced alignment. Note that there are no grips and you cannot graphically redefine this alignment. However, you can add labels using the contextual tab.

17. In the contextual tab>*Labels & Tables* panel, expand **Add Labels** and select **Station/Offset - Fixed Point**, as shown in Figure 2–26.

Figure 2–26

18. When prompted to select a point, select the end point of **Ascent PI,** as shown on the left in Figure 2-27. Select the label and move its location so that it is easier to read, as shown on the right in Figure 2-27. Note that the station is **6+98.72**.

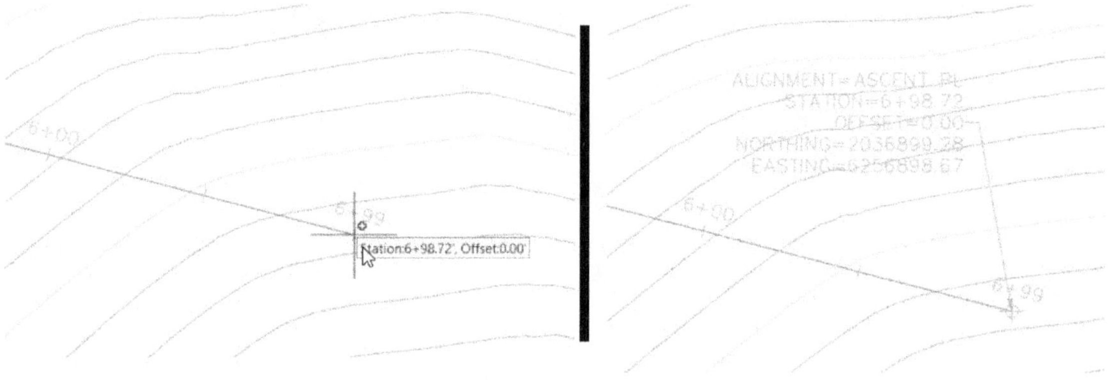

Figure 2-27

19. In the *TOOLSPACE>Prospector* tab, expand the *Surfaces> ExSurface* collection, as shown on the left in Figure 2-28. Note that it does not contain the definition elements that might otherwise be displayed in a surface that is not data-referenced, as shown on the right in Figure 2-28. Therefore, you cannot edit or make design changes to a referenced surface.

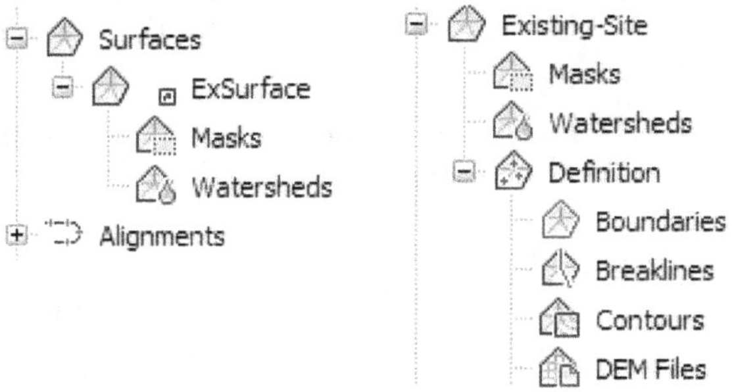

Figure 2-28

20. Save the drawing, but do not close it.

Task 3: Revise the original referenced object.

1. In the *TOOLSPACE>Prospector* tab, ensure that *Data Shortcuts* points to the *C:\Civil 3D Beyond\Data Shortcuts\Lesson\Ascent Phase 1* folder.

2. Ensure that the **Master View** is enabled in the Toolspace so that all of the drawings that are loaded display. Select **DS-A-Shortcuts**, right-click, and select **Switch to**, as shown in Figure 2-29. **DS-A-Shortcuts.dwg** is now the current drawing.

   • If you closed the drawing, you will need to open **DS-A-Shortcuts.dwg** again.

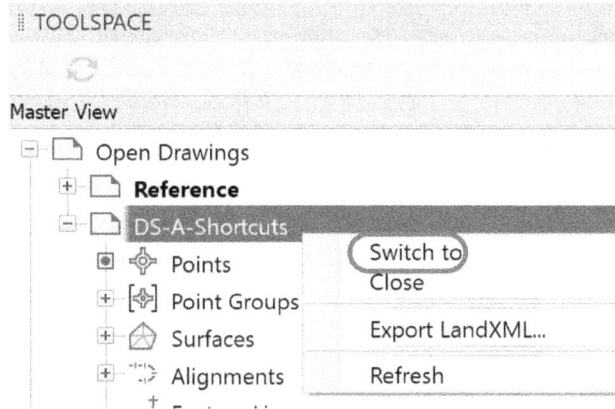

Figure 2–29

3. Zoom in to the end of **Ascent Pl** to get a better view of the cul-de-sac.

4. You will now change the length of this alignment. In Model Space, select the alignment, select the grip that signifies the end of the alignment, and move it to the intersection where it crosses the cul-de-sac bulb, as shown in Figure 2–30.

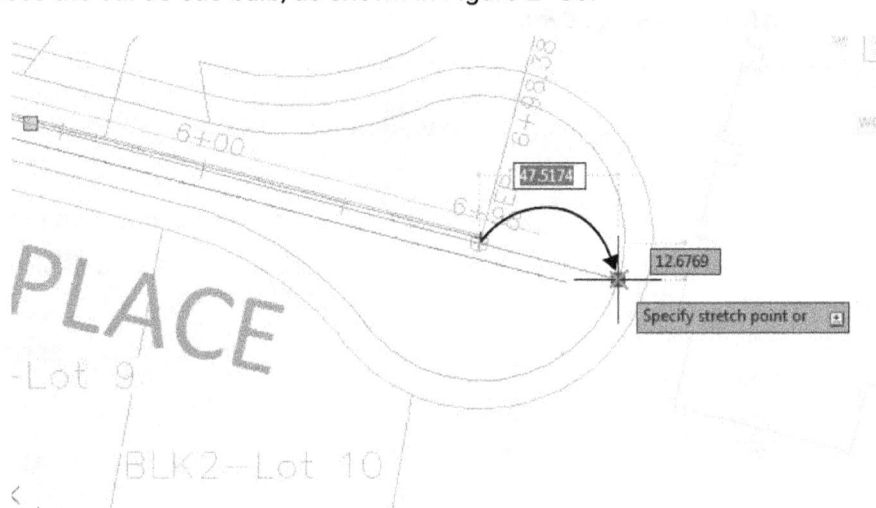

Figure 2–30

5. In the contextual tab>*Modify* panel, click **Alignment Properties**, as shown in Figure 2–31.

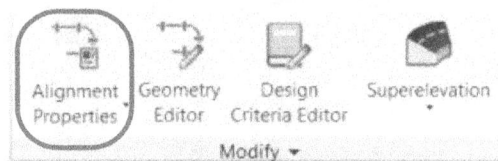

Figure 2–31

6. In the *Alignment Properties* dialog box, in the *Station Control* tab, set the *Reference point Station* to **100**, as shown in Figure 2–32. A warning displays prompting you that changing the station will affect objects and data that have already been created. Click **OK** to dismiss the warning, then click **OK** to close the *Alignment Properties* dialog box.

Figure 2–32

7. Save the drawing. This updates the data shortcut. If you closed the drawing used in Step 8, open the drawing **Reference File.dwg**.

8. If you are continuing with the drawing from the previous task, ensure that the **Master View** is enabled in the Toolspace so that you can see all of the drawings that are loaded. Select **Reference File**, right-click, and select **Switch to**. **Reference File.dwg** is now the current drawing.

9. In the *Status Bar*, you should see ⚐ (Data Shortcut Reference), as shown on the left in Figure 2–33. To synchronize your current drawing, right-click on ⚐ (Data Shortcut Reference) and select **Synchronize**, as shown on the right in Figure 2–33.

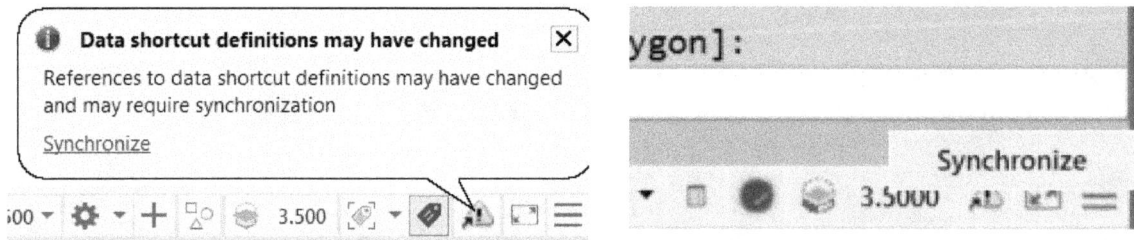

Figure 2–33

- Alternatively, in the *TOOLSPACE>Prospector* tab, select the alignment **Ascent Pl** in the *Alignments>Centerline Alignments* collection, right-click, and select **Synchronize**, as shown in Figure 2−34.

Figure 2−34

10. Note that the alignment has updated geographic information, as shown in Figure 2−35. The end of the alignment has been extended to intersect the cul-de-sac bulb, and the station label is updated to reflect the change to the original alignment design.

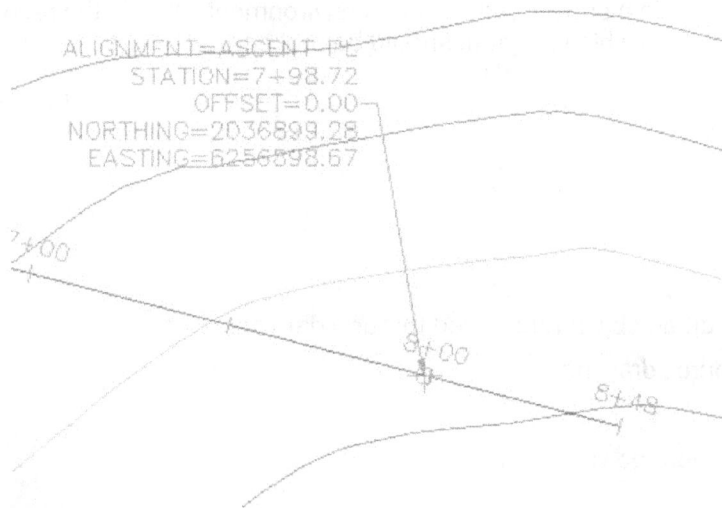

Figure 2−35

11. Save the drawing.

End of practice

Chapter Review Questions

1. In the Autodesk Civil 3D workflow, what are the two main methods of project collaboration (or the sharing of intelligent Autodesk Civil 3D design data)?

   a. Windows Explorer and XREFs

   b. Data shortcuts and Vault references

   c. XREFs and data shortcuts

   d. Vault references and XREFs

2. Why would you want to use Vault references over data shortcuts?

   a. Added security and version control.

   b. Permit more people to have access.

   c. It works more like regular AutoCAD.

   d. It works better with multiple offices.

3. When sharing data in a project collaboration environment, what is the recommended number of levels into which the data should be broken?

   a. 1 level

   b. 2 levels

   c. 3 levels

   d. 4 levels

4. How can you edit an object referenced through data shortcuts?

   a. Open the source drawing.

   b. With grips.

   c. Using the Panorama view.

   d. You cannot.

5. What is the file format that data shortcuts use to share design data between drawing files?

   a. .SHP

   b. .DWT

   c. .DWG

   d. .XML

Command Summary

Button	Command	Location
	Create Data Shortcuts	**Ribbon:** *Manage* tab>*Data Shortcuts* panel **Command Prompt:** CreateDataShortcuts
	Manager Reference Styles	• **Ribbon:** *Manage* tab>*Styles* panel • **Command Prompt:** AttachReferenceTemplate
	New Shortcuts Folder	**Ribbon:** *Manage* tab>*Data Shortcuts* panel **Command Prompt:** NewShortcutsFolder
	Set Shortcuts Folder	**Ribbon:** *Manage* tab>*Data Shortcuts* panel **Command Prompt:** SetShortcutsFolder
	Set Working Folder	**Ribbon:** *Manage* tab>*Data Shortcuts* panel **Command Prompt:** SetWorkingFolder

Parcels

In this chapter, you will learn how to create a subdivision plan using specific design criteria. Labels and tables will be added to the plan to correctly communicate the design to contractors and other stakeholders.

Learning Objectives

- Create parcels from objects in the drawing or in an external reference file.

- Change the properties and display order of parcels to ensure that the correct linetype and color display.

- Subdivide parcels into smaller lots using various tools.

- Change the parcel numbers so that they are numbered in order.

- Change area, line, and curve labels into tags and display in a table for better readability of the drawing.

- Create predefined reports to share useful engineering data about the parcels created in the drawing.

- Add annotations to parcels to communicate line bearing, distances, and areas for each lot.

3.1 Introduction to Parcels

A site (as shown in Figure 3−1) is the starting point for defining smaller parcels. The development's zoning agreement or covenants determine the size, setback, and other criteria for the new parcels. If a parcel is residential, there might be restrictions affecting minimum parcel areas, setbacks, and where to locate a house. If it is a commercial property, there might be restrictions or specific mandates for access, traffic control, parking spaces, etc. The **Parcel Layout** commands are used for subdividing larger parcels.

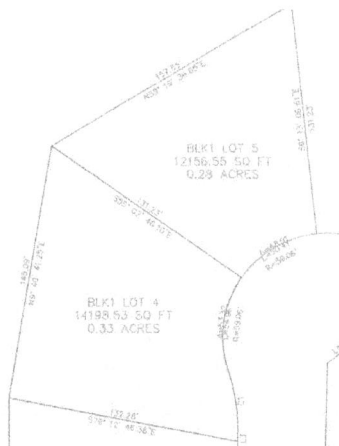

Figure 3−1

Sites, parcels, and alignments are closely related. Each can exist by itself and you do not need to have alignments associated with the parcels. However, you often start with a site boundary and then divide the site into smaller parcels by placing alignments within its boundary. In that case, it is recommended the parcels and alignments reside in the same Civil 3D site.

- Parcels are listed in the *TOOLSPACE>Prospector* tab in the *Sites* branch, as shown in Figure 3−2.

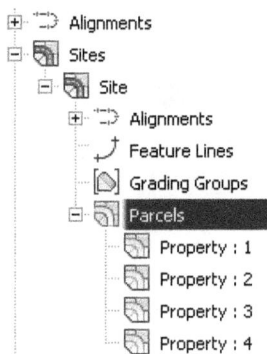

Figure 3−2

- When adding alignments to a Civil 3D site, the *Parcels* list is updated in the *TOOLSPACE>Prospector* tab.

- As in all other Autodesk Civil 3D objects, parcel object layers are controlled in the *Object Layers* tab of the *Drawing Settings* dialog box, as shown in Figure 3–3.

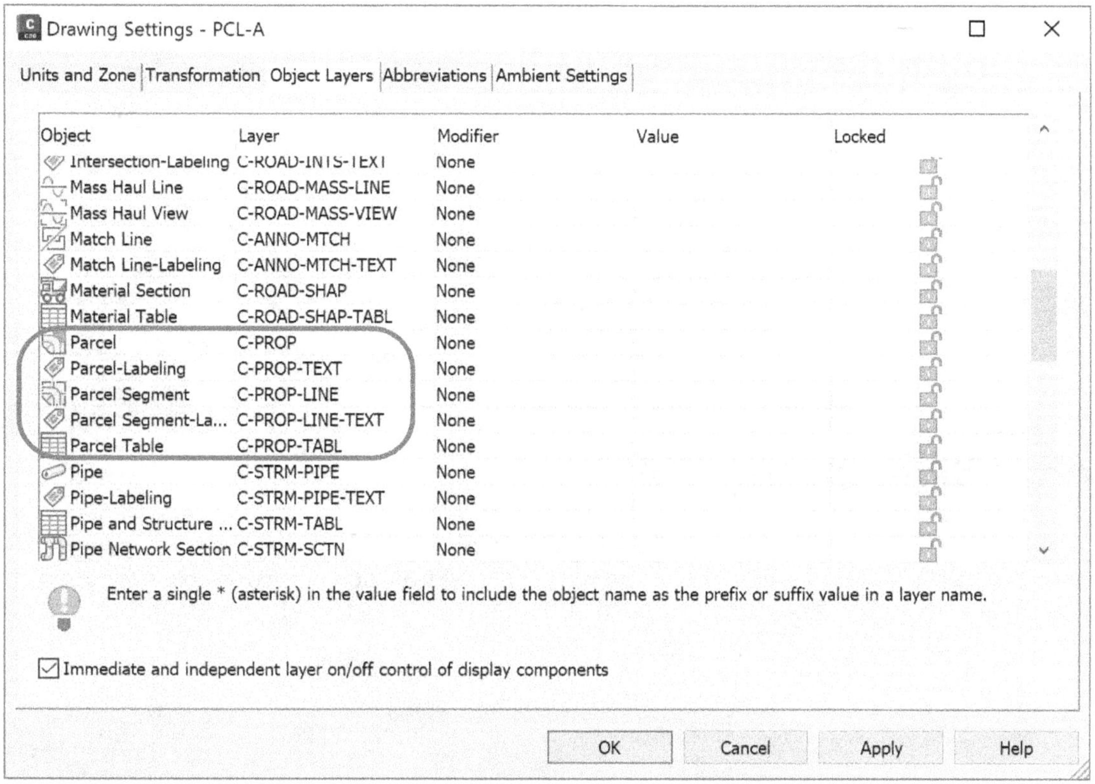

Figure 3–3

ROW Parcel

The right-of-way (ROW) parcel is related to the alignment and parcels. This special parcel represents land that is owned, maintained, and used for the community by a regulatory body (usually the local municipality or Department of Transportation). Typically, the ROW contains road, sidewalks, and utilities. The contents of the ROW depend on the covenants or agreements made before the site is developed. For example, in some cases, the sidewalks and utilities might be located within an easement outside the road ROW.

- The Autodesk Civil 3D software contains a **ROW** command, which creates a parcel using offsets from an alignment.

- A ROW parcel can represent the front yard definition of several potential parcels.

- While normal parcels automatically adjust to changes to an alignment, ROW parcels are static, as shown in Figure 3–4. Therefore, you should only create ROW parcels after determining a final location for an alignment.

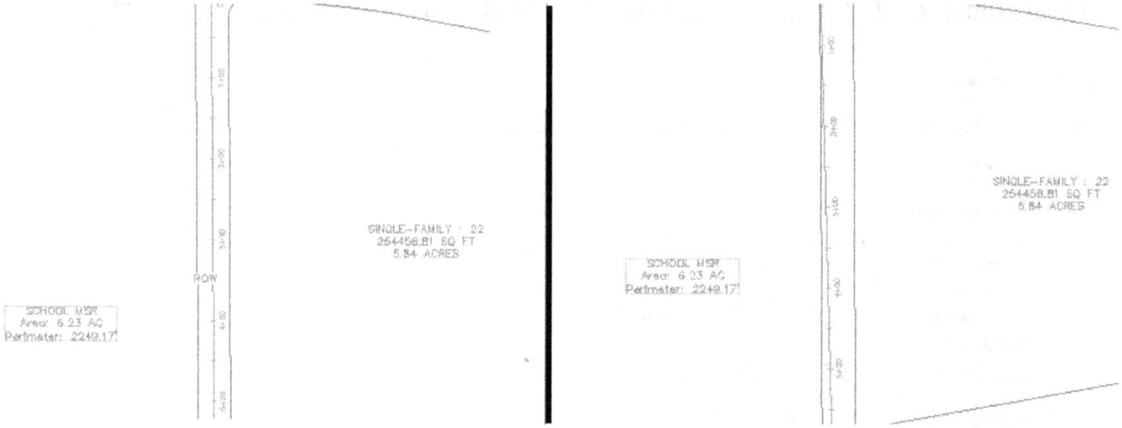

Figure 3–4

Parcel Style Display Order

Parcel segment display is controlled by parcel styles, and parcel lines can abut parcels with different styles. To open the *Site Parcel Properties* dialog box, select the **Parcels** collection (under *Sites*), right-click, and select **Properties**, as shown in Figure 3–5.

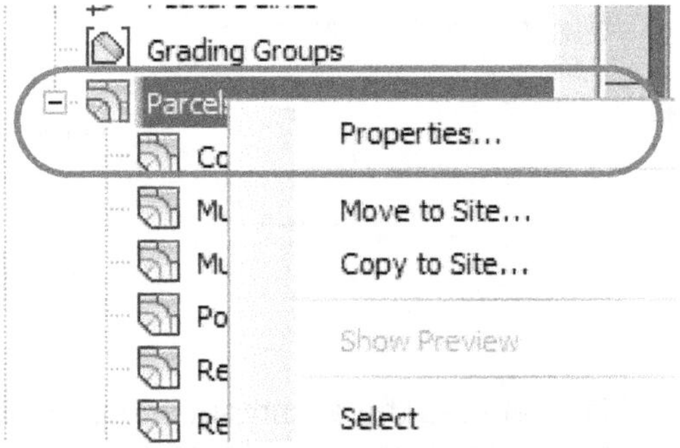

Figure 3–5

You can select which parcel style should take precedence in the *Parcel style display order* area of the *Site Parcel Properties* dialog box, as shown in Figure 3–6. Placing the style for the overall parent tract (the site parcel style) at the top of the list causes the outside parcel lines to display differently than those inside.

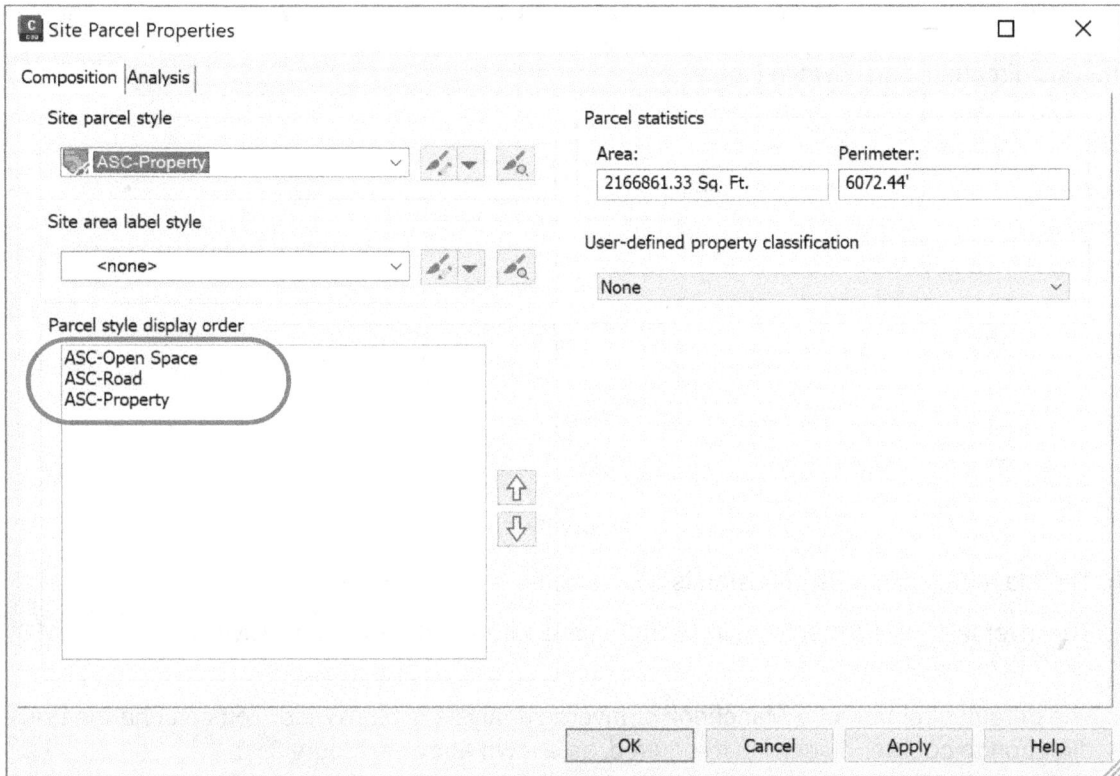

Figure 3-6

Parcel Properties

The properties of a parcel include its name, style, and the properties found on the *Analysis* tab, including the parcel's area, perimeter, and point-of-beginning (POB). The *Composition* tab of the *Parcel Properties* dialog box displays the label style, area, and perimeter, as shown in Figure 3-7.

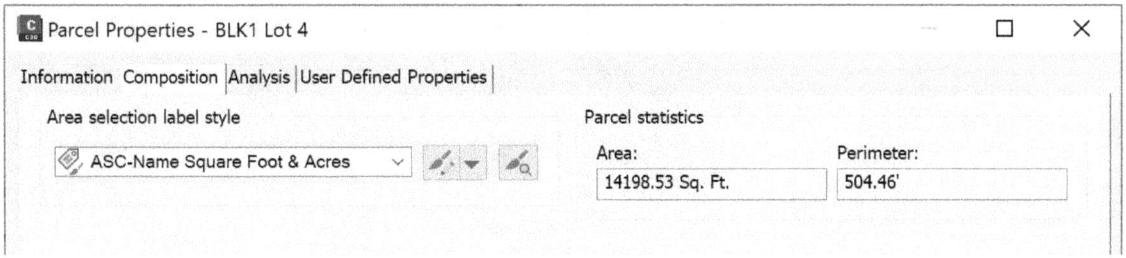

Figure 3-7

The *Analysis* tab contains a parcel boundary **Inverse analysis** or **Mapcheck analysis**. In the upper right area of the tab, you can change the *Point of beginning* (POB) location and the analysis direction, as shown in Figure 3-8.

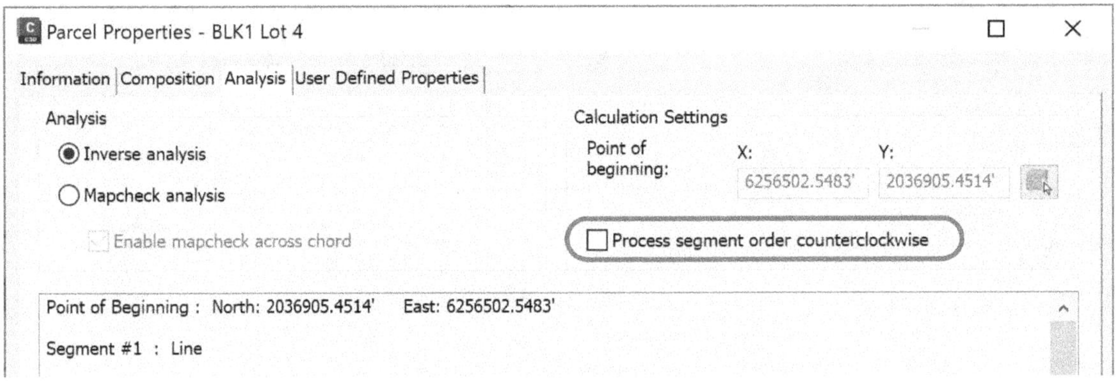

Figure 3-8

- The Mapcheck analysis precision is the same as the drawing distance precision.

- The Inverse analysis precision is set to the precision of the Autodesk Civil 3D software (10 to 12 decimal places).

- The default direction of a Mapcheck or Inverse analysis is clockwise. You can change the direction to counter-clockwise if required, as shown above in Figure 3-8.

- A POB can be any vertex on the parcel's perimeter.

The *User Defined Properties* tab contains site-specific details, such as the *Parcel Number, Parcel Address, Parcel Tax ID*, and other properties you might want to define, as shown in Figure 3-9. Custom properties can be assigned to a drawing by using the *User Defined Property Classifications* area in the *TOOLSPACE>Settings* tab, under the *Parcels* collection.

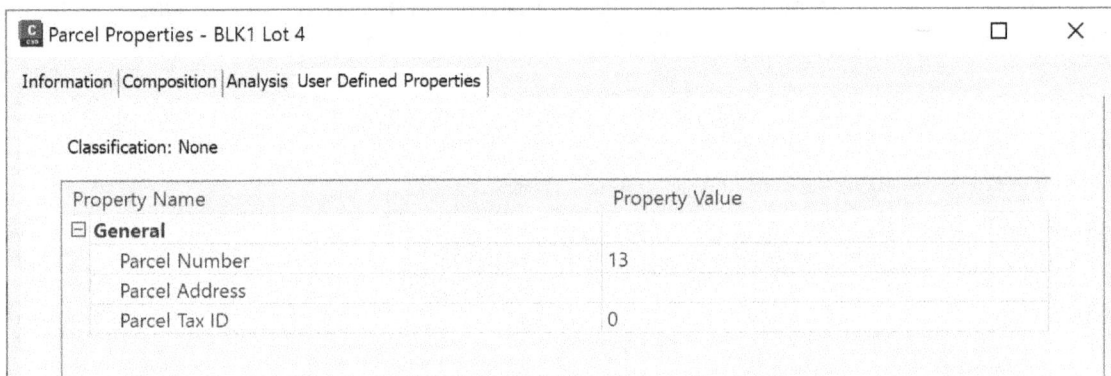

Figure 3-9

Parcel Labels and Styles

There are two types of parcel annotations: an area label for the parcel and the segments defining the parcel.

A parcel area label usually consists of a parcel's number or name, area, and perimeter, as shown in Figure 3–10. Most offices define their own parcel label styles. A parcel label style can include several additional parcel properties, address, PIN, site name, etc.

In the Autodesk Civil 3D software, you select a parcel by selecting a parcel area label, not the parcel segments.

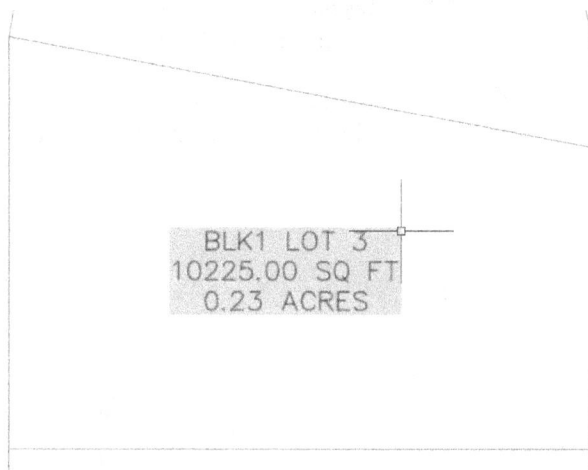

BLK1 LOT 3
10225.00 SQ FT
0.23 ACRES

Figure 3–10

Create Parcels from Objects

The Autodesk Civil 3D software can create parcels from AutoCAD objects, such as closed polylines and closed sequences of lines and arcs

Avoid gaps, multiple polyline vertices at the same location, and polylines that double-back over themselves, which might lead to errors in parcel layouts.

These objects can be selected in the current drawing or from an XREF. Note that Autodesk Civil 3D parcel lines in an XREF cannot be selected. You can only select AutoCAD lines, arcs, and polylines.

Note that Autodesk Civil 3D parcels created from AutoCAD objects do not maintain a relationship to the objects after creation.

Creating Right-of-Way Parcels

Once a site contains property that has been defined as a parcel and alignments have been generated, you are ready to start creating subdivision plans. One command that can speed up the process is **Parcels>Create ROW**. It automatically creates right-of-way parcels based on alignment setbacks.

ROW parcels do not automatically update when alignments change. Therefore, you may want to create ROWs after you are certain where you want the alignments to be for this alternative.

> ### 💡 Hint: Multiple Alternatives in the Same Drawing
>
> Sites enable you to organize alignments, parcels, and related data into separate containers, so that parcel lines from one site alternative do not clean up with parcel lines in others. However, sites do not offer layer or other kind of visibility control. Therefore, if you intend to have multiple parcel layout alternatives in the same drawing, you should consider placing parcel area labels and parcel segments on different layers.

Practice 3a
Create Parcels from Objects

Practice Objective

- Create parcels from objects in the drawing or external reference file.

Task 1: Create a site parcel from objects.

1. Open **PCL-A.dwg** from the *C:\Civil 3D Beyond\Working\ Parcels* folder.

2. Note that there are no sites within this drawing, as shown in Figure 3–11. There is no **+** symbol next to the *Sites* branch, indicating there are no sites.

Figure 3–11

3. In the *Home* tab>*Create Design* panel, expand **Parcel** and select **Create Parcel from Objects**, as shown in Figure 3–12.

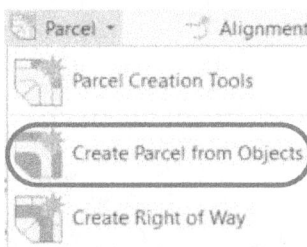

Figure 3–12

4. In the model, select the polyline that represent the property boundary, as shown in Figure 3–13, and press <Enter>.

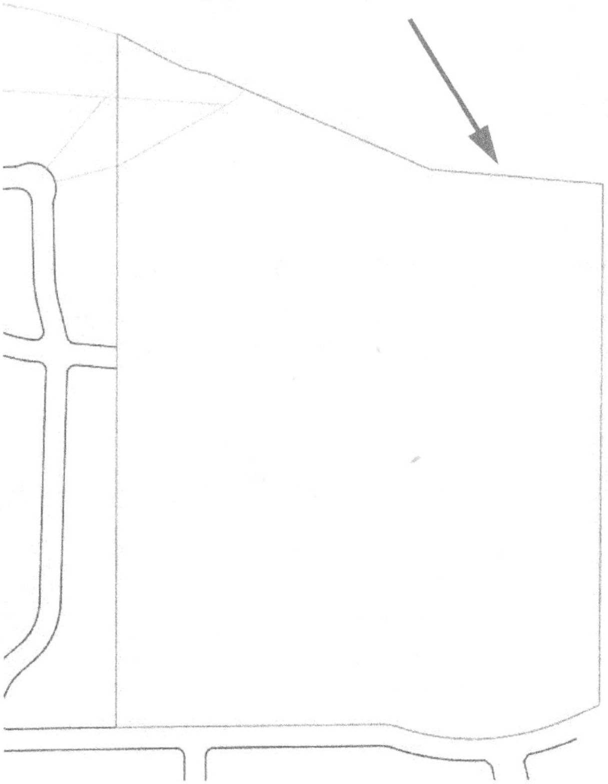

Figure 3–13

5. In the *Create Parcels* dialog box, set the following parameters, as shown in Figure 3-14, and then click **OK**.

*   *Site:* **Site 1**
*   *Parcel style:* **ASC-Property**
*   *Area label style:* **ASC-Name Area & Perimeter**
*   Select **Automatically add segment labels**.
*   *Line segment label style:* **ASC-(Span) Bearing and Distance with Crows Feet**
*   *Curve segment label style:* **ASC-Delta over Length and Radius (this is the default)**
*   Select **Erase existing entities**.

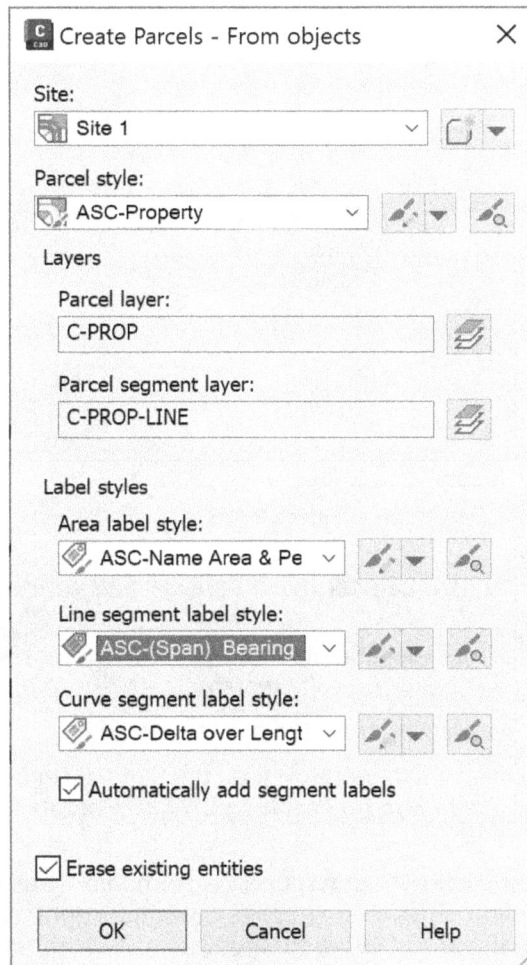

Figure 3-14

6. Civil 3D has created the new site (Site 1) and, within it, created the parcel. In the Toolspace>*Prospector* tab, expand the current drawing and select the **Sites>Site1>Parcels** node, as shown in Figure 3–15. Note that the new parcel is listed in the branch as well as in the preview area of the *Prospector* tab.If the + is not displayed next to Parcels, press <F5> to refresh the Toolspace>*Prospector* tab view.

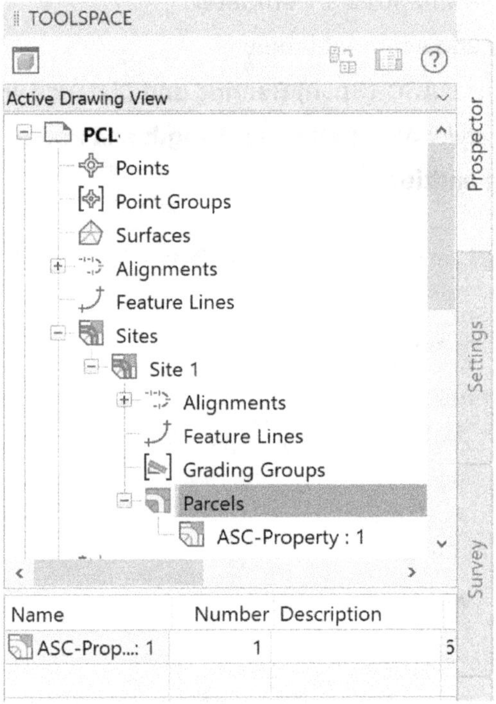

Figure 3–15

Task 2: Create a new site and parcel from referenced objects.

You have received a drawing from the land planning department that displays the street layout and different parcels. Using this plan, you will create parcels from XREF objects.

1. Continue working with the drawing from the previous task.

2. In the *TOOLSPACE>Prospector* tab, right-click on the *Sites* collection and select **New**. Type **C3D Training** as the name and **Site for teaching Civil 3D Parcels** for the description, then click **OK** to close the dialog box.

3. You now need to move the **ASC-Property:1** parcel from *Site 1* to the **C3D Training** site. Expand the *Site 1* collection, expand the *Parcels* collection, right-click on the **ASC-Property:1** parcel, and select **Move to Site...**, as shown on the left in Figure 3–16.

4. In the *Move to Site* dialog box, select **C3D Training** from the *Destination* site drop-down list, as shown on the right in Figure 3–16. Click **OK** to close the dialog box.

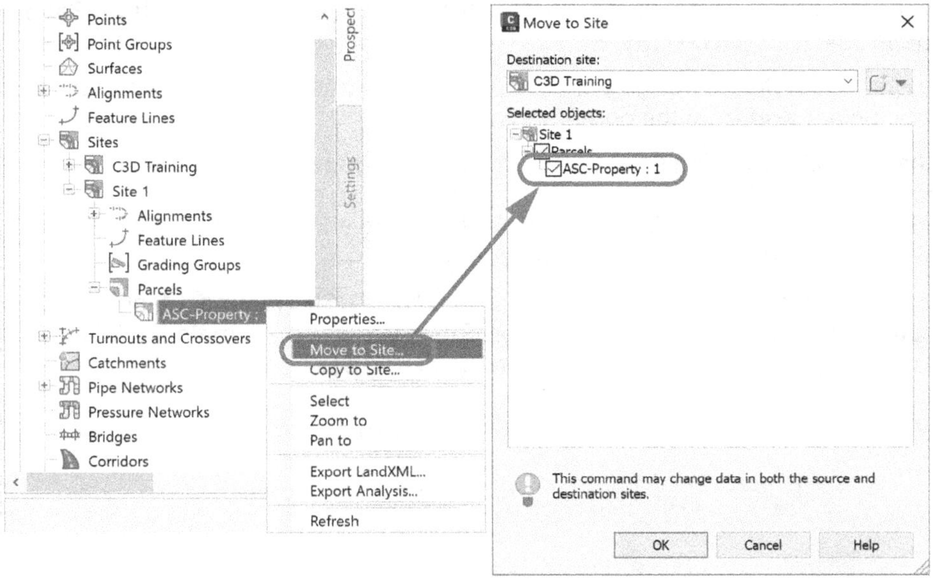

Figure 3–16

5. In the *TOOLSPACE>Prospector* tab, expand the current drawing and select the **Sites>C3D Training>Parcels** node, as shown in Figure 3–17. Note that the parcel is now listed in this branch and is no longer in the **Sites>Site1>Parcels** node. If the + is not displayed next to Parcels, press <F5> to refresh the *TOOLSPACE>Prospector* tab view.

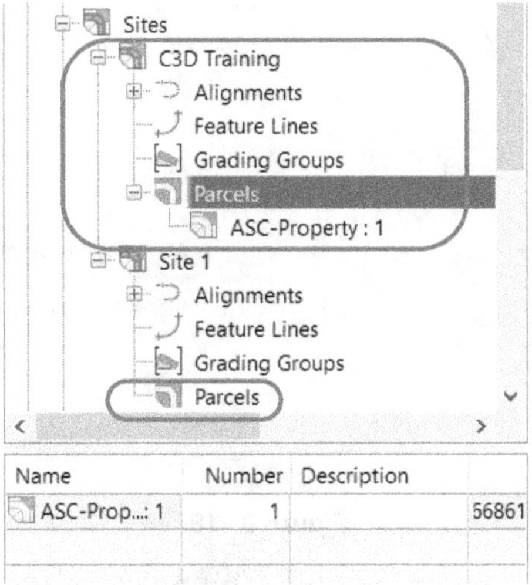

Figure 3–17

Note: To save time, the x-referenced drawing **Base-original Property** has already been referenced. The zone and units for the project drawings were set. This enables you to geo reference the drawings using **Locate using Geographic data**.

6. Thaw the layer **Base-originalProperty|C-PROP-LINE-N** and freeze the layer **Base-originalProperty|C-PROP-LINE-E**.

7. In the *Home* tab>*Create Design* panel, expand **Parcel** and select **Create Parcel from Objects**. Select **Xref** from the command options.

8. Use the AutoCAD crossing selection or the lasso crossing selection method (click and drag the cursor towards the left side of the screen) to select all the linework within the green boundary, as shown on the left in Figure 3-18. There should be a total of 39 or 40 objects. Press <Enter> to end the **Xref selection** command.

9. In the *Create Parcels* dialog box, verify that the *Site* is **C3D Training**. Clear the **Automatically add segment labels** option and keep the default values in the remaining fields, as shown on the right in Figure 3-18. Click **OK** to close the dialog box.

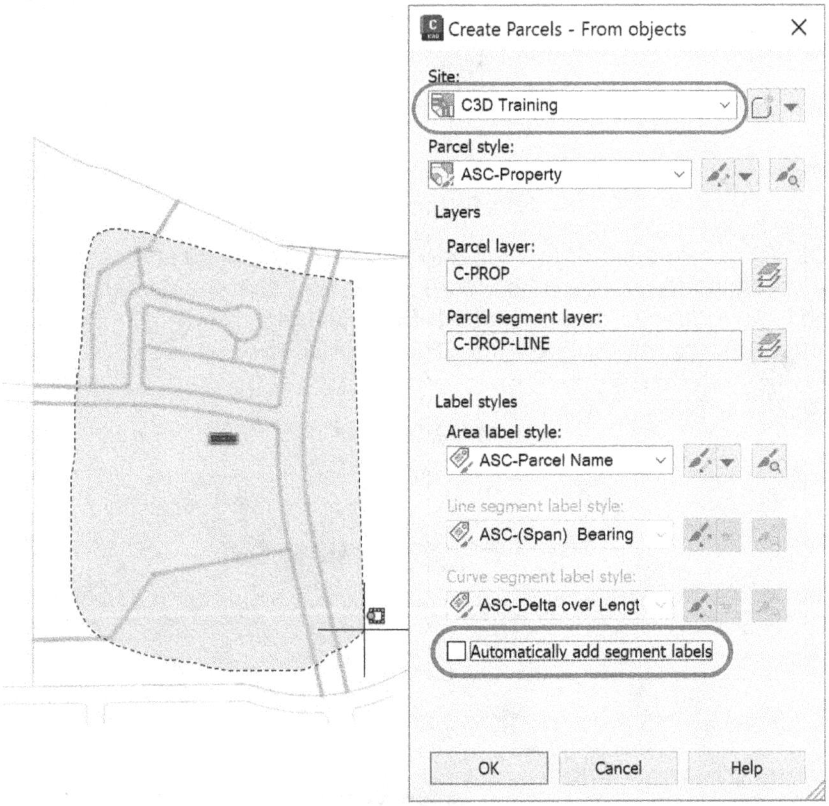

Figure 3-18

Note: You may need to refresh the Toolspace by pressing <F5>.

10. The project site now has nine parcels. In the drawing area, select each parcel label and click

(Parcel Properties) in the *Parcels* contextual tab>*Modify* panel.

11. In the *Parcel Properties* dialog box, in the *Information* tab, clear the **Use name template in parcel style** option, which will enable you to type in a new name for the parcel, as shown on the left in Figure 3–19. Note that the default parcel numbers may differ because they are randomly numbered.

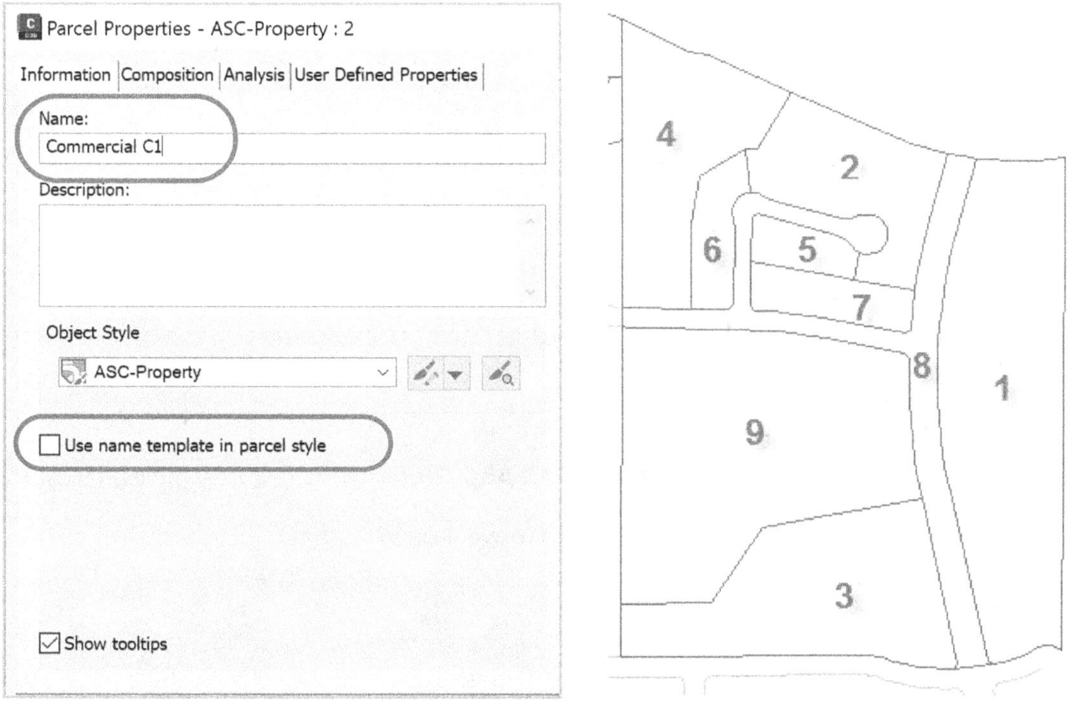

Figure 3–19

12. Using Figure 3–19 as a reference, set the parcel styles as follows:

Property Name	Style
1. Commercial C1	ASC-Property
2. Multi Family MF	ASC-Property
3. Municipal Reserve MR	ASC-Property
4. Pond PUL	ASC-Open Space
5. Residential BLK2 R1	ASC-Property
6. Residential BLK1 R1	ASC-Property
7. Residential BLK3 R1	ASC-Property
8. Right Of Way	ASC-Road
9. School MSR	ASC-Property

13. In the *TOOLSPACE>Prospector* tab, expand *Sites>C3D Training* site, right-click on **Parcels**, and select **Properties**, as shown in Figure 3−20.

Figure 3−20

14. In the *Site Parcel Properties* dialog box, select **ASC-Property** in the *Parcel style display order* area, as shown in Figure 3−21. Click ⬆ to move it up in the list.

Figure 3−21

Note: If the drawing does not look different after completing Step 14, you might need to adjust the draw order so that the XREF drawing is behind the existing drawing linework.

15. Click **OK**.

16. Save the drawing.

End of practice

3.2 Creating and Editing Parcels by Layout Overview

In addition to creating parcels from polylines, arcs, and lines, the Autodesk Civil 3D software can also intelligently create (and adjust) parcels using commands in the *Parcel Layout Tools* toolbar. To open the *Parcel Layout Tools* toolbar, expand **Parcel** in the *Create Design* panel and select **Parcel Creation Tools**, as shown in Figure 3–22.

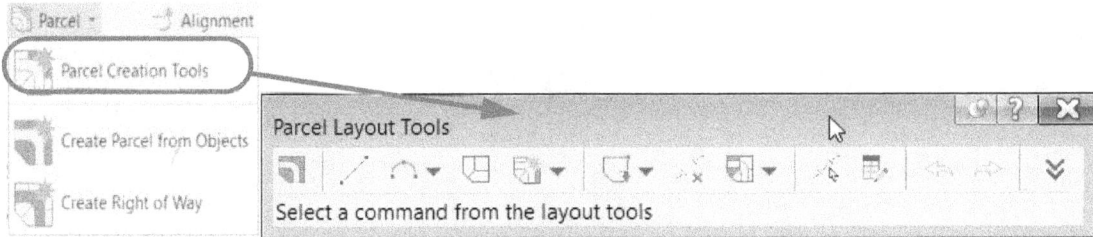

Figure 3–22

- (Create Parcel) assigns parcel creation settings, such as parcel type, labeling styles, and other parameters.

Hint: Closing Parcels

When drawing parcel line segments, it is essential to use the AutoCAD object snaps to ensure that the lines and curve segments touch existing parcel segments so that the enclosures are complete and parcels are created.

- The (Line) and (Curve) commands can be used to create individual line and curve parcel segments. Segments created with these tools are considered *fixed*.

- (Draw Tangent - Tangent with No Curves) enables you to create a series of connected parcel line segments.

- The Parcel Sizing flyout (shown in Figure 3-23) contains a list of commands for creating and editing parcels. The methods used to create parcels include defining the *last* parcel segment by slide direction, slide angle, swing line, or freehand drawing of a parcel boundary. The most frequently used method is **Slide Line**.

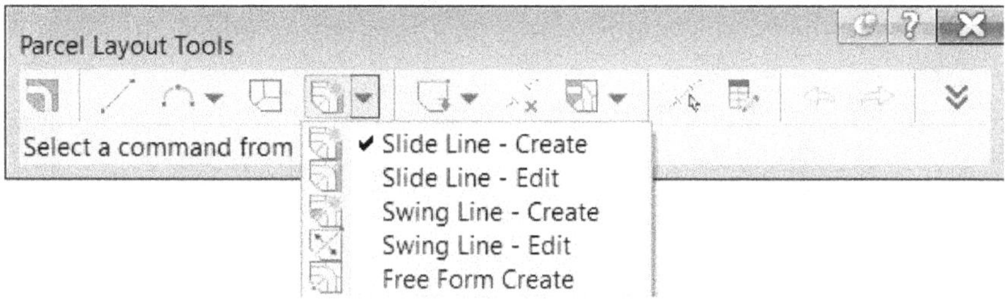

Figure 3-23

- The commands at the center of the toolbar (shown in Figure 3-24) enable you to further edit parcel segments. These commands include inserting or deleting points of intersection (PIs), deleting parcel segments, or creating or dissolving parcel unions.

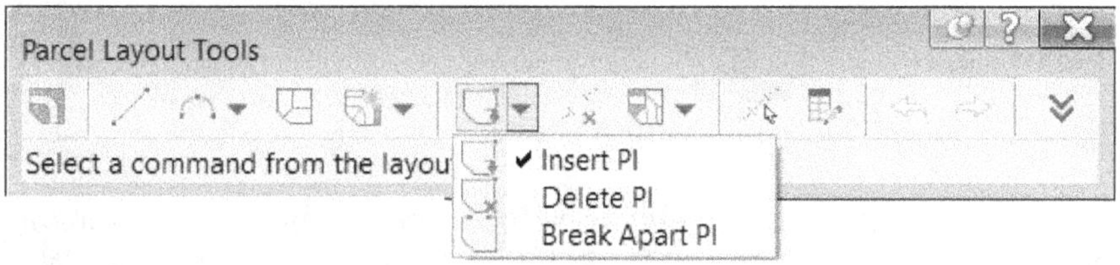

Figure 3-24

- (Pick Sub-Entity) enables you to select a parcel line and display its details in the *Parcel Layout Parameters* dialog box.

- (Sub-entity Editor) opens and closes the *Parcel Layout Parameters* dialog box.

- The next two commands enable you to **Undo** and **Redo** parcel edits. These can be used while the *Parcel Layout Tools* have been opened.

- The double down arrow (⯆) expands the toolbar to display the parcel creation parameters, as shown in Figure 3–25. (They are also accessible through the **Command Settings** of *CreateParcelByLayout* in the *TOOLSPACE>Settings* tab.)

Parcel Layout Tools

Parameter	Value
⊟ **Parcel Sizing**	
Minimum Area	10225.00 Sq. Ft.
Minimum Frontage	65.00'
Use Minimum Frontage At Offset	Yes
Frontage Offset	20.00'
Minimum Width	65.00'
Minimum Depth	20.00'
Use Maximum Depth	No
Maximum Depth	500.00'
Multiple Solution Preference	Use shortest frontage
⊟ **Automatic Layout**	
Automatic Mode	On
Remainder Distribution	Place remainder in last parcel

Figure 3–25

- The *Parcel Sizing* area sets the minimum area for parcels to be laid out. *Minimum Frontage* sets the minimum width of a parcel at the ROW or at a setback from the ROW.

- *Use Minimum Frontage At Offset* specifies whether or not to use frontage offset criteria.

- *Frontage Offset* sets the default value for the frontage offset from the ROW.

- *Minimum Width* sets the default minimum width at the frontage offset.

- *Minimum Depth* sets the minimum depth of new or existing parcels at the mid-point and is perpendicular to the frontage of the parcel.

- *Use Maximum Depth* specifies whether or not to use maximum depth criteria.

- *Maximum Depth* sets the maximum depth for new parcels or when editing parcels.

- *Multiple Solution Preference* specifies whether or not to use the shortest frontage or the smallest area when multiple solutions are encountered.

- *Automatic Layout* affects how parcel auto-sizing subdivides a parcel block.

3.3 Creating and Editing Parcels

The **Create Parcel by Layout** tools can help you to quickly create a subdivision plan. Although these tools can make your job easier and are faster than manual drafting, they are only effective in creating the *last* side of new parcels. Therefore, you might need to create additional (or adjust) parcel lines manually to guide the Autodesk Civil 3D software to the best solution. For example, the area shown in Figure 3–26 requires you to create minimum 10,225 sq. ft. (0.23 acre) parcels.

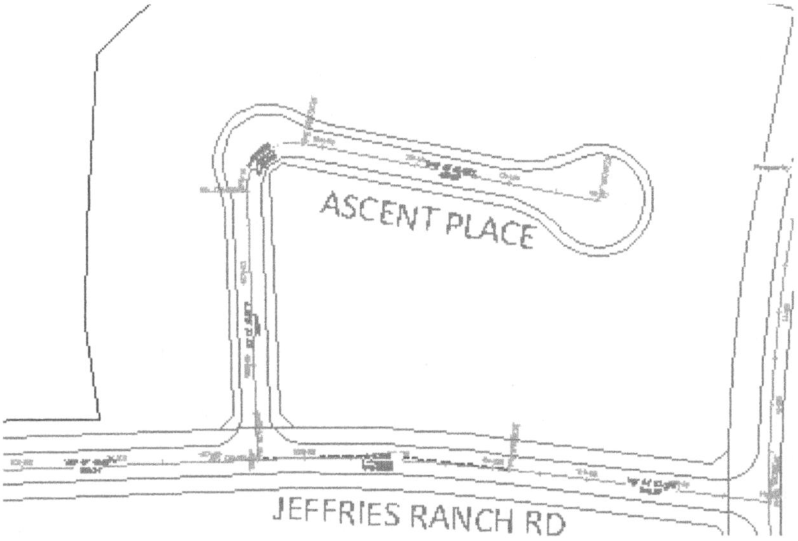

Figure 3–26

The back parcel lines (those along the west and south of the cul-de-sac area, and between Jeffries Ranch Rd and Ascent Place) were drawn manually and saved in a separate drawing file. Once inserted, they are used to guide the creation of the parcels next to Ascent Place. If you ask the Autodesk Civil 3D software to automatically subdivide this area, the result is a total of 15 residential lot parcels, as shown in Figure 3–27.

Figure 3–27

The various creation and editing techniques available in the *Create Parcel by Layout* toolbar include *Freehand* tools, *Slide Line* tools, *Swing Line* tools, and the **Free Form Create** command.

Freehand

The (Line), (Curve), and (Draw Tangent - Tangent with No Curves) commands enable you to create lot lines without having to specify an area. In contrast, the following commands all create parcels based on a specified area.

Slide Line

The **Slide Line - Create** command enables you to subdivide a larger parcel by creating new parcel lines that hold a specific angle relative to the ROW, such as 90° or a specific bearing or azimuth. The **Slide Line - Edit** command enables you to modify a parcel to a specified area while holding the same angle from the ROW or a specific bearing or azimuth. The commands are shown in Figure 3–28.

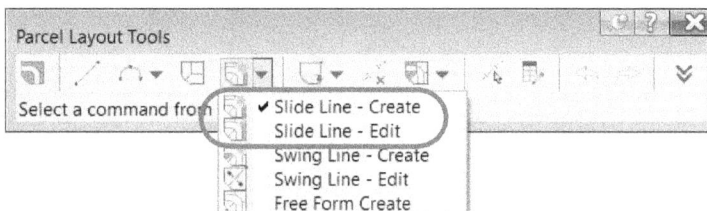

Figure 3–28

Swing Line

The **Swing Line - Create** command enables you to create a new parcel by creating a parcel segment that connects to a specified point, such as a property corner. The **Swing Line - Edit** command enables you to resize a parcel while specifying a lot corner. These commands are shown in Figure 3–29.

Figure 3–29

Free Form Create

The **Free Form Create** command enables you to create a new lot by specifying an area, attachment point and angle, or two attachment points.

Frontage

When using these tools, you are prompted to select a parcel interior point and trace its frontage geometry. This is a critical step. As you trace the frontage, the command creates a jig (heavy highlight) that recognizes the changing geometry of the frontage line work, as shown in Figure 3–30.

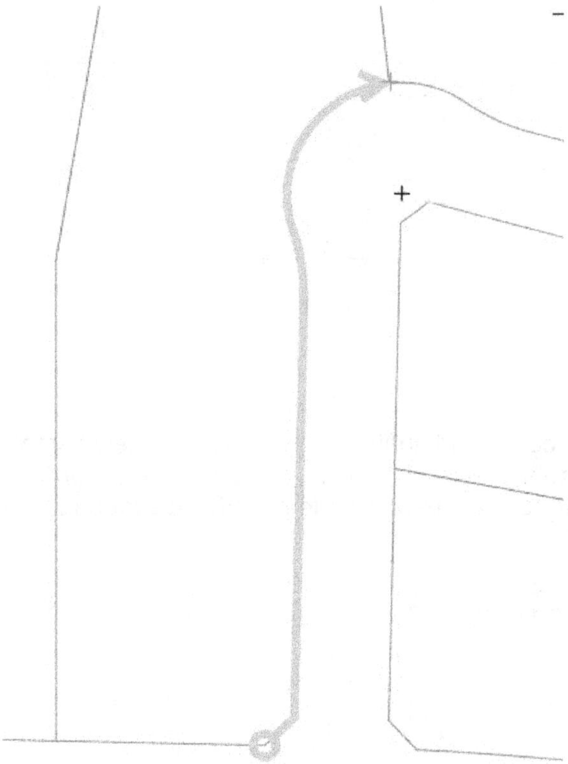

Figure 3–30

Practice 3b
Create and Edit Parcels

Practice Objective

- Create and edit parcels to maximize the number of lots you can create with the required area and frontage.

You have three parcels zoned as single-family residential: Block1 (1.31ac), Block2 (0.94ac), and Block3 (1.47ac). Your client, the land developer, requires you to maximize the number of lots in these three parcels, while noting the minimum area and frontages as required by the Land Use bylaws.

1. Continue working with the drawing from the previous practice or open **PCL-B.dwg** from the *C:\Civil 3D Beyond\Working\ Parcels* folder.

2. Select the preset view **Parcel-Create**.

3. In the *Home* tab>*Create Design* panel, expand **Parcel** and select **Parcel Creation Tools**. The *Parcel Layout Tools* toolbar displays.

4. Click ⩣ to expand the *Parcel Layout Tools* toolbar and enter the following values, as shown in Figure 3–31:

   • *Minimum Area:* **10225.00 Sq. Ft.**

   • *Maximum Frontage:* **65.00'**

   • *Use Maximum Frontage At Offset:* **Yes**

   • *Frontage Offset:* **20.00'**

   • *Minimum Width:* **65.00'**

   • *Minimum Depth:* **20.00'**

   • *Use Maximum Depth:* **No**

   • *Maximum Depth:* **500.00'**

   • *Multiple Solution Preference:* **Use shortest frontage**

   • *Automatic Mode:* **On**

   • *Remainder Distribution:* **Place remainder in last parcel**

Parameter	Value
Parcel Sizing	
Minimum Area	10225.00 Sq. Ft.
Minimum Frontage	65.00'
Use Minimum Frontage At Offset	Yes
Frontage Offset	20.00'
Minimum Width	65.00'
Minimum Depth	20.00'
Use Maximum Depth	No
Maximum Depth	500.00'
Multiple Solution Preference	Use shortest frontage
Automatic Layout	
Automatic Mode	On
Remainder Distribution	Place remainder in last parcel

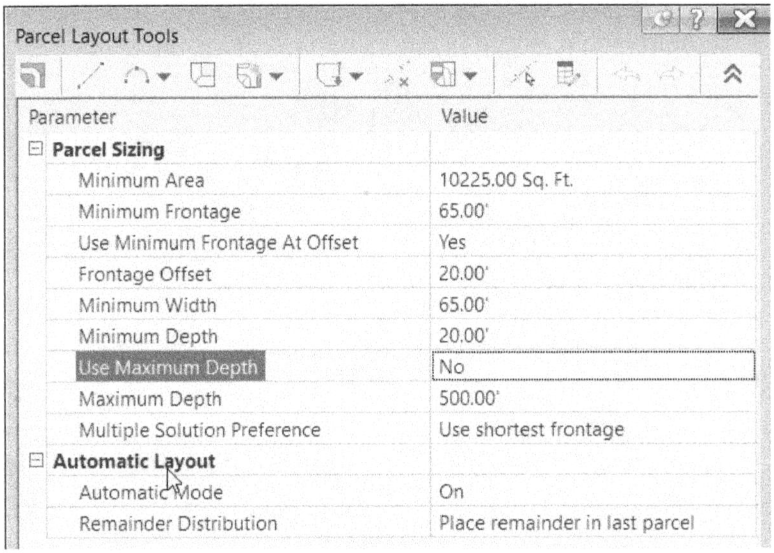

Figure 3–31

5. When finished, click ⩓ to collapse the expanded toolbar.

6. In the *Parcel Layout Tools* toolbar, expand 🗔 and select **Slide Line - Create**, as shown in Figure 3–32.

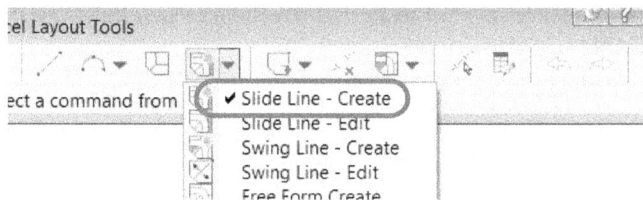

Figure 3–32

7. In the *Create Parcels - Layout* dialog box, set the following parameters, as shown in Figure 3–33:

   - *Site:* **C3D Training**
   - *Parcel style:* **ASC-Single-Family**
   - *Area label style:* **ASC-Name Square Foot & Acres**
   - Leave **Automatically add segment labels** unchecked

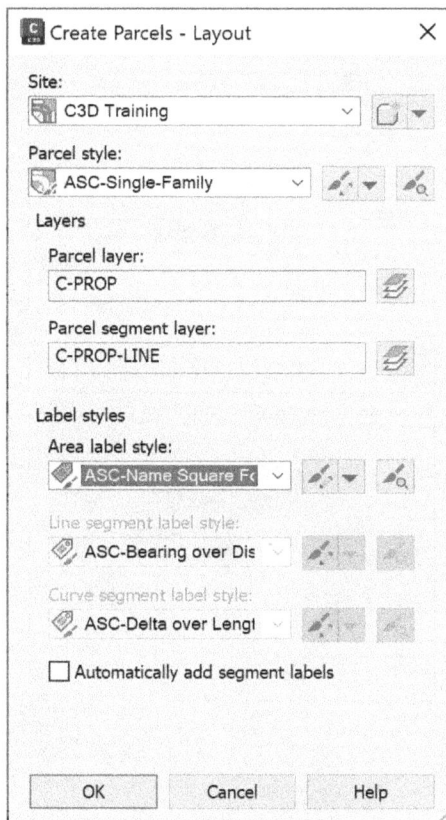

Figure 3–33

8. Click **OK** to accept the changes and close the dialog box.

9. When prompted to select the parcel to be subdivided, select the area label for parcel **RESIDENTIAL BLK1 R1**, as shown in Figure 3–34.

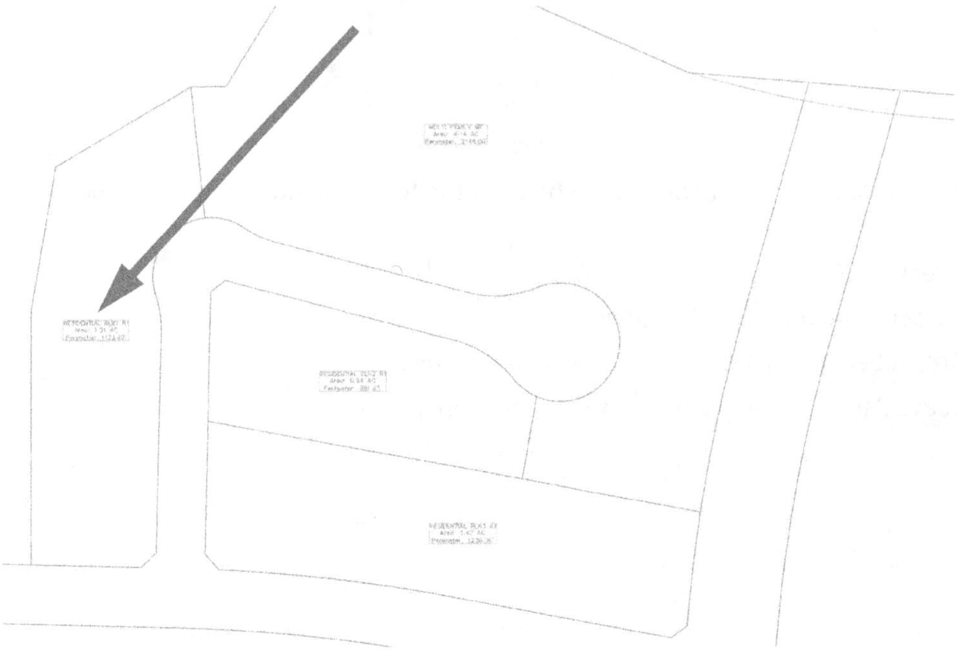

Figure 3–34

10. When you are prompted for the *starting point on frontage*, select the south end of the corner cut. Press <Ctrl>, right-click, and select **endpoint** from the right-click menu, then select the corner cut at **Pt 1**, as shown in Figure 3−35.

11. When prompted for the *end point of the frontage*, set the end point of the property line to the north, **Pt 2**, as shown in Figure 3−35. Use the same process as the previous step to set the end point.

12. When prompted for the *angle of the property line* that will be used to define each lot, select a point east of the parcel near **Pt 3**, as shown in Figure 3−35. For the second point, press <Ctrl>, right-click, and select **Perpendicular**, then select the line at **Pt 4**.

Figure 3−35

13. When prompted to *Accept results*, press <Enter>.

14. When prompted to select another parcel to subdivide, press <Esc> to end the command.

- The result is shown in Figure 3–36.

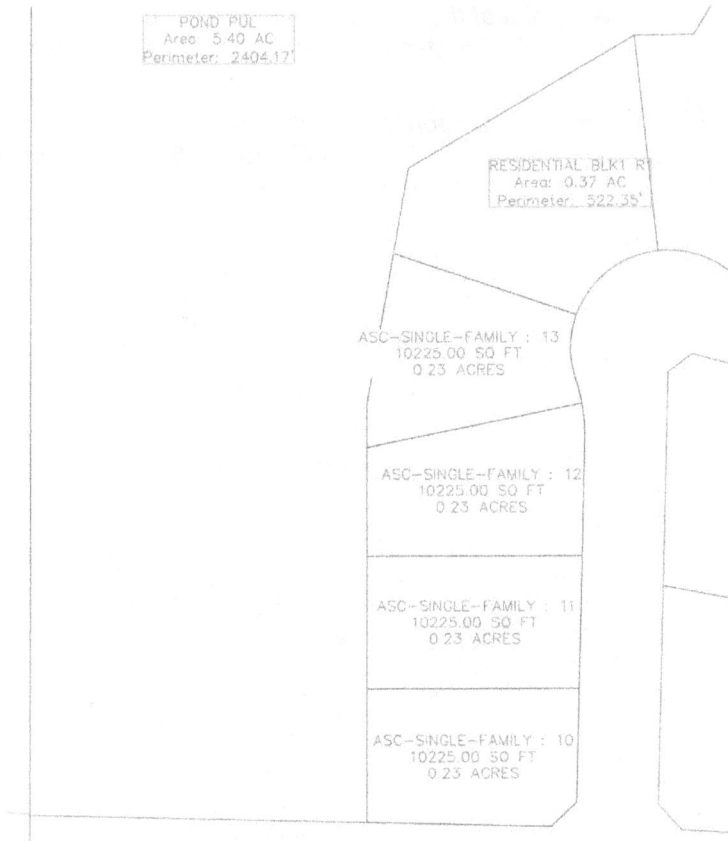

Figure 3–36

15. Save the drawing.

End of practice

3.4 Renumbering Parcels

Creating parcels using the methods that have already been taught results in inconsistent parcel numbering. Autodesk Civil 3D parcels can be renumbered individually using Parcel Properties or in groups using **Modify>Parcel>Renumber/Rename**.

This command enables you to specify a starting parcel number and the increment you want to have between parcels. (It also enables you to rename your parcels based on a different name template.) When renumbering, the command prompts you to identify parcels in the order in which you want to have them numbered. The *Renumber/Rename Parcels* dialog box is shown in Figure 3–37.

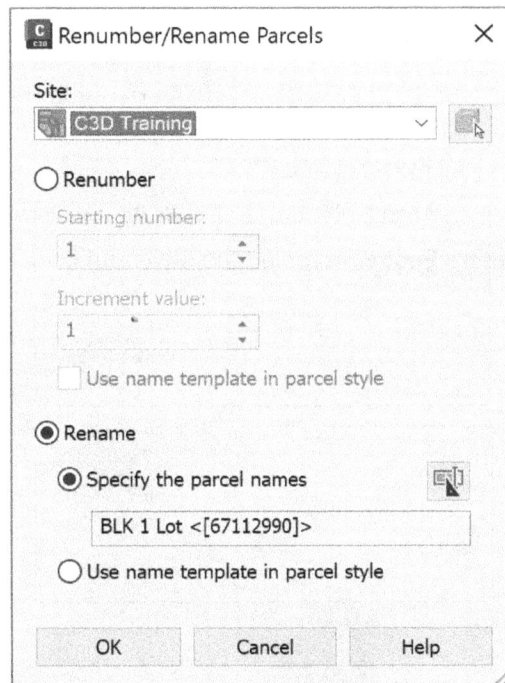

Figure 3–37

💡 **Hint: Renumber Odd and Even Parcels**

If you need to have odd numbered lots on one side of the street, you can set the *Starting Number* to an odd number and the *Incremental Value* to **2**. Repeat the procedure for even numbered lots on the opposite side and set the *Starting Number* to an even number.

Practice 3c
Rename/Renumber Parcels

Practice Objective

* Renumber the lots created so they are in sequential order.

Task 1: Rename and renumber parcels.

1. Continue working with the drawing from the previous practice or open **PCL-C.dwg** from the *C:\Civil 3D Beyond\Working\ Parcels* folder.

2. Select the preset view **Parcel-Create**.

3. Before renaming the newly created parcels, you need to change the label style of the original parcel:

   * Select the parcel label **RESIDENTIAL BLK1 R1**.

   * Right-click and select **Edit Area Selection Label Style**, as shown in Figure 3–38.

   * Select **ASC-Name Square Foot & Acres** as the style and click **OK** to apply the changes and close the dialog box.

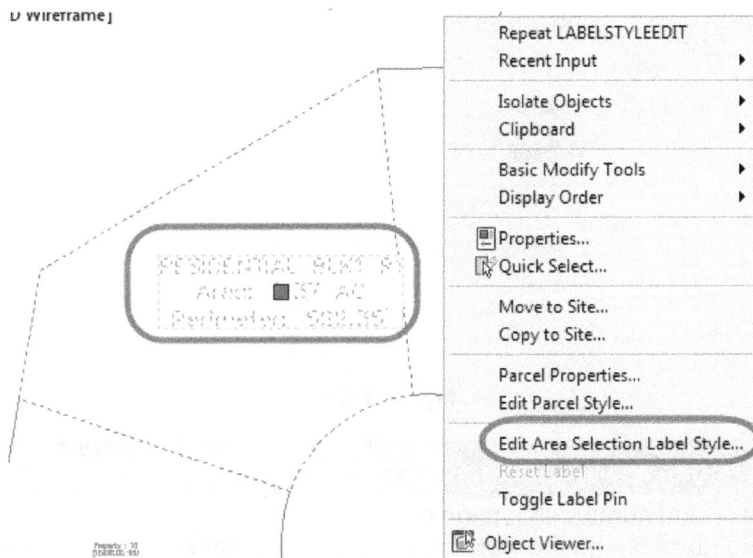

Figure 3–38

Note: Do not use the Parcel contextual tab from a selected parcel to select the command because it will only rename the parcel you picked rather than multiple parcels.

4. Rename and renumber the lots so that you have the same numbering system. In the *Modify* tab>*Design* panel, select **Parcel**. The *Parcel* contextual tab displays.

5. In the *Parcel* tab>*Modify* panel, click (Renumber/Rename), as shown in Figure 3–39.

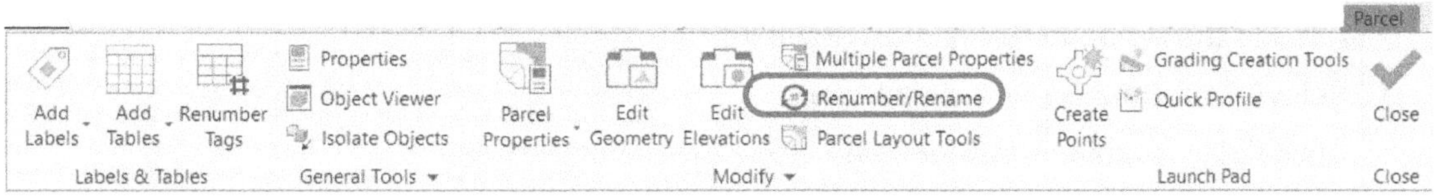

Figure 3–39

6. In the *Renumber/Rename Parcels* dialog box, do the following (as shown in Figure 3–40):

    *   Select **Rename**.
    *   Select **Specify the parcel names**.
    *   Click (Click to edit name template).

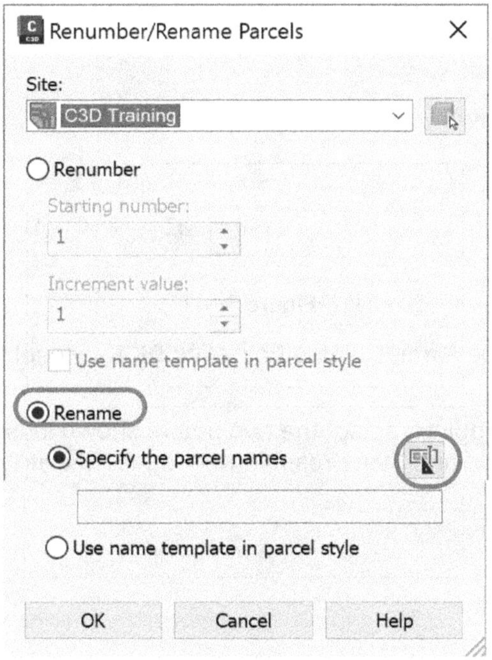

Figure 3–40

7. In the *Name Template* dialog box, do the following (as shown in Figure 3–41):

   - Type **BLK1 Lot** followed by a space in the *Name* field.
   - Expand the *Property Fields* drop-down list.
   - Select **Next Counter** and click **Insert**.
   - Click **OK** to apply the changes and close the dialog box.

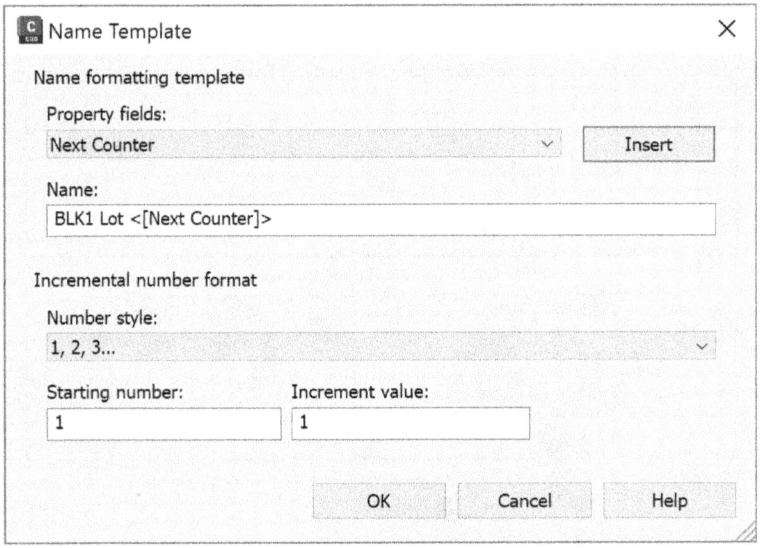

Figure 3–41

8. In the *Renumber/Rename Parcels* dialog box, click **OK** to accept the changes and close the dialog box.

9. When prompted for the points, select the two points shown in Figure 3–42. Press <Enter> to complete the selection and then press <Enter> again to exit the command.

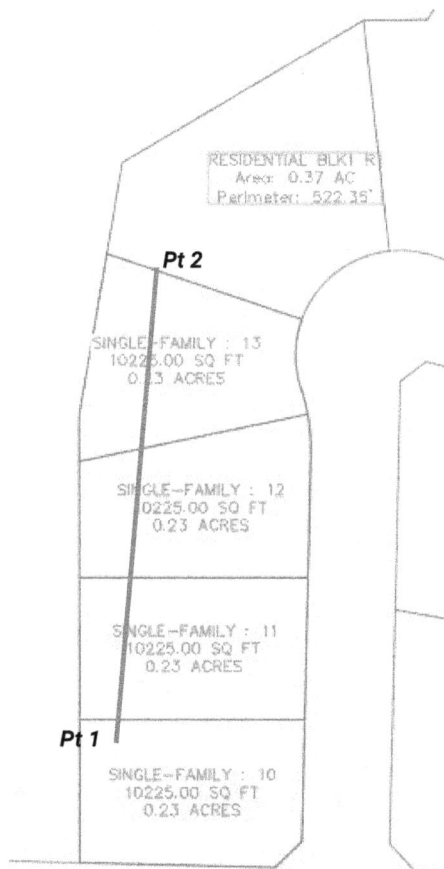

Figure 3–42

10. Save the drawing.

Task 2: Edit parcels using Swing Line - Edit.

In this task, you adjust the last three lots of the parcel suddivision so that they are more marketable.

1. Continue working with the drawing from the previous task.

2. You first need to adjust the lot line between Parcel 3 and Parcel 4. In the *Home* tab>*Create Design* panel, expand **Parcel** and select **Parcel Creation Tools**.

3. Expand the *Parcel Layout Tools* toolbar and ensure the *Minimum Area* is set to **10225**, as shown in Figure 3–43. Keep the other settings as they were previously and click ⚊ to collapse the expanded toolbar.

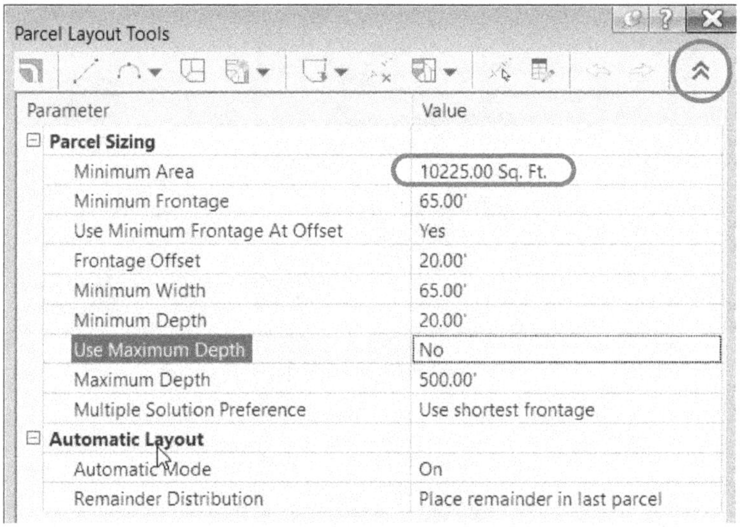

Figure 3–43

4. Select **Swing Line - Edit**, as shown in Figure 3–44.

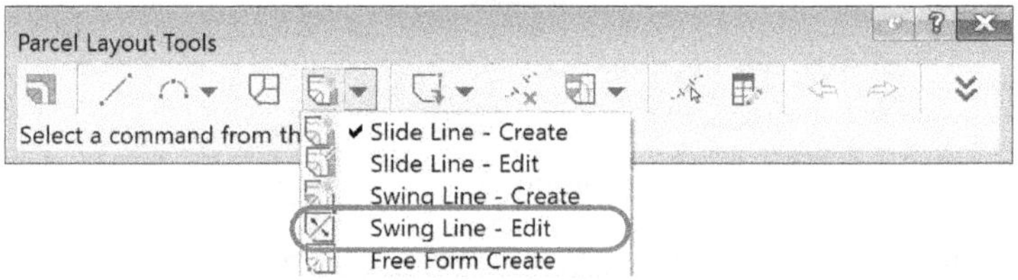

Figure 3–44

5. In the *Create Parcel - Layout* dialog box, set the following parameters:

    *   *Site:* **C3D Training**
    *   *Parcel style:* **ASC-Single-Family**
    *   *Area label style:* **ASC-Name Square Foot & Acres**

    You do not want to label segments, so do not enable this option. Click **OK** when done.

6. When prompted, complete the following, as shown in Figure 3–45:

- To select the parcel line to adjust, select the parcel line between Lot 3 and Lot 4.
- For the parcel to adjust, select **Lot 3**.
- For the *start frontage*, select the bottom right corner of **Lot 3, Pt 1**.
- For the *end of the frontage*, select the top right corner of **Lot 4, Pt 2**.
- For the *swing point*, select the end point of the rear vertical lot line labeled **Pt 3** in the figure.
- To accept the results, select **Yes**.

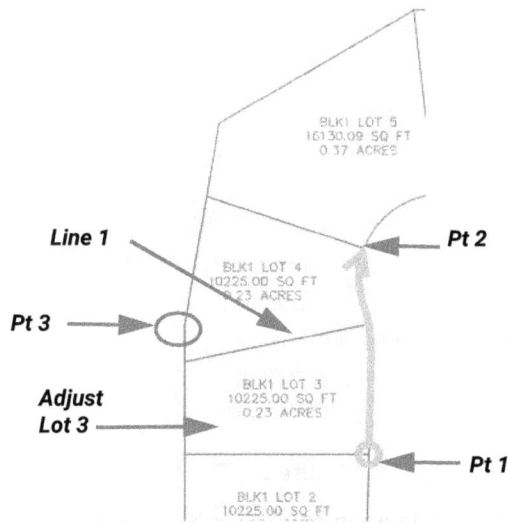

Figure 3–45

7. You have the required results for Lot 3. However, Lot 5 is larger than Lot 4. You want to create more evenly sized lots. Display the *Parcel Layout Tools* toolbar, if it is not open.

8. You could use the **Swing Line - Edit** command, but instead you will use a more graphical approach. Erase the parcel line between Lot 4 and Lot 5 using the ✕ (Delete Sub-entity) command in the *Parcel Layout Tools* toolbar. This causes both parcels to merge into one.

9. Add a new parcel line by selecting the **Add Fixed Line - Two Points** command, as shown in Figure 3–46.

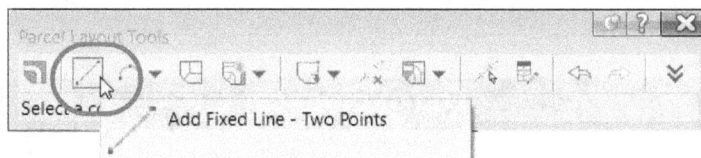

Figure 3–46

10. In the *Create Parcels - Layout* dialog box, leave all the default options as they are. You will correct them after the parcels are created. Click **OK** to close the dialog box.

11. For the start point, select the endpoint of the western lot line. Use the <Shift> + right-click option to bring up the AutoCAD Object Snap overrides menu.

12. For the end point, select (with the AutoCAD **Perpendicular** object snap) the arc of the knuckle curve, as shown in Figure 3–47.

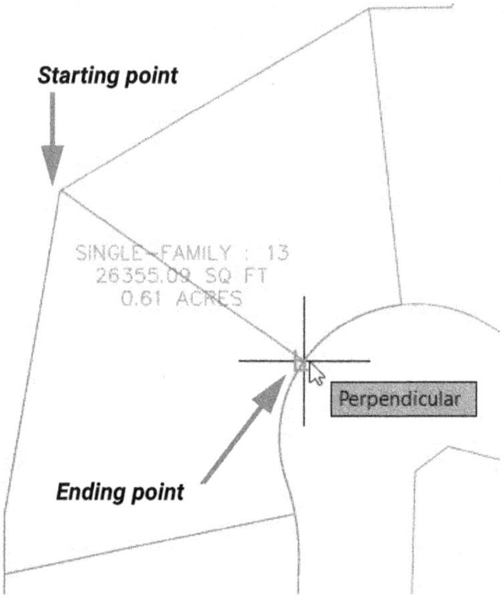

Figure 3–47

13. Press <Esc> to stop drawing fixed lines, then type X (or press <Enter>) to exit the *Parcel Layout Tools*.

14. Select the top parcel and use the *Parcel Properties* to rename it to **BLK1 LOT 5**.asyou had done previously,

15. Click **OK** to exit the *Parcel Properties* dialog box.

16. Repeat the procedure for the newly created lot (#14), rename it to **BLK1 LOT 4**. Remember to uncheck the *Use name template in parcel style* box in order to be able to rename it.

17. If time permits, repeat the steps above to subdivide the Block 1 and Block 3 parcels. If you do not complete the subdivisions for Block 1 and Block 3, you will need to open **PCL-D1-Parcels.dwg** in the next practice.

18. Save the drawing.

End of practice

3.5 Parcel Reports

The Autodesk Civil 3D software contains several types of parcel reports. Parcel inverse and mapcheck data is available in the *Analysis* tab in the *Parcel Properties* dialog box, as shown in Figure 3–48. The report can be generated clockwise or counter-clockwise, and the point of beginning can be specified.

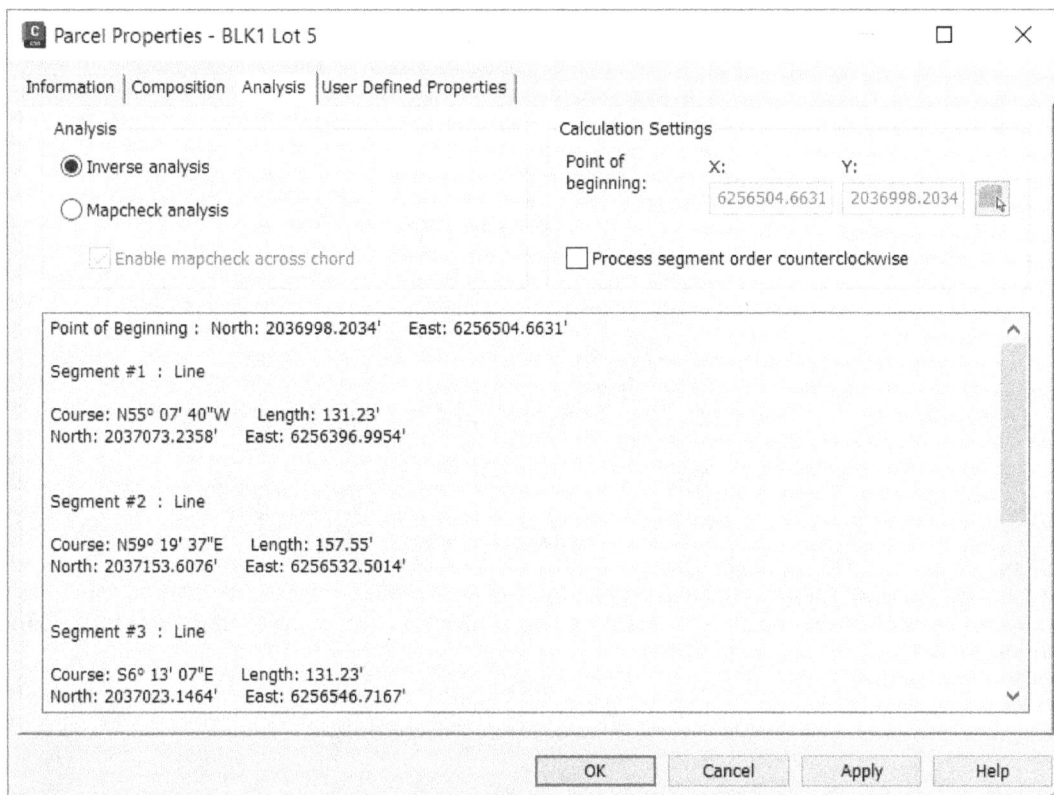

Figure 3–48

This dialog box does not enable output. You can copy the results to your Windows clipboard and paste them into your own report. However, if you want to generate a printable report "out of the box," use the Autodesk Civil 3D Toolbox. It includes several stock parcel-related reports (such as surveyors certificates, inverse and mapcheck reports, and metes and bounds), as shown in Figure 3–49.

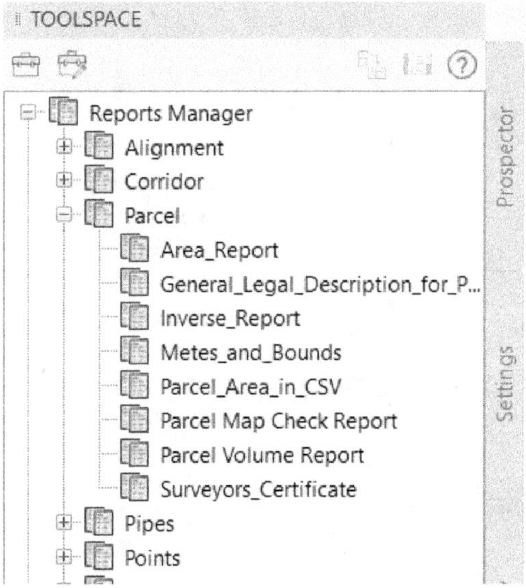

Figure 3–49

Once a report is run, it can be opened in a web browser, word processor, or spreadsheet application. Report settings (such as the preparer's name) can be assigned by selecting **Report Settings** in the Toolspace.

3.6 Parcel Labels

Parcel area labels are a means of graphically selecting a parcel, such as when creating right-of-ways. In the parcel creation and editing examples, the parcel segment labels are created for you automatically. This section explores the functionality of these labels in more depth.

The *Add Labels* dialog box (**Annotate>Add Labels>Parcel>Add Parcel Labels...**) can be used to assign the required label styles and place labels in the drawing. It can set the line and curve styles, toggle between single and multiple segment labeling, and be used to access the **Table Tag Numbering**. The dialog box is shown in Figure 3–50.

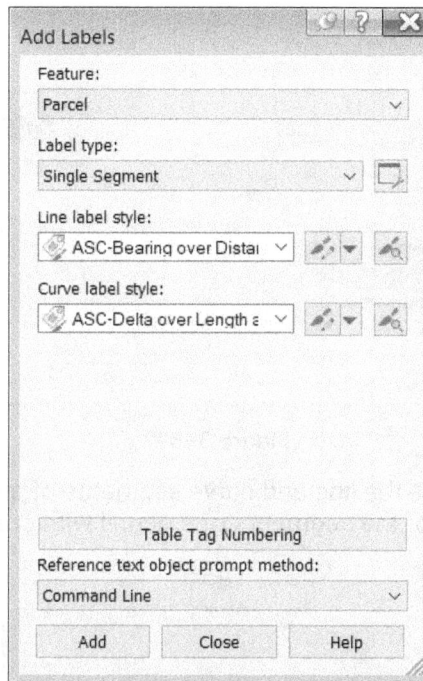

Figure 3–50

- Parcel labels, as with all Autodesk Civil 3D labels, are capable of rotating and resizing to match changes in the viewport scale and rotation.

- A segment label has two definitions: composed and dragged state. A dragged state can vary rather significantly from the original label definition.

- The Autodesk Civil 3D software can label segments while sizing parcels.

- Labeling can be read clockwise or counter-clockwise around the parcel.

- Labels can be added through an external reference file using the same commands that label objects in their source drawing. This makes it easier to have multiple plans that need different label styles.

- The **Replace Multiple Labels** option is useful when you want to replace a number of parcel segment labels with another style. However, if you are labeling through an external reference file, labels created in the source drawing cannot be modified.

Parcel area labels are controlled using parcel area label styles, which control the display of custom information (such as the parcel number, area, perimeter, address, etc.). For example, you can create more than one parcel area label if you need to show different parcel information on different sheets, as shown in Figure 3–51.

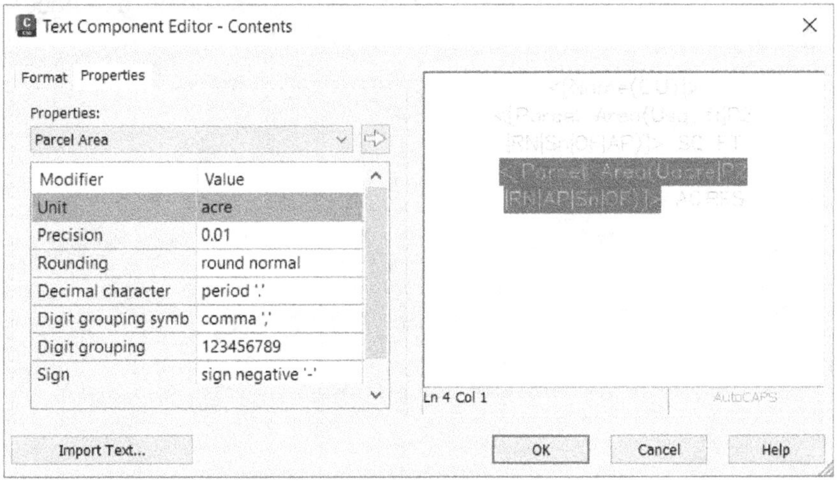

Figure 3–51

Parcel segment labels annotate the line and curve segments of a parcel, as shown in Figure 3–52. You can label all of the segments of a parcel with one click or only label selected parcel segments.

Figure 3–52

All labels have two definitions: one for the original location and another when it is moved from its original location. A dragged label can remain as originally defined or can be changed to stacked text. This is defined in the label style definition.

3.7 Parcel Tables

Parcel tables are an alternative to labeling individual parcel areas and segments. An example is shown in Figure 3–53.

Parcel Line and Curve Table			
Line #/Curve #	Length	Bearing/Delta	Radius
L2	6.42	N43° 08' 59.63"W	
L1	6.36	S46° 18' 04.79"W	
L3	1.08	S1° 18' 04.79"W	
L4	5.58	N52° 59' 46.62"E	
C1	11.38	19.75	33.00

Figure 3–53

When creating a table, the Autodesk Civil 3D software changes the parcel segment labels to an alpha-numeric combination, called a *tag*. In a tag, an **L** stands for line and a **C** stands for curve. A segment's tag has a corresponding entry in the table.

- A table can only represent a selected set of label styles.

- The **Add Existing** option (shown in Figure 3–54) creates a table from existing objects. New objects are not added to the table. The **Add Existing and New** option creates a table with existing and new objects.

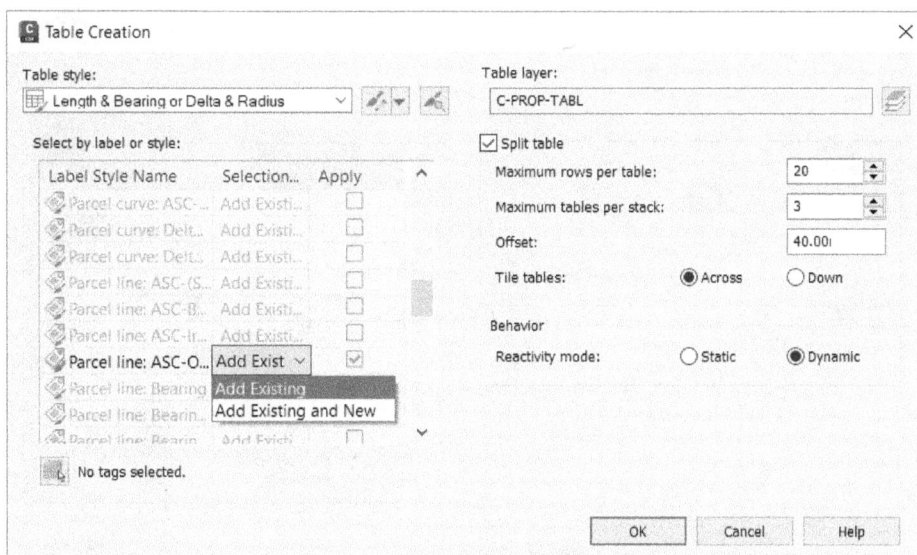

Figure 3–54

- A table can have a dynamic link between a segment's tag and table entry. If the segment changes, the table entry updates.

- The Autodesk Civil 3D software switches a label to a tag by changing the *Used in* mode from **Label and Tag Modes** to **Tag Mode**, as shown in Figure 3–55.

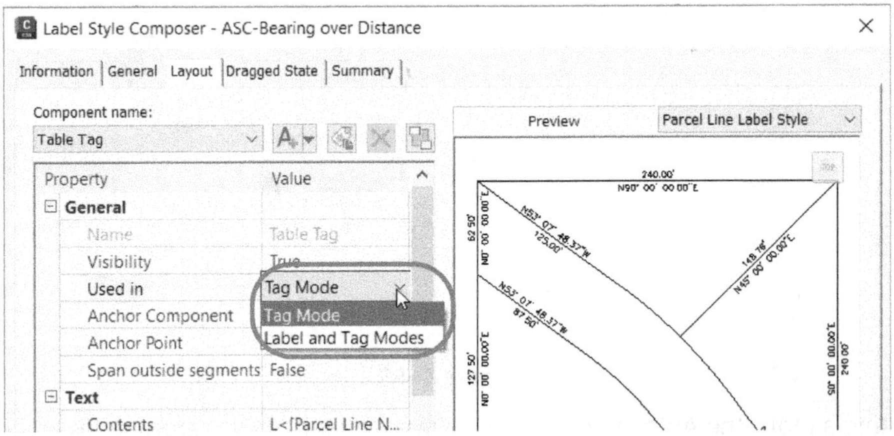

Figure 3–55

Practice 3d
Report On and Annotate the Parcel Layout

Practice Objectives

* Add labels, tags, and tables to the drawing to display useful parcel information.
* Create predefined reports to share useful parcel information in a textual format.

Task 1: Add parcel labels.

1. Continue working with the drawing from the previous practice or open **PCL-D1.dwg** from the *C:\Civil 3D Beyond\Working\ Parcels* folder.

2. In the *Annotate* tab>*Labels & Tables* panel, click (Add Labels), as shown in Figure 3–56.

Figure 3–56

3. In the *Add Labels* dialog box, set the following parameters (as shown in Figure 3–57):

* *Feature:* **Parcel**
* *Label type:* **Multiple Segment**
* *Line label style:* **ASC-Bearing over Distance**
* *Curve label style:* **ASC-Delta over Length and Radius**

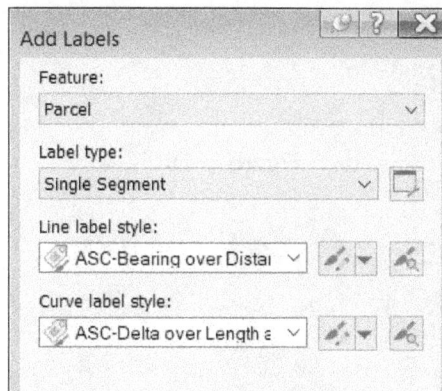

Figure 3–57

4. Once the parameters are set, click **Add**.

5. When prompted to select the parcels that you want to annotate, select the single-family parcel labels in the **BLK1** lot area.

6. When prompted for the label direction, select **Clockwise**.

7. Continue selecting single-family parcels and labeling them clockwise until all of the single-family parcels are labeled, including the parcels in BLK2 and BLK3.

8. Press <Enter> when finished labeling the parcels.

9. Click **Close** in the *Add Labels* dialog box to close the dialog box.

10. The final result should look similar to that shown in Figure 3–58.

Figure 3–58

11. Save the drawing.

Task 2: Create line and curve segment tables.

The labels are overlapping in a number of locations, making the drawing difficult to read. In this task, you will try two methods to fix this. In the first method, you will drag the label to a location in which there is no conflict. In the second method, you will add a label tag and an associated table.

1. Select the preset view **Parcel-Tag1**. Note that the annotation scale has decreased as when restoring the view.

2. Select the label **11.70'**, select the square grip, and drag it to place the label in a location in which there is no conflict. Do the same for the label **21.48'**, as shown in Figure 3–59.

Figure 3–59

3. Select the preset view **Parcel-Create**. Note that the annotation scale has increased as when restoring the view.

4. You will now add tags and a table. In the *Annotate* tab>*Label & Tables* panel, expand

   (Add Tables) and select **Parcel>Add segment**, as shown in Figure 3–60.

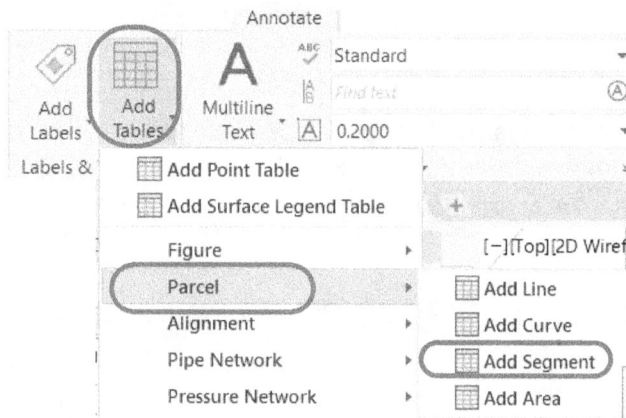

Figure 3–60

---

5. In the *Table Creation* dialog box, click ![icon] (Pick on screen) and select the four line labels and one curve label shown in Figure 3–61. Press <Enter> when done.

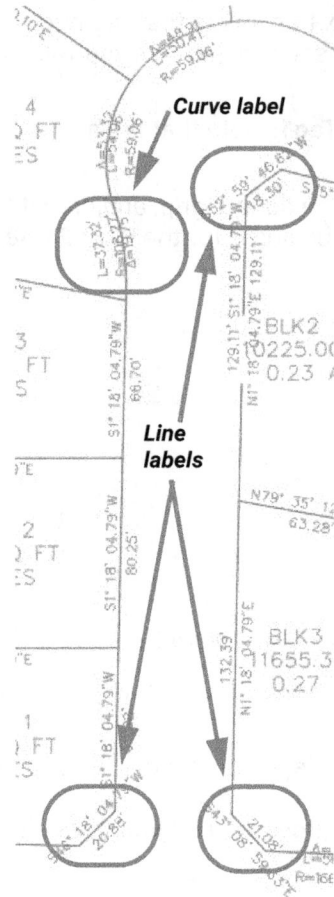

Figure 3–61

6. When prompted to convert labels to tags or to not add labels, select **Convert all selected label styles to tag mode**.

7. Click **OK** to close the *Table Creation* dialog box.

8. When prompted for a location for the table, select a location in an open space, as shown in Figure 3–62.

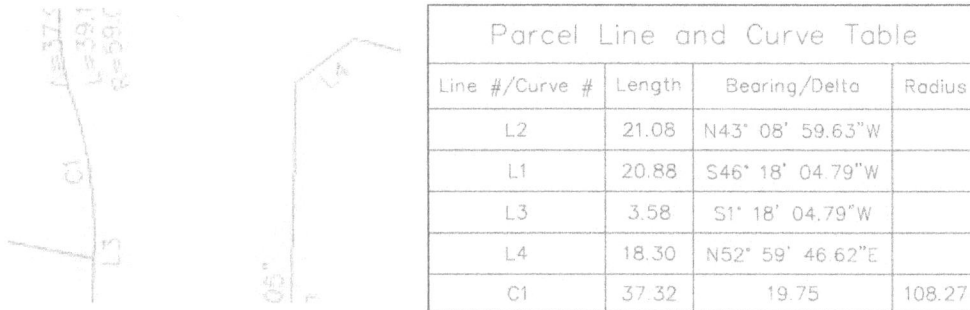

Parcel Line and Curve Table			
Line #/Curve #	Length	Bearing/Delta	Radius
L2	21.08	N43° 08' 59.63"W	
L1	20.88	S46° 18' 04.79"W	
L3	3.58	S1° 18' 04.79"W	
L4	18.30	N52° 59' 46.62"E	
C1	37.32	19.75	108.27

Figure 3–62

9. Save the drawing.

Task 3: Create a parcel area table.

1. Continue working with the drawing from the previous task or open **PCL-D2.dwg** from the *C:\Civil 3D Beyond\Working\Parcels* folder.

2. In the *Annotate* tab>*Label & Tables* panel, expand ▦ (Add Tables) and select **Parcel>Add Area**.

3. In the *Table Creation* dialog box, leave the *Table style* as **Area Perimeter Length and Bearing** and in the *Select by label or style* area, select the style name **ASC-Name Square Foot & Acres**, as shown in Figure 3–63. All parcels with this style will be selected. Click **OK** to close the dialog box.

Figure 3–63

4. Select a location to insert the table into the drawing, as shown in Figure 3−64.

Parcel Area Table				
Parcel #	Area	Perimeter	Segment Lengths	Segment Bearings
9	10227.70	407.80	47.65 11.70 36.39 123.83 4.70 70.72 29.81 82.99	N79° 24' 32.62"W N79° 35' 12.54"W N79° 35' 12.54"W N10° 24' 47.46"E S75° 18' 31.56"E S56° 35' 41.15"E S52° 20' 32.14"E 59° 48' 22.81"W
10	10225.00	407.10	80.86 126.51 69.02 20.88 109.83	N0° 01' 55.61"W N89° 58' 04.39"E S1° 18' 04.79"W S46° 18' 04.79"W N88° 41' 55.21"W
11	10225.00	415.37	80.23 128.38 80.25 126.51	N0° 01' 55.61"W N89° 58' 04.39"E S1° 18' 04.79"W S89° 58' 04.39"W
12	10225.00	418.87	91.51 132.28 66.70	N0° 01' 55.61"W S79° 12' 46.38"E S1° 18' 04.79"W

Figure 3−64

5. Save the drawing.

Task 4: Create a parcel report.

1. If the *TOOLSPACE>Toolbox* tab is not displayed, go to the *Home* tab>*Palettes* panel and click (Toolbox), as shown in Figure 3−65.

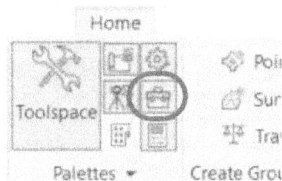

Figure 3−65

2. In the *TOOLSPACE>Toolbox* tab, expand the *Reports Manager* and *Parcel* collections. Right-click on **Surveyor's Certificate** and select **Execute**.

3. In the *Export to LandXML* dialog box, click (Pick from drawing), located at the bottom left of the dialog box.

4. When prompted to select a parcel, select one of the single-family lots that you created earlier and press <Enter>.

   Note: For a surveyor's certificate report, you can only create a report for a single parcel. If you want reports for multiple parcels, you need to repeat the command.

5. In the *Export to XML Report* dialog box, note that only the lot you selected now displays a checkmark. Click **OK** to close the dialog box.

6. In the *Save As* dialog box, stay in the default folder and type **ASC-Parcel-Report** for the report name. Click **Save**.

7. Review the report (shown in Figure 3–66), then close the web browser. Note that you can customize the various fields produced in the report and even the verbiage used within the report.

Parcel BLK1 Lot 4

SURVEYOR'S CERTIFICATE

I, Preparer Registered Land Surveyor, do hereby certify that I have surveyed, divided, and mapped

_____

_____

more particularly described as:

    Commencing at a point of Northing 2036905.451 and Easting 6256502.548 ;
    thence bearing N 79-12-46.378 W a distance of 132.282 feet ;
    thence bearing N 9-40-41.250 E a distance of 145.091 feet ;
    thence bearing S 55-7-40.098 E a distance of 131.233 feet ;
    thence along a curve to the LEFT, having a radius of 59.055 feet, a delta angle of 53° 19' 14.83",
    and whose long chord bears S 8-12-42.487 W a distance of 52.996 feet ;
    thence along a curve to the RIGHT, having a radius of 108.267 feet, a delta angle of 19° 44' 59.72",
    and whose long chord bears S 8-34-25.067 E a distance of 37.135 feet ;
    thence bearing S 1-18-4.794 W a distance of 3.580 feet to the point of beginning.

Said described parcel contains 14198.535 square feet (0.326 acres), more or less, subject to any and all easements, reservations, restrictions and conveyances of record.

Figure 3–66

8. Save and close the drawing.

End of practice

Chapter Review Questions

1. Where are parcels listed?

   a. Under the *Survey* collection in the *TOOLSPACE>Prospector* tab.

   b. In a site under the *Sites* collection in the *TOOLSPACE>Prospector* tab.

   c. Under the *Figures* collection inside the Survey Database.

   d. In the *Layers* panel in the *Home* tab.

2. What does a parcel style assign in the *Display* tab?

   a. The layer to which parcel segments are assigned.

   b. How big the parcel can be.

   c. The label text that describes the line segments.

   d. The label text that describes the area and name of the parcel.

3. What is the default direction of a mapcheck or inverse report?

   a. Clockwise

   b. Counter-clockwise

   c. Always starts going north

   d. Always starts going south

4. How do you adjust parcel display order?

   a. Select the parcel segments, right-click, and select **Draw Order**.

   b. Move the parcel up or down in the parcel preview list in the *TOOLSPACE>Prospector* tab.

   c. Select the parcel area label, right-click, and select **Draw Order**.

   d. Under *Sites*, right-click on **Parcels** and select **Properties**.

5. How do you create or subdivide parcels interactively?

   a. Draw parcel segments at each location in which you want a parcel line.

   b. Use the **Create** and **Edit** tools in the *Parcel Layout Tools* toolbar.

   c. Select the parcel, right-click, and select **Subdivide**.

   d. Used the AutoCAD **Measure** or **Divide** commands to help place lot lines and even intervals.

6. Which parcel **Create** command enables you to hold a specified angle relative to the right-of-way?

   a. Slide Line - Create

   b. Swing Line - Create

   c. Free Form Create

   d. Add fixed line

7. What are the types of Autodesk Civil 3D parcel labels that can be set up in the *Settings* tab? (Select all that apply.)

   a. Parcel Line

   b. Parcel Area

   c. Parcel Curve

   d. Parcel Perimeter

8. What does the *Add Labels* dialog box do?

   a. Creates label styles.

   b. Add or change labels interactively after parcel creation.

   c. Add or change labels during parcel creation.

   d. Creates static text describing what you want to label.

9. What are parcel tables an alternative to? (Select all that apply.)

   a. Drawing the parcels.

   b. Creating tags.

   c. Labeling parcel areas in an already crowded drawing.

   d. Labeling parcel segments in an already crowded drawing.

Command Summary

Button	Command	Location
	Add Labels	• **Ribbon:** *Annotate* tab>*Labels & Tables* panel
	Add Tables	• **Ribbon:** *Annotate* tab>*Labels & Tables* panel
	Bearing Distance	• **Toolbar:** Transparent Commands • **Command Prompt:** 'bd
	Create Parcel from Objects	• **Ribbon:** *Home* tab>*Create Design* panel • **Command Prompt:** ParcelFromObjects
	Parcel Creation Tools	• **Ribbon:** *Home* tab>*Create Design* panel • **Command Prompt:** CreateParcelByLayout
	Rename/ Renumber	• **Contextual Ribbon:** *Parcels*>Modify • **Command Prompt:** EditParcelNumbers
	Slide Line - Create	• **Toolbar:** Parcel Layout Tools
	Swing Line - Edit	• **Toolbar:** Parcel Layout Tools

Surfaces - Beyond the Basics

In this chapter, you will learn how to create surfaces in multiple ways: from contours and survey data, from feature lines, from GIS data, and from a point cloud. You will also edit and fine-tune a surface and then calculate volumes between two surfaces.

Learning Objectives

- Add existing contour data to a surface to take advantage of data created by someone else.
- Add drawing objects to a surface to improve the accuracy of a TIN model.
- Create feature lines and create a new surface from them.
- Create a surface from GIS data.
- Make adjustments to a surface.
- Calculate the volume of cut and fill or adjusted cut and fill between two surfaces.
- Create Autodesk Civil 3D surfaces from point cloud data files.

4.1 Contour Data

Contour data is available from many sources. Large sites are often surveyed using aerial photogrammetry, which provides contour polylines and spot elevations. Contour data can also be obtained from other civil engineering applications.

Polylines with elevation can represent contours, which Autodesk Civil 3D can use to build a surface by triangulating between contours. The end of each triangle side connects to a vertex of two different contours.

When processing contours for surface data, the Autodesk Civil 3D software inspects the contour vertices for two conditions: too many data points representing similar data (e.g., 10 vertices on 15 units of contour length in an almost straight line) and not enough data points over the length of a contour.

You can set the values for these conditions in the *Add Contour Data* dialog box (shown in Figure 4–1) when you add contour data.

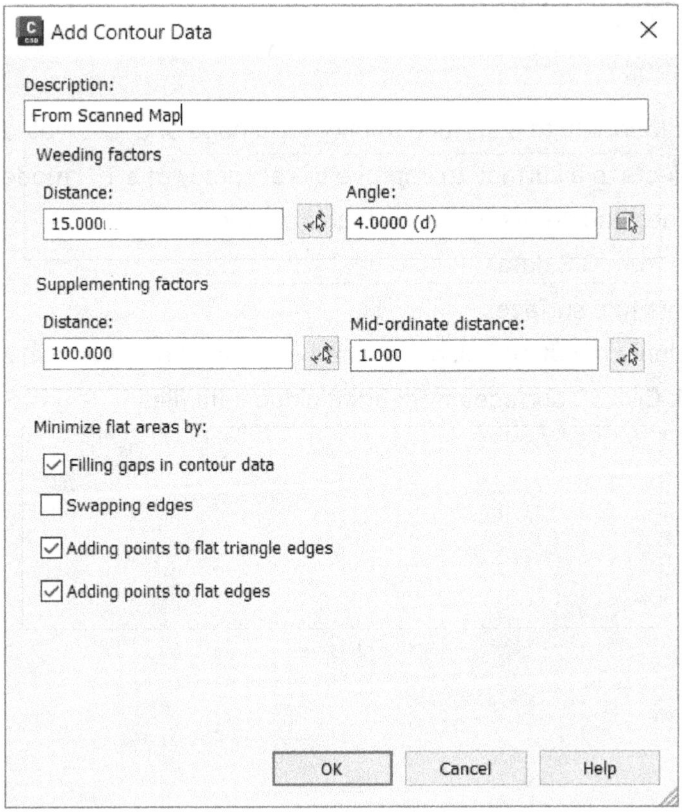

Figure 4–1

Weeding Factors

The *weeding* process removes redundant vertices from contours. The first step in the weeding process is to inspect three adjacent contour vertices, whose overall distance is shorter than a user-specified distance (e.g., three vertices in less than 15 units of contour). When encountering this situation, the weeding process prompts you about the change in direction between the three vertices.

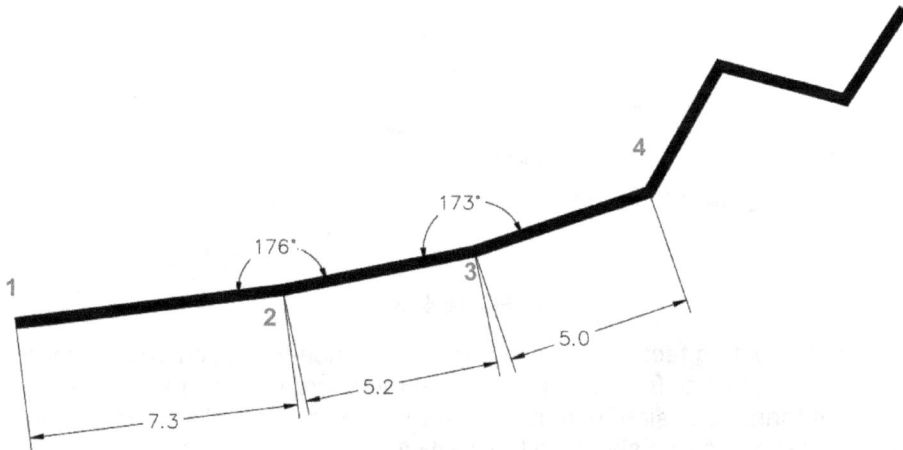

Figure 4–2

For example, in Figure 4–2 above, does the direction from vertex 1 to vertex 2 change more than four degrees when going from vertex 2 to vertex 3? If not, the vertices are almost in a straight line and are too close. The Autodesk Civil 3D software considers vertex 2 to be redundant and removes it from the surface data. This process repeats for the next three vertices. If the distance is under 15 units and the change of direction is less than four degrees, the next vertex 2 is removed from the data.

If a contour has three vertices in less than 15 units and turns more than four degrees, vertex 2 is kept because the change in direction is significant. If there are more than 15 units between the three vertices, the Autodesk Civil 3D software moves on to the next group.

Therefore, the higher the number for distances and angles, the more vertices will be removed.

An important feature of weeding is not what it removes from the data, but what is left over. If not enough data remains, the numbers for the weeding factors should be set to lower values.

Supplementing Factors

When the Autodesk Civil 3D software inspects contour data, it uses supplementing factors to add vertices to the surface data. The first supplementing factor is the distance between contour vertices. When the distance between vertices is over 100 units, the Autodesk Civil 3D software adds a vertex to the data along the course of the contour, as shown in Figure 4–3.

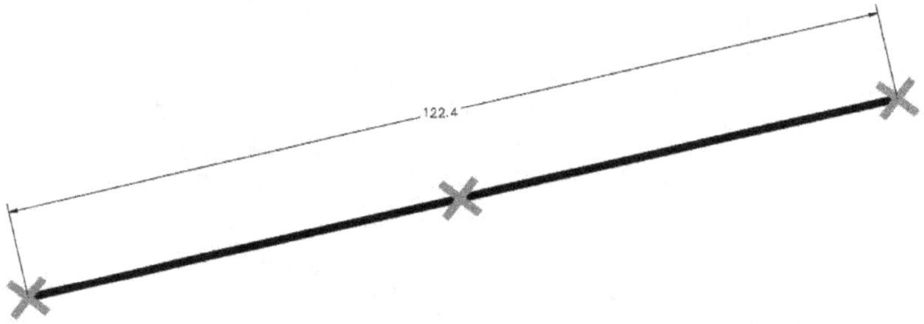

Figure 4–3

The second supplementing factor is a mid-ordinate distance for the curve segments of a contour. If the length of a line from the mid point of the chord length of the arc to perpendicular to the arc is more than the desired distance, a new vertex is inserted at the midpoint of the arc and the process is repeated, as shown in Figure 4–4.

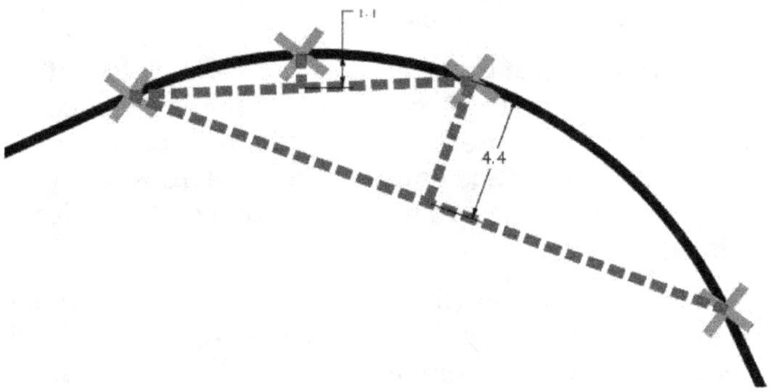

Figure 4–4

If curves are distributed throughout the contour data, a setting of 0.1 is a good starting point.

- All weeding and supplementing factors are user-specified.

- Weeding and supplementing does not modify the contours or polylines in a drawing, only their data.

- There is no *correct* setting for weeding and supplementing. Varying the values creates more or less surface data.

Contour Issues

You should be aware of two issues when working with contour data: bays and peninsulas within the contours and the lack of high and low point elevations. These two issues affect triangulation and the quality of a surface.

Bays and peninsulas within contours represent gullies or isolated high points on a surface. As long as there is data to work with, the Autodesk Civil 3D software builds a surface by triangulating between contours of different elevations. When the software cannot triangulate between different contours, the triangulation switches to connecting vertices on the same contour.

The **Minimize Flat Areas** command helps mitigate this situation by forcing the triangulation to target different contours, as shown in Figure 4–5. However, this method, similar to the swap edge method, does not correct every problem on a contour surface.

- To launch the **Minimize Flat Areas** command, in *TOOLSPACE>Prospector* tab, right-click on the *Edits* heading in the *Definition* collection of a surface and select the command.

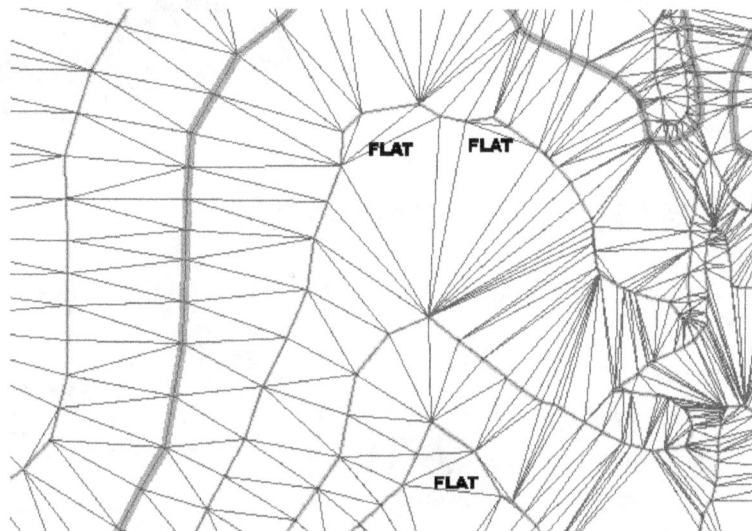

Figure 4–5

The second issue with contour data regards the loss of high and low points. Contours represent an elevation interval (120, 122, 123, etc.). However, the top of a hill could be 123.04 or 136.92 and the only contours present are for the elevations of 123 or 136. Spot elevations are required in the surface data to help correctly resolve the high and low spots of a surface.

- Flat spots and the loss of high and low points affect the calculation of volumes for earthworks, as shown in Figure 4−6.

Figure 4−6

Minimizing Flat Triangle Strategies

By default, the *Add Contour Data* dialog box suggests using the **Minimize flat areas by:** options shown in Figure 4−7.

Figure 4−7

Together, these three methods attempt to detect and resolve peninsulas, bays, and other issues by adding additional points and filling in gaps based on surface trends. Generally, these provide the most expected results. The **Swapping edges** option is provided as a way of emulating how other terrain modeling software traditionally approached minimizing flat areas.

Practice 4a
Create the Existing Ground Surface

Practice Objectives

- Define a new surface.
- Add contour data to a surface.
- Create a surface style.

In this practice, you will create a surface from contour data. A drawing has already been inserted for you as a block and exploded. It contains AutoCAD polylines on specific layers representing major and minor existing contours. For reference, the drawing is *C:\Civil 3D Beyond\References\DWG\Existing\Site-Contours.dwg*.

Task 1: Create a surface and set properties.

1. Open **SUF-A1.dwg** from the *C:\Civil 3D Beyond\Working\ Surface* folder.
2. In *TOOLSPACE>Prospector* tab, select **Surfaces**, right-click, and select **Create Surface**.
3. In the *Create Surface* dialog box, set the following, as shown in Figure 4-8:
   - *Type*: **TIN surface**
   - *Name:* **ExTopo**
   - *Description*: **Existing Topology**
   - *Style:* **ASC-Contours 2' and 10' (Background)**

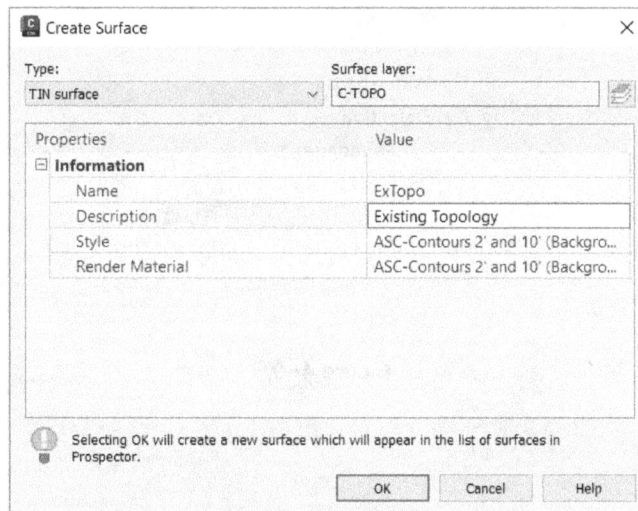

Figure 4-8

4. Click **OK** to accept the changes and close the dialog box.

5. Save the drawing.

Task 2: Define a surface with contour data.

1. Thaw the layers **A-TOPO-MAJR** and **A-TOPO-MINR**. These layers contain AutoCAD polylines representing existing contours of a surface.

2. In the *Home* tab>*Layers* panel, click   (Isolate). Do the following before selecting the layers:

   - Type **S** for **Settings**.
   - Select **Off** and then select **Off** again to ensure that **layiso** does not lock the layer by changing the settings to toggle off isolated layers. If this setting is not changed, the **C-TOPO** layer will lock and the Autodesk Civil 3D software will not create the surface.

3. Select one major and one minor contour from the **Site-Contours.dwg** to isolate the layers **A-TOPO-MAJR** (dark gray color) and **A-TOPO-MINR** (light gray color), and press <Enter>.

4. Expand the *Surfaces* collection in *TOOLSPACE*>*Prospector* tab.

5. Expand the *ExTopo* collection and the *Definition* collection.

6. Select the **Contours** data element, right-click, and select **Add...**, as shown in Figure 4–9.

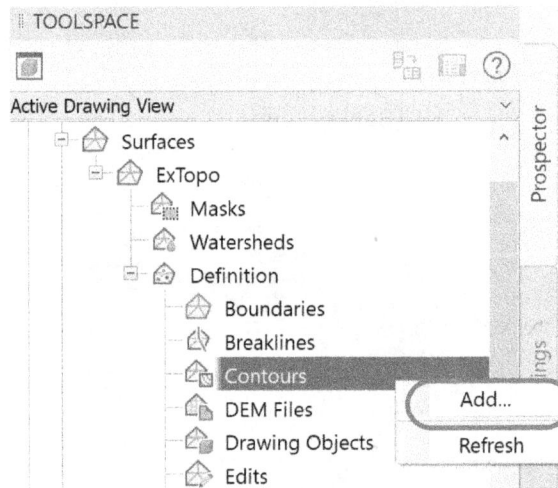

Figure 4–9

7. In the *Add Contour Data* dialog box, accept the defaults, as shown in Figure 4–10, and click **OK**.

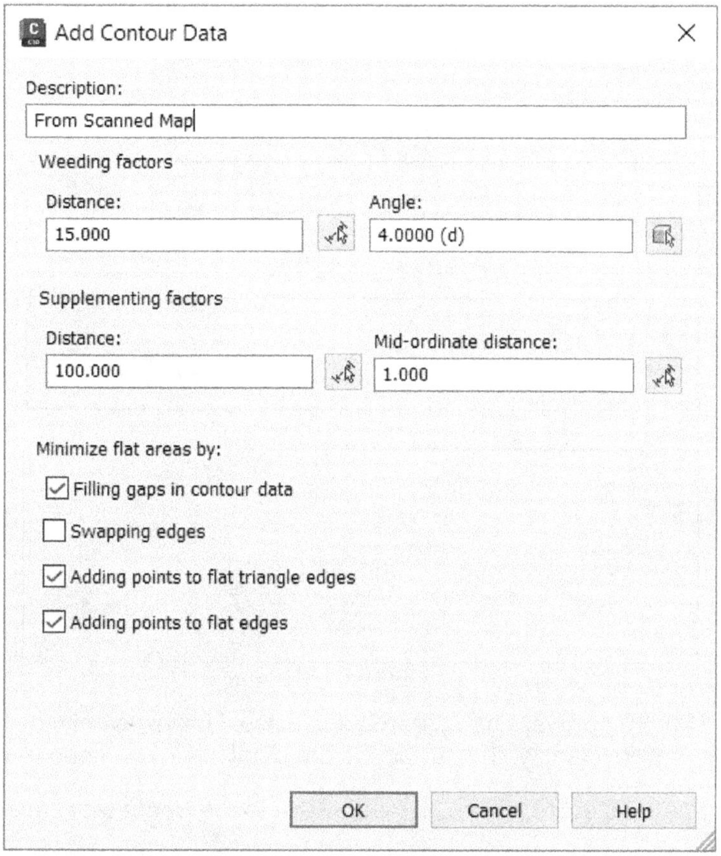

Figure 4–10

8. When prompted to select contours, use the AutoCAD window or crossing selection method to select all of the AutoCAD contour objects on the screen, as shown in Figure 4–11. Press <Enter> to end the command.

Figure 4–11

9. The Autodesk Civil 3D software has created a surface. However, only the original two isolated contour layers display; the surface is not displayed. You need to restore the previous layer state. To do so, click ⬚ (Unisolate) in the *Home* tab>*Layer* panel, as shown in Figure 4–12.

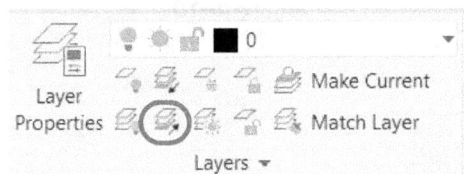

Figure 4–12

10. Freeze the layers **A-TOPO-MAJR** and **A-TOPO-MINR** by clicking ⬚ (Layer Freeze) and selecting the contours you selected when adding contours to the surface. This will clean up the drawing while ensuring that you do not accidentally modify the surface by changing any of the original contour polylines.

Note: After freezing the original contours, if the contours for the new surface are not displayed, verify that the C-TOPO layer is not frozen.

11. If you select the green surface boundary or any contour line, the *Tin Surface: ExTopo* contextual tab displays, as shown in Figure 4–13.

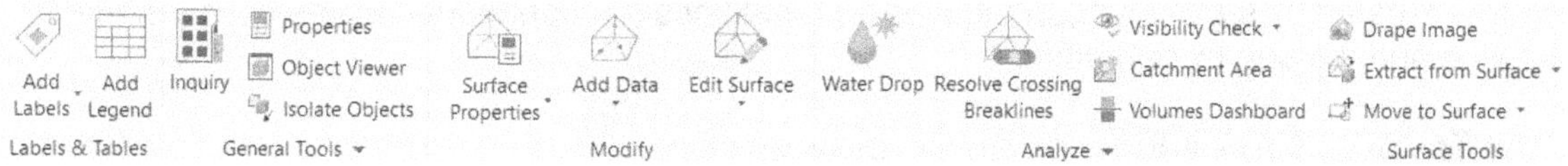

Figure 4–13

12. Press <Esc> to clear the selection. The *Tin Surface: ExTopo* contextual tab closes and reverts back to the previous tab you had opened, which is the *Home* tab.

13. Save the drawing.

End of practice

4.2 Survey Figures as Breaklines

Figures created by surveyors can be used as breaklines if a connection exists between the drawing and the survey database.

How To: Add Survey Figures as Breaklines

1. Open the survey database for editing.

2. In the *TOOLSPACE>Survey* tab, expand the *Survey Data* collection and select **Figures**. The list of figures in the grid view displays at the bottom of the Toolspace.

3. Select the figures, right-click, and select **Create breaklines...**, as shown in Figure 4–14.

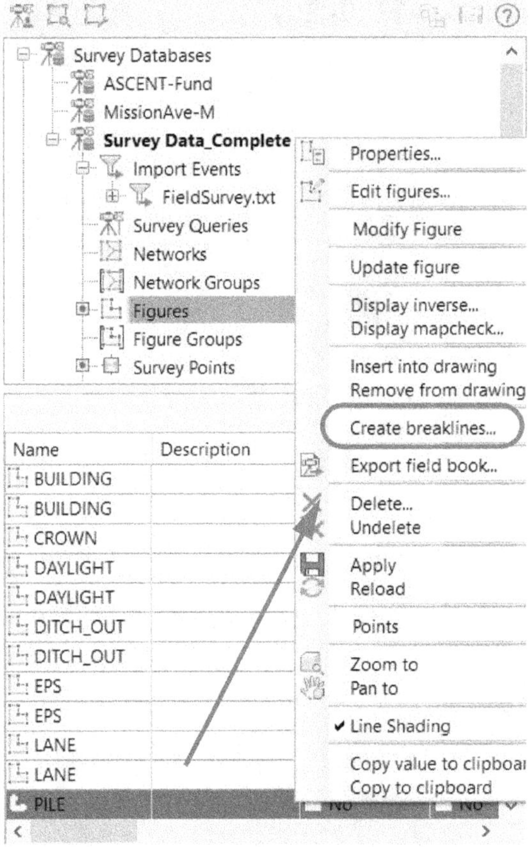

Figure 4–14

4. In the *Create Breaklines* dialog box, select the surface on which to place the breaklines, and then in the *Breakline* column, select **Yes** to create the breaklines, as shown in Figure 4–15. Click **OK** to close the dialog box.

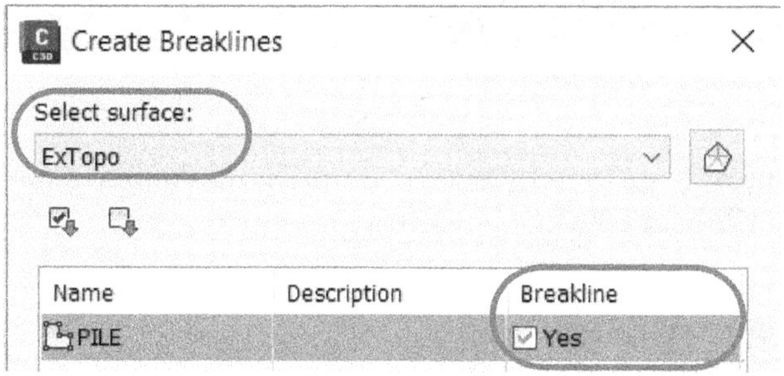

Figure 4–15

Practice 4b
Add Additional Data to the Existing Ground Surface

Practice Objective

*   Improve the accuracy of a surface by adding various breaklines, such as standard breaklines, wall breaklines, and breaklines from survey figures.

Task 1: Set up the survey database.

In this practice, you will need to incorporate survey data into the surface. To do so, you must first establish a connection to the survey database. You will need to open the survey database **Survey Data_Complete** to open the connection.

1. Continue working with the drawing from the previous practice or open **SUF-A2.dwg** from the *C:\Civil 3D Beyond\Working\ Surface* folder. If the *TOOLSPACE*>Survey tab is not open,

    click in the *Home* tab>*Palettes* panel to toggle it on.

2. In the *TOOLSPACE*>Survey tab, right-click on **Survey Databases** and select **Set working folder...**, as shown in Figure 4–16.

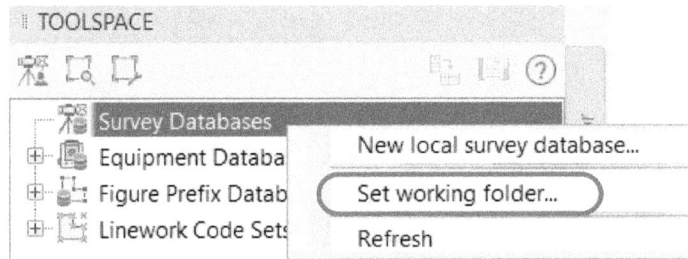

Figure 4–16

3. If need be, select the *Survey Databases* folder in the *C:\Civil 3D Beyond\Survey Databases* folder, and click **Select Folder**.

4. In the *TOOLSPACE>Survey* tab, select the survey database **Survey Data_Complete**, right-click, and select **Open for edit**, as shown in Figure 4–17. (Do not double-click as this would open the survey database as read-only.)

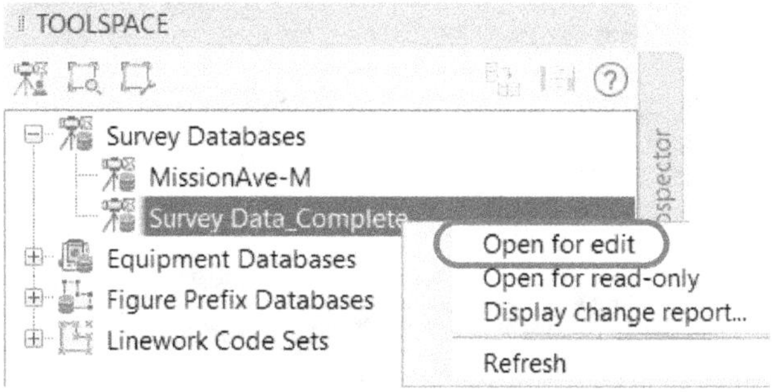

Figure 4–17

5. In the *TOOLSPACE>Survey* tab, expand the *Survey Data_Complete* collection and select **Figures**. The list of figures in the grid view displays at the bottom of the Toolspace.

6. Select the figure **PILE**, right-click, and select **Create breaklines…**, as shown in Figure 4–18.

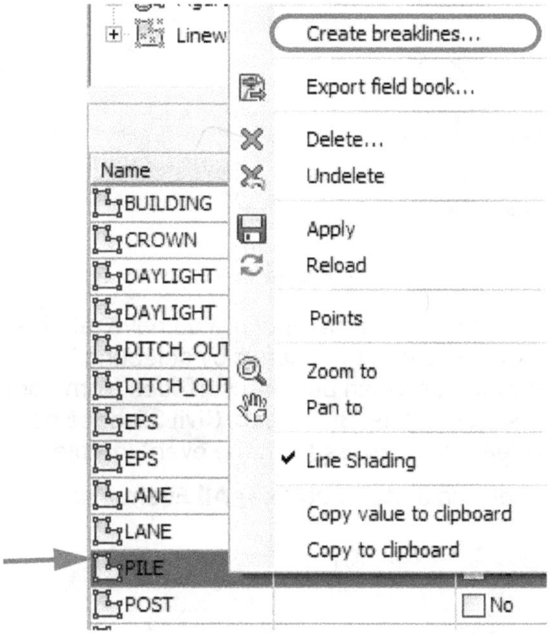

Figure 4–18

7. In the *Create Breaklines* dialog box, select **ExTopo** for the surface, and select the **Yes** option in the *Breakline* column to create breaklines, as shown in Figure 4–19. Click **OK** to close the dialog box.

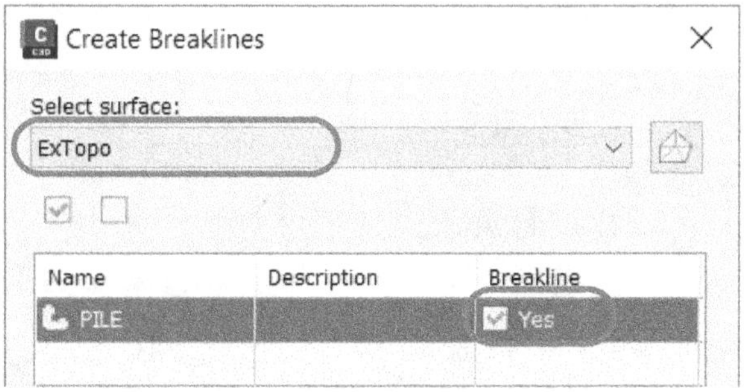

Figure 4–19

8. The Autodesk Civil 3D software will zoom in to the location of the breakline and open the *Add Breaklines* dialog box. Type **Rock pile from site survey** in the *Description* field and ensure that **Standard** is selected in the *Type* drop-down list, as shown in Figure 4–20. Click **OK** to close the dialog box.

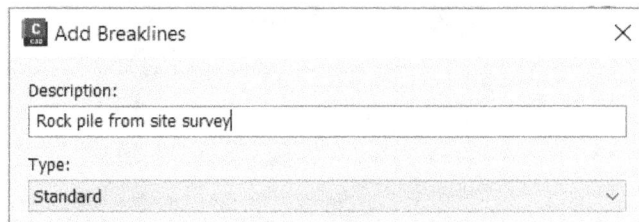

Figure 4–20

9. The *Event Viewer* vista in the Panorama opens. You have received a number of errors with crossing breaklines. You can zoom to the error by selecting **Zoom to** in the far right column. The reason for this error is that when building surfaces from contour-type objects, each of these objects becomes a breakline. By default, Civil 3D does not allow crossing breaklines. For now, you need to clear these errors from the event log file.

10. Click **Action** in the Panorama and select **Clear All Events**, as shown in Figure 4–21.

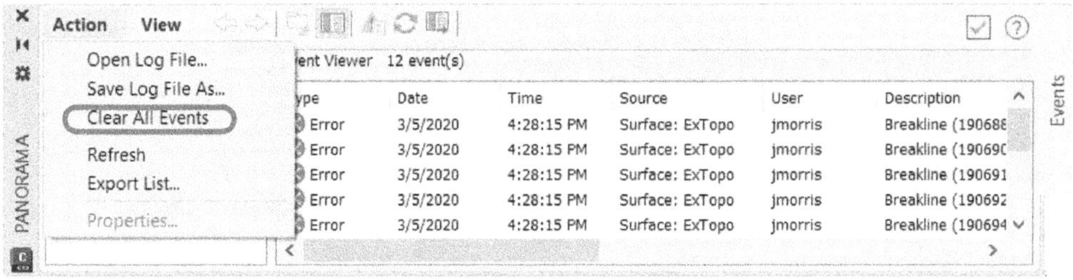

Figure 4–21

11. Close the Panorama by clicking ☑ in the dialog box.

12. In Model Space, select the **ExTopo** surface. The *Tin Surface: ExTopo* contextual tab displays. In the *Modify* panel, click ⌂ (Surface Properties), as shown in Figure 4–22.

Figure 4–22

13. The *Surface Properties - ExTopo* dialog box opens. In the *Definition* tab, expand the *Build* collection and set the value of *Allow crossing breaklines* to **Yes**. Set the value for the *Elevation to use* field to **Use last breakline elevation at intersection**, as shown in Figure 4–23. When you have finished, click **OK**.

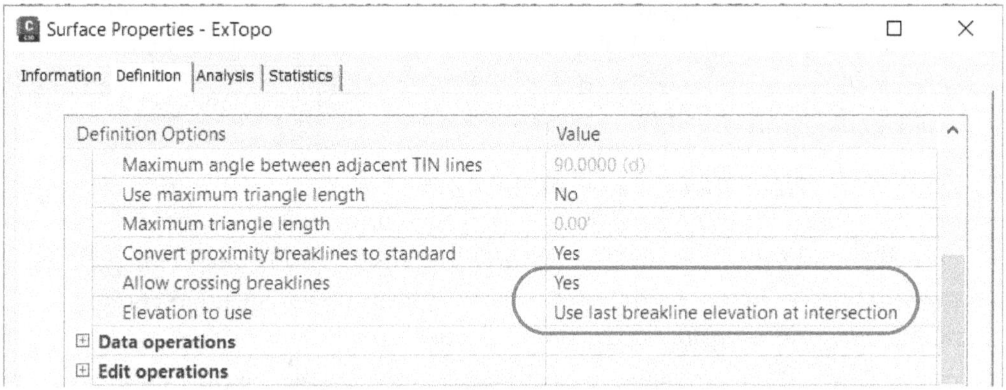

Figure 4–23

14. When prompted to *Rebuild the surface* or *Mark as out of Date*, select **Rebuild the surface**. When you review the surface contours, note that the surface has used the figure as a breakline.

> ⚲ **Hint: Use with Caution**
>
> In practice, you should use this option with caution. Unless you use contours to build a surface, this option can produce unexpected results.

15. Save the drawing.

End of practice

4.3 Surface Editing

There are three ways of adjusting surfaces graphically:

* lines

* points

* area edit tools (such as **Minimize Flat Areas** and **Smooth Surface**)

Simplify Surface

As the collection methods of surface data continue to evolve, yielding significantly larger data sets, the drawing file size increases in proportion to the surface data contained in the drawing. The Autodesk Civil 3D software has a limit of 2.5 million vertices for a surface. Once it exceeds this limit, the software prompts you to store surface data to an external file with an .MMS extension. The resulting external surface files can be quite large. To avoid this, you can simplify your surface using the *Simplify Surface* wizard. Extra points can be removed from a surface without compromising its accuracy. Points that you might want to remove include points that are in an external point file or database, or redundant points in areas of high data concentration where the value of this extra information is minimal. There are two simplification methods available:

* **Edge Contraction:** This method simplifies the surface by using existing triangle edges. It contracts triangle edges to single points by removing one point. The location of the point to which an edge is contracted is selected so that the change to the surface is minimal.

* **Point Removal:** This method simplifies the surface by removing existing surface points. More points are removed from denser areas of the surface.

When you simplify a surface, you specify which regions of the surface the operation should address. The region options include using the existing surface border or specifying a window or polygon. The **Pick in Drawing** option enables you to select the region from the drawing. If a closed polyline exists in the drawing that you want to use as the region boundary, you can select the **Select objects** option and then use the **Pick in Drawing** option to select the boundary. Curves in the boundary are approximated by line segments. The line segment generation is governed by a *Mid Ordinate Distance* value that you determine.

Once you have selected the region, the dialog box displays the *Total Points Selected In Region* value. You can refine the surface reduction options by setting a percentage of points to remove, the maximum change in elevation, or the maximum edge contraction error.

Smooth Surface

The Smooth Surface edit introduces new, interpolated elevations between surface data. It is used to create a more realistic-looking terrain model, though not necessarily a more accurate one. Generally, surface smoothing works best with point-based surface data.

The Autodesk Civil 3D software has two smoothing methods: **Natural neighbor interpolation** and **Kriging**.

- **Natural neighbor interpolation** interpolates a grid of additional data points that produce a smoother overall terrain model.

- **Kriging** reads surface trends to add additional data in sparse areas.

Surface smoothing is applied by right-clicking on the *Edits* collection under a surface's *Definition* and selecting **Smooth Surface**. The *Smooth Surface* dialog box and an example of surface smoothing are shown in Figure 4–24.

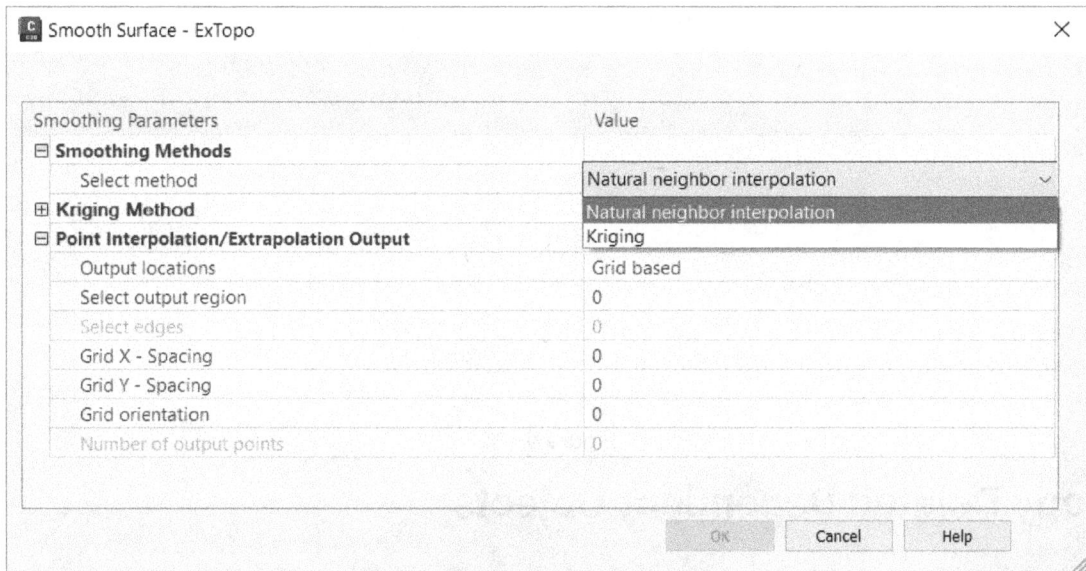

Figure 4–24

Raise/Lower Surface

The **Raise/Lower Surface** command adds or subtracts a specified elevation value. This adjustment is applied to the entire surface. It is useful for modeling soil removal and changing a surface's datum elevation.

Adjusting Surfaces Through Surface Properties

In addition to the graphical edit methods, you can adjust surfaces by changing their surface properties. Surface property adjustments include setting a *Maximum triangle length* or certain values for *Exclude elevations greater than* or *less than*. You can also enable or disable the effects of certain surface data (such as breaklines and boundaries) by disabling them in the dialog box.

To locate these options in the *Surface Properties* dialog box, select the *Definition* tab and expand the **Build** branch, as shown in Figure 4–25.

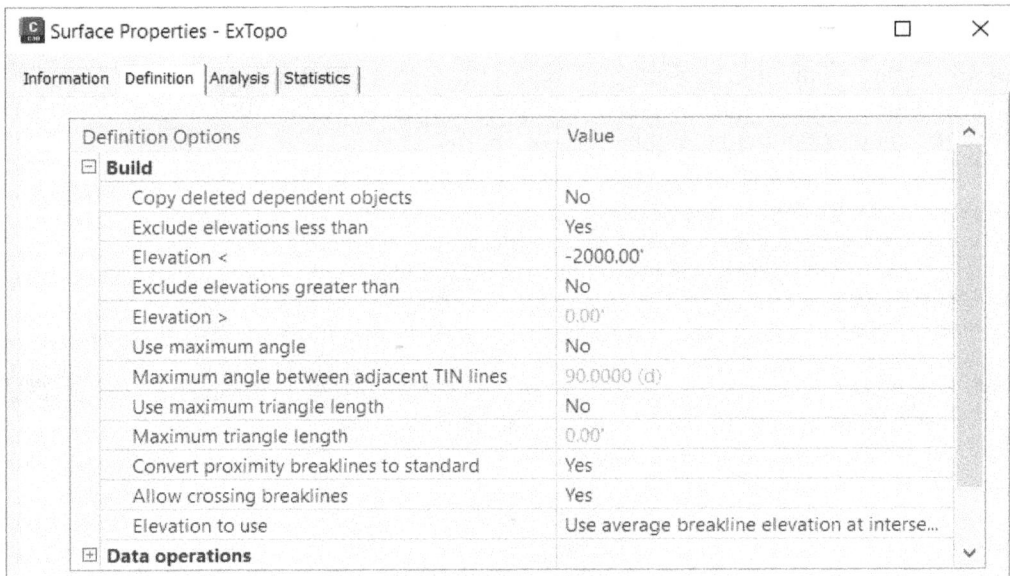

Definition Options	Value
⊟ **Build**	
Copy deleted dependent objects	No
Exclude elevations less than	Yes
Elevation <	-2000.00'
Exclude elevations greater than	No
Elevation >	0.00'
Use maximum angle	No
Maximum angle between adjacent TIN lines	90.0000 (d)
Use maximum triangle length	No
Maximum triangle length	0.00'
Convert proximity breaklines to standard	Yes
Allow crossing breaklines	Yes
Elevation to use	Use average breakline elevation at interse...
⊞ **Data operations**	

Figure 4–25

Copy Deleted Dependent Objects

If dependent objects, such as polylines (used for contour definitions), breaklines, or any AutoCAD objects (used to define the surface), are deleted from the drawing, this option will copy the definition of those objects into the surface object. The surface will remain unaffected.

However, if such dependent objects are removed from the drawing without this option enabled, the surface will lose the definition those objects had provided and update to reflect the removal of these objects it was dependent on.

Practice 4c
Surface Edits

Practice Objectives

- Edit a surface using definition options in the surface properties.
- Use commands found in the Toolspace.
- Set limits to surface definition information.

In this practice, you will refine a previously created surface. The **ExTopo** surface has some triangulations that are not valid. You will eliminate these TIN lines using three methods: you will set options for the surface properties, delete TIN lines (triangle edges), and add a boundary to the surface. Each of these methods has advantages and disadvantages and should be used appropriately.

Task 1: Copy deleted dependent objects.

1. Open **SUF-B.dwg** from the *C:\Civil 3D Beyond\Working\ Surface* folder.
2. In the *View* tab>*Named Views* panel, select the preset view **Surface-Edit**.
3. In Model Space, select the **ExTopo** surface. The *Tin Surface ExTopo* contextual tab will display. In the *Modify* panel, click (Surface Properties), as shown in Figure 4–26.

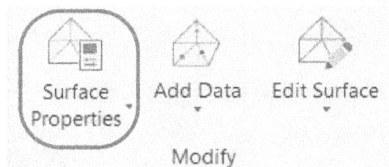

Figure 4–26

4. The *Surface Properties* dialog box opens. Select the *Definition* tab and expand the **Build** branch in the *Definition Options* area.

5. Set the *Copy deleted dependent objects* value to **Yes**, as shown in Figure 4–27. Click **OK** to close the dialog box and accept the changes.

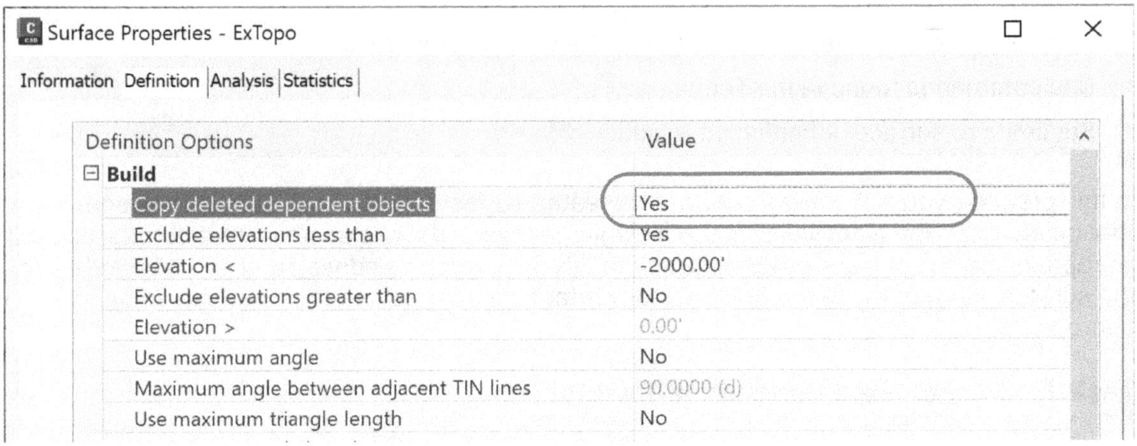

Figure 4–27

6. When prompted to *Rebuild the surface* or *Mark the surface as out-of-date*, select **Rebuild the surface**.

7. If the *Event Viewer* vista opens in the *Panorama*, click **Action** and select **Clear All Events**, then close the *Panorama* in the dialog box.

8. Save the drawing.

Task 2: Set the elevation range.

In reviewing the drawing, you need to address an error in the site. The original topographical contour file contains an invalid piece of data that has transferred to the surface.

1. Select the preset view **Surf Elev Edit**.

2. In Model Space, as shown on the left in Figure 4–28, select the **ExTopo** surface, right-click, and select **Object Viewer**.

3. In *Object Viewer*, click and drag the view, as shown on the right in Figure 4–28, to rotate the 3D view to identify the issue. Change the visual style to **Conceptual** using the drop-down list in the top left corner.

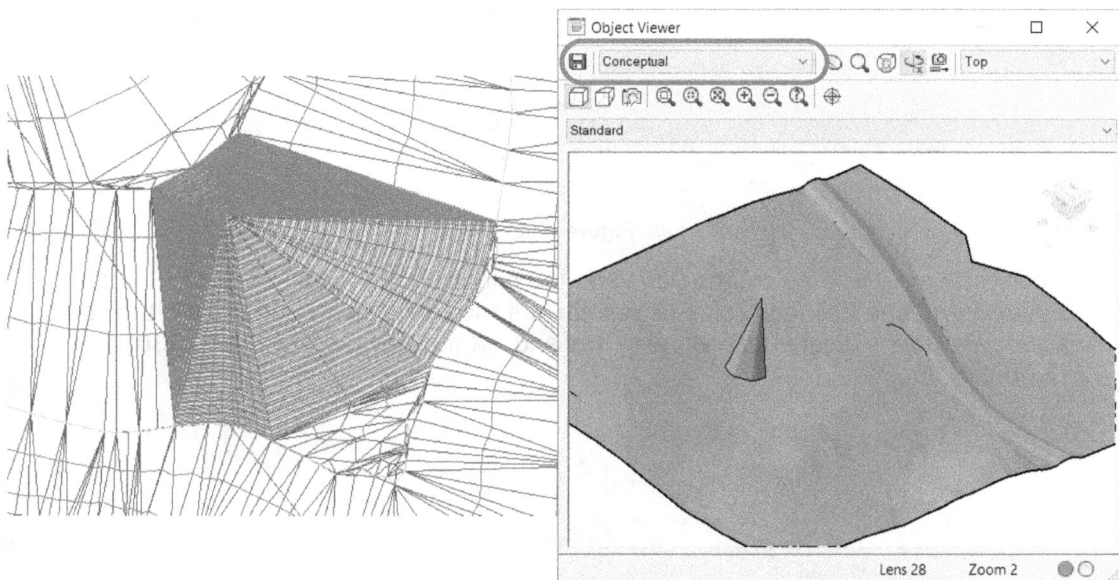

Figure 4–28

4. Close *Object Viewer* by clicking the **X** in the top right corner of the dialog box.

5. With the **ExTopo** surface still selected, select **Surface Properties** in the *Tin Surface ExTopo* contextual tab. The *Surface Properties* dialog box opens.

6. Select the *Statistics* tab and expand the **General** branch to display the value list.

7. When you review the site conditions, note that the site ranges from an elevation of roughly **124' to 310'**. However, the statistics indicate that the surface ranges from an elevation of **115' to 492.12'**, as shown in Figure 4–29.

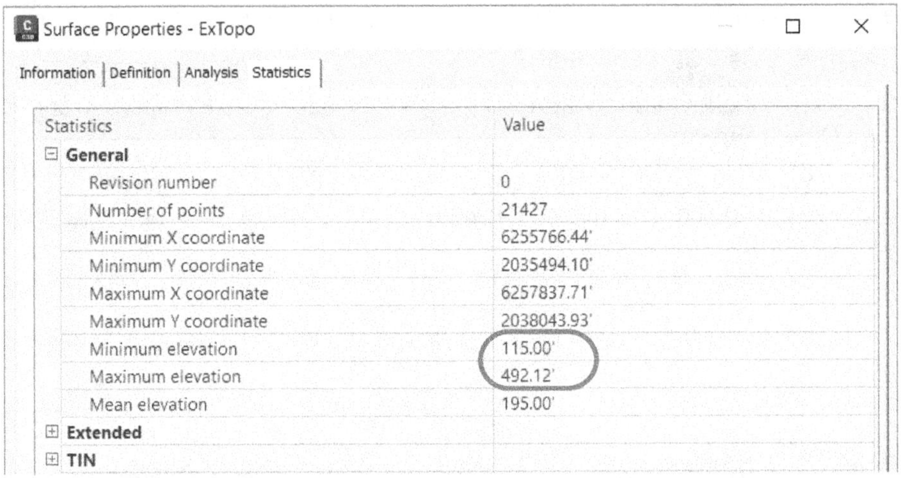

Figure 4–29

8. To correct the surface, select the *Definition* tab and expand the **Build** branch. Set the *Exclude elevations less than* value to **Yes** and set the *Elevation <* value to **100'**, then set the *Exclude elevations greater than* value to **Yes** and set the *Elevation >* value to **330'**, as shown in Figure 4–30.

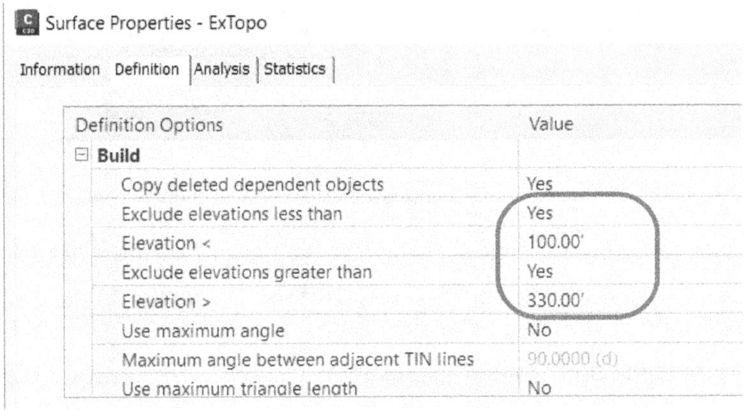

Figure 4–30

9. Click **OK** to accept the changes and close the dialog box.

10. When prompted to *Rebuild the surface* or *Mark the surface as out-of-date*, select **Rebuild the Surface**.All points that are above an elevation of 330' are removed and the error is fixed.

11. The *Event Viewer* vista opens again in the Panorama. Click **Action** and select **Clear All Events**, then close the Panorama in the dialog box.

12. Save the drawing.

End of practice

4.4 Feature Lines

Feature Line Contextual Tab

The *Feature Line* contextual tab (shown in Figure 4–31) contains commands to edit and modify feature lines. These commands include tools to edit feature line elevations and feature line geometry, such as **Break**, **Trim**, **Extend**, and **Fillet** (which creates a true 3D curve).

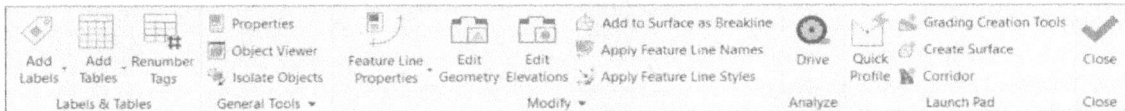

Figure 4–31

There are multiple ways of creating feature lines, such as:

- **Create Feature Lines from Objects**

- **Create Feature Lines from Alignment** (linked or unlinked)

- **Create Feature Lines from Corridor** (linked or unlinked)

- **Create Feature Lines from Stepped Offset**

These commands are available in the *Home* tab>*Create Design* panel, expanded **Feature Line** flyout, as shown in Figure 4–32.

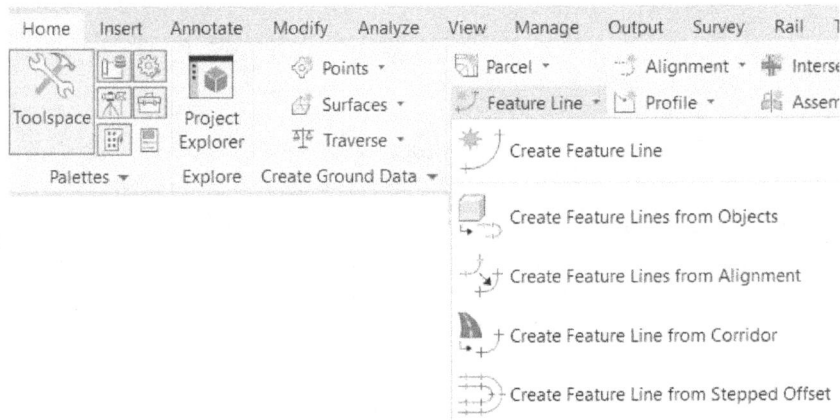

Figure 4–32

Linking feature lines to alignments or corridors makes the feature lines uneditable. This can have advantages in that as the alignments or corridors change, the feature lines will automatically update. However, the inability to edit the feature line (e.g., using Break, Trim, Extend, and Fillet) often makes this option less attractive.

> **💡 Hint: Updating Feature Lines**
>
> If feature lines derived from corridors are unlinked, you can always update the feature lines to the new corridor elevations through the feature line contextual ribbon.

Elevation Editor

The *Grading Elevation Editor* vista (shown in Figure 4–33) enables you to add, modify, or vary the elevations of a feature line. The feature line data is organized into rows; each row lists the data for a specific vertex.

Station	Elevation(R...	Elevation(Actual)	Length	Grade Back	Grade Ahead	Elevation Derived From
0+00.00	0.50'	247.94'	27.57'		1.81%	Relative to Surface
0+27.57		248.44'	282.02'	-1.81%	2.00%	Absolute Elevation
3+09.58		254.08'	76.44'	-2.00%	-3.00%	Absolute Elevation
3+86.03		251.79'	176.77'	3.00%	-3.27%	Absolute Elevation
5+62.79		246.00'	176.77'	3.27%	-2.73%	Absolute Elevation
7+39.56		241.18'	76.44'	2.73%	-3.00%	Absolute Elevation
8+16.00		238.89'	282.02'	3.00%	3.21%	Absolute Elevation
10+98.02	0.50'	247.94'		-3.21%		Relative to Surface

Figure 4–33

- **(Select a Feature Line Or Lot Line):** Enables you to change the feature line that you are editing.

- **(Zoom to):** Zooms in to a highlighted vertex.

- **(Quick Profile):** Creates a quick profile along the feature line.

- **(Raise/Lower):** Raises or lowers all of the feature line vertices by the elevation entered in the edit field on the right.

- **(Raise/Lower Incrementally):** Changes the elevations by the elevation increment entered (the default is 1).

- **(Set Increment):** Sets the increment value.

- **(Flatten Grade or Elevations):** Enables you to flatten selected vertices to a specified grade or single elevation.

- (**Insert Elevation Point**): (Green) Adds an elevation control to the feature line. Elevation points provide an elevation control without creating a new vertex. These points are Z-controls without X- or Y-components.

- (**Delete Elevation Point**): (Red) Removes elevation points.

- (**Elevations from Surface**): Takes the elevations of all of the vertices from the surface if no rows are selected. If a row is selected, it only takes the surface elevation for that vertex.

- (**Reverse the direction**): Changes the direction of the feature line by reversing the order of its points.

- (**Show Grade breaks only**): Only displays rows for vertices where there is a change to grade.

- (**Unselect All Rows**): Clears selected vertices. With no rows selected, the **Raise/Lower** commands apply to all rows.

- (**Select from List**): When elevations are set to be relative to a surface, select the surface that is in control using the drop-down list, as shown in Figure 4–34.

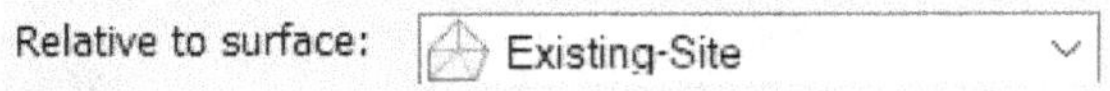

Relative to surface: Existing-Site

Figure 4–34

- (**Select from the drawing**): Select the controlling surface (for Relative to surface) from the drawing.

You can edit the elevations of a feature or parcel line before or after it becomes part of a grading group.

Practice 4d
Create Feature Lines

Practice Objectives

- Create feature lines from a drawing object.
- Extract feature lines from corridors.

The first step in grading is to establish an interim design surface based on existing site conditions. In this practice, you will define feature lines from the parcel boundary and corridors, from which you will create a surface. Next, feature lines defining design features are created, to be used for grading purposes to meet the interim design surface.

Task 1: Create a feature line for the western edge based on existing surface elevations.

To establish an interim design surface, you will create a feature line from an existing polyline along the western and southern edges of the school parcel. Then, you will create one feature line from the southern edge of the **Jeffries Ranch Rd** corridor, as shown in Figure 4–35.

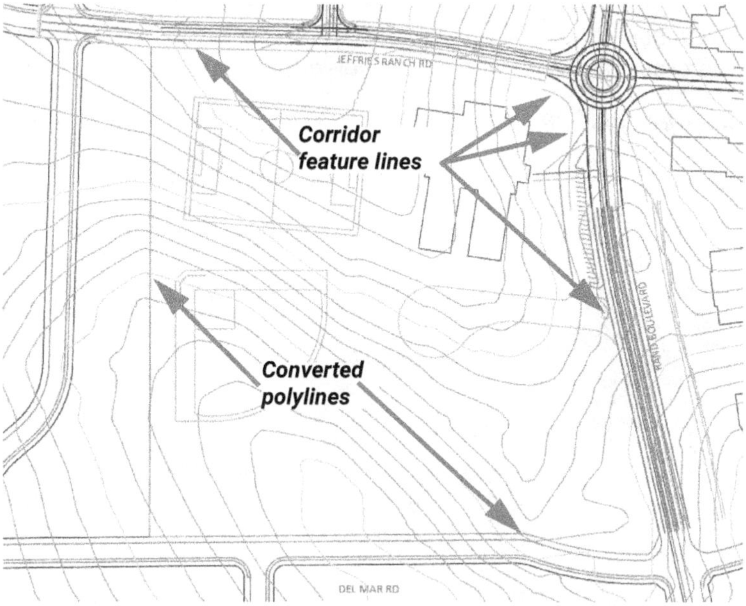

Figure 4–35

The other corridor feature lines will be added, trimmed, and joined together to form one feature line. This is beyond the scope of this practice simply because it is too time-consuming. You will, however, join the polyline feature line with the corridor feature line.

---

1. Open **SUF-C.dwg** from the *C:\Civil 3D Beyond\Working\ Surface* folder.

2. In the *Home* tab>*Create Design* panel, expand **Feature Line** and select (Create Feature Lines from Objects), as shown in Figure 4–36.

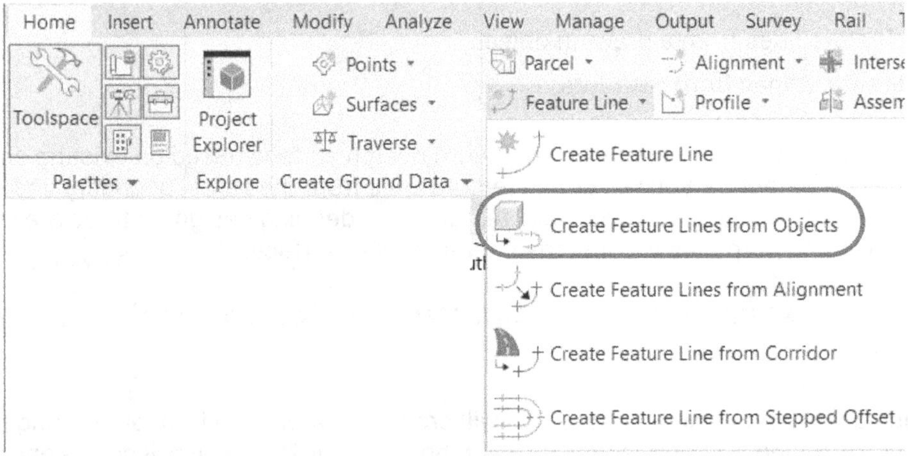

Figure 4–36

3. When prompted to *select the object,* pick the cyan polyline as indicated previously in Figure 4–35 and press <Enter> to finish the selection.

4. In the *Create Feature Lines dialog* box, click (New Site) to create a new site.

5. In the *Site Properties* dialog box, do the following (as shown on the right in Figure 4–37):

   • For the *Name*, enter **School-Site-A**.

   • For the *Description*, enter **Option A for developing Site for School**.

   • Click **OK** to close the *Site Properties* dialog box.

6. In the *Create Feature Lines* dialog box, do the following (as shown on the left in Figure 4–37):

   • Check the **Name** box and name the feature line **School-SW Bound**.

   • Leave the **Style** box unchecked to keep the default style.

   • In the *Conversion options* area, select **Erase existing entities** and **Assign elevations**.

   • Click **OK** to continue.

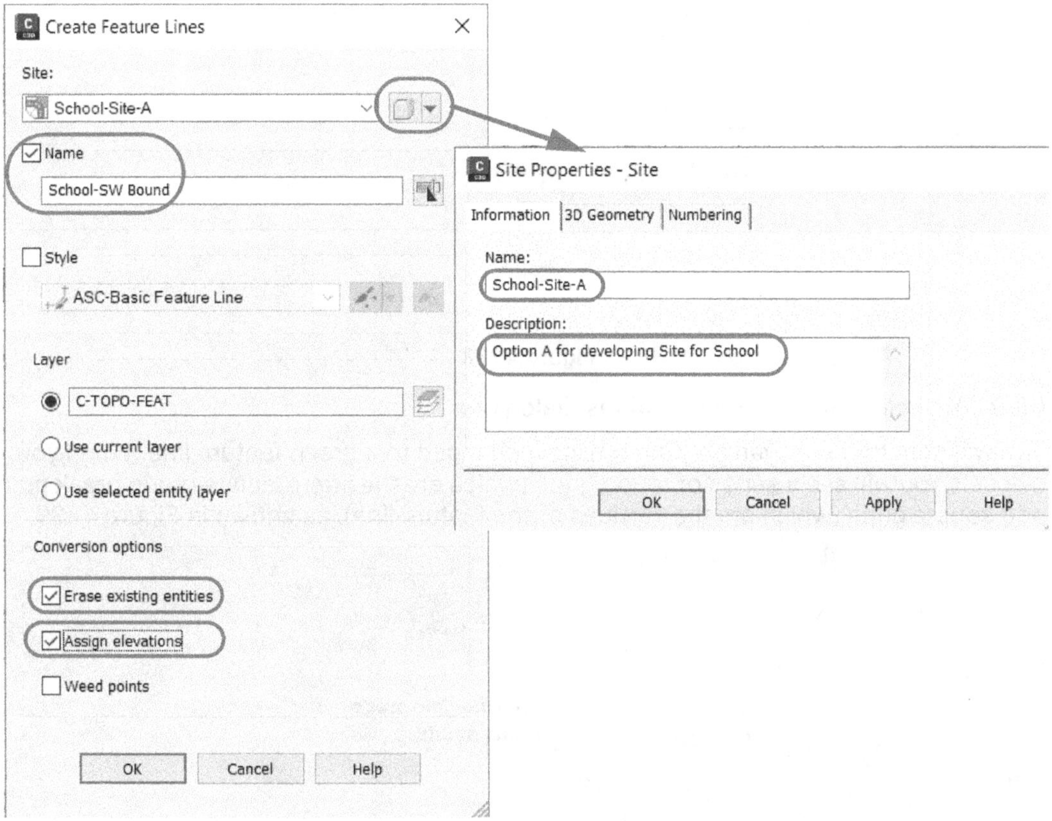

Figure 4–37

7. In the *Assign Elevations* dialog box that opens, ensure the following are set, as shown in Figure 4–38:

   - *From surface:* toggled on and set to **Existing-Site**
   - *Insert intermediate grade break points:* **checked**
   - *Relative elevation to surface:* **unchecked**

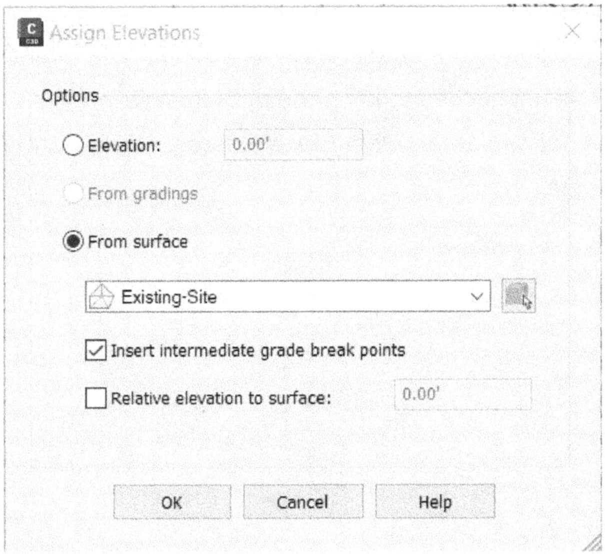

Figure 4–38

8. Click **OK** to close the *Assign Elevations* dialog box.

9. You will note that the cyan polyline has now changed to a green feature line. When you select it, you will see a series of round grips (which are the intermediate grade break points) and square grips (which are the vertices of the feature line), as shown in Figure 4–39.

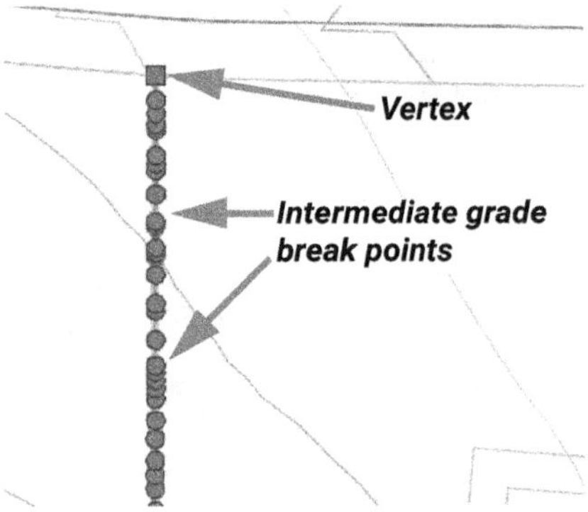

Figure 4–39

10. Save the drawing.

Task 2: Extract feature line from corridor.

In this task, you will create a feature line from the southern edge of the **Jeffries Ranch Rd** corridor to form the northern edge of the school design surface.

1. Continue to work in the drawing from the previous task.

2. Zoom and pan to the southern edge of the **Jeffries Ranch Rd** corridor, as shown in Figure 4–40.

3. In the *Home* tab>*Create Design* panel, expand **Feature Line** and select (Create Feature Lines from Corridor).

4. Select the **Jeffries Ranch Rd** corridor. The *Code Set Style* has been set to **ASC-All Codes - No Display**, so you will need to select one of the parallel segments of the road, which are the links, as shown in Figure 4–40.

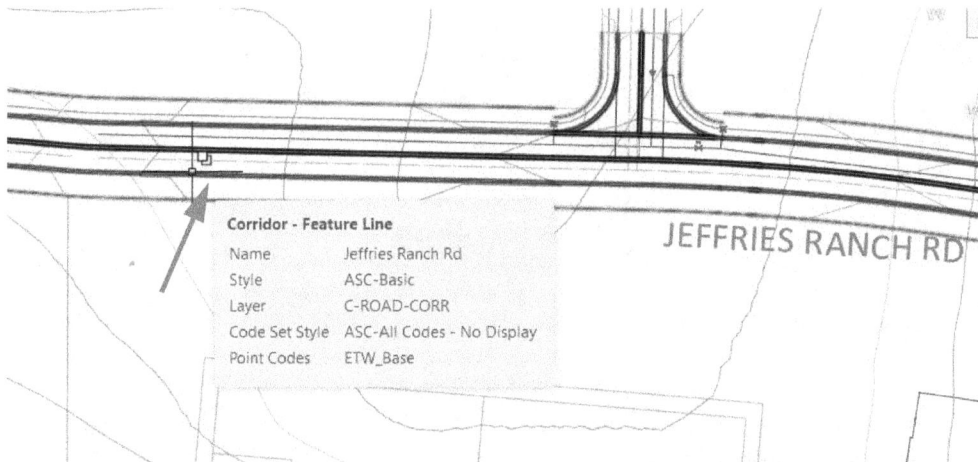

Figure 4–40

5. When prompted to select the corridor feature line, hover over the various parallel links and note how they turn red and their code appears as a tooltip. Select the southernmost one, which is **P2**, as shown in Figure 4–41. Press <Enter> to finish the selection.

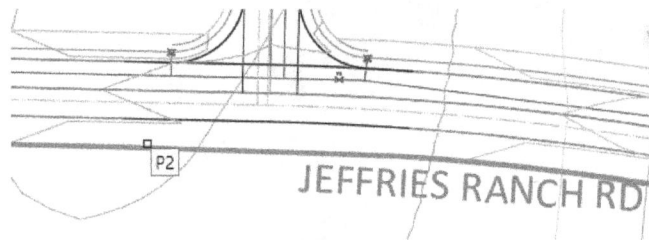

Figure 4–41

6. In the *Extract Corridor Feature Lines* dialog box that opens, click the **Settings** button to open the *Extract Corridor Feature Lines Settings* dialog box, then set the following (as shown in Figure 4–42):

- *Dynamic link to corridor:* **unchecked**
- *Apply Smoothing:* **unchecked**
- Name: **checked** and type the name **FL - <[Corridor Name]> South Edge**

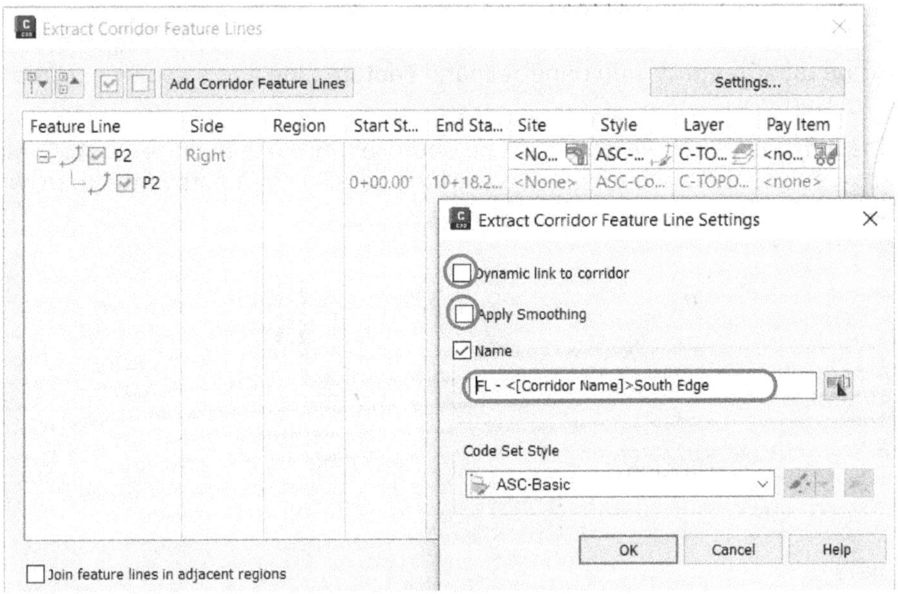

Figure 4–42

7. Click **OK** to close the *Extract Corridor Feature Lines Settings* dialog box, then click **Extract** to close the *Extract Corridor Feature Lines* dialog box.

8. Save the drawing.

End of practice

4.5 Create Design Surfaces from Feature Lines

A common practice in land development is to create an interim base surface for design purposes. For hilly, irregular project sites with many natural grade changes and topologies, it can be a challenge to provide preliminary design grading directly to the existing site. An interim surface can be used to make it easier to come up with design proposals, as can be seen in the quick profile of both the existing grade and the interim design grade in Figure 4-43.

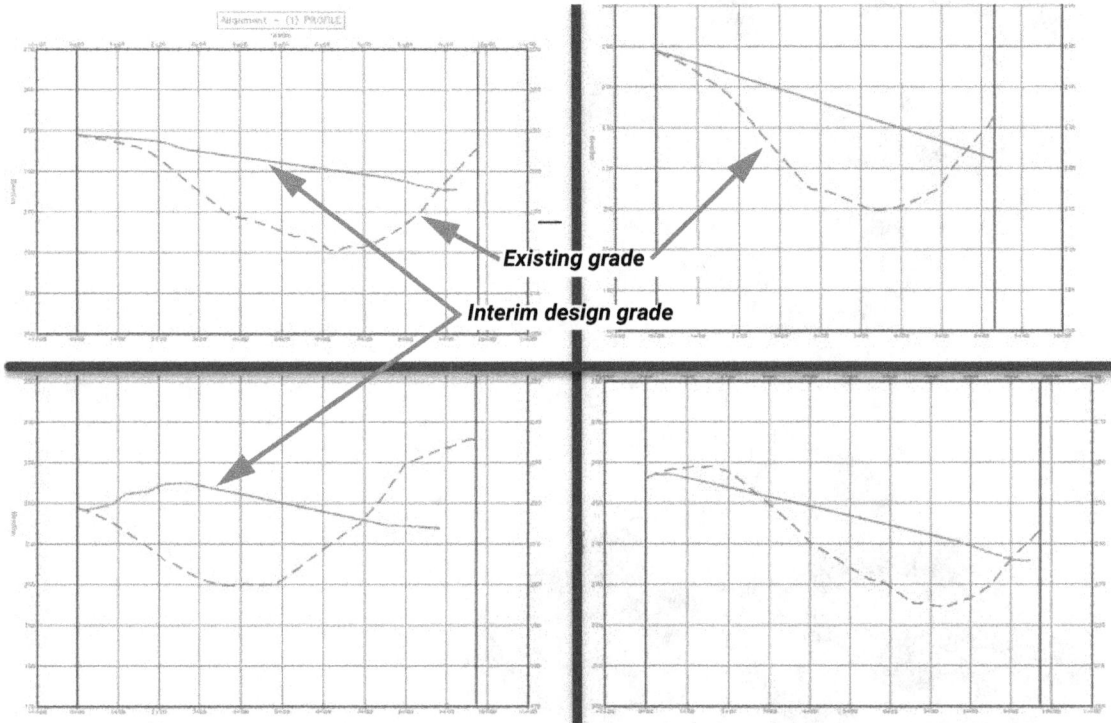

Figure 4-43

The interim surface will intersect the existing surface at the project site's boundary. If the boundary is a corridor, extracted feature lines from the corridor are used to create the interim surface. If the boundary is open space, a feature line created with elevations from the existing ground will be used.

The result is a less complex grading surface, which is often flatter with lesser elevation changes. Compare the existing surface in Figure 4–44 with the interim design surface in Figure 4–45.

Figure 4–44

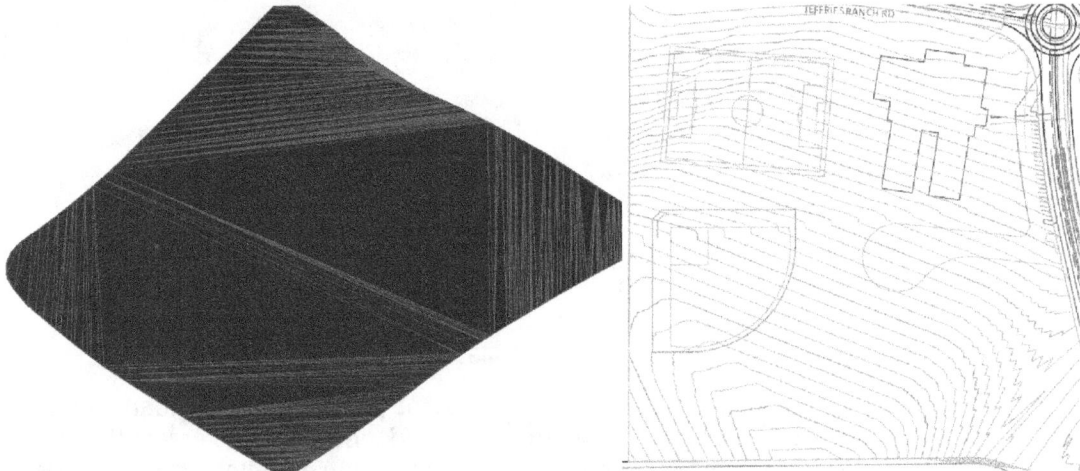

Figure 4–45

In practice, it is recommended that an interim design grade be refined with other features deemed necessary for the final design. Such features may include streams and waterways, proposed pathways, etc.

The first step of creating such feature lines has been done in the previous practices. The next step is to create a interim surface with these feature lines. With such an interim design grade, preliminary grading of building pads, parking lots, irrigation or retention ponds, and sports fields can be done and studied.

Practice 4e
Create the Interim Design Surface

Practice Objective

- Create grading objects to design the finished ground and display the finished ground contours.

In this next drawing, the boundary feature line has been completed. More corridor feature lines were extracted, but not linked to the corridors. Then, the feature lines were trimmed and the endpoint vertices were adjusted to meet other endpoint vertices from other feature lines, both in elevation and location (by using the Endpoint Osnap). Finally, the feature lines were joined together, as shown in Figure 4–46. The name of the resulting feature line is **School-Site Boundary**.

Figure 4–46

1. Open **SUF-D.dwg** from the *C:\Civil 3D Beyond\Working\Surface* folder. Do not continue from the previous drawing.

2. In the *TOOLSPACE>Prospector* tab, select **Surfaces**, right-click, and select **Create Surface**.

3. In the *Create Surface* dialog box, set the following (as shown in Figure 4–47):

- *Type*: **TIN surface**
- *Name*: **IDG**
- *Description*: **Interim Design**
- *Style*: **ASC-Contours 2' and 10' (Background)**
- *Render Material:* **Sitework.Planting.Grass.Thick**

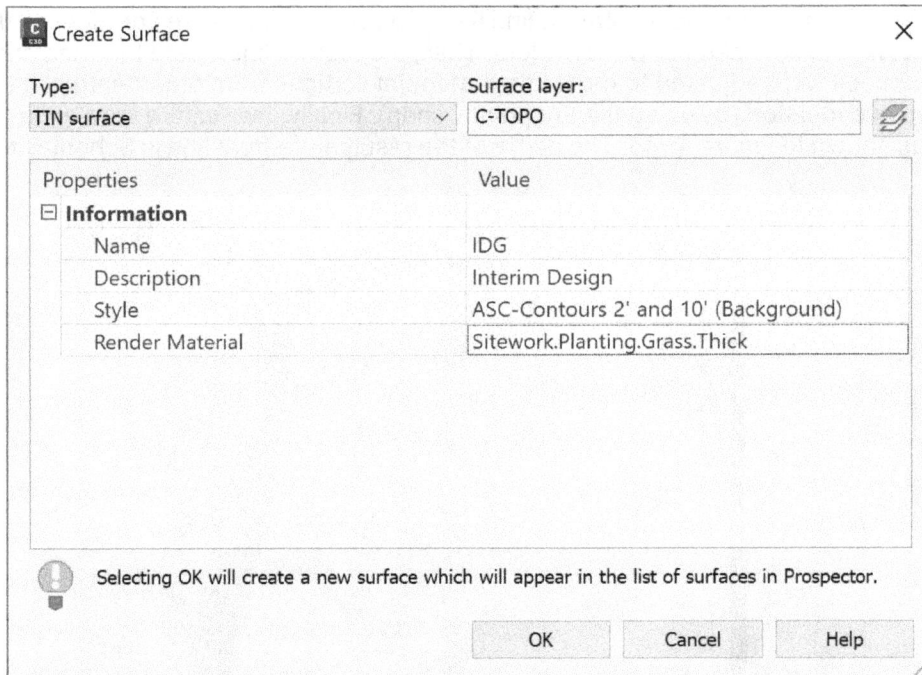

Figure 4–47

4. Click **OK** to accept the changes and close the dialog box.

5. Expand the *IDG* surfaces collection and the *Definition* collection.

6. Select the **Breaklines** data element, right-click, and select **Add...**.

7. In the *Add Breaklines* dialog box, enter **Boundary from feature lines** for a description and leave all other options as default, then click **OK**.

8. Select the perimeter feature line, as shown previously in Figure 4–46, and press <Enter> to finish the selection.

9. The surface is built. You may have to regenerate the drawing to see it.

10. Select the **Existing-Site** surface and in *Surface Properties*, set the surface style to **ASC-Border Only**.

11. The result is shown in Figure 4–48.

Figure 4–48

12. Save and close the drawing.

End of practice

4.6 Surface Volume Calculations

You can generate volume calculations in the Autodesk Civil 3D software in many ways. Surface-to-surface calculations are often used to compare an existing ground surface to a proposed surface to determine cut and fill quantities. In the Autodesk Civil 3D software, quantities can be adjusted by an expansion (cut) or a compaction (fill) factor. Surfaces representing different soil strata can be compared to each other to determine the volume between the soil layers. There are multiple ways of comparing surfaces to each other in the Autodesk Civil 3D software.

Volumes Dashboard

In the *Analyze* tab>*Volumes and Materials* panel, click ⊤ (Volumes Dashboard).

The Volumes Dashboard creates a volume surface based on a graphical subtraction of one surface from the other, as shown in Figure 4–49.

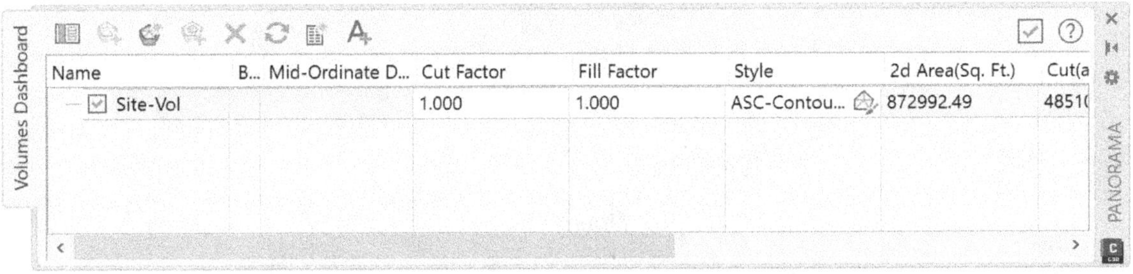

Figure 4–49

The *Net Graph* column color displays in red if the surface difference results in a net cut and in green if it is a net fill. You can have multiple volume entries listed if you are comparing multiple surfaces. If any surfaces change, return to this vista and click ♺ (Recompute Volumes) to update the calculations. Alternatively, you can add another volume entry. Select the same two surfaces and compare before and after volume calculations.

Bounded Volumes

The area to calculate cut and fill can be limited by clicking ⛁ (Add Bounded Volume). This limits the calculations to the area defined by a polyline, polygon, or parcel.

Volume Reports

The dashboard's cut/fill summary contents can be placed directly into the drawing by clicking A₊ (Insert Cut/Fill Summary) inside the Volumes Dashboard. In addition, you can create a volume report from the dashboard contents to include in specifications or other project documents by clicking 🗒 (Generate Volume Report) inside the Volumes Dashboard.

Grid Volume or TIN Volume Surface

This method enables you to assign the surfaces you want to compare as object properties of a volume surface. The volume between the surfaces is calculated and included in the volume surface object properties. The TIN surface calculation is the same one conducted in the Volumes Dashboard. The grid surface calculation is based on a grid of points interpolated from both surfaces, rather than all of the surface points of both. Grid surfaces tend to be less accurate, but faster to calculate and easier to prove by manual methods.

A grid of spot elevation labels that lists the elevation differences between two surfaces can be generated from either a grid volume surface or a TIN volume surface. Once the volume surface is established, create the labels. In the *Annotate* tab>*Labels & Tables* panel, expand **Add Labels>Surface** and select **Spot Elevations on Grid**, as shown in Figure 4-50.

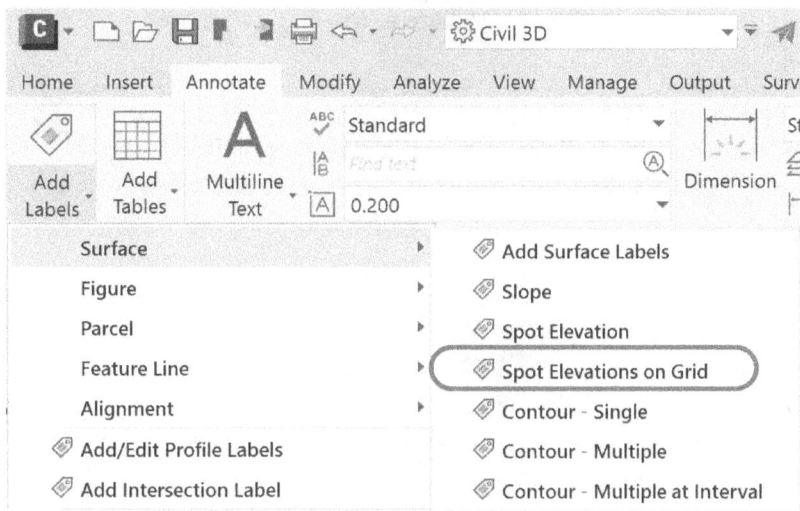

Figure 4-50

Practice 4f
Calculate Surface Volumes

Practice Objective

- Communicate information about the surface by labeling and analyzing it.

A primarily final surface has been established, so now you can get an idea of the overall volumes for the entire site. You already discovered finding the volumes of grading groups or individual grading objects; this will calculate the volumes of the extents of the final ground you have established.

1. Open **SUF-E.dwg** from the *C:\Civil 3D Beyond\Working\ Surface* folder.

2. In the *Analyze* tab>*Volumes and Materials* panel, click ▆ (Volumes Dashboard).

3. In the Volumes Dashboard, click 🥣 (Create new volume surface), as shown in Figure 4−51.

Figure 4−51

4. In the *Create Surface* dialog box, enter the following, as shown in Figure 4–52:

   * *Name:* **Vol-School Site**
   * *Description:* **Volume of EG-FG for school site**
   * *Style:* **ASC-Cut and Fill Banding 1' Interval (2D)**
   * *Base Surface:* **Existing-Site**
   * *Comparison Surface:* **FG**

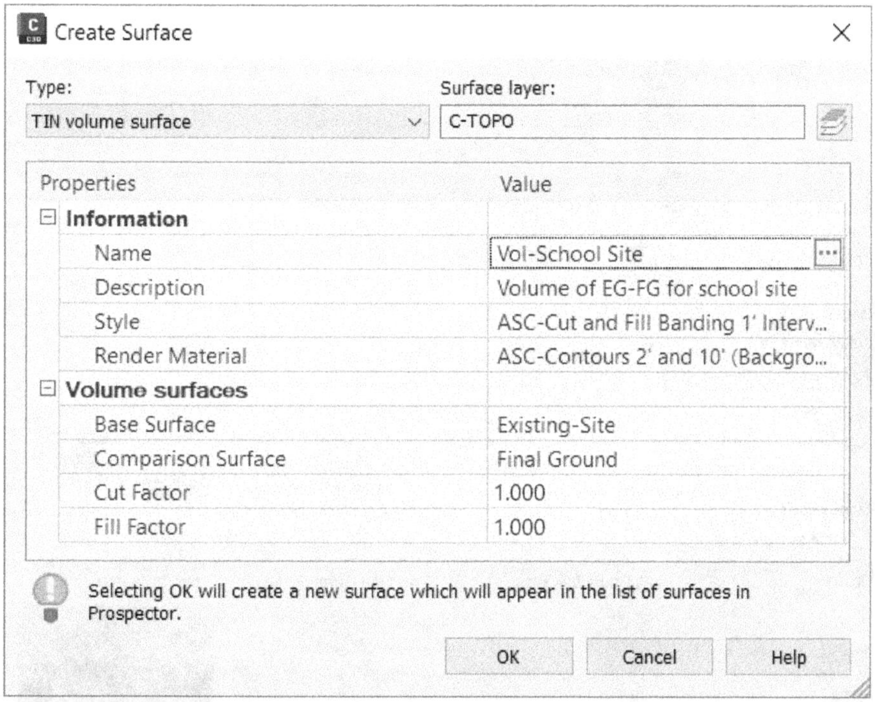

Figure 4–52

5. Click **OK** to close the *Create Surface* dialog box. The new volume surface is displayed in a series of green and red blotches. The reason is the intervals for the elevation ranges are too small.

6. Select the volume surface and launch **Surface Properties**.

7. In the *Surface Properties* dialog box, select the *Analyze* tab and do the following (as shown in Figure 4–53):

- Set the *Analysis type* to **Elevations**.
- Set *Create ranges by:* to **Range interval with datum**.
- Set the number of intervals to **5**. Note: Do not press <Enter> when entering 5 as this will close the dialog box.
- Click ▣ (Run Analysis) to run the analysis.

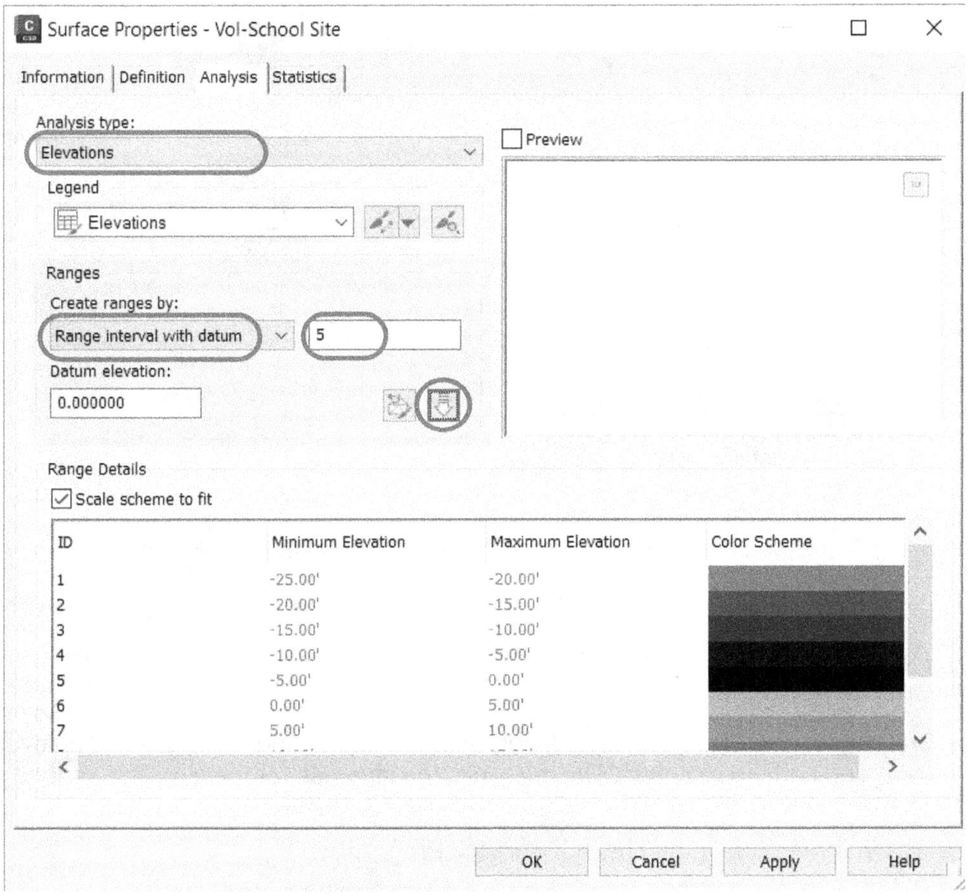

Figure 4–53

8. Click **OK** to close the *Surface Properties* dialog box. The surface will rebuild, as shown in Figure 4–54.

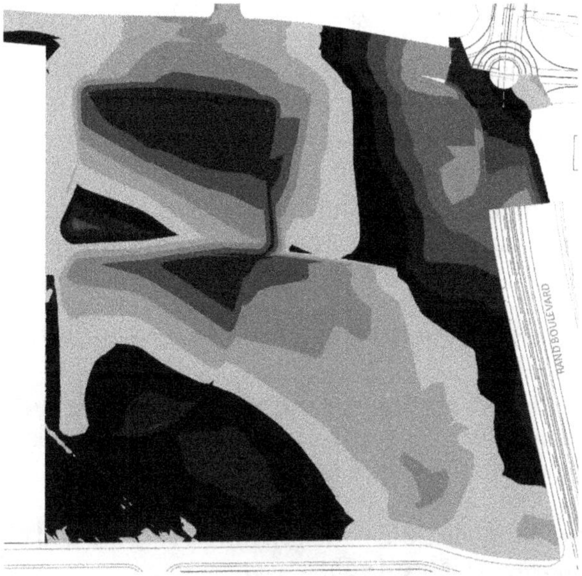

Figure 4–54

Note: A cut/fill table could also be generated, which would be useful.

9. Save the drawing.

10. Open **SUF-E1.dwg** from the *C:\Civil 3D Beyond\Working\ Surface* folder to see the final result.

11. Close the drawing.

End of practice

4.7 Create a Surface from GIS Data

An Autodesk Civil 3D surface can be created from GIS data. Once created, the surface can be used to create surface profiles and act as a target for corridor models and grading groups. It is recommended that you request any available metadata when obtaining GIS layers that could be used for creating a 3D surface model. The metadata should indicate how accurate the data is and whether it can be used in detailed design drawings. GIS surfaces are not often used for detailed design because they are typically mapping grade rather than survey grade.

Having a surface from GIS data can be useful in the project planning phase of a project, even if it is not survey grade. Data source types that can be used to create a surface include ArcSDE, Oracle, and ESRI shape files.

How To: Create an Autodesk Civil 3D Surface from SHP Files

1. Ensure you are in the **Civil 3D** workspace and not the **Planning and Analysis** workspace. The **Planning and Analysis** workspace is the customary workspace for GIS type tasks, but to create a surface from GIS data, the **Civil 3D** workspace is required.

2. In the *Home* tab>*Create Ground Data* panel, expand **Surfaces** and click 📧 (Create Surface from GIS Data), as shown in Figure 4–55.

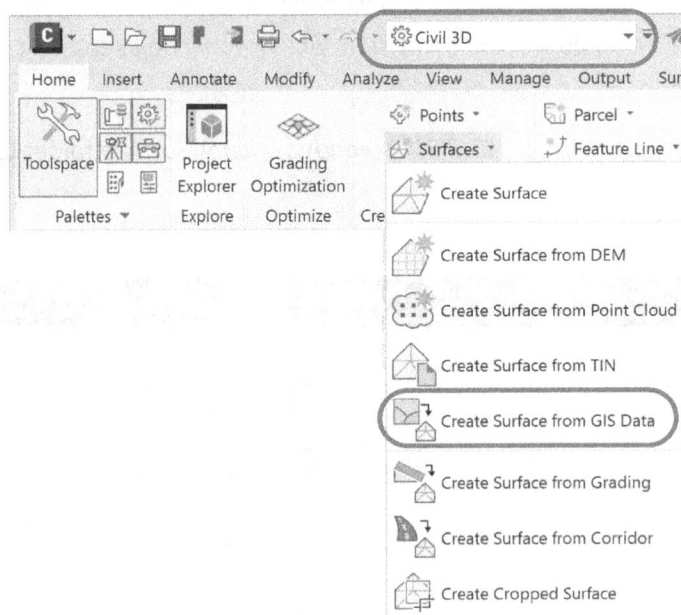

Figure 4–55

3. In the *Create Surface from GIS Data* wizard, on the *Object Options* page, set the *Civil 3D object type* to **Surface**. Type a name and select the required styles for displaying the surface, as shown in Figure 4–56. Click **Next**.

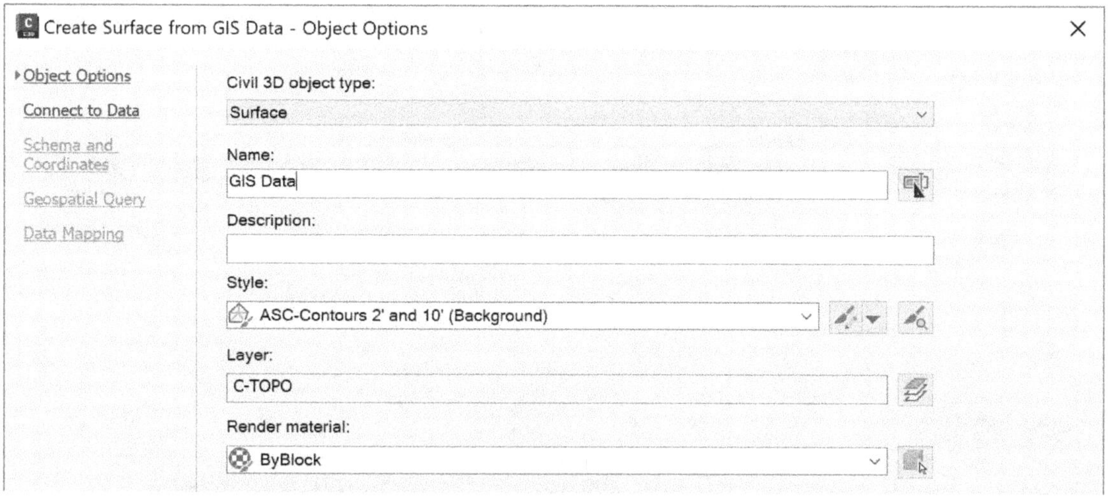

Figure 4–56

4. On the *Connect to Data* page, for the *Data source type*, select **SHP**. For the *SHP path*, click ⋯ (Browse for file) and select a shape file that includes vector data for the contours and elevation data in the database file, as shown in Figure 4–57. Click **Login**.

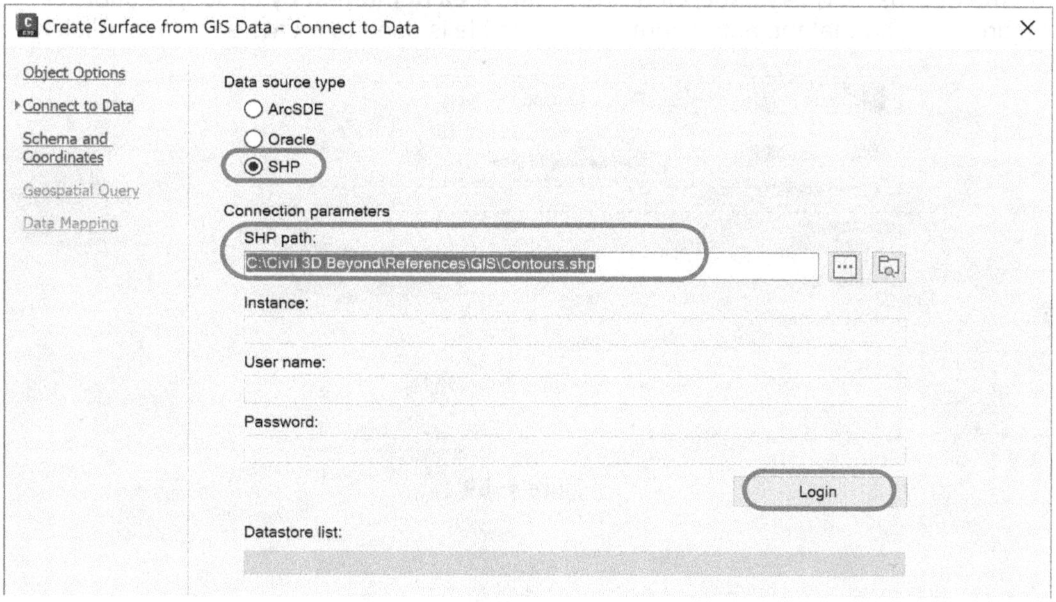

Figure 4–57

5. On the *Schema and Coordinates* page, select the **Contours** feature class and ensure that the *Coordinate system* is set, as shown in Figure 4–58. Click **Next**.

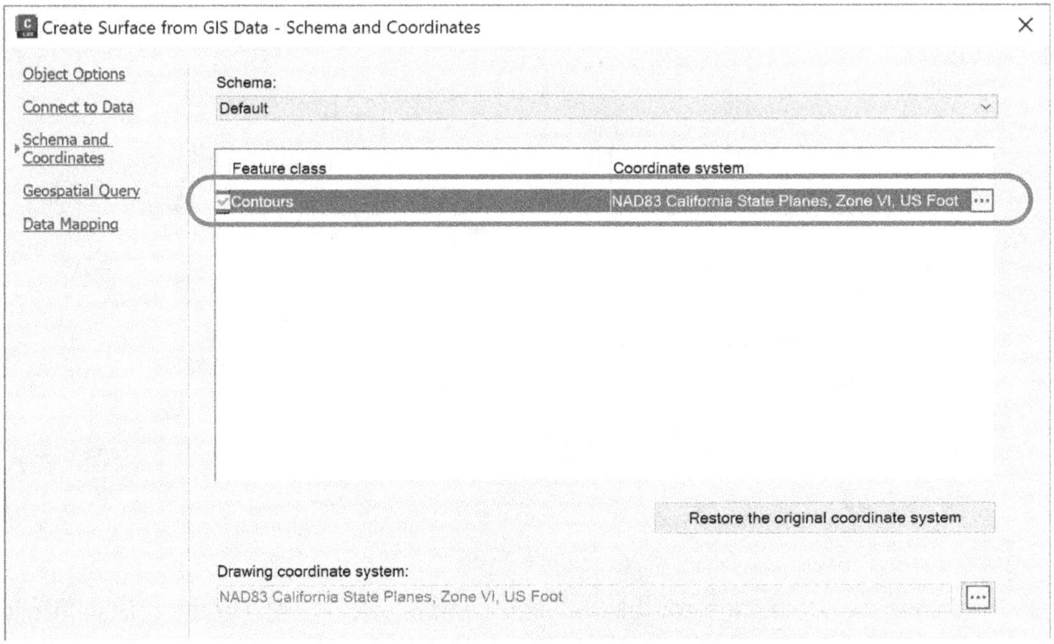

Figure 4–58

6. On the *Geospatial Query* page, clear the **Define area of interest by** option, as shown in Figure 4–59, so that the entire contours shape file is used to create a surface. Click **Next**.

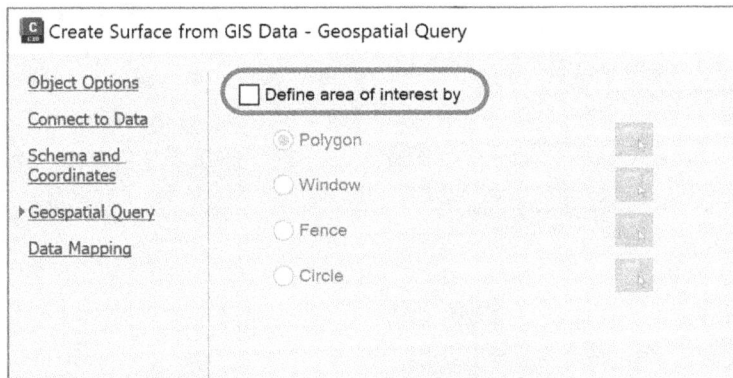

Figure 4–59

7. On the *Data Mapping* page, expand the drop-down list and select the field that holds the surface elevation values, as shown in Figure 4–60. Click **Finish**.

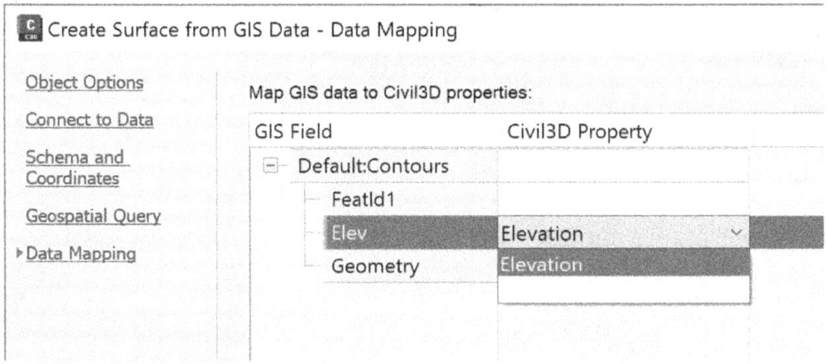

Figure 4–60

Contour data is available from many sources. Large sites are often surveyed using aerial photogrammetry, which provides contour polylines and spot elevations. When contour data is used from other GIS data types, the Autodesk Civil 3D software interprets the imported linework as polylines with elevations.

In the Autodesk Civil 3D software, polylines with elevation are useful as custom contour objects. Whether using polylines or other GIS contour objects, the Autodesk Civil 3D software builds a surface by triangulating between contours. The end of each triangle side connects to a vertex of two different contours.

Practice 4g
Create a Surface from a Shape File

Practice Objectives

* Examine GIS data in the drawing.

* Create a surface from a shape file containing elevation data.

In this practice, you will create surface from a shape file that contains elevation data.

1. Open **SUF-F.dwg** from the *C:\Civil 3D Beyond\Working\ Surface* folder.

2. Ensure you are in the **Civil 3D** workspace and not the **Planning and Analysis** workspace.

3. The drawing contains a series of parcels which are derived from a GIS Shape (SHP) file. Select any of the parcels and examine its properties through the AutoCAD *Properties Panels*, as shown in Figure 4–61. You can open the *Properties Panel* using the right-click menu or the **<Ctrl 1>** keyboard shortcut.

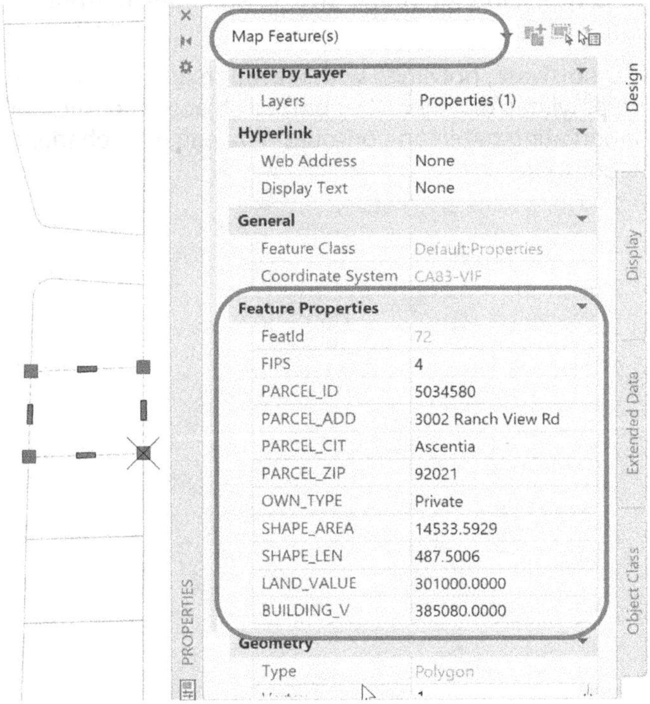

Figure 4–61

4. Notice that the object is a *Map Feature,* and the GIS information is listed in the *Feature Properties* section, i.e. Land Value, Parcel ID, etc.

5. Press the <Esc> key to clear the selection.

6. In the *Home* tab>*Create Ground Data* panel, expand **Surfaces** and click ⬛ (Create Surface from GIS Data), as shown in Figure 4–62.

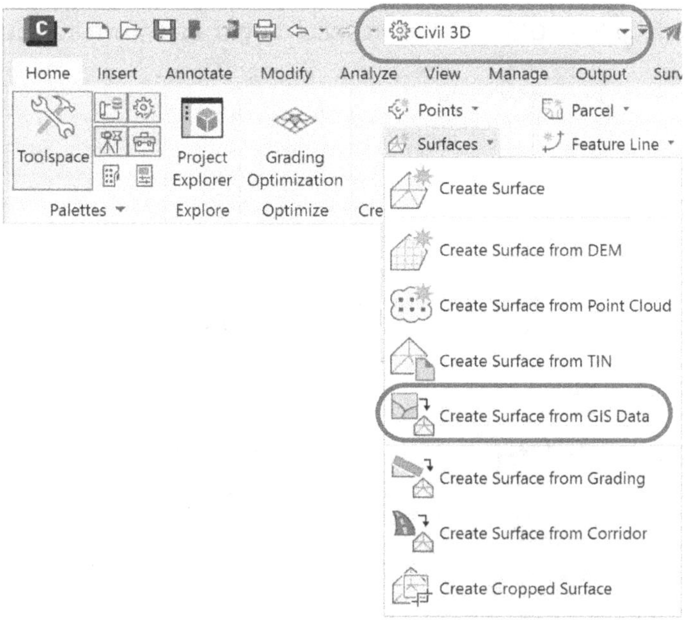

Figure 4–62

7. In the *Create Surface from GIS Data* wizard, on the *Object Options* page, for the *Name*, type **GIS Data**. Leave all of the other settings as their defaults, as shown in Figure 4–63. Click **Next**.

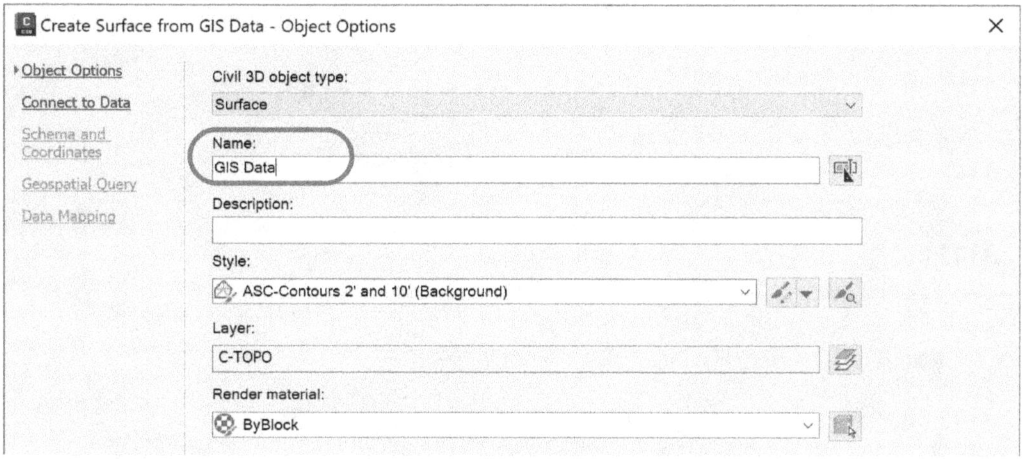

Figure 4–63

8. On the *Connect to Data* page, set the *Data source type* to **SHP**, as shown in Figure 4–64. For the *SHP path*, click ⋯ (Browse for file) and in the Select an *SHP File* dialog box, select **Contours.shp** from the *C:\Civil 3D Beyond\ References\GIS* folder and click **Open**.

9. In the *Create Surface from GIS Data* wizard, click **Login**, as shown in Figure 4–64.

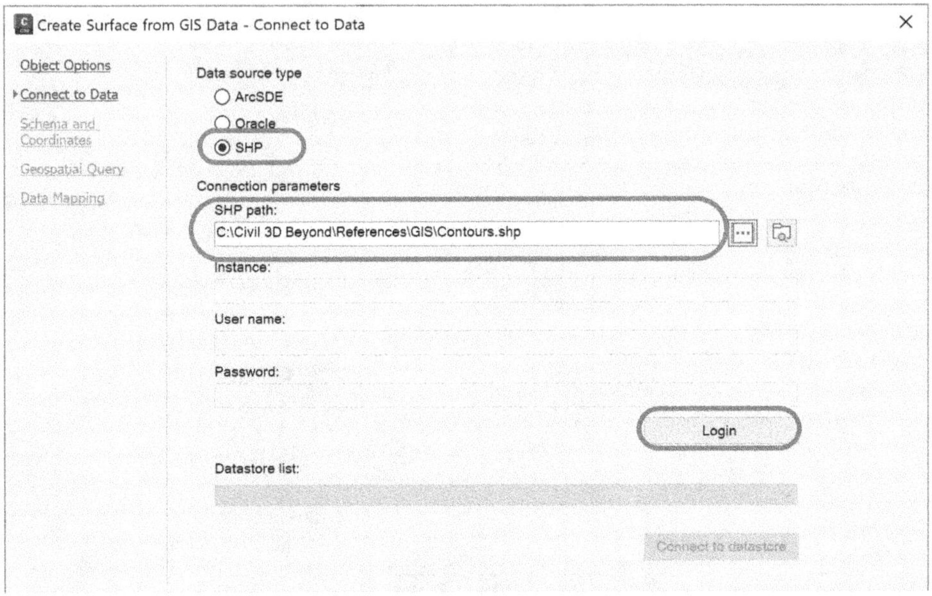

Figure 4–64

10. On the *Schema and Coordinates* page, select the **Contours** feature class and ensure that the *Coordinate system* is set to **NAD83 California State Planes, Zone VI, US Foot**, as shown in Figure 4–65. Click **Next**.

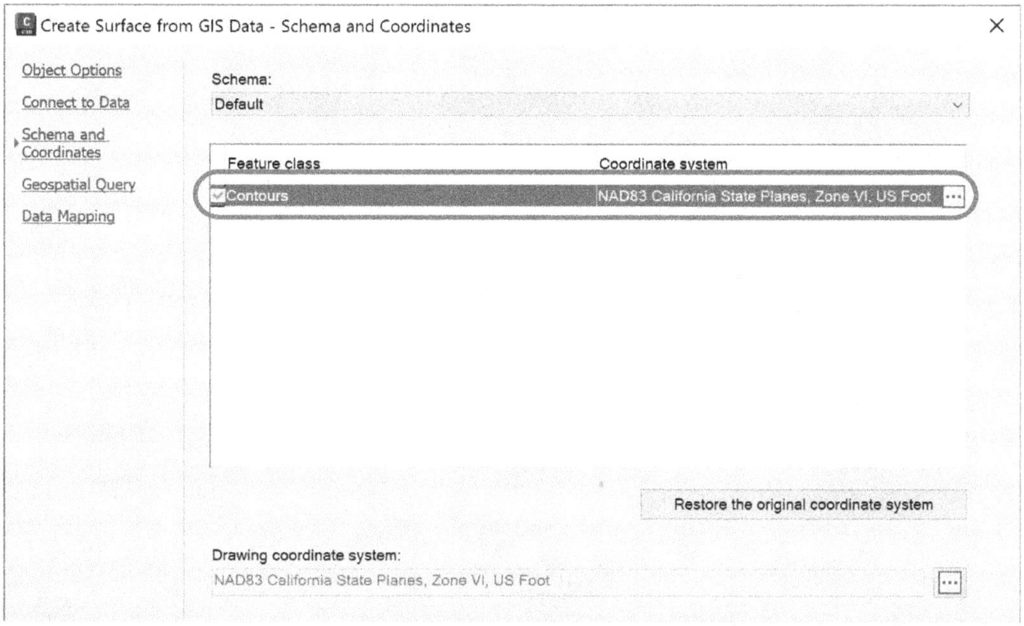

Figure 4–65

11. On the *Geospatial Query* page, clear the **Define area of interest by** option, as shown in Figure 4–66, so that the entire contours shape file is used to create a surface. Click **Next**.

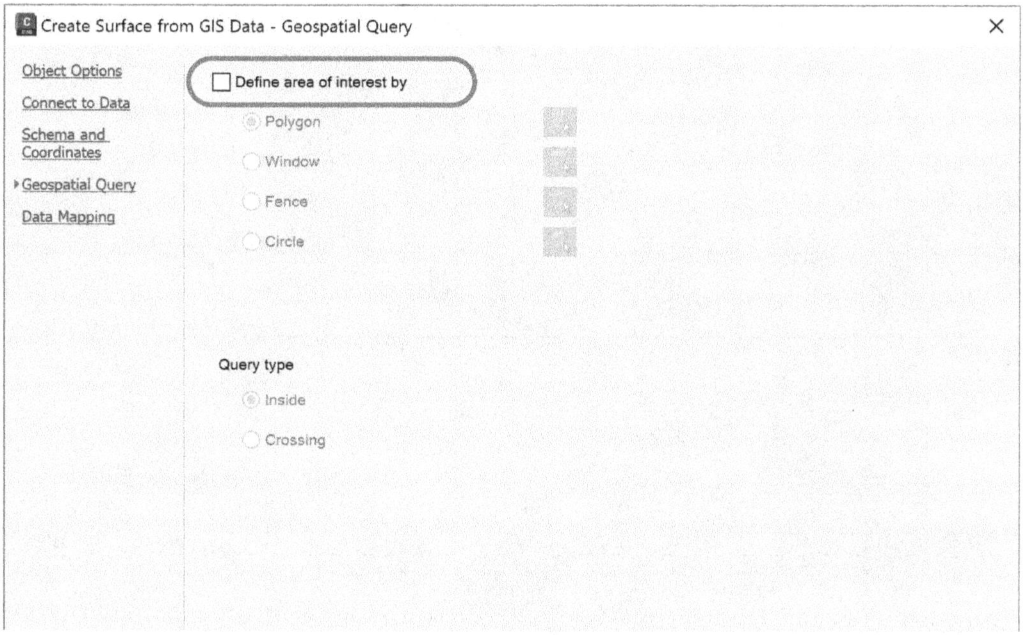

Figure 4–66

12. On the *Data Mapping* page, expand the *Elev* drop-down list and select **Elevation**, as shown in Figure 4-67.

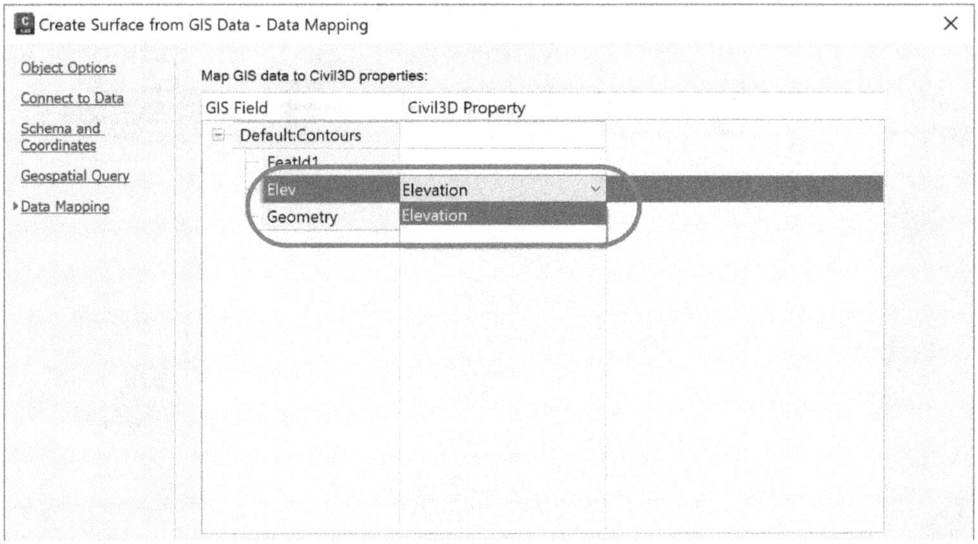

Figure 4-67

13. Click **Finish** to close the wizard. The surface will be built, as shown in Figure 4-68.

Figure 4-68

14. Save and close the drawing.

15. Open **SUF-F1.dwg** from the *C:\Civil 3D Beyond\Working\ Surface* folder to see the final result.

End of practice

4.8 Point Cloud Surface Extraction

Point clouds are dense groupings of points created by 3D scanners. The AutoCAD software has been capable of working with point clouds. The accepted point cloud file formats are .RCP and .RCS. They are faster and more efficient than the previous file formats and are created using the Autodesk Recap software.

- As with XREFs, images, and other externally referenced files, you can attach and manage point clouds using the External References Manager.

- Point cloud object snaps have been added to the *3D Object Snap* tab in the *Drafting Settings* dialog box and the 3D Object Snap options in the *Status Bar*.

- In a point cloud, you can use the **Object** option in the **UCS** command to align the active UCS to a plane.

- Dynamic UCS now aligns to a point cloud plane according to point density and alignment.

Attach Point Cloud

In the *Attach Point Cloud* dialog box, you can preview a point cloud and its detailed information (such as its classification and segmentation data) before attaching it, as shown in Figure 4–69. You can also use a geographic location for the attachment location (if the option is available).

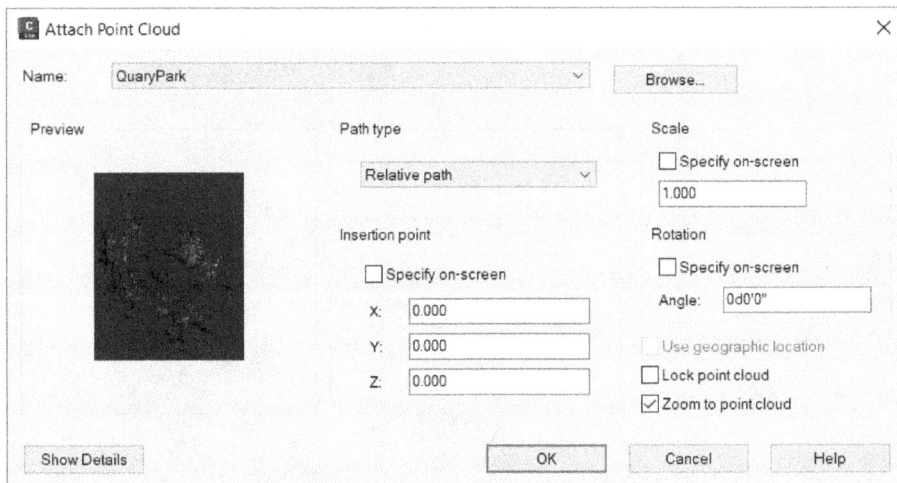

Figure 4–69

How To: Attach a Point Cloud

1. In the *Insert* tab>*Point Cloud* panel, click ⬚ (Attach).

2. In the *Select Point Cloud File* dialog box, expand the *Files of type* drop-down list and select a file type. In the *Name* area, select a file and click **Open**.

- The AutoCAD software can attach Point Cloud Project (.RCP) and Scan (.RCS) files (which are produced by the Autodesk ReCap software).

- The Autodesk ReCap software enables the creation of a point cloud project file (.RCP) that references multiple indexed scan files (.RCS). It converts scan file data into a point cloud format that can then be viewed and modified in other products.

3. In the *Attach Point Cloud* dialog box, click **Show Details** to display the point cloud information

4. In the *Path type*, *Insertion point*, *Scale*, and *Rotation* areas, set the options that you want to use to attach the point cloud, as shown in Figure 4–70. Click **OK**.

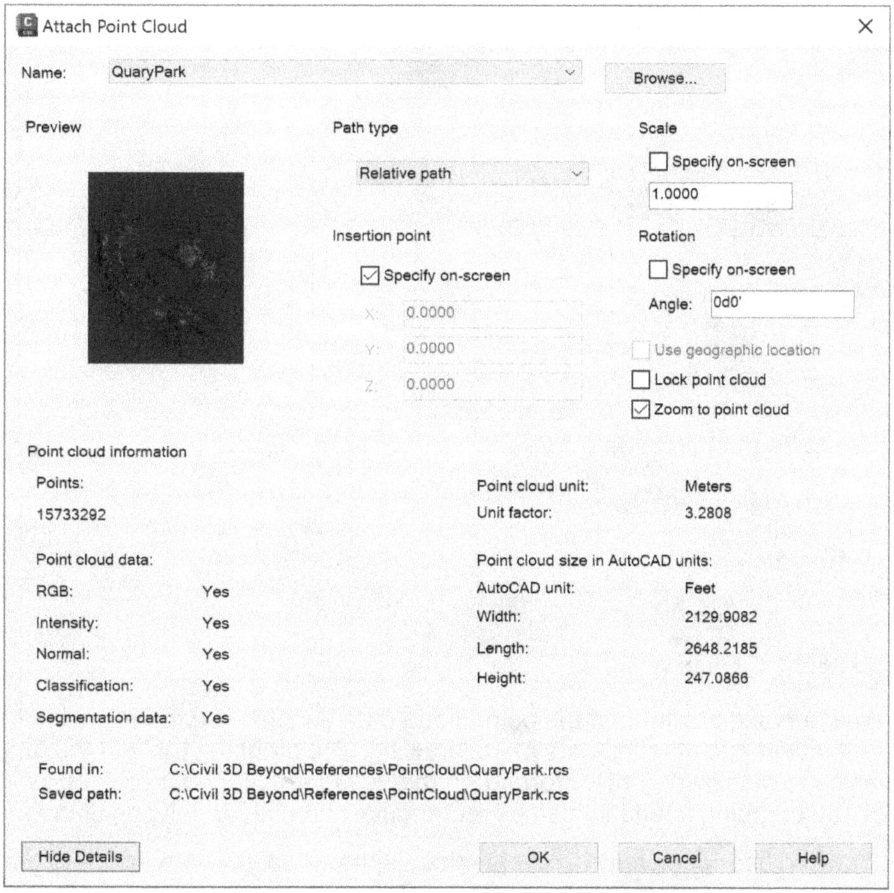

Figure 4–70

5. At the *Specify insertion point* prompt, click in the drawing to locate the point cloud.

Point Cloud Transparency

When point clouds exist in a drawing with other geometry, it can be difficult to see anything behind the point cloud. A tool in the *Point Cloud* contextual tab>*Visualization* panel enables you to adjusts the transparency of the point cloud, as shown in Figure 4–71. Alternatively, you can adjust the point cloud transparency in the *Properties* palette, as shown in Figure 4–71.

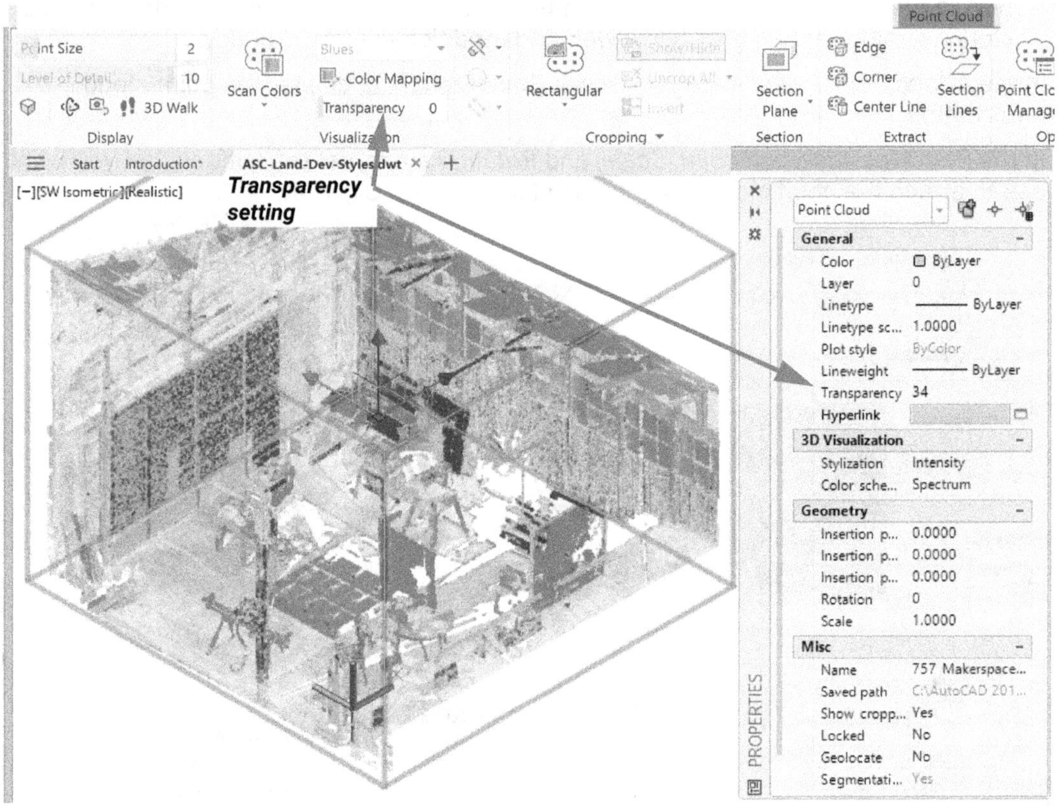

Figure 4–71

Cropping Point Clouds

Displaying the bounding box around the point cloud data enables you to determine its position in 3D space relative to the other objects in the drawing. The cropping tools in the *Cropping* panel enable you to display only the information that is required for your project, as shown in Figure 4–72. The cropping boundary can be rectangular, circular, or polygonal and is normal to the screen. You can use ⊕ (Invert) to reverse the displayed points from inside to outside the boundary.

Figure 4–72

A tool in the *Cropping* panel (displayed by expanding the panel) enables you to save and restore named cropping states. Both the visibility of the scans and regions as they are displayed and the cropping boundary are maintained in named cropping states, as shown in Figure 4–73.

Figure 4–73

💡 **Hint: List Crop States**

The **POINTCLOUDCROPSTATE** command can be used to **S**ave, **R**estore, and **D**elete crop states, as shown in Figure 4–74. Using the **?** option will list all of the available crop states.

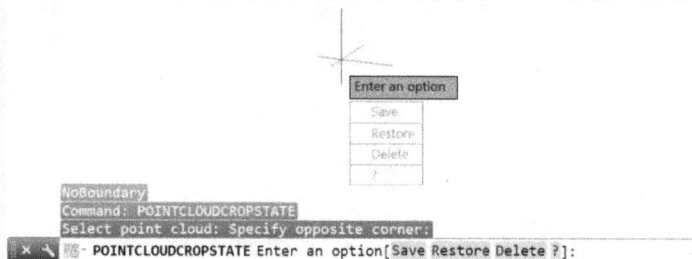

Figure 4–74

How To: Save a Named Crop State

1. Once a point cloud has been attached, select it in the model.

2. In the *Point Cloud* contextual tab>*Cropping* panel, select an appropriate crop boundary, as shown in Figure 4−75.

Figure 4−75

3. In the model, pick points to draw the boundary. If a **Polygonal** boundary was selected, press <Enter> when done.

4. At the cursor, select either **Inside** or **Outside** to indicate which points to keep.

5. Expand the *Point Cloud* contextual tab>*Cropping* panel and click ⬚ (New Crop State).

6. Enter a name for the new crop state.

Surfaces from Point Clouds

Point clouds can be used to create Autodesk Civil 3D surfaces. Once a point cloud has been attached to the drawing, it can be used to create a surface. In the *Home* tab>*Create Ground Data* panel, expand **Surfaces** and select ⬚ (Create Surface from Point Cloud), as shown in Figure 4−76.

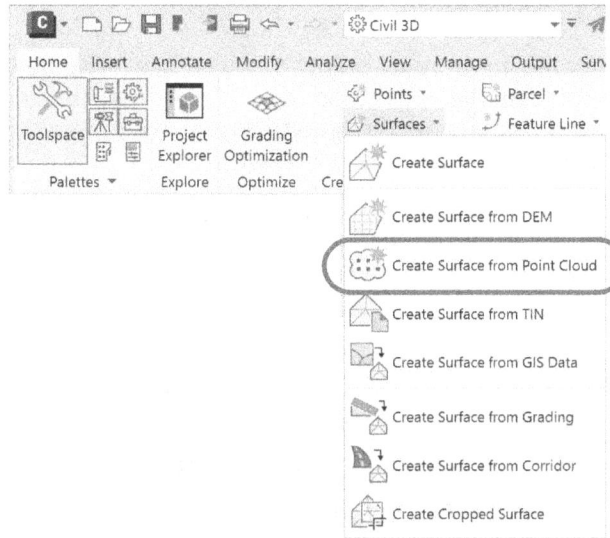

Figure 4–76

(Create Surface from Point Cloud) extracts point data from the point cloud to create a TIN surface. During the surface creation process, you can:

* Name the surface.

* Select a style for the surface.

* Select a render material.

* Select part or all of a point cloud.

* Select a filter method for non-ground points.

Point Cloud Selection

If there are one or more point clouds in the model, it is important to communicate to the software which points from the point clouds to use in the surface. The three available options for this are described as follows:

Button	Description
	Add an entire point cloud
	Remove a selection from the list
	Add a selected area of a point cloud

Non-Ground Point Filtering

When point clouds are created, they create points on any and every object visible in the scan area. This means that points can fall at the tops of buildings, trees, and other structures. In order to create a surface that represents the ground terrain, the points that are not on the ground must be filtered out. Three filter methods exist when creating a surface from point clouds.

1. **Planar average:** Predicts the elevation of a surface by finding the average elevation of a plane of points. An example is shown in Figure 4–77.

Figure 4–77

2. **Kriging interpolation:** Predicts the elevation of a surface by computing a weighted average of the elevations of neighboring points. An example is shown in Figure 4–78. This is usually the most accurate option.

Figure 4–78

3. **No filter:** Uses the point cloud point elevations for the surface elevations. An example is shown in Figure 4–79.

Figure 4–79

How To: Create a Surface from Point Clouds

1. In the *Home* tab>*Create Ground Data* panel, expand **Surfaces** and select (Create Surface from Point Cloud).

2. In the model, select the point cloud or select any of the following options in the command line, as shown in Figure 4–80:

- **Window**
- **polyGon**
- **polyLIne**

CREATESURFACEFROMPOINTCLOUD
Select a point cloud or [Window polyGon polyLIne]:

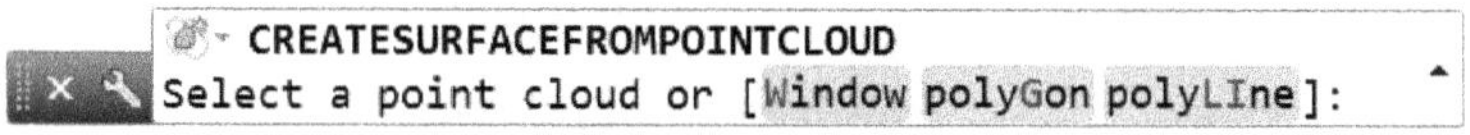

Figure 4–80

3. In the *Create TIN Surface from Point Cloud* wizard, on the *General* page, type a surface name and set the surface style and render material, as shown in Figure 4–81. Click **Next>**.

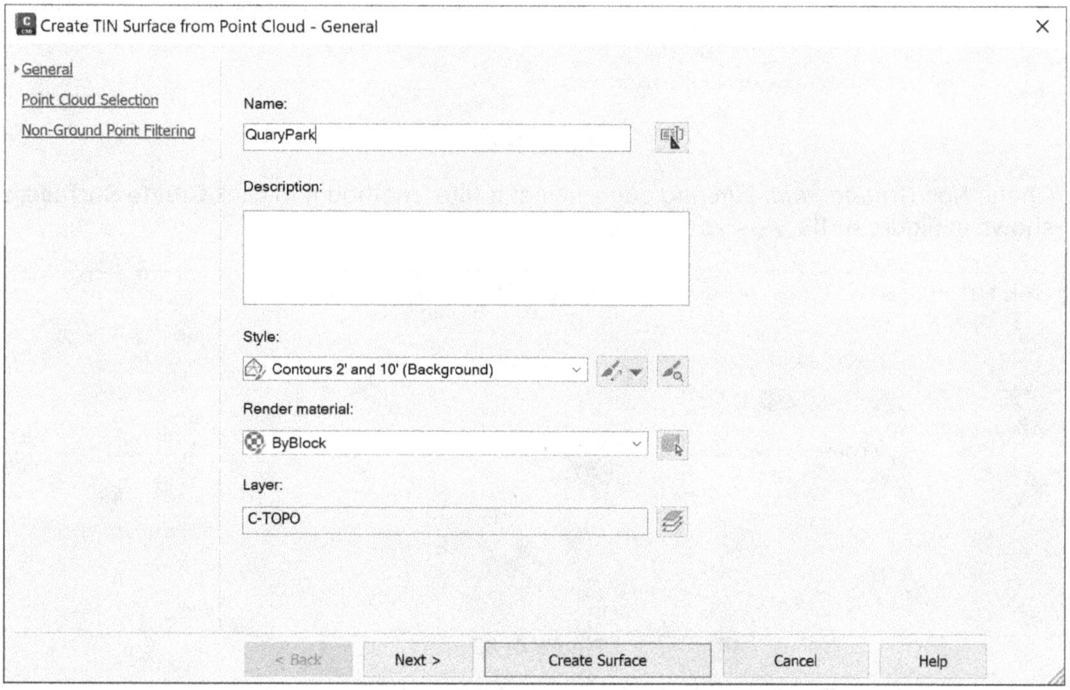

Figure 4–81

4. On the *Point Cloud Selection* page, select the point clouds or parts of the point clouds, as shown in Figure 4–82. Click **Next>**.

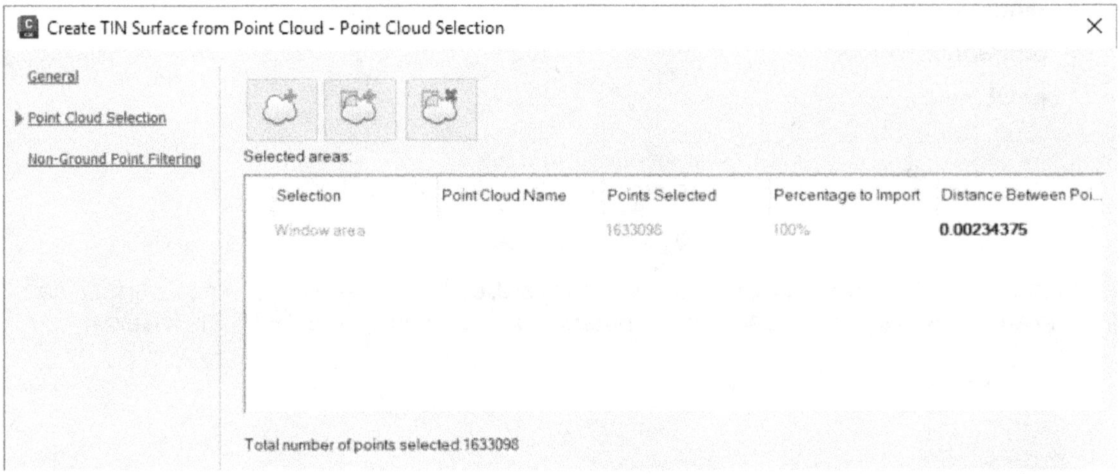

Figure 4–82

5. On the *Non-Ground Point Filtering* page, select a filter method and click **Create Surface**, as shown in Figure 4–83.

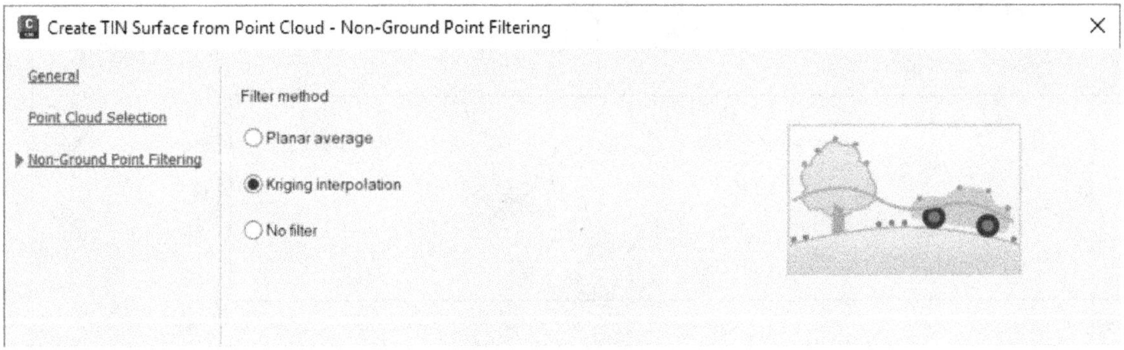

Figure 4–83

6. In the *Point Cloud Processing in Background* message box, click **Close**.

Practice 4h
(Optional) Create a Point Cloud Surface

Practice Objectives

- Gain familiarity with point clouds.
- Examine a point cloud in Civil 3D.
- Create a Civil 3D surface from point cloud data.

In this practice, you will attach a point cloud to a new drawing file, as shown in Figure 4–84. You will then create a surface from the point cloud.

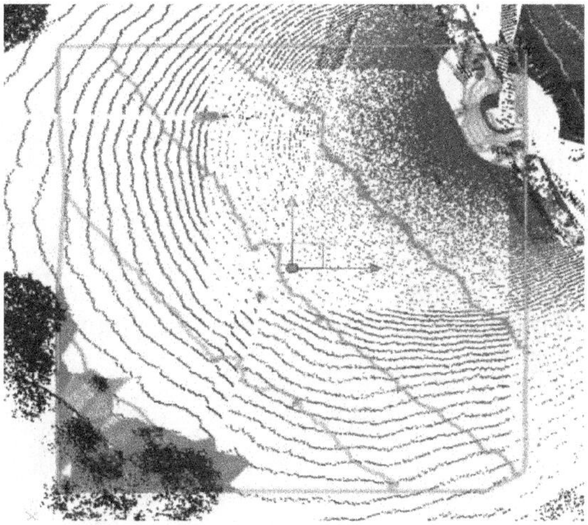

Figure 4–84

Task 1: Attach a point cloud.

1. Start a new drawing with the default Civil 3D template by clicking on ▢ (Qnew) in the top left corner, as shown in Figure 4–85.

Figure 4–85

2. In the *Insert* tab>*Point Cloud* panel, click 🔡 (Attach).

3. In the *Select Point Cloud File* dialog box, navigate to the *C:\Civil 3D Beyond\References\ PointCloud* folder. Change the *Files of type* to ***.rcs**, as shown in Figure 4–86.

Figure 4–86

4. In the *File name* area, select **Quarry Park.rcs** and click **Open**.

5. Accept the default options in the *Attach Point Cloud* dialog box, click **OK**, and use an insertion point of **0,0**. This point cloud is not geo-referenced, so the insertion point is arbitrary.

6. Save the file.

Task 2: Analyze the point cloud.

1. Select the point cloud.

2. In the *Point Cloud* contextual ribbon>*Visualization* panel, locate the *Scan Colors* drop-down list and experiment with different options, as shown in Figure 4–87.

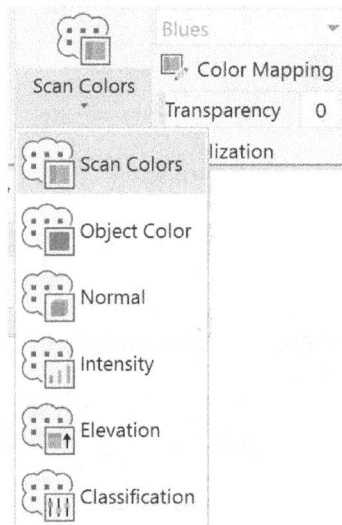

Figure 4–87

3. In the *Point Cloud* contextual ribbon>*Visualization* panel, select **Elevation** from the drop-down list and experiment with different color options, as shown in Figure 4–88.

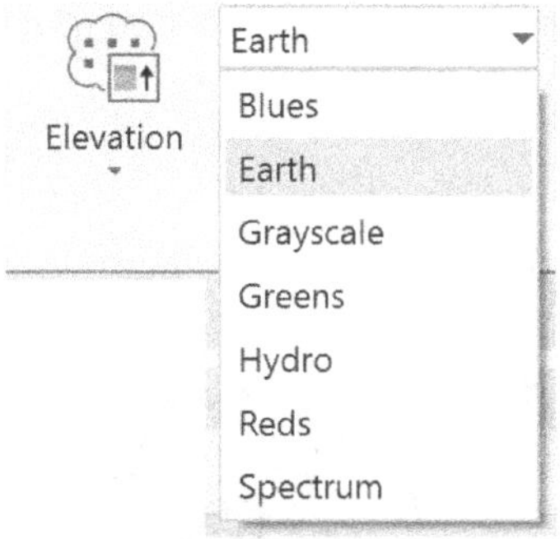

Figure 4–88

4. In the *Home* tab>*Create Ground Data* panel, expand **Surfaces** and select ⊛ (Create Surface from Point Cloud).

5. In the model, select the point cloud.

6. In the *Create TIN Surface from Point Cloud* wizard, on the *General* page, type **Quarry Park** for the surface name. Leave all other defaults and click **Next>**.

7. On the *Point Cloud Selection* page, note that the entire point cloud is already in the *Selected areas* list, which we do not want. Therefore, click ⊠ (Remove a selection from the list), as shown in Figure 4–89.

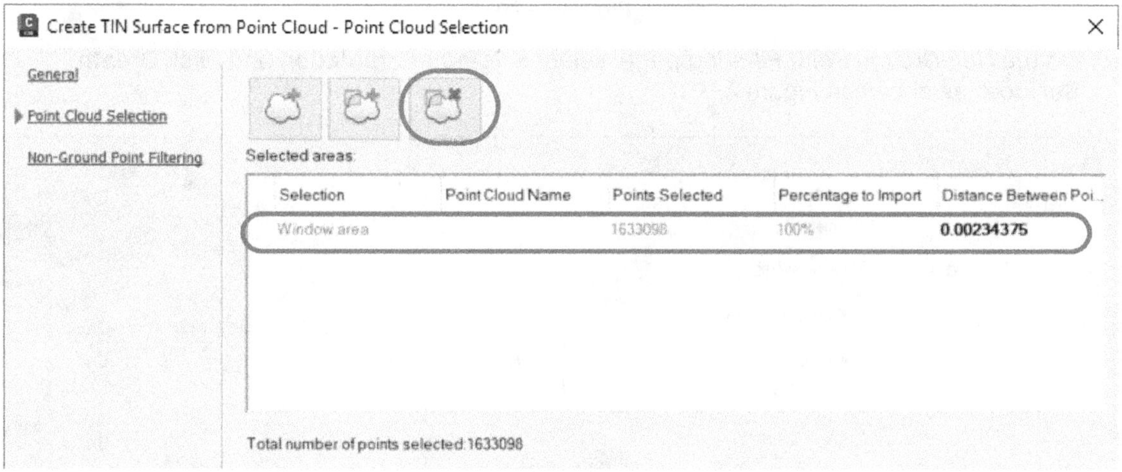

Figure 4–89

8. In the drawing area, select the point cloud and hit <Enter>. The *Point Cloud Selection* page,

   Note that the *Selected areas* list is now empty. Click ⬚ (Add a selected area of a point cloud). In the model, draw a window around the area indicated in Figure 4−90. When finished, click **Next>**.

Figure 4−90

9. On the *Non-Ground Point Filtering* page, select **Kriging interpolation** and click **Create Surface**., as shown in Figure 4−91.

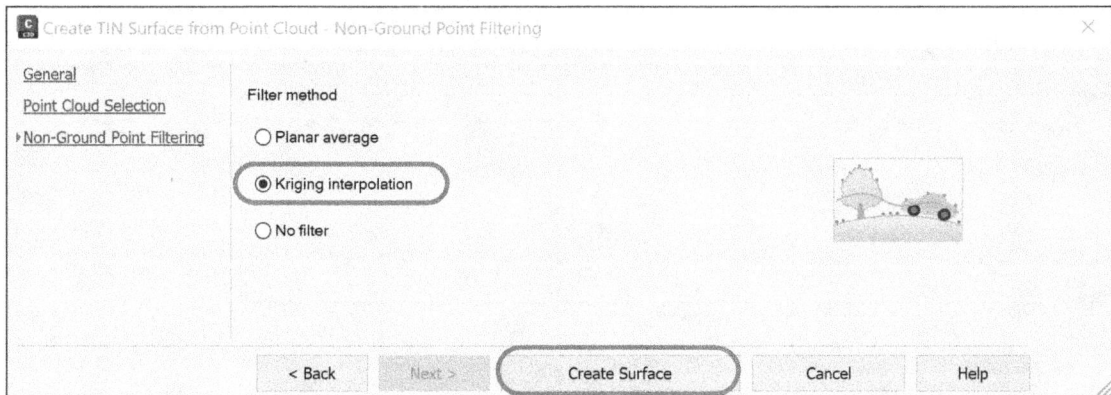

Figure 4−91

10. In the Point Cloud Processing in Background message box, click **Close**. It may take a few minutes to process the points.

11. Close the file without saving.

End of practice

4.9 3D Solid Surface from TIN Surface

The Autodesk Civil 3D software has the capability to extract an AutoCAD 3D solid surface from any TIN surface. During the extraction process, you can define the vertical properties, the output properties, and which surface to extract.

Vertical Definition

Three options are available for setting the vertical definition of a 3D solid from a TIN surface, as shown in Figure 4−92.

1. The first option creates a solid with a consistent depth across the entire surface. This may be used to quickly calculate the volume of top soil to be removed.

2. The second option creates a solid with a fixed elevation. This option may be used to quickly calculate the water volume of a pond, which will have a consistent water elevation.

3. The last option creates a solid between two surfaces. This could be used to create various solids from soil report point. Doing so provides a solid for each type of material.

Depth   *Fixed Elevation*   *Surface*

Figure 4−92

Output Properties

Multiple output settings enable you to define where the solid is created during the extraction process. The layer and color for the solid can also be set. Then, you can create the solid in the current drawing or in a new drawing. If you select a new drawing, you can set the file path and name of the new drawing by clicking (Browse).

How To: Create a 3D Solid Surface

1. In the model, select a **TIN** surface.

2. In the contextual *Surface* tab>*Surface Tools* panel, expand (Extract from Surface) and select (Extract Solids from Surface).

3. In the *Extract Solid from Surface* dialog box, shown in Figure 4–93, set the vertical definition and the required drawing output.

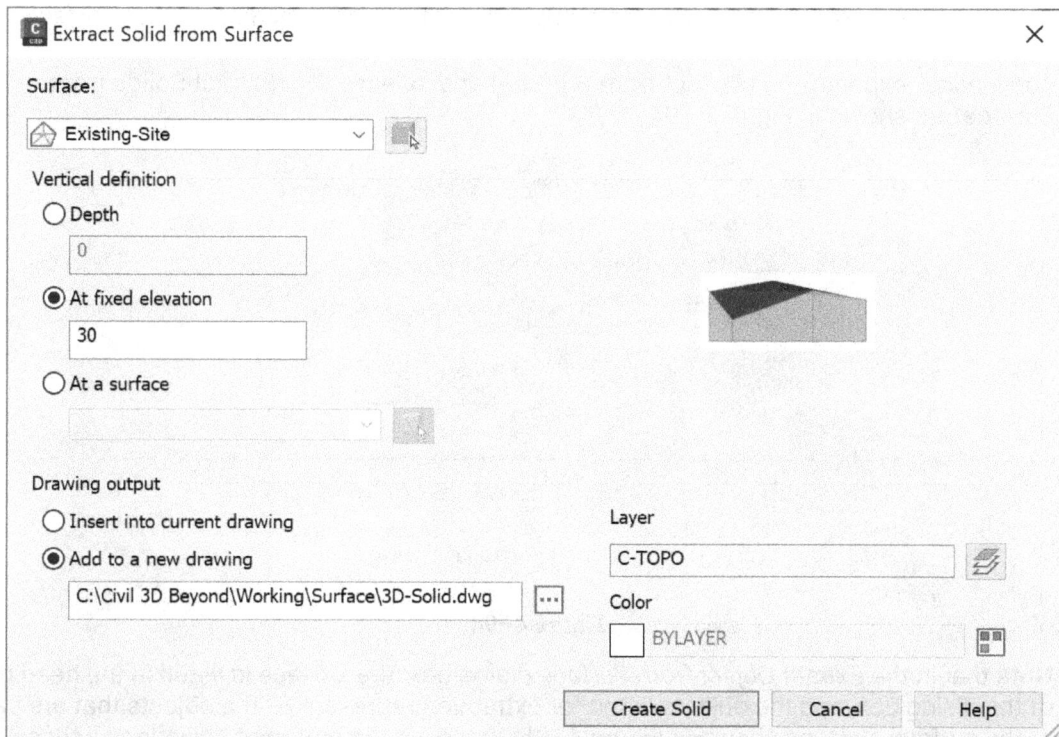

Figure 4–93

4. Click **Create Solid**.

Practice 4i
Create 3D Surface Solids

Practice Objectives

- Output the surface as a solid object.
- Adjust the readability of contour labels.

1. Open **SUF-G.dwg** from the *C:\Civil 3D Beyond\Working\ Surface* folder.

2. Select the **Existing-Site** surface in Model Space. In the contextual *Surface* tab>*Surface Tools* panel, expand ![icon] (Extract from Surface) and select ![icon] (Extract Solids from Surface), as shown in Figure 4–94.

Figure 4–94

3. Note that in the *Extract Object from Surface* dialog box, the surface is listed in the heading of the dialog box, and the objects listed for extraction represent all the objects that are part of the surface style, as shown in Figure 4–95. You have the option of selecting all these objects using the down arrow to select only specific objects.

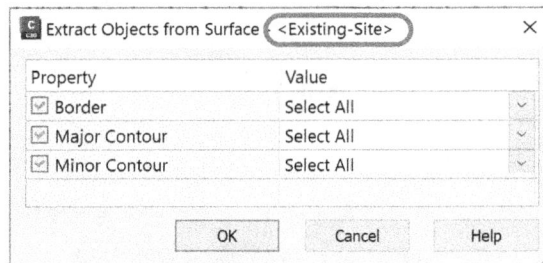

Figure 4–95

4. Click **Cancel** to exit the In the *Extract Object from Surface* dialog box, since you don't want to extract this information.

5. In the contextual *Surface* tab>*Surface Tools* panel, select ⌂ (Extract Solids from Surface)

6. In the *Extract Solid from Surface* dialog box, set the following (as shown in Figure 4–96):

    *   *Surface:* **Existing-Site**
    *   *Vertical definition:* **At fixed elevation** =100
    *   *Drawing output:* **Add to a new drawing** and save it as *C:\Civil 3D Beyond\Working\ Surface\3D-Solid.dwg*.

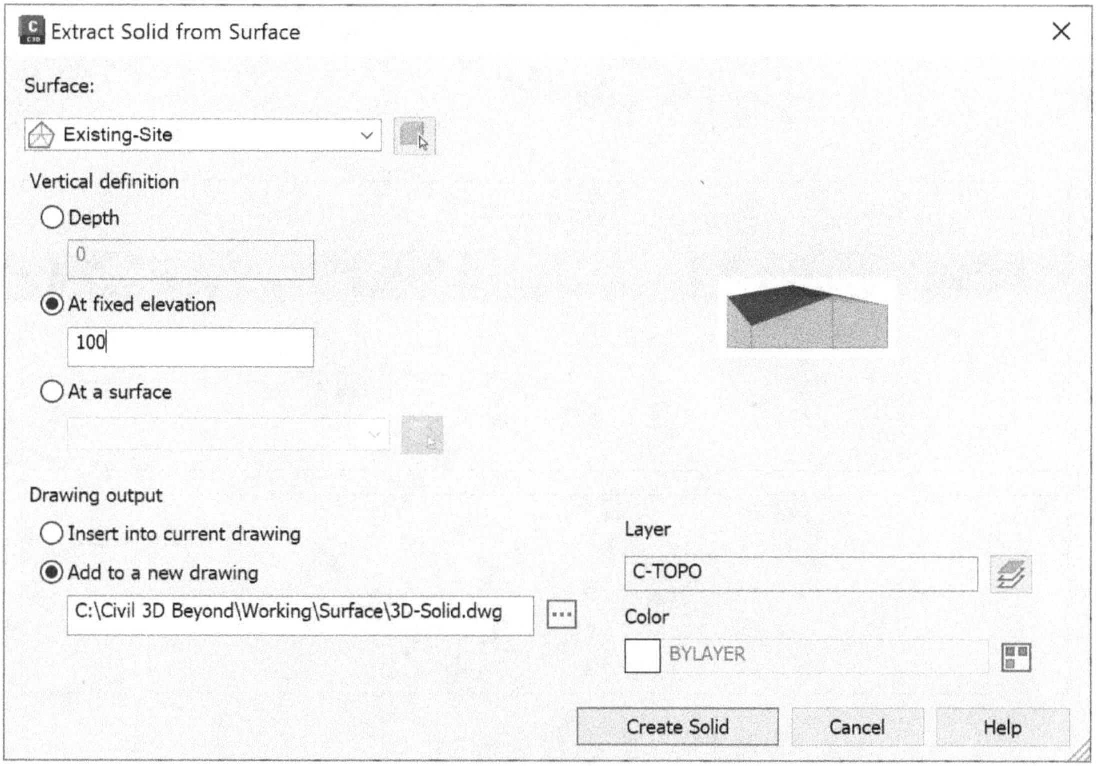

Figure 4–96

7. Click **Create Solid**, then click **OK** when prompted.

8. Open **3D-Solid.dwg** from the *C:\Civil 3D Beyond\Working\ Surface* folder. Orbit the model and verify that the bottom of the solid surface is at elevation 100, as shown in Figure 4–97.

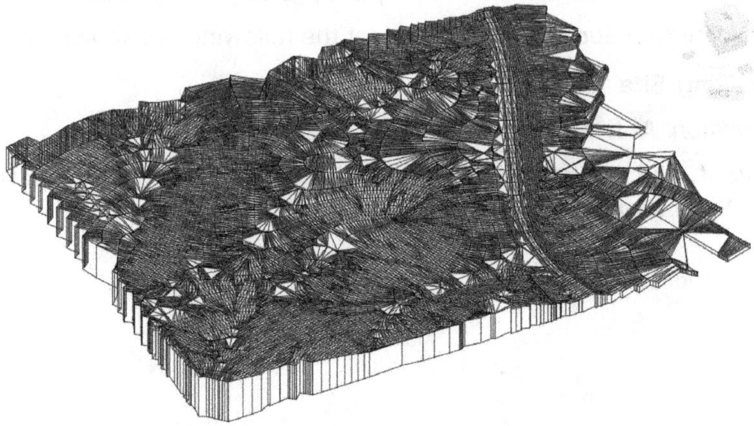

Figure 4–97

End of practice

Chapter Review Questions

1. Put the following steps in the order suggested for building a surface.

Step	Answer
a. Add breaklines, assign more data, modify the data, or edit the surface, as required.	
b. Assign data to a surface.	
c. Accumulate data.	
d. Evaluate the resulting surface.	

2. Where would you set the lowest and highest acceptable elevations for a surface?

    a. In the *Create Surface* dialog box when you are first creating the surface.

    b. In the *Definition* tab in the *Surface Properties* dialog box.

    c. In the *Analysis* tab in the *Surface Properties* dialog box.

    d. Under *Edits* within the surface definition.

3. Select which type of breakline this statement defines: *This type of breakline is a 3D polyline or feature line. It does not need a point object at each vertex because each has its own elevation.*

    a. Non-Destructive

    b. Proximity

    c. Wall

    d. Standard

4. What are the types of edits that can be done to a surface? (Select all that apply.)

    a. Line Edits

    b. Point Edits

    c. Simplify Surface

    d. Grip Edits

5. How do you remove an edit from a surface? (Select all that apply.)

   a. Clear it in the Operations Type list in the Surface Properties in the *Definition* tab.

   b. Remove it from the *Edits* list in the *Prospector* tab's preview area.

   c. Select it and press <Delete>.

   d. Delete it from the Operations Type list of the Surface Properties in the *Definition* tab.

6. Which type of boundary would you use to ensure that any data that you add to a surface is ignored if it falls outside that boundary?

   a. Hide

   b. Show

   c. Data Clip

   d. Outer

7. How do you calculate the volume between two surfaces in a specific parcel?

   a. Bounded Volumes

   b. Grid Volume Surface

   c. TIN Volume Surface

   d. Show Cut/Fill Labels in a grid pattern

8. Which of the following is NOT a vertical definition option when creating a solid surface from a TIN surface?

   a. Kriging interpolation

   b. Depth

   c. Fixed elevation

   d. Surface

Command Summary

Button	Command	Location
	Add Data	• **Contextual Ribbon:** *Surface* tab>*Modify* panel
	Create Surface	• **Ribbon:** *Home* tab>*Create Ground Data* panel • **Command Prompt:** CreateSurface
	Create Surface from Point Clouds	• **Contextual Ribbon:** *Point Cloud* tab>*Civil 3D* panel
	Edit Surface	• **Contextual Ribbon:** *Surface* tab>*Modify* panel
	Resolve Crossing Breaklines	• **Contextual Ribbon:** *Surface* tab>*Analyze* panel • **Command Prompt:** BreaklineTool
	Surface Properties	• **Contextual Ribbon:** *Surface* tab>*Modify* panel • **Command Prompt:** EditSurfaceProperties
	Volumes Dashboard	• **Ribbon:** *Analyze* tab>*Volumes and Materials* panel • **Contextual Ribbon:** *Surface* tab>*Analyze* panel • **Command Prompt:** VolumesDashboard

Corridors - Beyond the Basics

Corridors are complex Civil 3D® objects representing roads and other travel ways, dams, breakwaters, and much more. In some cases, corridors are used for strip-mining and grading.

In this chapter, you will explore more tools for creating and managing assemblies and additional features for profiles and profile views, then create a roundabout portion of a corridor. You will also create a mass haul diagram of the corridor to study the cumulative cut and fill material volumes. Finally you will change the way the corridor looks in the drawing.

Learning Objectives

- Create new assemblies from copies of existing ones.
- Manage assemblies for distribution.
- Superimpose profiles to calculate elevation points.
- Create a roundabout intersection.
- Review and edit corridor sections to make changes to a selected station.
- Create a mass-haul diagram.
- Change code sets.

5.1 Subassembly Composer

The Autodesk® Civil 3D® software comes with stock subassemblies covering a wide variety of situations. In most cases, these will suffice for any situation land development or road projects encounter.

However, these stock subassemblies are not dynamic. Dynamic subassemblies can be created using the dot net (.net) programming language using the Subassembly Composer, which is an additional program that is included with Autodesk Civil 3D.

The *Subassembly Composer* is rather complex and is not covered in extensive detail in this guide; however, an overview is provided for you to understand its capabilities and potential use.

The *Subassembly Composer* interface is broken down into four major areas plus a toolbox side panel, as shown in Figure 5-1.

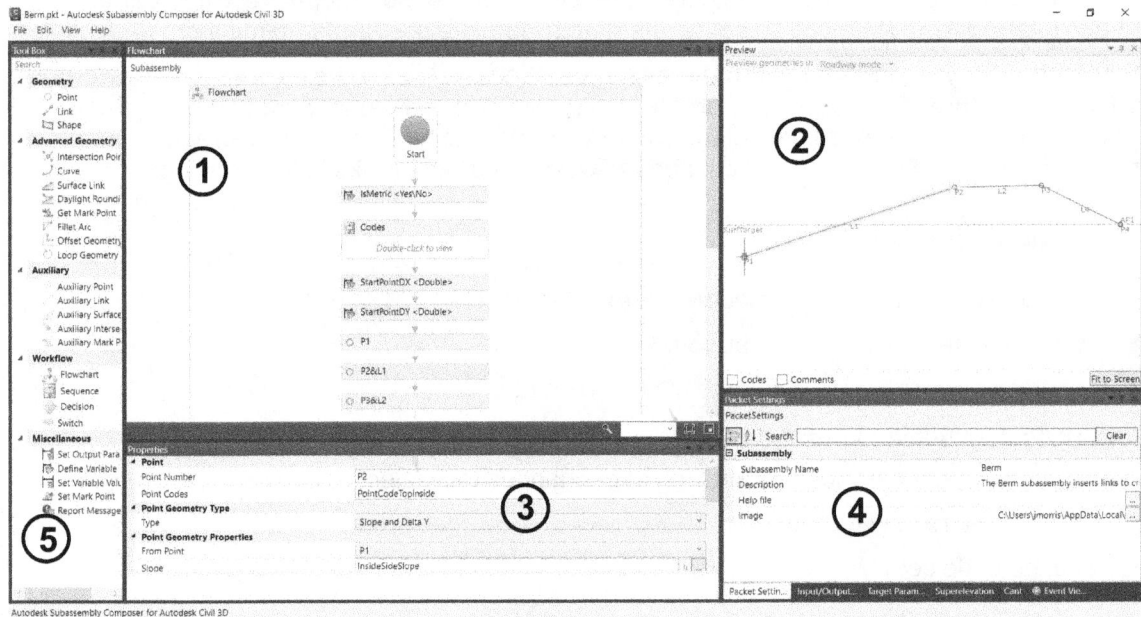

Figure 5-1

1. **Flowchart:** This area provides a logical, graphical overview of the subassembly. Place and rearrange the various elements that make up the subassembly. Parts can be moved by clicking and dragging them to their new position.

2. **Preview:** This area provides a preview of the selected element of the subassembly. As the properties of the element are altered (in the *Properties* panel), the preview updates to provide a graphical view of the element.

3. **Properties:** This area is where the details of the selected element are manipulated. Many of the entries are controlled through populated lists and defaults to ensure the proper variables are entered to prevent mistakes and typos. Ordinary values can also be entered.

4. **Multi-use panel:** This area contains the following tabs:

   - *Packet Settings:* General information of the packet.
   - *Input/Output Parameters:* Tabular view of the various input and output parameters along with their default values.
   - *Target Parameters:* Tabular view of the various target parameters along with their values used for the preview panel.
   - *Superelevation:* Settings for the superelevations, their values used for the preview panel, and a toggle if they are enabled for the preview.
   - *Cant:* Settings for the cants (superelevations for rail) and their values used for the preview panel.
   - *Event Viewer:* A record of all the events (errors and triggers) that have occurred.

5. **Toolbox:** This is a collection of various generic, auxiliary, and advanced geometry elements, flowchart components, and miscellaneous tools.

5.2 Modifying Assemblies

Attaching Subassemblies

The easiest way to add an Autodesk Civil 3D subassembly to an assembly is using *TOOL PALETTES*. You can open *TOOL PALETTES* by clicking [icon] (Tool Palettes) in the *Home* tab>*Palettes* panel (shown in Figure 5–2) or in the *View* tab>*Palettes* panel. You can also use <Ctrl>+<3>.

Figure 5–2

The Autodesk Civil 3D software provides a number of stock subassembly tool palettes, as shown in Figure 5–3. In addition, it is continually updating and adding new subassemblies with every release.

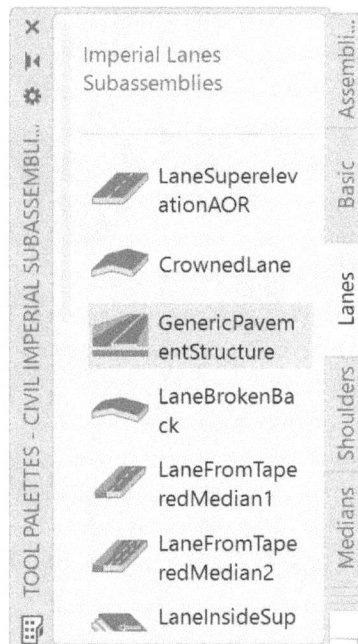

Figure 5–3

There are separate tool palettes for metric and imperial units. Ensure that you are using the correct palette. To select the correct palette, right-click on the *TOOL PALETTES* band (top or side of palettes) and select the required palette, as shown in Figure 5–4.

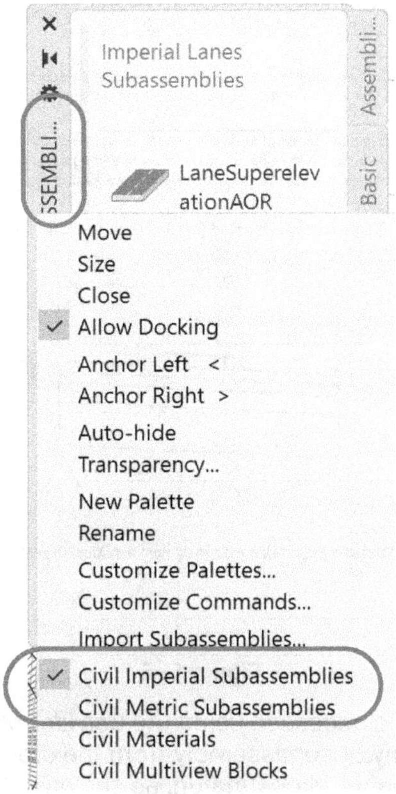

Figure 5–4

The Help file is an invaluable resource for an updated list and information about the specific attributes and properties of each subassembly, as shown in Figure 5–5.

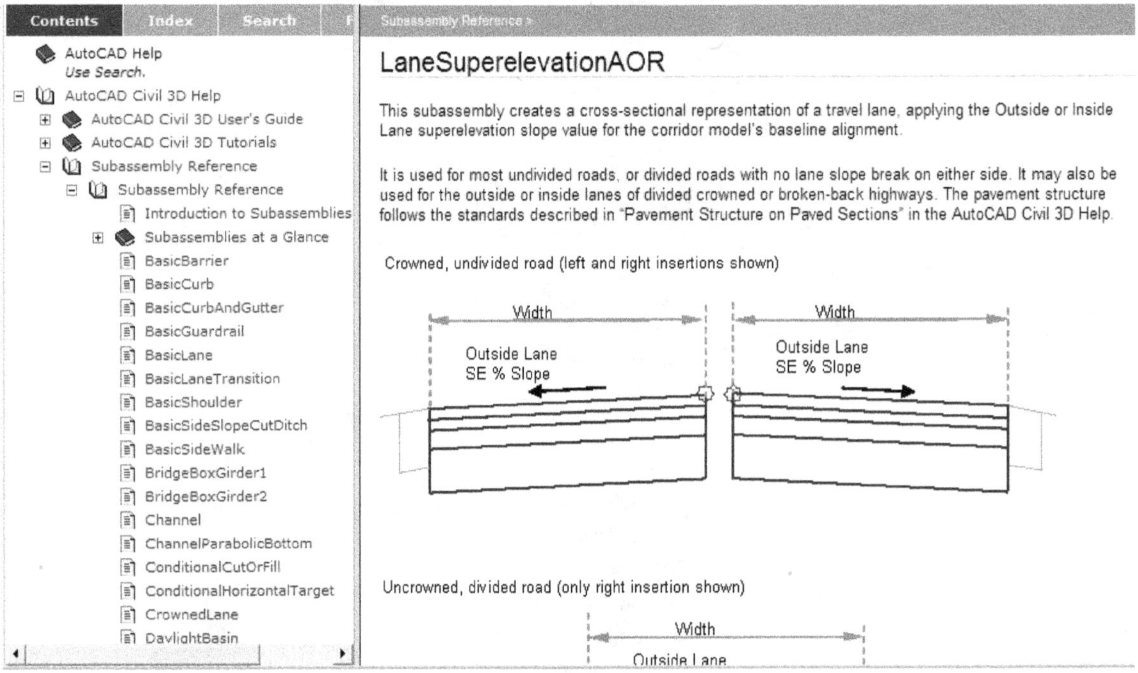

Figure 5–5

Additional subassemblies can be accessed using the *Corridor Modeling* catalogs. Open the catalog by selecting an assembly or subassembly from the drawing, then in the *Assembly/Subassembly* tab>*Launch Pad* panel, click **Catalog**, as shown in Figure 5–6.

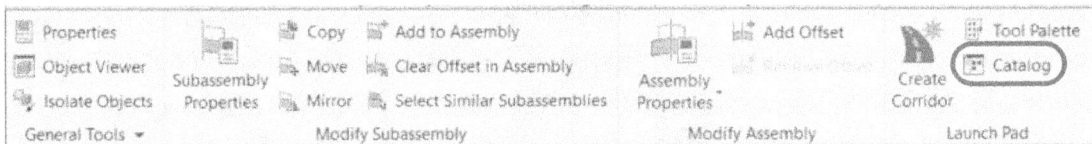

Figure 5–6

You can drag and drop the catalog onto a tool palette, if required. When working with *TOOL PALETTES* and the *Properties* palette, you might find it helpful to toggle off the **Allow Docking** option to prevent them from docking on the sides of the screen. Right-click on the palette's title bar to set the option, as shown in Figure 5–7.

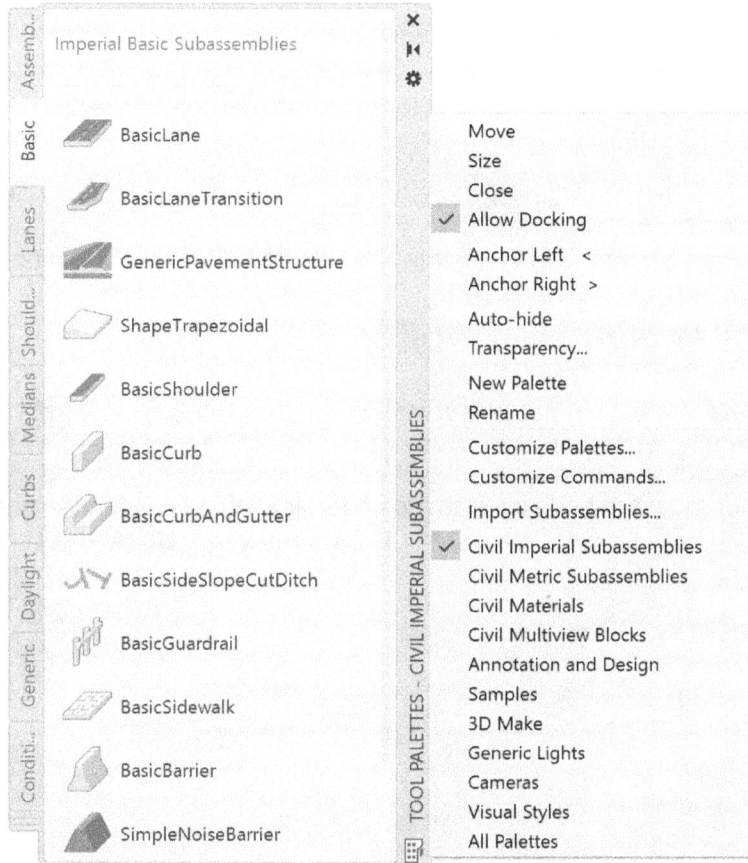

Figure 5–7

Detaching Subassemblies

Individual subassemblies can be deleted directly from an assembly with the AutoCAD® **Erase** command or using **Assembly Properties**. Assemblies can also be deleted with the **Erase** command.

Copying Assemblies

Assemblies can be copied with the AutoCAD **Copy** command. Copying an assembly creates an independent assembly without a relationship to the original. Select the assembly by selecting the **Assembly Baseline**.

Modifying Subassemblies

In the Autodesk Civil 3D software, subassemblies can be mirrored, copied, and moved across the assembly to which it is attached by selecting the subassemblies, right-clicking, and

selecting **Mirror, Copy to,** or **Move to**. Alternatively, you can click ▧ (Mirror), ▧ (Copy), or

▧ (Move) in the *Assembly* tab>*Modify Subassembly* panel. This enables you to create one side of the roadway and create a mirrored image for the other side in one step.

> 💡 **Hint: AutoCAD Mirror, Move, and Copy Commands**
>
> The basic AutoCAD **Mirror**, **Move,** and **Copy** commands do not work for subassemblies. You need to use the special commands from the shortcut menu or Modify Subassembly panel.

Select Similar Subassemblies

It is often necessary to create multiple assemblies with the same subassemblies for various purposes. For example, a corridor that includes an intersection might need a full assembly that includes both sides of the road, an assembly that includes just the right side of the road, and another that includes just the left side of the road. It might also include two other assemblies that require the assembly marker to be placed at the edge of pavement rather than the crown, as shown in Figure 5–8.

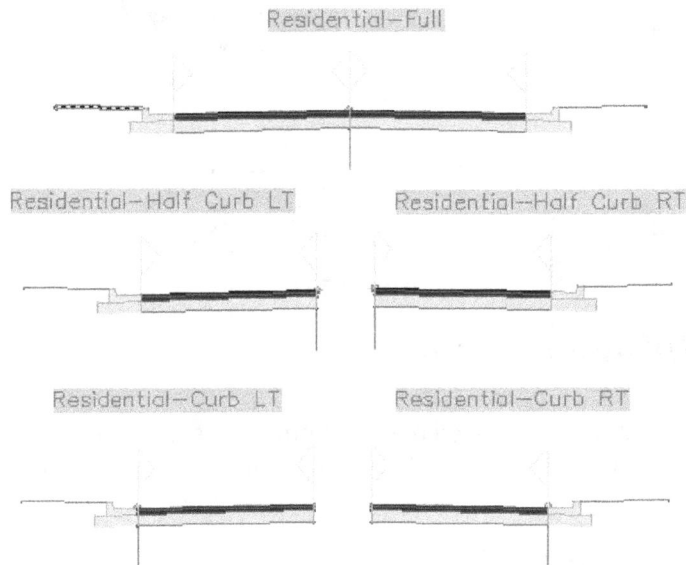

Figure 5–8

However, making changes to all of the assemblies when a design parameter changes can be time-consuming. To ensure that all similar subassemblies are modified at the same time when

a design change occurs, you can select one subassembly, click ⬚ (Select Similar Subassemblies) in the *Assembly* tab>*Modify Subassembly* panel, and change the parameter in the AutoCAD *Properties* palette.

Getting More Information on Subassemblies

Many subassemblies have a large number of parameters. If you want to read the documentation on a subassembly, right-click on its tool icon in *TOOL PALETTES* and select **Help**. You can also find out more from *Subassembly Properties* and *Assembly Properties* using the **Subassembly help** icon, as shown in Figure 5–9.

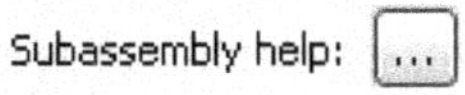

Subassembly help: [...]

Figure 5–9

Practice 5a
Create New Assemblies from Existing Ones

Practice Objective

- Create and modify assemblies for use in an intersection model.

In this practice, you will create assemblies from copies of the existing assemblies. **Note:** There are AutoCAD fields that contain the names of the assemblies for easy identification.

Task 1: Create the assemblies required for the intersection.

1. Open **COR-A.dwg** from the *C:\Civil 3D Beyond\Working\ Corridors* folder.
2. In the *View* tab>*Named Views* panel, select the preset view **Assemblies-Collector**.
3. Start the AutoCAD **Copy** command. Copy the **Collector-Full** assembly and its name (which is an AutoCAD field) to two locations below the original, as shown in Figure 5–10.

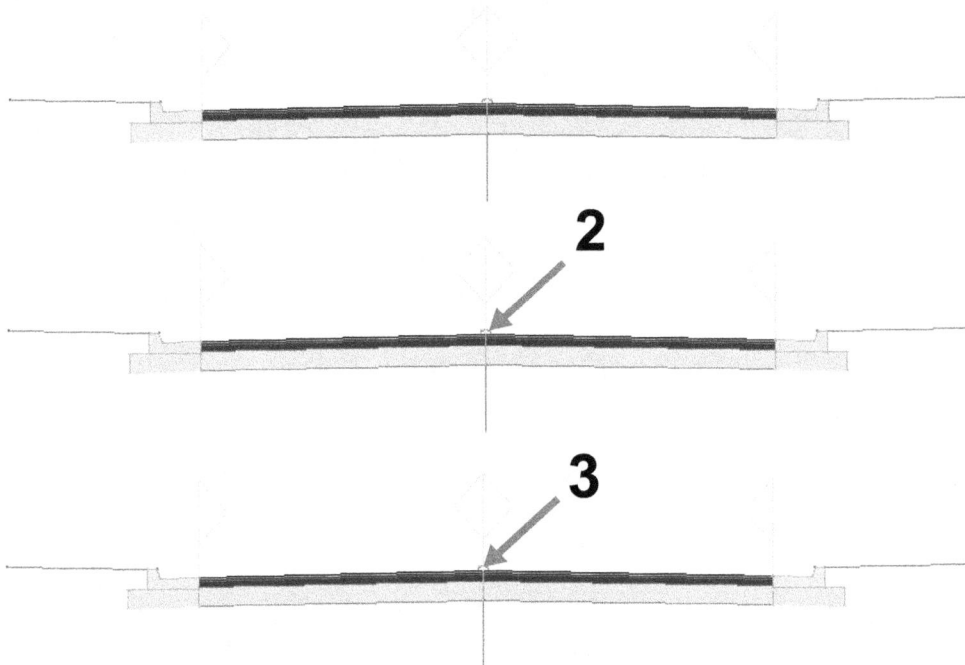

Figure 5–10

4. Select the second assembly baseline, right-click, and select **Assembly Properties**. In the *Information* tab, change the *Name* to **Residential-Half Curb LT** and click **OK**. When you regenerate the drawing, the name in the field will update.

5. Use the AutoCAD **Erase** command to erase the right **LaneSuperelevationAOR**, the right **UrbanCurbGutterGeneral**, and the right **LinkWidthAndSlope**. Select each subassembly individually rather than using the window or crossing selection method.

6. Select the third assembly baseline, right-click, and select **Assembly Properties**. In the *Information* tab, change the *Name* to **Residential-Half Curb RT** and click **OK**.

7. Regenerate the drawing so the name in the field will update.

8. Start the AutoCAD **Erase** command and erase the left **LaneSuperelevationAOR**, the left **UrbanCurbGutter General**, and the left **LinkWidthAndSlope**, as shown in Figure 5-11.

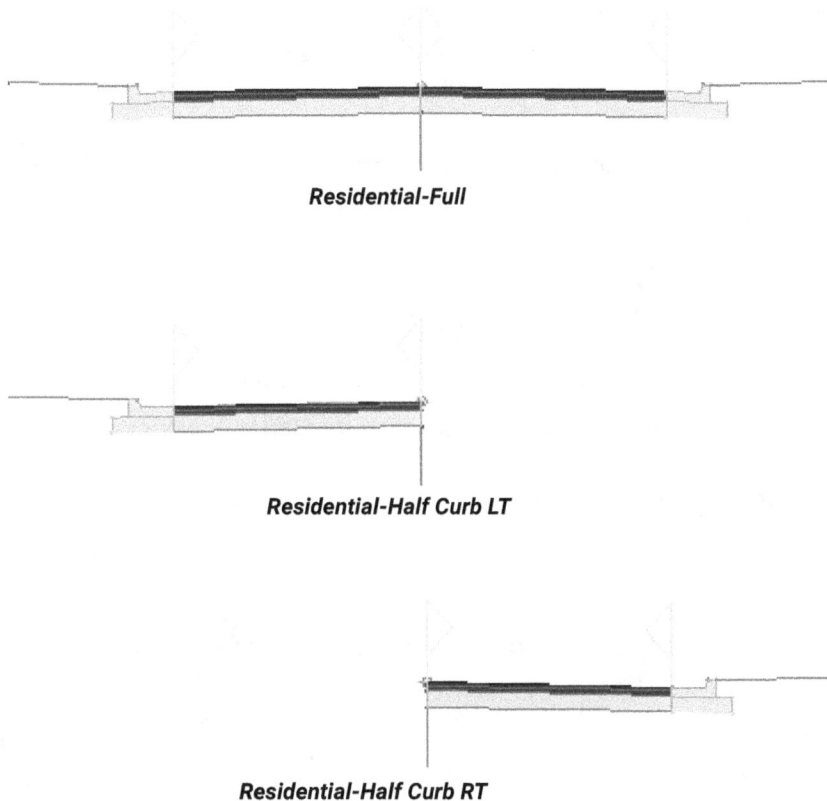

Residential-Full

Residential-Half Curb LT

Residential-Half Curb RT

Figure 5-11

Task 2: Create a curb return assembly.

To include the intersection in the corridor model, you need another assembly to go around the curb returns. This assembly will have the assembly baseline at the edge of pavement or flange of the curb and gutter. It is important to create the assembly with the lane inserted first for the **Intersection** tool to be able to set the correct transitions at the centerline.

> **Note:** *Open TOOL PALETTES by clicking* ⬚ *in the View tab>Palettes panel, if it is not already open.*

1. In the *Home* tab>*Create Design* panel, expand **Assembly** and select **Create Assembly**.

2. In the *Create Assembly* dialog box, name the new assembly **Residential-Curb Return**. Leave the other settings at their defaults, and click **OK**. Click in the drawing to place the new assembly.

3. In the *Lanes* tool palette, select the **LaneSuperelevationAOR** subassembly to add it to your assembly. In the AutoCAD *Properties* palette, confirm that the following are set:

    *   *Side:* **Left**
    *   *Width*: **14.75'**
    *   *Slope*: **+2**

4. To add the left lane subassembly, select the assembly baseline object.

5. In the *Curbs* tool palette, select the **UrbanCurbGutterGeneral** subassembly to add it to your assembly.

6. In the AutoCAD *Properties* palette, confirm that the following are set:

    *   *Side*: **Right**
    *   *Dimensions B*: **24"**

7. Select the assembly baseline to add the curb and gutter, as shown in Figure 5–12.

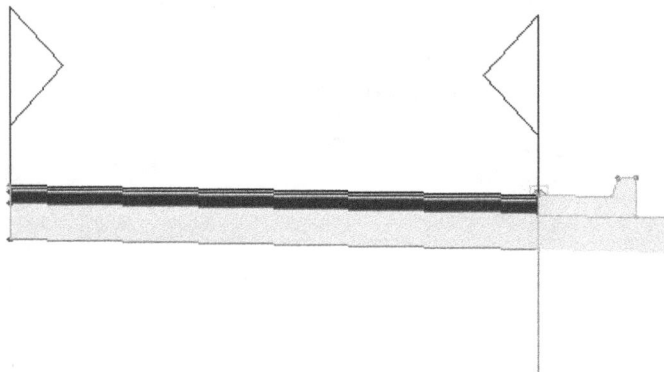

Figure 5–12

You will now create a subassembly that links the back of curb to the property line.

8. In the *Subassemblies* tool palette, select the *Generic* tab and select the **LinkWidthAndSlope** subassembly. In the AutoCAD *Properties* palette, in the *Advanced Properties*, set the following:

- *Side*: **Right**
- *Width*: **7.193'**

9. Insert the subassembly at the end of the **UrbanCurbGutterGeneral** subassembly, as shown in Figure 5–13.

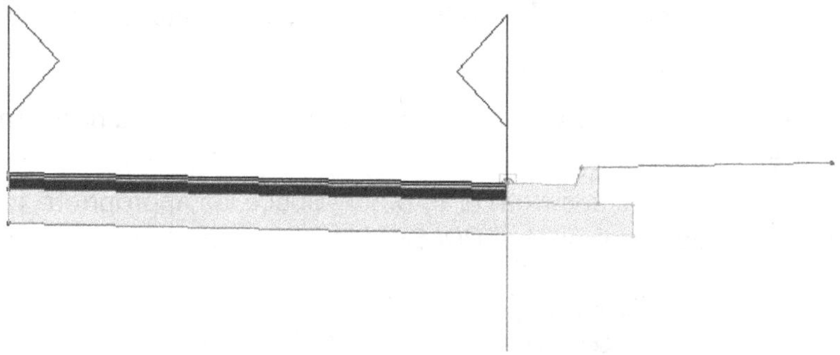

Figure 5–13

10. Press <Esc> to exit the subassembly command and save the drawing.

End of practice

5.3 Managing Assemblies

Assemblies are small in size but very important components to a road design project. They are often standardized to meet requirements spelled out by the various governing agencies or project requirements; hence, the more they can be reused on a company-wide basis, the more efficient the overall design workflow becomes.

Identifying Assemblies

Assemblies are small and tend to get lost in the overall Model Space of the project. The following are some tips to make it easier to find, identify, and manage assemblies in a project:

- Name the assemblies with fields so the identification is easier.

- Establish AutoCAD named views where the assemblies are and name the views appropriately.

- Remove or insert assemblies from or to Model Space, as appropriate, using the right-click menu of the assembly in the *TOOLSPACE>Prospector* tab, as shown in Figure 5-14.

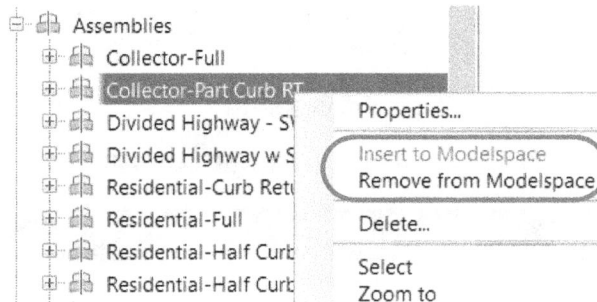

Figure 5-14

- Note that in the right-click menu of the assembly in *TOOLSPACE>Prospector* tab, there is also a **Zoom to** feature.

Sharing Assemblies

Assemblies can be shared with the Autodesk Civil 3D software in three ways:

- Assemblies can be dragged from the drawing area to a tool palette. The tool palette can then be shared, as shown in Figure 5–15.

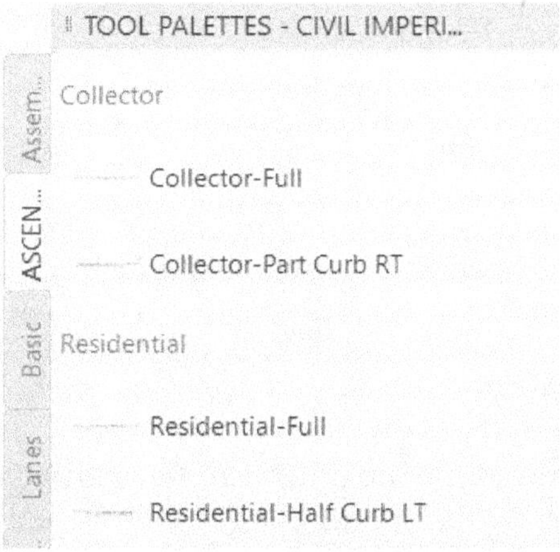

Figure 5–15

- The *Content Browser* can be used to add assemblies to a catalog.

- Assemblies can be placed in their own drawing files and shared by dragging the assembly drawing into the destination drawing file. If this method is used, the assembly drawing must only contain the assemblies that you want to share.

Practice 5b
Manage Assemblies

Practice Objectives

- Modify assemblies from another project.
- Create an assembly library in *TOOL PALETTES*.
- Create AutoCAD named views to find the assemblies.
- Insert fields for the assembly names.

In this practice, you will open a drawing containing other assemblies. You will modify one of them and then create a palette to share the assemblies. Finally, you will study ways of finding the assemblies within your project.

Task 1: Modify an assembly.

1. Open **Assem-Reference.dwg** from the *C:\Civil 3D Beyond\Ascent-Config\Assembly Sets* folder.

2. In the *View* tab>*Named Views* panel, select the preset view **Assemblies-BLVD**.

3. Locate the assembly named **Divided Highway - SW - DL**, as shown in Figure 5–16.

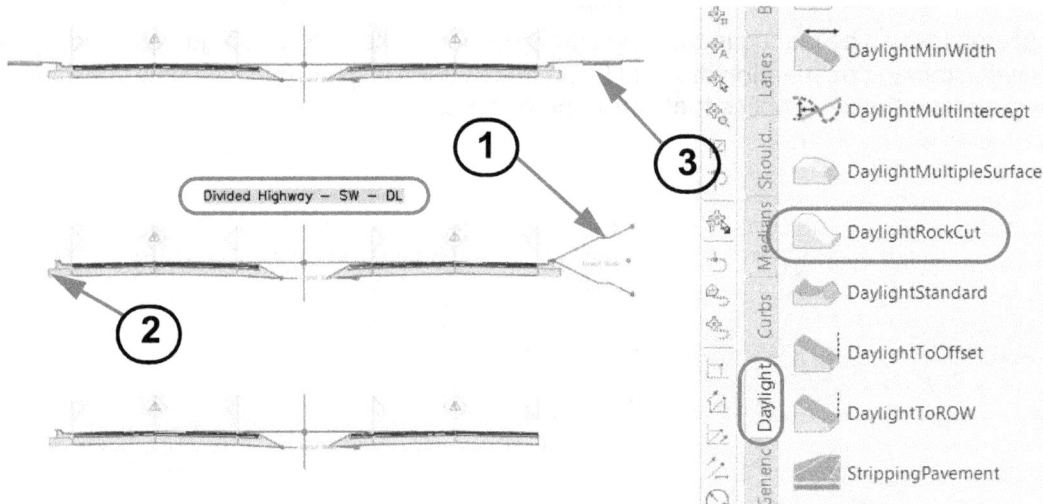

Figure 5–16

4. If needed, open *TOOL PALETTES* by clicking ![Tool Palettes icon] (Tool Palettes) in the *Home* tab>*Palettes* panel.

5. In the *Daylight* tool palette, select the **DaylightRockCut** subassembly.

6. When prompted for a marker point, select **Replace** (either from the command line or the right-click menu) instead. Then, select the existing daylight subassembly to be replaced, as marked **(1)** in Figure 5−16.

7. Press <Enter> to finish the command.

8. Select the newly inserted daylight subassembly, right-click, and select **Mirror**. At the *select marker point within assembly:* prompt, select the far left marker, as marked **(2)** in Figure 5−16.

9. Select the first **DaylightRockCut** subassembly (on the right side) and erase it.

10. Select the **Sidewalk** subassembly marked **(3)** in Figure 5−16. In the *Subassembly* contextual tab>*Modify Subassembly* panel, click ![icon] (Copy). For the marker point, select the far right point where you had just erased the *Daylight* subassembly. Figure 5−17 shows the final result.

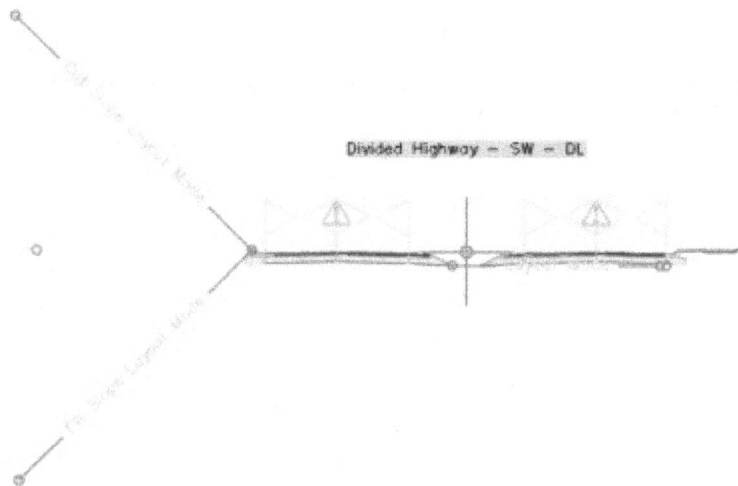

Divided Highway − SW − DL

Figure 5−17

11. Save the drawing.

Task 2: Create an Assembly palette.

In order to share assemblies throughout an organization, the drawings containing the assemblies need to be centrally located so all users have access to them. They can then be used to create an *Assembly* palette to serve as a library.

1. Save the drawing as **<Your Initials>-Assemblies.dwg** in the *C:\Civil 3D Beyond\Ascent-Config\Assembly Sets* folder.

2. In *TOOL PALETTES*, right-click on the top tab (*Assemblies*) and select **New Palette** from the menu, as shown in Figure 5–18. Name the new palette **<Your Initials>- Assemblies**.

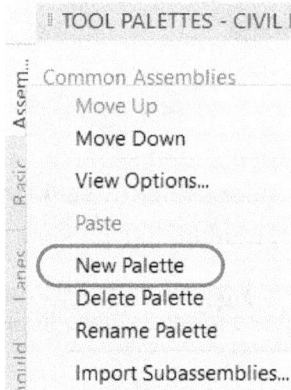

Figure 5–18

3. In the new palette, from the right-click menu, select **Add Text**, as shown in Figure 5–19. Type **Collector** for the text.

Figure 5–19

4. In the *TOOLSPACE>Prospector* tab, expand the *Assemblies* branch, right-click on **Collector-Full**, and select **Zoom to**, as shown in Figure 5–20.

Figure 5–20

5. Select the assembly by picking the red vertical centerline, then click on the lower part of the red centerline and drag it into *TOOL PALETTES*, as shown in Figure 5–21. Release it there. Do NOT select the grip when clicking and dragging.

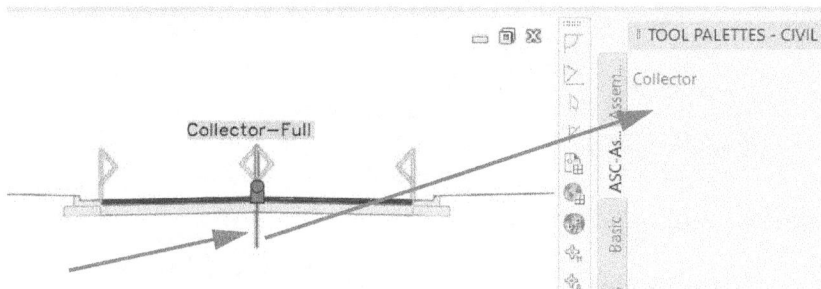

Figure 5–21

6. Repeat this for **Collector-Part Curb RT**.

7. Create a **Residential** text and drag the following under it:

   • **Residential-Full**

   • **Residential-Half Curb LT**

   • **Residential Half Curb RT**

   • **Residential-Curb Return**

8. Create a **Boulevard** text and drag the following under it:

   • **Divided Highway w SW**

   • **Divided Highway -SW - DL**

   • **Divided Highway Curb - NoCurb**

9. The final result should look like Figure 5–22.

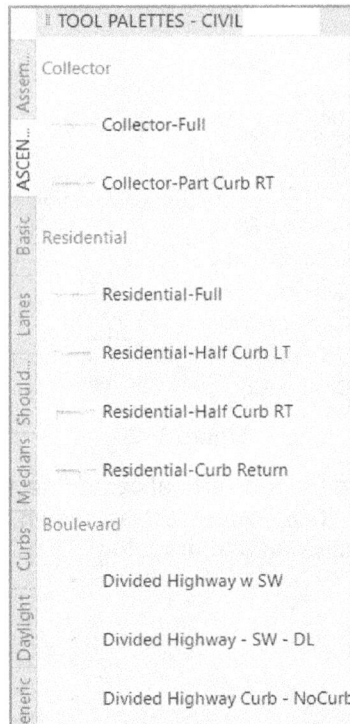

Figure 5–22

10. Save and close the drawing.

Task 3: Insert assemblies from a tool palette.

If you did not complete the previous task with the tool palettes, you must skip this task.

1. Open **COR-B.dwg** from the *C:\Civil 3D Beyond\Working\ Corridors* folder.

2. Zoom and pan to the lower left corner of the **Rand Boulevard** profile view.

3. In your Assembly tool palette that you created in the previous task, select the **Divided Highway w SW** assembly and release the mouse button (do not click and drag).

4. In Model Space, select a point left of the profile view to place the assembly. Place the **Divided Highway -SW - DL** assembly by clicking the left mouse button.

5. Save the drawing.

Task 4: Manage assemblies.

1. Continue working with the previous drawing if you completed Task 3 or open **COR-C.dwg** from the *C:\Civil 3D Beyond\ Working\Corridors* folder.

2. Zoom and pan to the lower left corner of the **Rand Boulevard** profile view, if not already there.

3. In the *View* tab>*Named Views* panel, click (New View).

4. In the *New View / Shot Properties* dialog box, name the view **Assem-Boulevard**. If the dialog box is not expanded, click on the down arrow to expand it, as shown in Figure 5–23. Clear the **Save layer snapshot with view** checkbox.

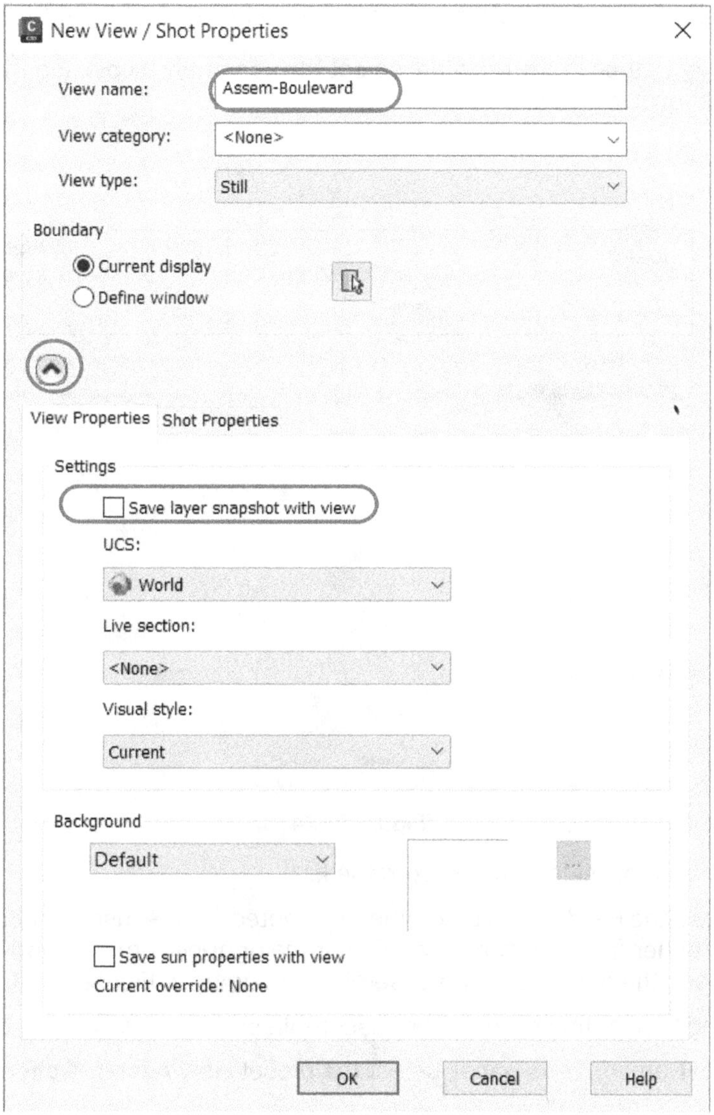

Figure 5–23

5. Click **OK** to close the *New View / Shot Properties* dialog box.

6. Pan to the lower left corner of the **Ascent Place** profile view and repeat the process to create an **Assem-Residential** view.

7. Pan to the lower left corner of the **Jeffries Ranch Rd** profile view and repeat the process to create an **Assem-Collector** view.

8. In the *Insert* tab>*Data* panel, click ⌐A (Field).

9. In the *Field* dialog box, in the *Field names* column, select **Object** from the list. Click

   (Select Object), then in the drawing, select the assembly by picking the red vertical centerline, as shown in Figure 5–24.

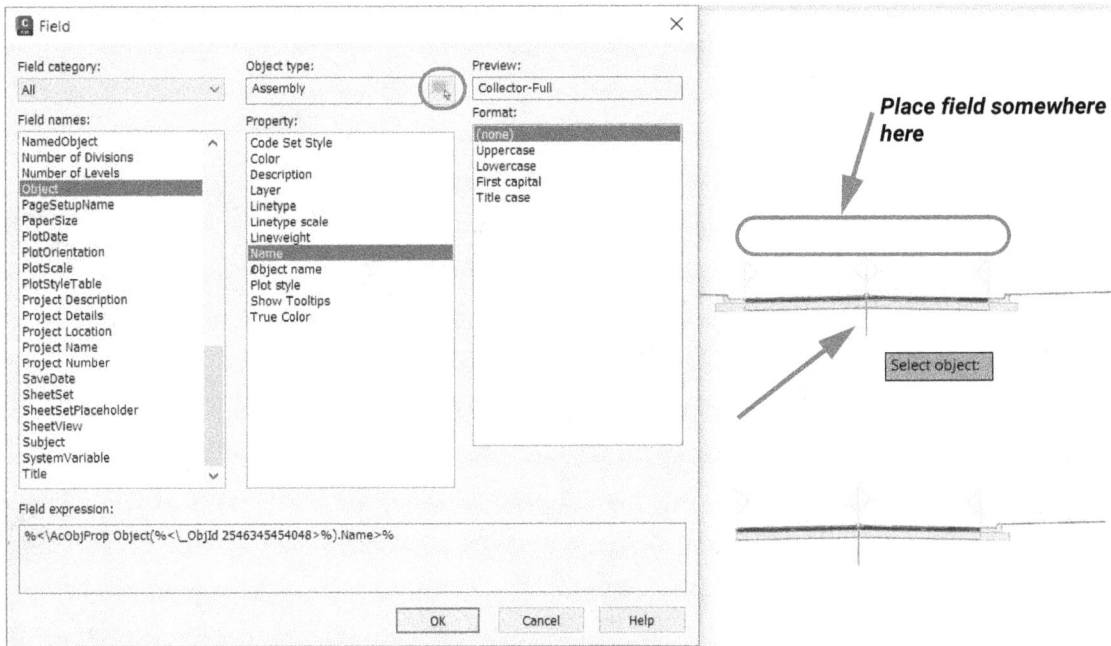

Figure 5–24

10. In the *Property* column, select **Name** from the list.

11. Click **OK** to close the *Field* dialog box. When prompted for the insertion point for the field, select **Height** (either from the command line or the right-click menu) and enter 1.2 for the height, then place the field above the assembly, as shown in Figure 5–24.

12. Time permitting, repeat this for the other assemblies.

13. In the *View* tab>*Named Views* panel, select the preset view **Assem-Collector** that you created earlier.

14. In the *TOOLSPACE>Prospector* tab, expand the *Assemblies* branch, right-click on **Collector-Full**, and select **Remove from Modelspace**, as shown in Figure 5–25.

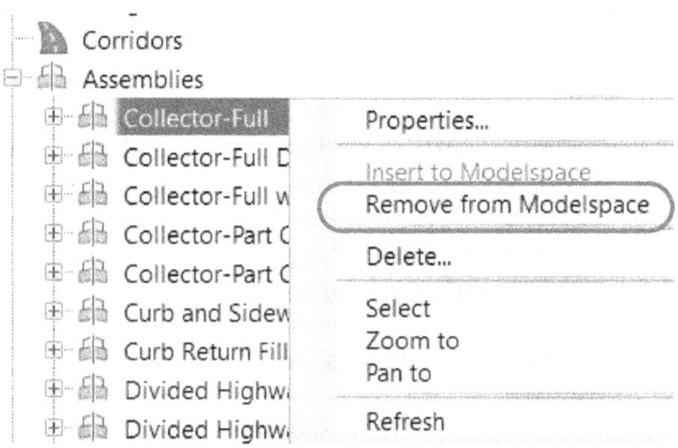

Figure 5–25

15. Right-click on **Collector-Full**, select **Insert to Modelspace**, and select a point to insert the assembly.

💡 **Hint: Help with Views and Fields**

For more information on AutoCAD fields and AutoCAD named views, consult the AutoCAD Help documentation or the *AutoCAD: Beyond the Basics* guide (published by ASCENT).

16. Save and close the drawing.

End of practice

5.4 Superimposing Profiles

When there are multiple design profiles in a project, it may become necessary to see the different profiles together to understand how they relate and at which elevations they may intersect.

You select a profile in the originating profile view, and then select the profile view you want the profile superimposed on. The *Superimpose Profile Options* dialog box opens. It contains two tabs: *Limits* and *Accuracy*. The *Limits* tab prompts for the limits of the profile, meaning the extents the superimposed profile is displayed. If you do not want the entire length of the profile to be superimposed, enable the **Select start** and/or **Select end** checkboxes in order to type in the station values. You can also select the stations in Model Space by clicking (Pick station), as shown in Figure 5–26.

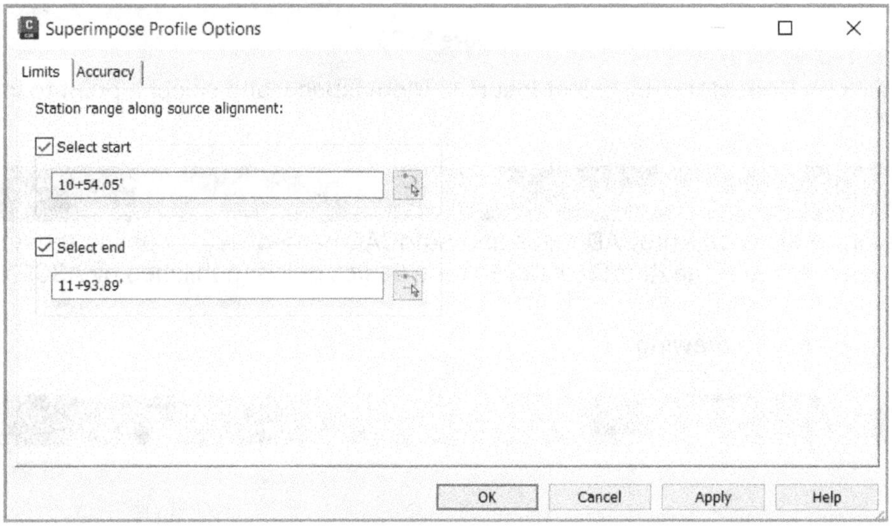

Figure 5–26

The *Accuracy* tab is for setting the horizontal and vertical accuracy. You can set the mid-ordinate distances based on the source profile, as shown in Figure 5–27.

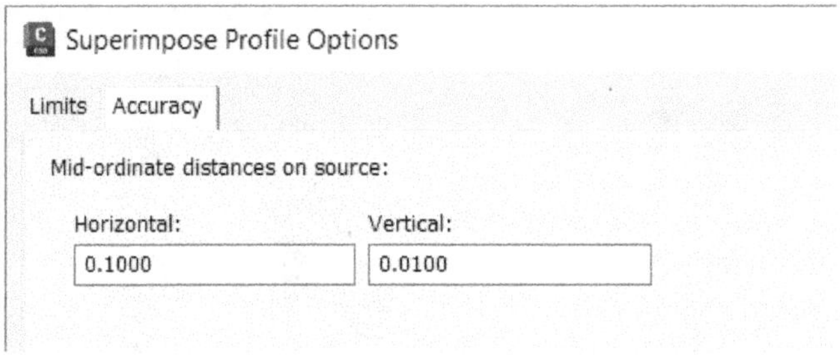

Figure 5–27

Practice 5c
Create and Superimpose Profiles

Practice Objectives

- Create a simple design profile.
- Superimpose another profile for reference.
- Modify the design profile.

In this task, you will create a rough design grade for **Rand Boulevard**. To do this, you will use Civil 3D to determine the stations and elevations. You will first draw a simple tangent from the start to the end of the surface profile in the profile view, then you will superimpose a small segment of the Jeffries Ranch Road FG profile into the profile view in order to see where they intersect. Finally, you will insert a PVI at the intersection point and place a vertical curve.

1. Open **COR-D1.dwg** from the *C:\Civil 3D Beyond\Working\ Corridors* folder.

2. In the top left corner of the drawing window, select the - symbol for Viewport Control, expand **Viewport Configuration List** and select **Plan-Profile-Rand**.

3. In the *Home* tab>*Create Design* panel, expand **Profile** and click ⌁ (Profile Creation Tools). When prompted to select a profile view, select the **Rand Boulevard** profile view.

4. The *Create Profile* dialog box opens. Do the following:
   - Type **Rand Boulevard-DGN** for the *Name*.
   - Set the *Profile style* to **ASC-Design Profile**.
   - Set the *Profile label set* to **ASC-Complete Label Set**.
   - Click **OK**.

5. In the *Profile Layout Tools* toolbar, select ⁄ (Draw fixed tangent by two points).

6. Use the Endpoint Osnap to snap to the beginning and the end of the red **Existing Site** surface profile.

7. Press <Enter> to exit the command, and note that now the labels update. Leave the *Profile Layout Tools* toolbar open for later use.

8. In the *Home* tab>*Create Design* panel, expand **Profile** and click ⌳ (Create Superimposed Profile).

   *Note: The **Create Superimposed Profile** command is also available in the Profile View contextual tab.*

9. For the **source profile**, pan up to the **Jeffries Ranch Rd** profile view and select the cyan **Jeffries Ranch Rd-DGN** profile in the drawing.

10. For the **destination profile view**, select the **Rand Boulevard** profile view in the drawing.

11. In the *Superimpose Profile Options* dialog box, click on the checkboxes for **Select start** and **Select end**, then click 🔖 (Pick station) for both the **Select start** and **Select end** values, as shown in Figure 5–28.

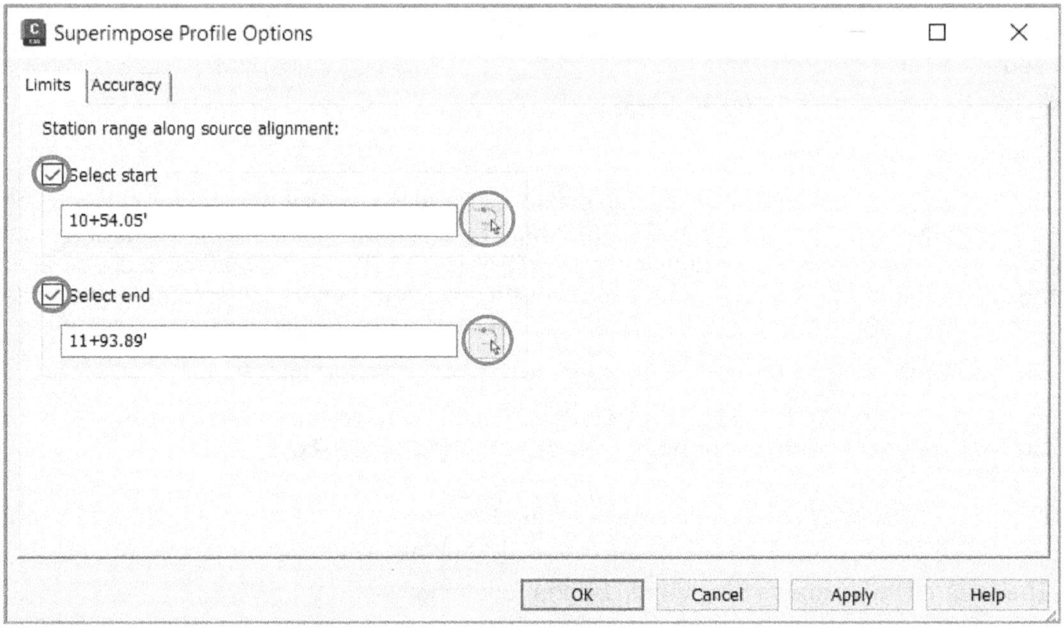

Figure 5–28

12. Select near the incoming and outgoing islands of the sketched roundabout for the start and end stations, respectively, as shown in Figure 5–29.

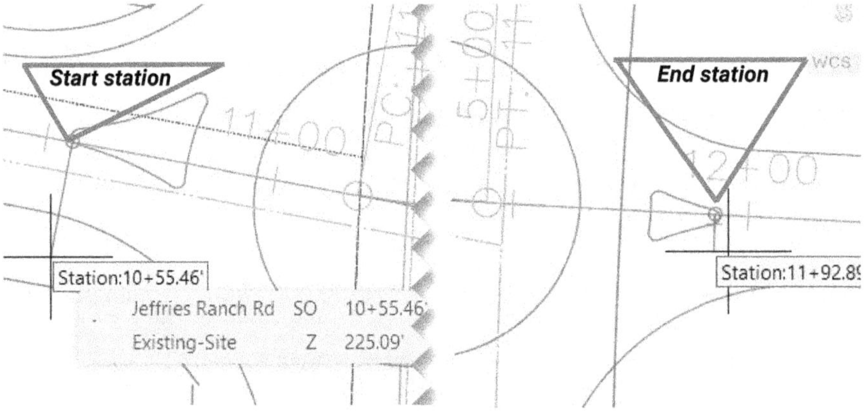

Figure 5–29

13. Click **OK** to close the *Superimpose Profile Options* dialog box.

14. Near station **5+33** and elevation **200'**, you will note a small cyan line segment, which is the superimposed profile, as shown in Figure 5–30.

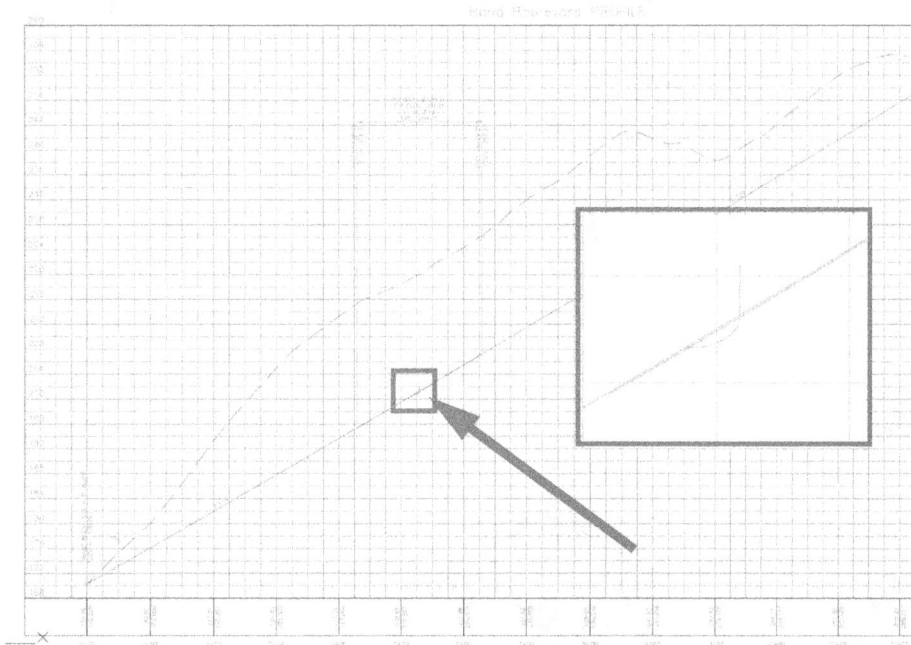

Figure 5–30

15. In the *Profile Layout Tools* toolbar, select (Insert PVI).

16. For the *point for new PVI*, select near the middle of the superimposed profile. Press <Enter> to finish the **Insert PVI** command.

17. In the *Profile Layout Tools* toolbar, in the *Curves* drop-down list, expand **More Free Vertical Curves** and select **Free Vertical Parabola (PVI based)**, as shown in Figure 5–31.

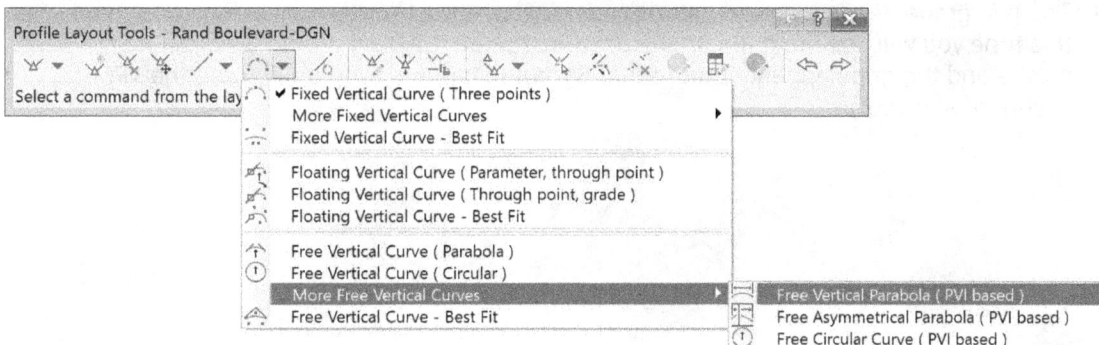

Figure 5–31

18. Select near the new PVI you just created to add the curve. Make the curve length **200.0'** and press <Enter> to finish the command.

19. Select the curve label and drag it into the profile view by its grip, as shown in Figure 5–32.

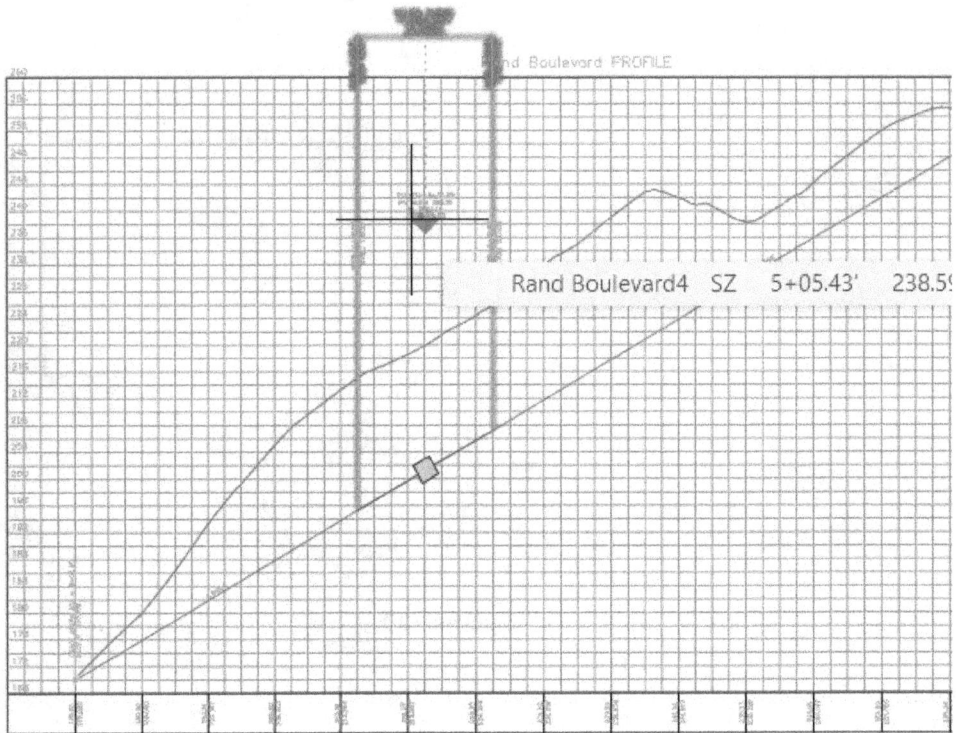

Figure 5–32

20. Adjust the curve labels in the other two profile views as well so they do not interfere with other labeling.

21. The last grade needs to be adjusted. You could use the Panorama as done previously, but this time you will use the grips. In the **Jeffries Ranch Rd-DGN** profile view, select the design profile and the grips appear. Ensure that **Dynamic Input** is toggled on (use the <F6> keyboard shortcut).

22. Select the last square grip. The tooltip displays, specifying the station. Press <Tab> to toggle to the elevation, as shown in Figure 5–33.

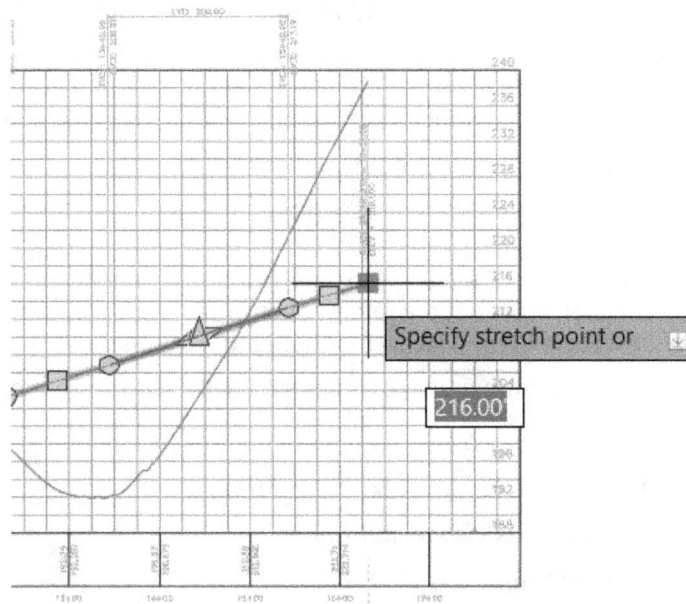

Figure 5–33

23. Type **225.0** for the final elevation and press <Enter>.

24. Save and close the drawing.

End of practice

Practice 5d
Build a Boulevard Corridor with Daylighting

Practice Objectives

- Create a corridor model using previously created alignments, profiles, and assemblies.

- Split profiles to make room for a roundabout.

- Modify a corridor region to use a different assembly.

In this practice, you will create a corridor that has daylighting on one side in a particular region. You will create the full corridor, split it at the intersection, and then apply another assembly to the newly created region. This is in preparation for creating a roundabout in later practices.

1. Continue to work on the previous drawing or open **COR-D2.dwg** from the *C:\Civil 3D Beyond\Working\Corridors* folder.

2. In the *Home* tab>*Create Design* panel, click ⬛ (Corridor).

3. In the *Create Corridor* dialog box, do the following:

    - Name the corridor **Rand Boulevard.**

    - For the *Alignment*, select **Rand Boulevard.**

    - For the *Profile*, select **Rand Boulevard-DGN.**

    - For the *Subassembly*, select **Divided Highway - SW -DL.**

    - For the *Target Surface*, select **Existing Site**.

    - **Do not** select the **Set baseline and region parameters** option. You will be using the corresponding tools within the contextual ribbon instead.

4. Click **OK** to close the *Create Corridor* dialog box. The corridor is built with the default settings.

5. You now need to split the corridor to make room for the roundabout. Select the newly built corridor.

6. Split the sole region to make two regions, then pull the two regions apart using the grips. In the *Corridor* contextual tab>*Modify Region* panel, select ▲ (Split Region), as shown in Figure 5–34.

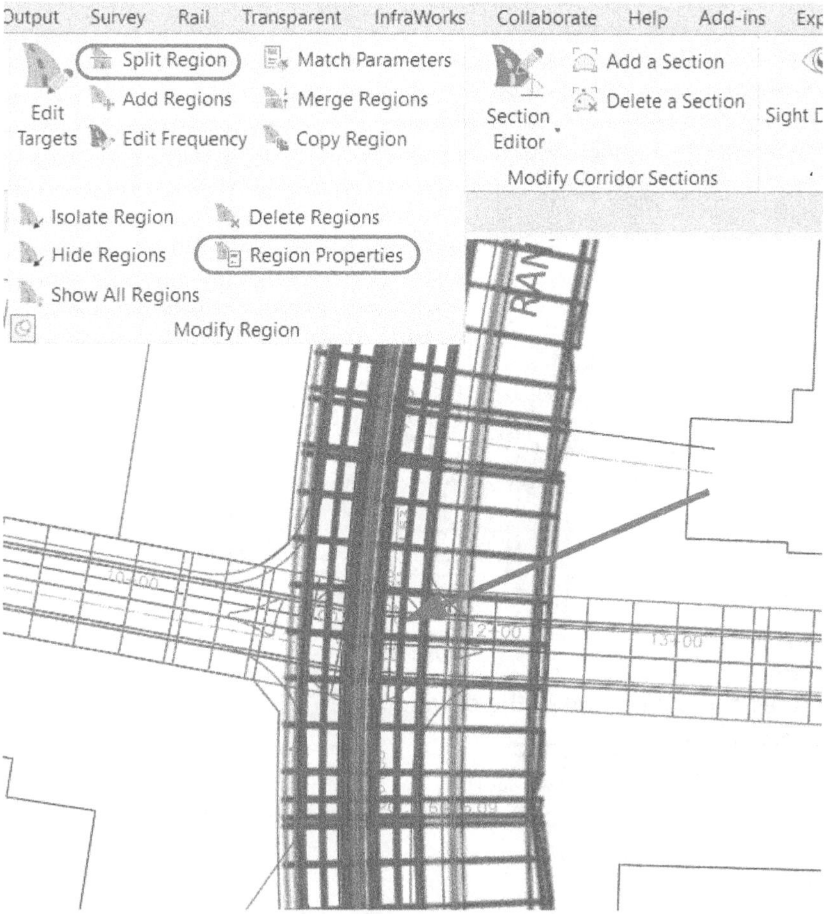

Figure 5–34

7. The first click will select the region you want to split (even though there is only one region) and the second selects the station where the split occurs.

8. Press <Enter> to finish the command.

9. Zoom in more to see the grips better. Select the triangular grip pointed downward, as shown in Figure 5–35, and drag it so it is just barely beyond the boulevard island.

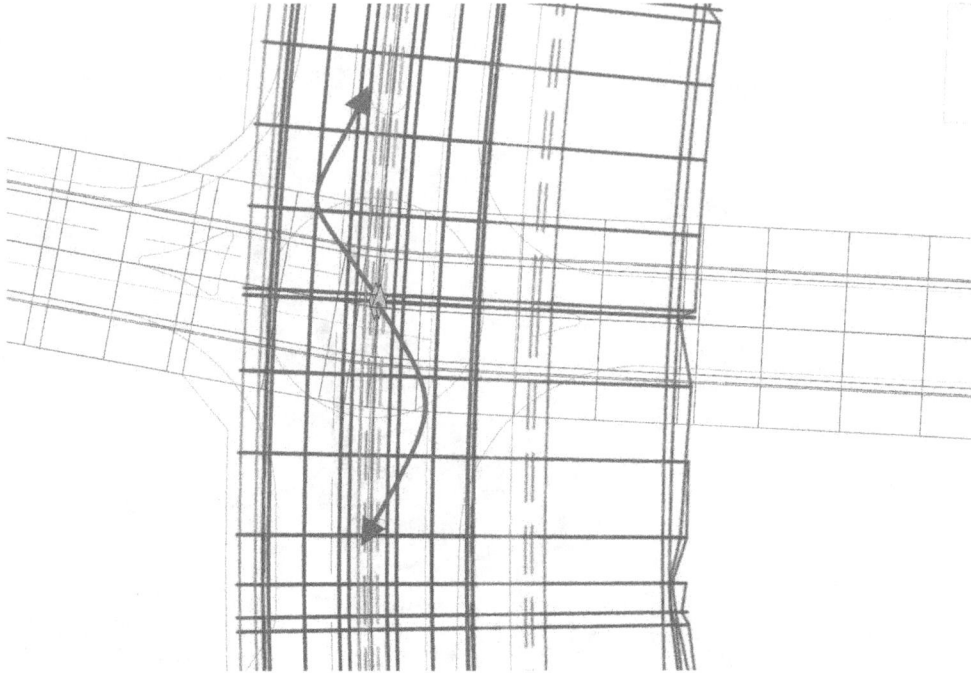

Figure 5–35

10. Repeat for the northern portion of the corridor.

11. Press <Esc> to deselect the corridor.

12. Select the **Jeffries Ranch Rd** corridor and repeat Steps 6 to 9 to split the corridor and drag it beyond the intersection. The result should be similar to Figure 5–36. The exact position of the regions is not important as they can be adjusted later.

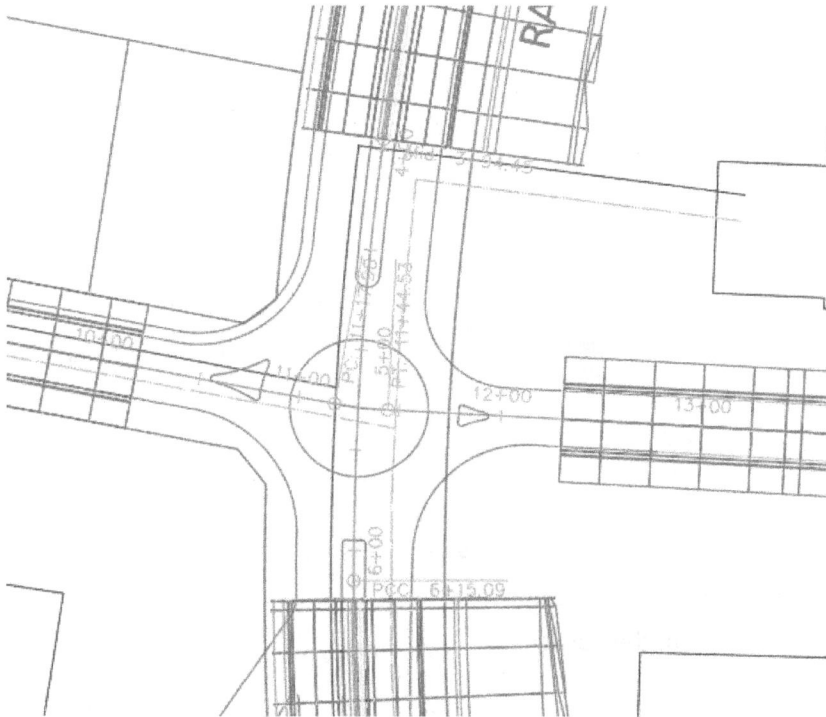

Figure 5–36

13. Press <Esc> to deselect the corridor.

14. Select the **Rand Boulevard** corridor.

15. In the *Corridor* contextual tab>expanded *Modify Region* panel, select (Region Properties).

16. You are prompted for a region to edit. Select the northern region.

17. In the *Corridor Region Properties* dialog box, click in the *Value* column for the *Assembly*, and in the *Edit Corridor Region* dialog box that opens, select the **Divided Highway w SW** assembly, as shown in Figure 5–37.

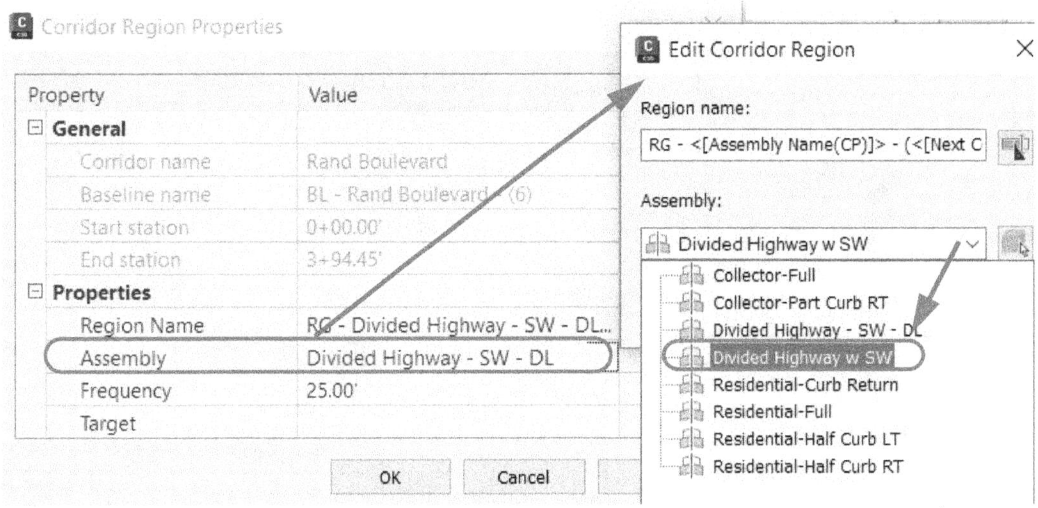

Figure 5–37

18. Click **OK** twice to get back to the drawing.

19. Press <Esc> to deselect the corridor

20. Save the drawing.

End of practice

5.5 Exporting Corridors

Civil 3D corridors can be exported to:

- InfraWorks via the IMX format

- A file geodatabase (FGDB) that can be used in ArcGIS

- ArcGIS directly via the ArcGIS Connector

- A LandXML exchange file

- A regular AutoCAD drawing with the intelligent Civil 3D objects translated to regular AutoCAD objects

These export utilities are accessible though the *Output* and the *InfraWorks* tabs shown in Figure 5–38.

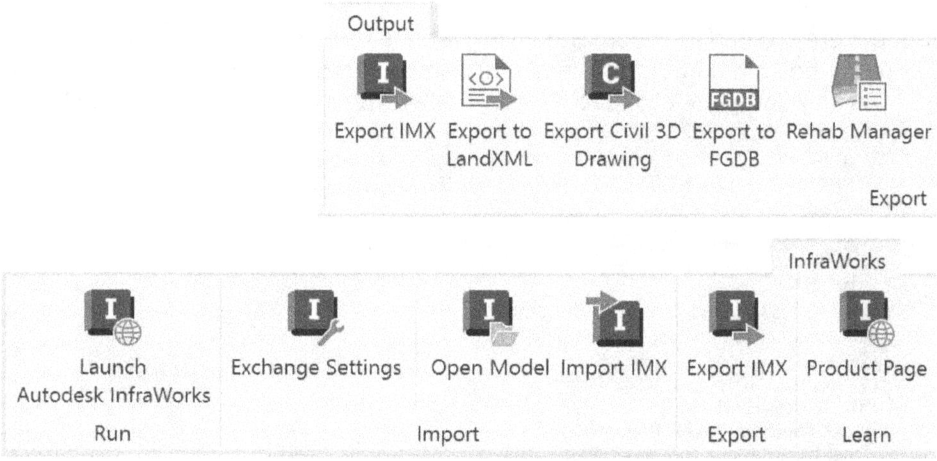

Figure 5–38

5.6 Roundabouts

Roundabouts are becoming very popular everywhere. Many existing intersections are routinely being upgraded to more efficient and safer roundabout designs.

Autodesk Vehicle Tracking has a very robust set of roundabout tools and editing features. The roundabout tools within Civil 3D are a subset of the Autodesk Vehicle Tracking tools. For more information on Autodesk Vehicle Tracking, refer to the *Autodesk Vehicle Tracking: Fundamentals* guide (published by ASCENT).

Civil 3D has powerful features to simplify preliminary layout of roundabout geometry. Editing options are also available, and as you make changes to the layout, you will see the dynamic nature of the objects, as well as the adherence to design standards. Using the geometrically constrained roundabout objects makes it viable to explore multiple design solutions.

Roundabout Standards

All roundabouts are created in accordance with defined rules or standards. The Roundabout Standard Explorer holds a number of these standards from several countries, as shown in Figure 5–39. All standards are grouped by nationality, and custom standards can be created as well.

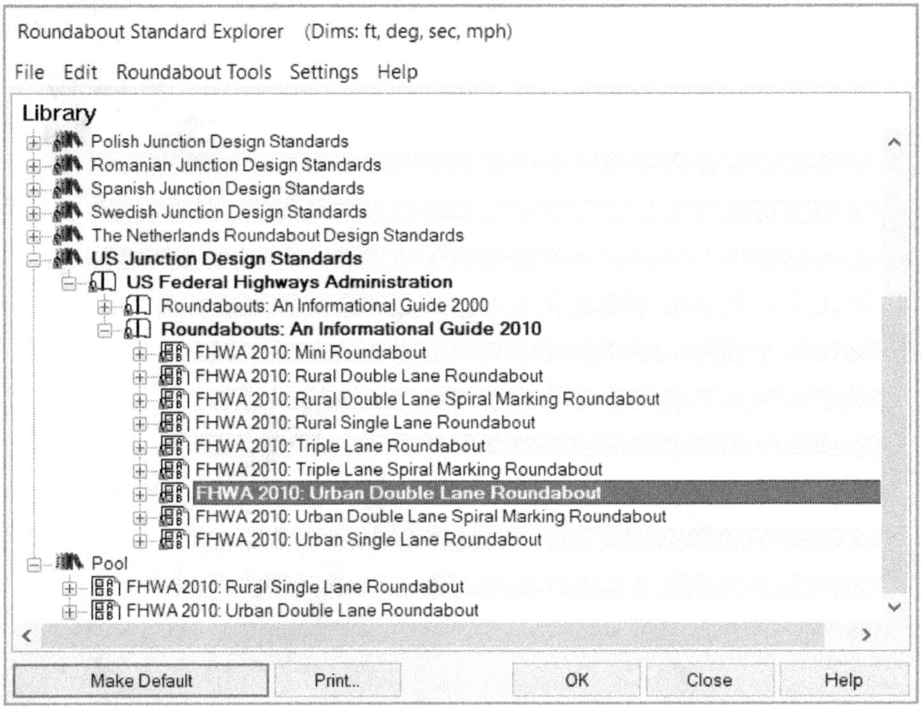

Figure 5–39

Creating Roundabouts

The **Create Roundabout** command is found in the *Home* tab>expanded *Intersection* panel. Before you create your roundabout, there are some elements required, such as:

- Civil 3D existing and final surfaces (optional)
  - If no surfaces are available, only a 2D roundabout will be created without any corridor segments.
- Alignments
- Profiles (optional)
  - If no profiles are available, only a 2D roundabout will be created.

When the **Create Roundabout** command is launched, the *New Roundabout Details* dialog box will open, as shown in Figure 5–40. Set all the appropriate settings.

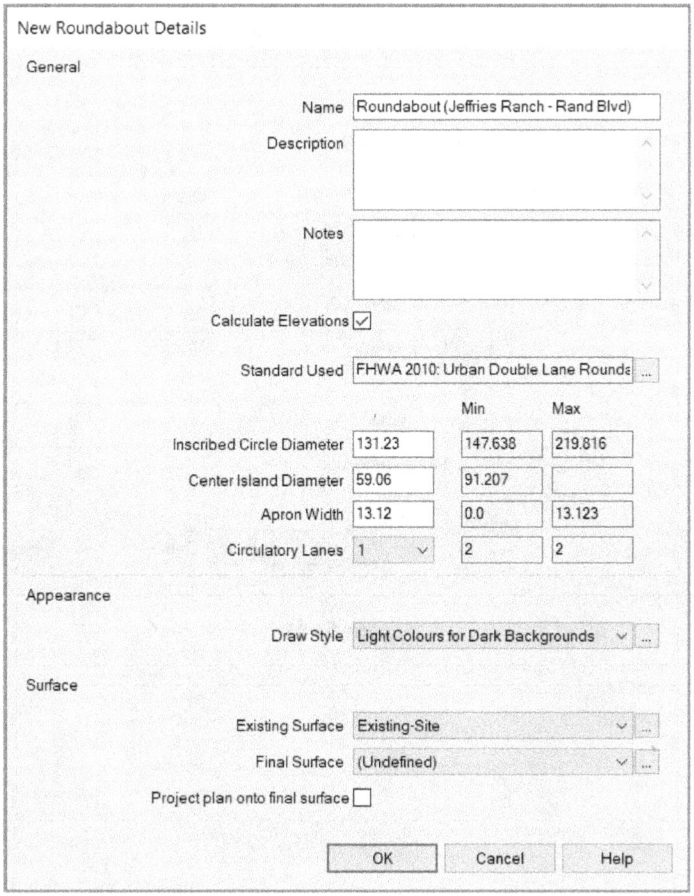

Figure 5–40

Place the center point of the roundabout in the drawing, then add the arms (or approaches) of the roundabout by clicking on (or near) the intersection of the Civil 3D alignments.

When adding each approach, the New Arm dialog box will appear, as shown in Figure 5–41. Enter a unique name for each new arm created.

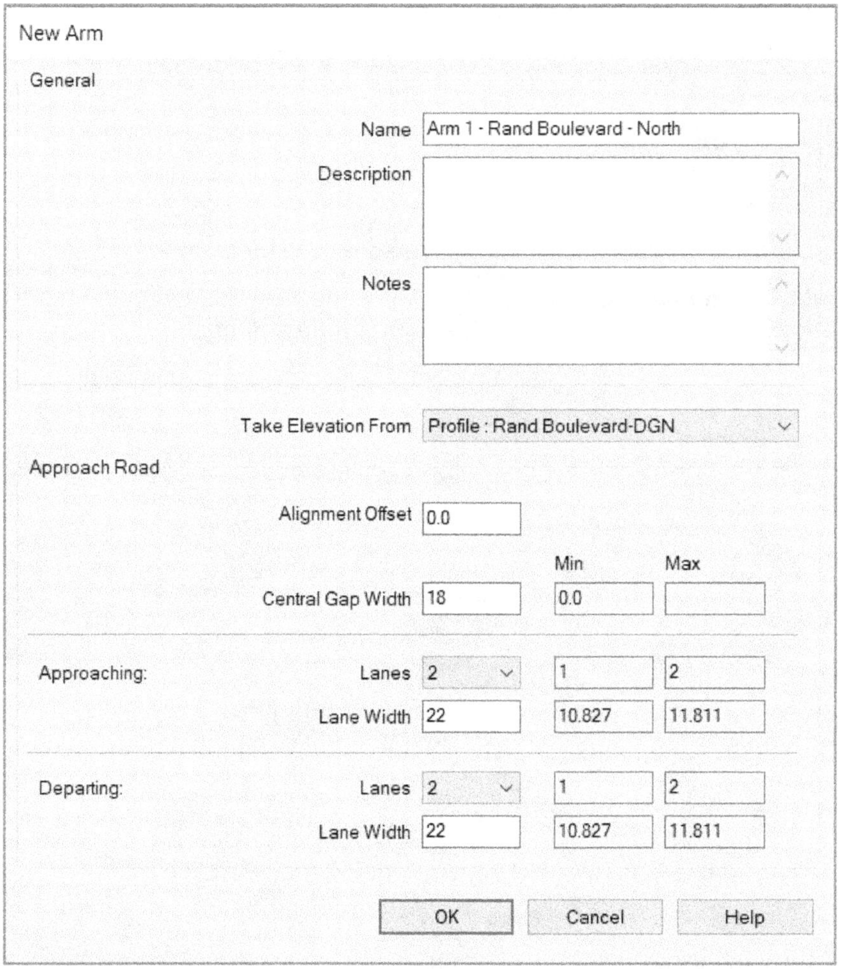

Figure 5–41

Each new approach creates the full geometry necessary for the roundabout. As the roundabout is created, either a 2D vehicle roundabout or a full 3D corridor model is created, as shown in Figure 5–42. The corridor model settings can be turned on at any time during the creation or editing process.

With corridor model settings turned off   **With corridor model settings turned on**

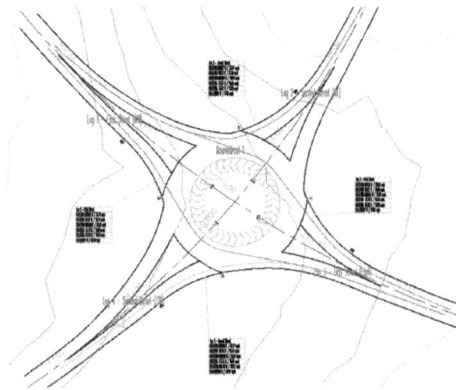

Figure 5–42

Real-time feedback is also added when the roundabout is created. A table is provided for each arm of the roundabout, providing fastest path and performance data. All tables stay up to date as the roundabout is being created and edited.

If using the corridor model creation while creating the roundabout, the *Corridor Properties* will populate with all of the appropriate baselines and regions, as shown in Figure 5–43.

Figure 5–43

Heads Up Display

As you create the roundabout, little boxes appear for each approach arm, as shown in Figure 5–44. This is called a Heads Up Display (HUD). HUDs show the critical design values related to each approach arm. These include radii and calculated speeds.

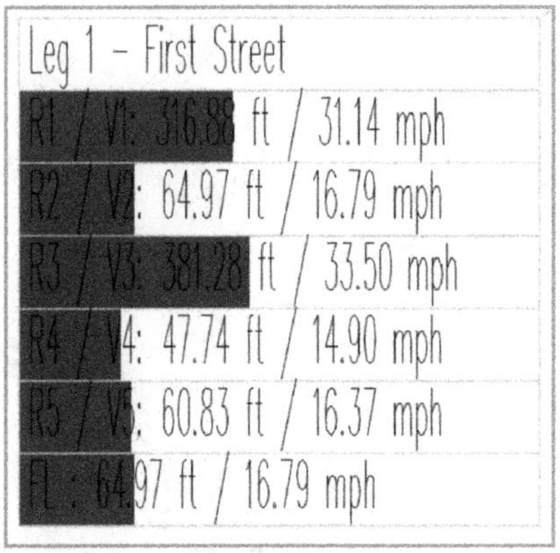

Figure 5–44

The data is color coded:

- **Green**: Values are within the limits specified in the standards.

- **Amber**: Values are getting close to the limiting value.

- **Red**: Values are outside of the limits.

The HUDs are dynamic tables. If you adjust the roundabout, the values will update. You will also notice color changes as limits are approached.

Practice 5e
Roundabout with Corridor

Practice Objectives

- Create a 3D roundabout.

- Turn off the Civil 3D corridor aspects of the roundabout for easy viewing.

In this practice, you will create a 3D roundabout using Civil 3D alignments and the existing surface. Then, upon studying the roundabout and its specifications, you will simplify the drawing by turning off the Civil 3D corridor and its surface.

To create a roundabout with proper elevations, an interim design surface named **IDG-Roundabout** has been created.

1. Open **COR-E.dwg** from the *C:\Civil 3D Beyond\Working\ Corridors* folder.

2. Select the preset view **Corr-Round**.

3. In the *Home* tab>*Create Design* panel, expand **Intersection** and select ⚒ (Create Roundabout).

4. If *Roundabout Standard Explorer* opens, expand *US Junction Design Standards>US Federal Highways Administration>Roundabouts: An Informational Guide 2010* and select **FHWA2010 Urban Double Lane Roundabout**, as shown in Figure 5–45. Click **Make Default**, then click **OK**.

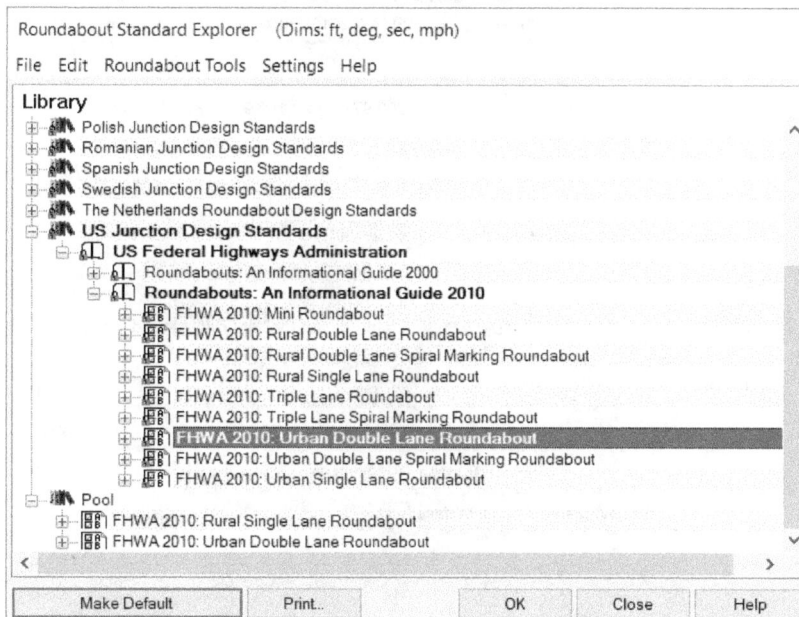

Figure 5–45

---

5. In the *New Roundabout Details* dialog box, set the following, as shown in Figure 5–46:

- *Name:* **Roundabout (Jeffries Ranch - Rand Blvd)**
- *Notes:* **For training purposes only**
- *Calculate Elevation:* **Checked**
- *Standards Used:* **FHWA2010 Urban Double Lane Roundabout** (as shown above in Figure 5–45)
- *Existing Surface:* **IDG-Roundabout** (from drop-down list)
- *Final Surface:* **(Undefined)**
- *Project plan onto final surface:* **Unchecked**

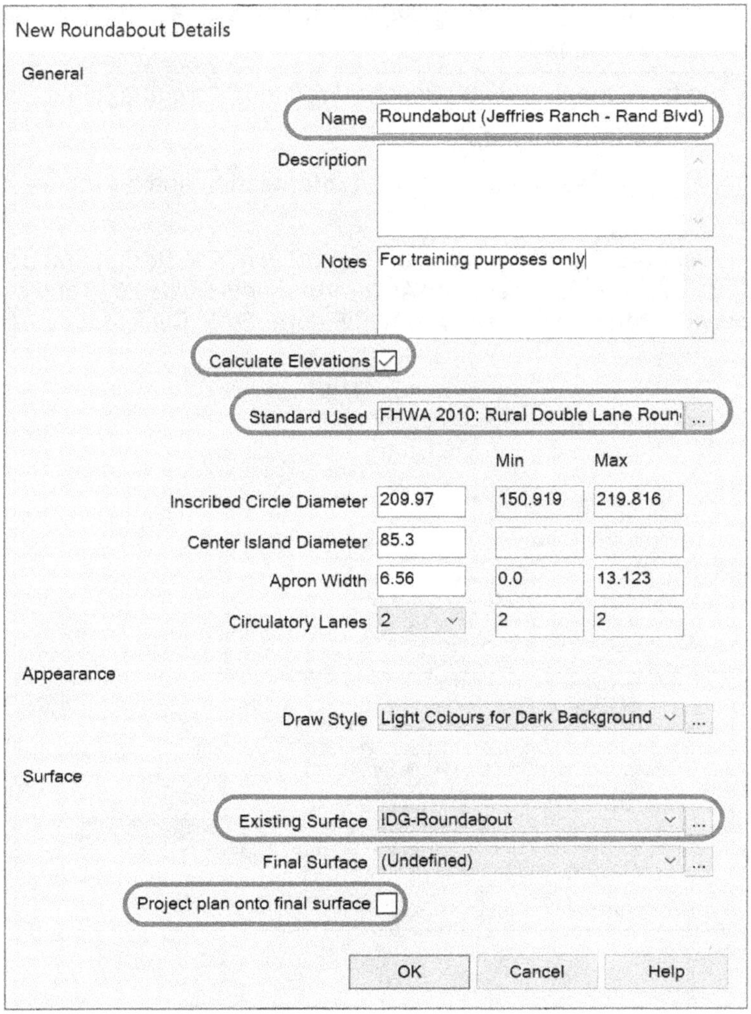

Figure 5–46

6. Click **OK** to close the *New Roundabout Details* dialog box. You are now prompted for *the location for the center of the roundabout*. Select a point on (or near) the intersection of the alignments, as shown in Figure 5–47.

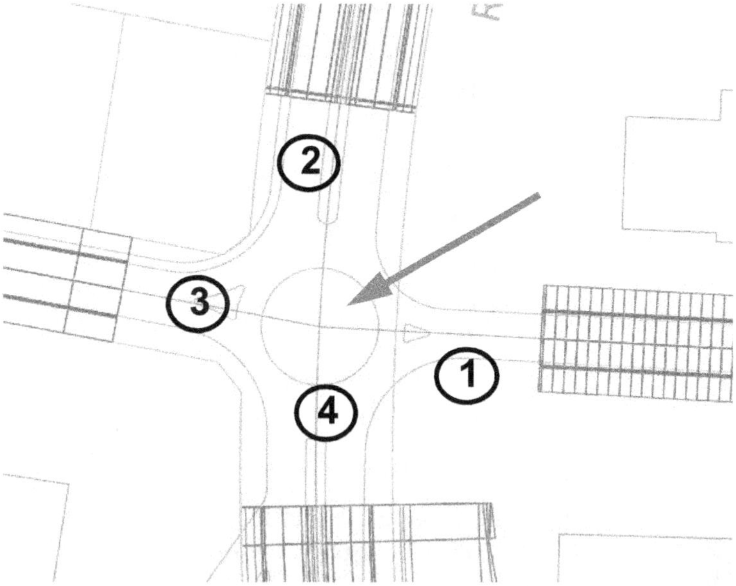

Figure 5–47

7. You are prompted for the line defining the new access road center line. Select the alignment labeled **(1)** in Figure 5–47.

8. Continue to select arms 2 through 4 and enter the following information:

	Name	Central Gap Width	Approaching and Departing Lanes
Arm 1	Arm - Jeffries Ranch Rd East	0	Lanes: 1 Lane Width: 15.5'
Arm 2	Arm - Rand Boulevard - North	18.0'	Lanes: 2 Lane Width: 11.0'
Arm 3	Arm - Jeffries Ranch Rd West	0	Lanes: 1 Lane Width: 15.5'
Arm 4	Arm - Rand Boulevard - South	18.0'	Lanes: 2 Lane Width: 11.0'

Note: It can take quite a while for Civil 3D to preform the calculations, so be patient.

9. When you are finished selecting all four approaches, press <Enter>.

10. The roundabout, corridor, and corridor surface are created, as shown in Figure 5–48.

Figure 5–48

11. In the *TOOLSPACE>Prospector* tab, expand the *Surfaces* branch and note the new **Roundabout (Jeffries Ranch - Rand Blvd) Top** surface that has been created. Right-click on it and select **Surface Properties**.

12. Set the *Surface style* to **_No Display** and click **OK** to close the dialog box.

13. Review the roundabout and the HUDs for each branch.

14. Restore the **Roundabout-Hide** layer state by selecting it from the *Layer States* drop-down list, as shown in Figure 5–49 .

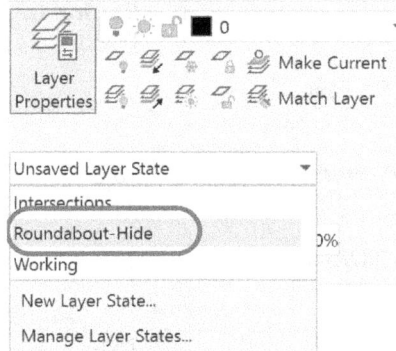

Figure 5–49

15. Save the drawing.

End of practice

5.7 Corridor Section Review and Edit

Creating complex corridors can be greatly simplified using ![icon] (Corridor Section Editor). It is accessed through the shortcut menu or contextual ribbon after selecting a corridor, as shown in Figure 5–50.

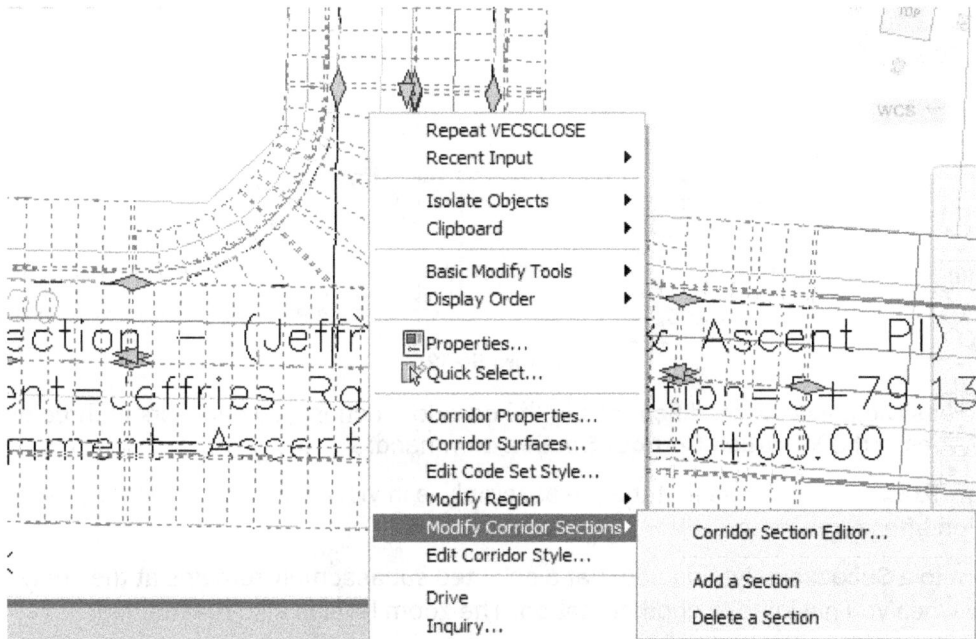

Figure 5–50

This command launches the *Section Editor* contextual tab, which enables you to review and edit sections interactively using the appropriate panels. The **Parameter Editor**, as shown in Figure 5–51, enables you to review and change most subassembly parameters.

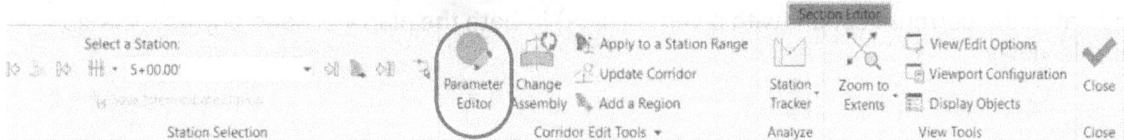

Figure 5–51

The editor enables you to modify those sections that need special attention, such as different daylight slopes. The editor also enables you to add and remove some subassemblies or links directly to and from a section. These parameter changes, additions, and deletions can be done for a single section or for a range of sections. An example is shown in Figure 5–52.

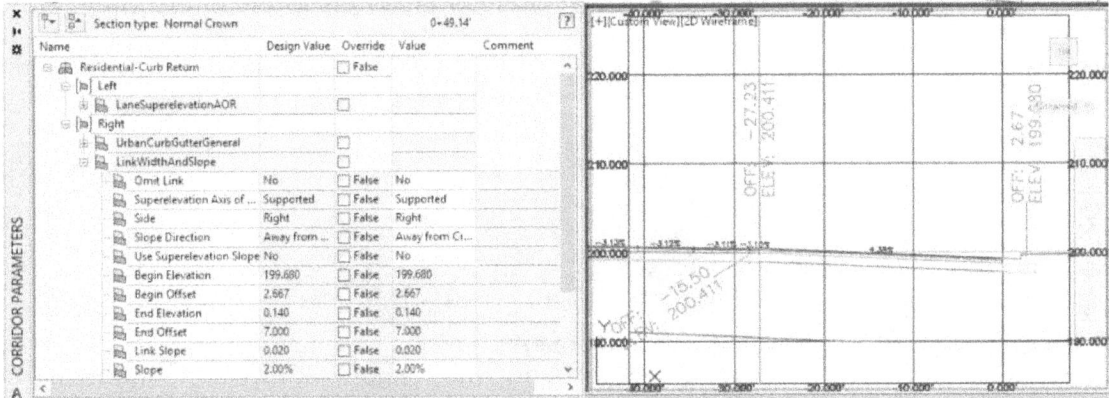

Figure 5–52

To more easily display the modifications in the corridor section, you can work in three different zoom modes in the **View/Edit Corridor Section** command:

- **Zoom To Extents:** Ensures that the full assembly is in view when you navigate to another station after zooming in.

- **Zoom to a Subassembly:** Ensures that a selected subassembly remains at the center of the view when you navigate to another station. The zoom level is also maintained.

- **Zoom to an Offset and Elevation:** Ensures that the current zoom level is maintained when you navigate to another station after a zoom.

Before launching the **Corridor Section Editor** command, you can set up multiple viewports using ▦ (Edit Viewport Configuration) for viewing the plan, profile, and section during the **Section Edit** command. Then, while in the **Corridor Section Editor** command, a Station Tracker indicates the current section (with a vertical line) in both the plan view and any associated profile views.

Practice 5f
Corridor Section Editor

Practice Objectives

- Inspect a corridor with the *Section Editor* to review and adjust the corridor.
- Show what is happening with existing and proposed surface data at predefined intervals along an alignment using section views.

1. Open **COR-F.dwg** from the *C:\Civil 3D Beyond\Working\ Corridors* folder.

2. Select the preset view **Corr-Inter**.

3. Select the **Jeffries Ranch Rd** corridor.

4. Open the **Corridor Section Editor**, either by clicking the ▶ icon in the corridor contextual ribbon or through the right-click menu (**Modify Corridor Section>Section Editor**).

5. In the *Section Editor* tab>*View Tools* panel, click 🔲 (Viewport Configuration) and set the following, as shown in Figure 5–53:

   - *Layout*: **Three Above**
   - *Horizontal Split*: **60%**
   - *Vertical Split*: **40%**
   - *Viewport 1*: **Section**
   - *Viewport 2*: **Profile**
   - *Viewport 3*: **Plan**

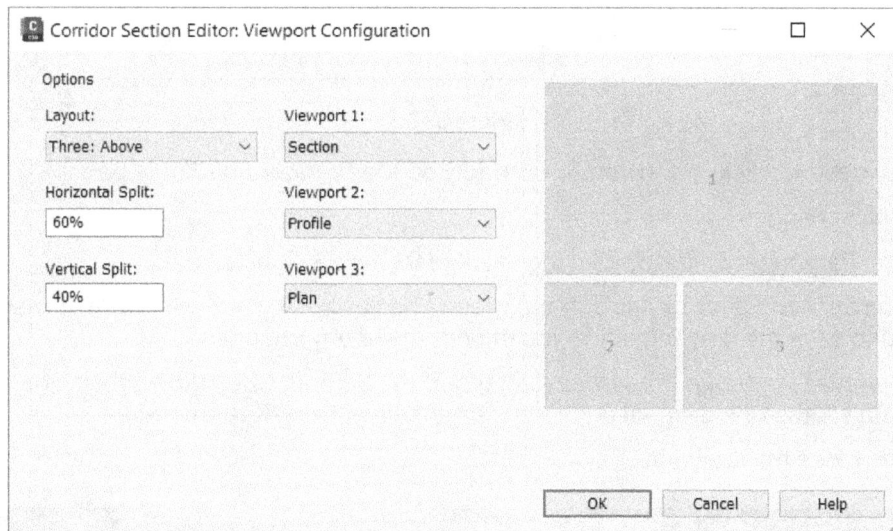

Figure 5–53

6. Click **OK**.

7. Select station 6+50.00' from the *Station* drop-down list in the *Station Selector* panel.

8. In the *Corridor Edit Tools* panel, click ◯ (Parameter Editor).

9. Navigate to *Right>LaneSuperelevationAOR>Sub-base Depth*. Change the *Value* to 2.00' and add an appropriate comment in the *Comment* space. Note that as you change the value, the section updates in the *Section Editor*.

Clear the **True** toggle checkbox, as shown in Figure 5–54, and note how the section returns to its previous state.

📄	Pave2 Depth	0.08'	☐ False	0.08'	
📄	Sub-base Depth	**2.00'**	ℹ️ ☑ True	2.00'	testing different thi...
📄	Width	**15.50'**	ℹ️ ☐ False	15.50'	
📄	Version	R2013	☐ False	R2013	

Figure 5–54

10. In the *Section Editor* contextual ribbon>*Corridor Edit Tools*, select ⬆ (Apply to a Station Range).

11. In the *Apply to a Range of Stations* dialog box, change the starting station to 6+50.00'and the ending station to 8+00.00', as shown in Figure 5–55 and click **OK**.

Apply to a Range of Stations ✕

Start station:
6+50.00'

End station:
8+00.00'

OK   Cancel   Help

Figure 5–55

12. You may need to click △ (Update Corridor) on the *Corridor Edit Tools* panel.

13. Review the changes

14. Close the *Parameter Editor* by clicking the **X** in the upper right corner.

15. Close the *Section Editor* by clicking the **green checkmark** in the upper right corner. There is no need to save the drawing since you did not make any changes.

16. In the *Sample Line Group Properties* dialog box, the *Sample Lines* tab enables you to change the swath widths of individual sections numerically. Click **OK** to exit.

17. Save and close the drawing.

End of practice

5.8 Mass Haul Calculations

When the appropriate surfaces for the existing site and the corridor datum are assigned to sample lines, cut and fill quantities can be calculated. These quantities are for the entire corridor. However, to manage the earthwork during the actual construction, the ability to generate cumulative quantities along the corridor is necessary.

This is the purpose of a mass haul diagram. It can be generated and used as a visual representation of the cumulative cut and fill material volumes along a corridor. Contractors use mass haul diagrams as a primary tool in determining and balancing haulage costs when bidding on an earthwork job. Mass haul is the volume of excavated material multiplied by the distance it is required to be moved. When the mass haul line is above the balance line, it indicates how much cut there is going to be at that station. When the mass haul line is below the balance line, it indicates the volume to be filled. To generate a mass haul diagram, you need an alignment, a sample line group, and a materials list. The mass haul diagram calculates and displays the following:

* The distance over which cut and fill volumes balance

* Free haul and overhaul volumes

* Volumes offset by borrow pits and dump sites

Construction costs can be reduced by enabling the designer to compare alternative designs and add dump sites and borrow pits at key locations in the free haul distance, thus eliminating a portion of the overhaul volume. An example of a mass haul diagram is shown in Figure 5–56.

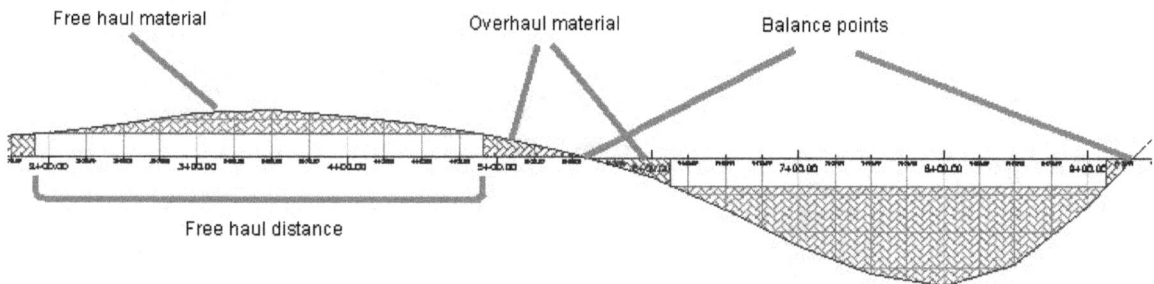

Figure 5–56

Create Mass Haul Diagram Wizard

You can create a mass haul diagram after the earthwork surfaces have been assigned to the

appropriate sample lines. In the *Analyze* tab>*Volumes and Materials* panel, select ⌄ (Mass Haul). All of the settings selected in the wizard can be reassigned later using *Mass Haul View Properties* (except for the alignment on which they are based).

The *General* page in the *Create Mass Haul Diagram* wizard enables you to select the *Alignment* that you want to work with and its associated *Sample line group* and to assign the mass haul view a name, description, view style, and layer, as shown in Figure 5–57.

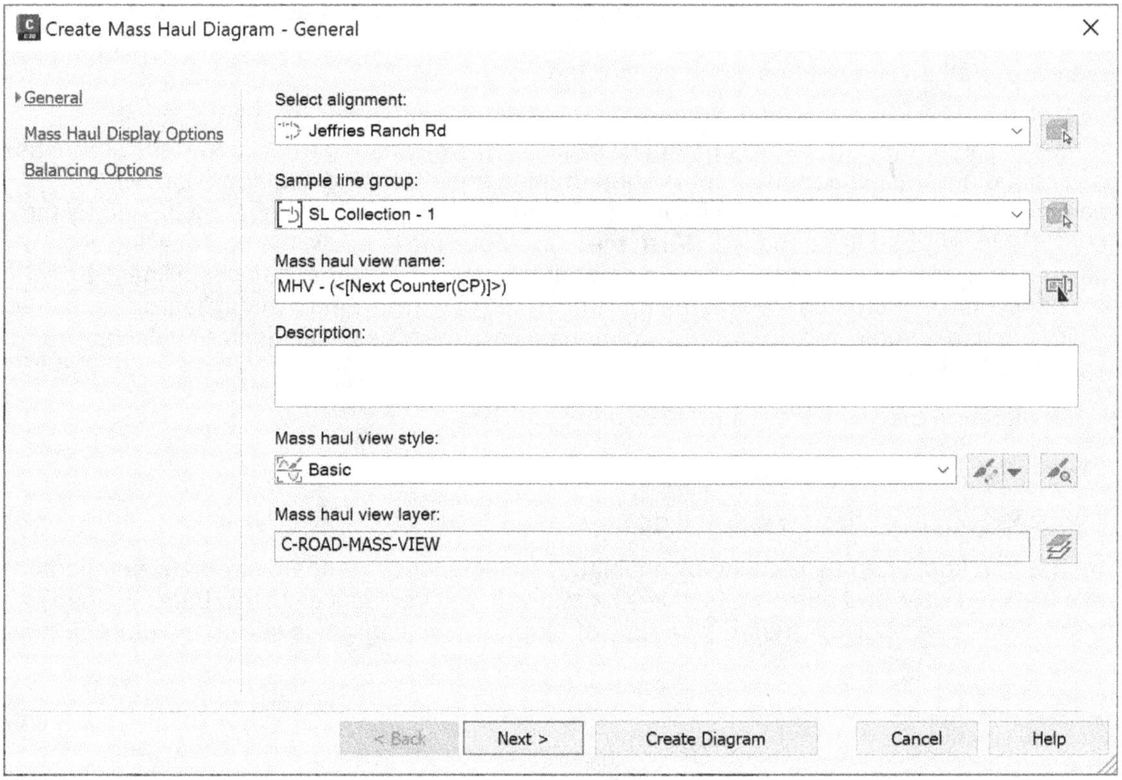

Figure 5–57

The next page in the *Create Mass Haul Diagram* wizard is for setting the *Mass Haul Display Options*, as shown in Figure 5–58. Here you can assign the material list (part of the chosen sample line group) and choose the material to use to generate the mass haul line. Select from:

- Total Volume

- Total Cut Volume

- Total Fill Volume

- Total Unusable Volume

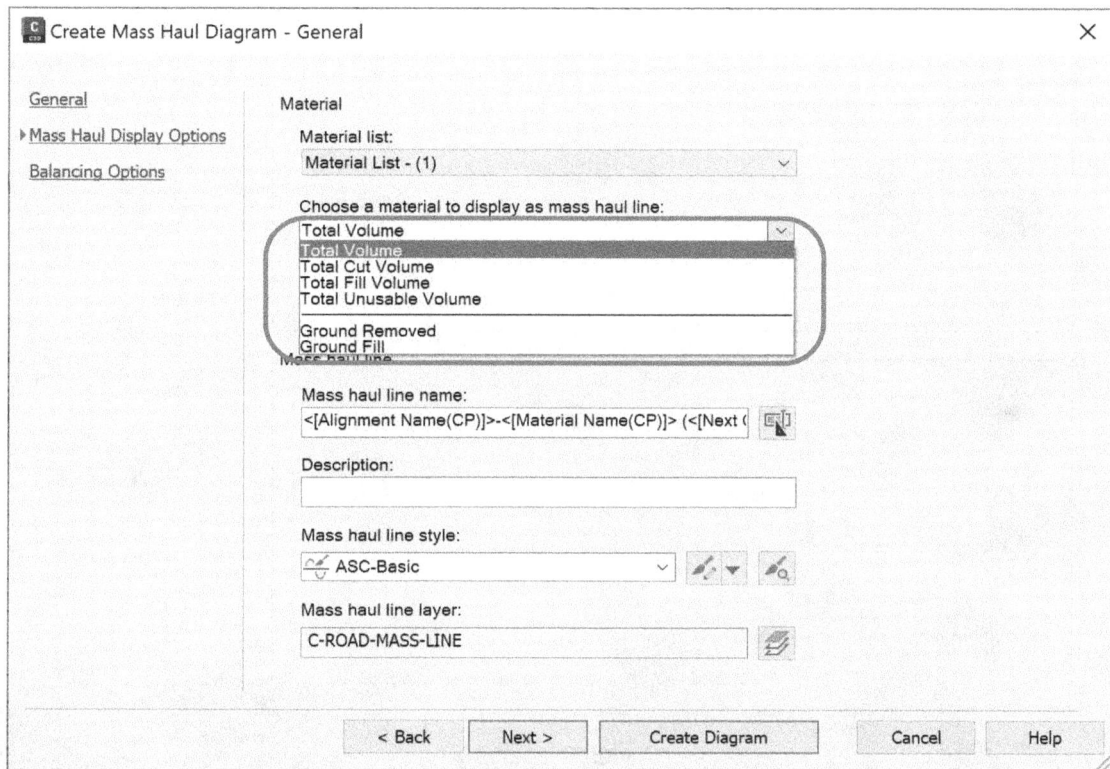

Figure 5–58

Assign a proper name to the mass haul line and select the proper mass haul line style.

The next page in the *Create Mass Haul Diagram* wizard is for *Balancing Options*, as shown in Figure 5−59. Here you can enable and specify the *Free haul distance*. You can also add borrow pits or dump sites, specifying the following:

- *Type* (borrow pit or dump site)

- *Station* (of the alignment where it is located)

- *Capacity* (in volume)

Figure 5−59

Mass Haul Line

The mass haul line is controlled through its style, as shown in Figure 5–60. The free haul can be measured either from the **balance point** or from the **grade point**.

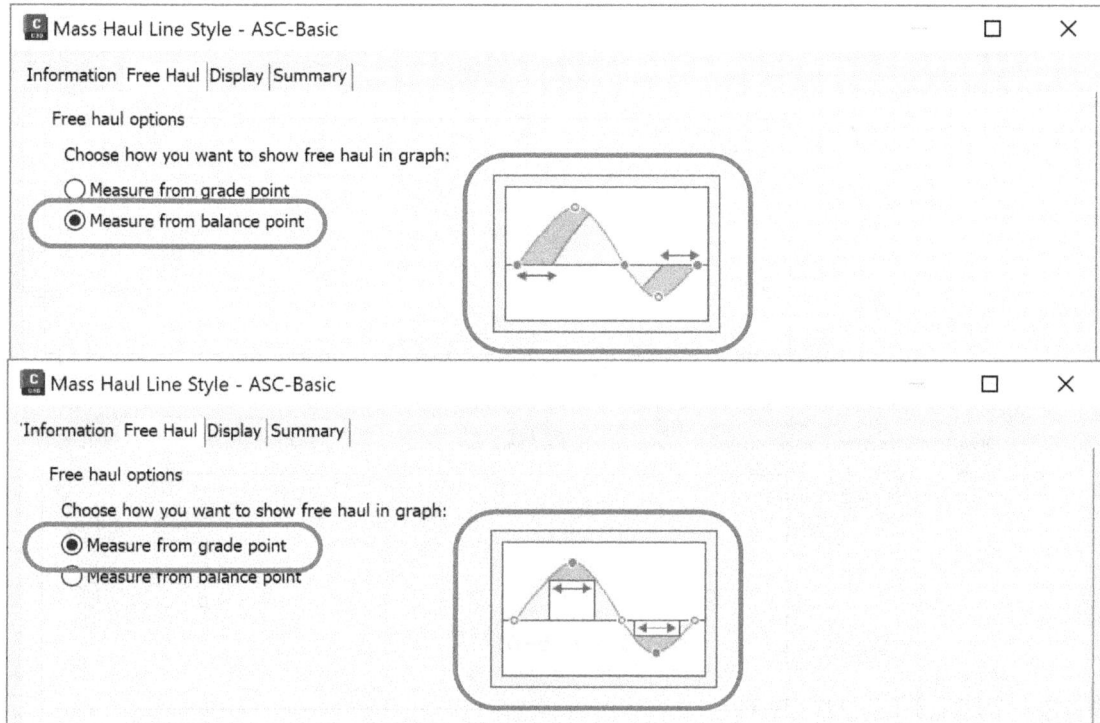

Figure 5–60

The colors for the free haul and overhaul areas are assigned in the *Display* tab of the Mass Haul Line Style dialog box, as shown in Figure 5–61.

Figure 5–61

Mass Haul Diagram

In the example shown in Figure 5–62, there are no balancing options assigned. The *Free Haul Area* is assigned blue and the *Overhaul Area* is assigned salmon.

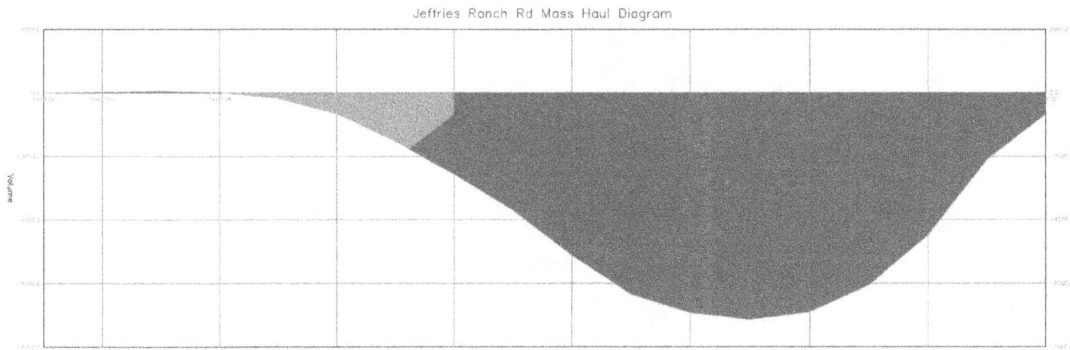

Figure 5–62

In the example shown in Figure 5-63, the balancing options are shown as assigned.

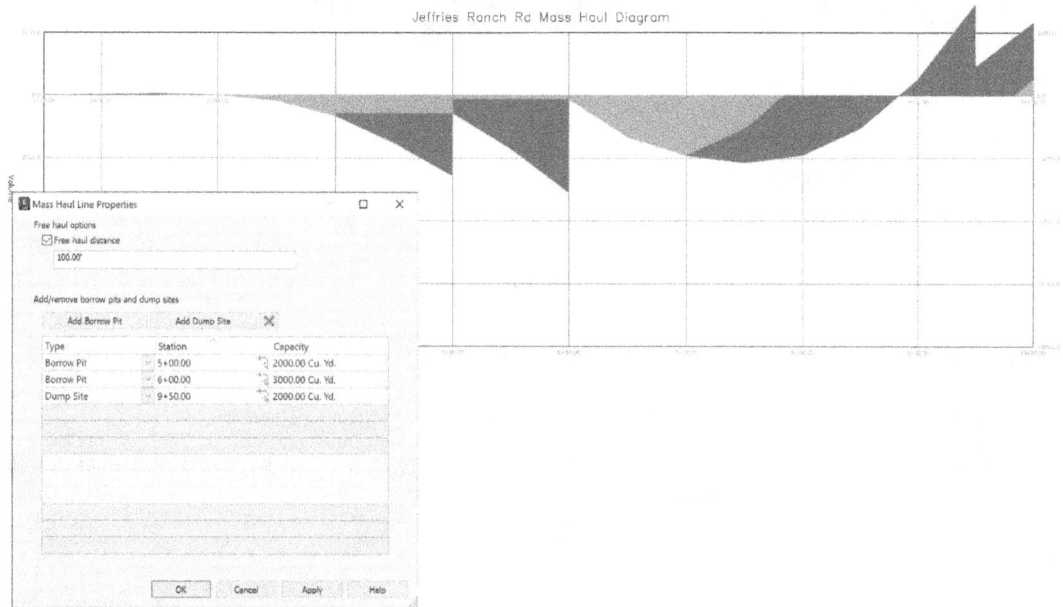

Figure 5-63

Practice 5g
Create a Mass Haul Diagram

Practice Objectives

- Create a mass haul diagram.
- Change the balancing options.

In this practice, you will generate a mass haul diagram to study methods of controlling the accumulating earthwork volumes along the corridor. You will then study different balancing options for the mass haul diagram.

1. Open **COR-G.dwg** from the *C:\Civil 3D Beyond\Working\ Corridors* folder.

2. In the *Analyze* tab>*Volumes and Materials* panel, click ⌄ (Mass Haul).

3. On the *General* page of the *Create Mass Haul Diagram* wizard, leave all the settings as their defaults and click **Next**, as shown in Figure 5–64.

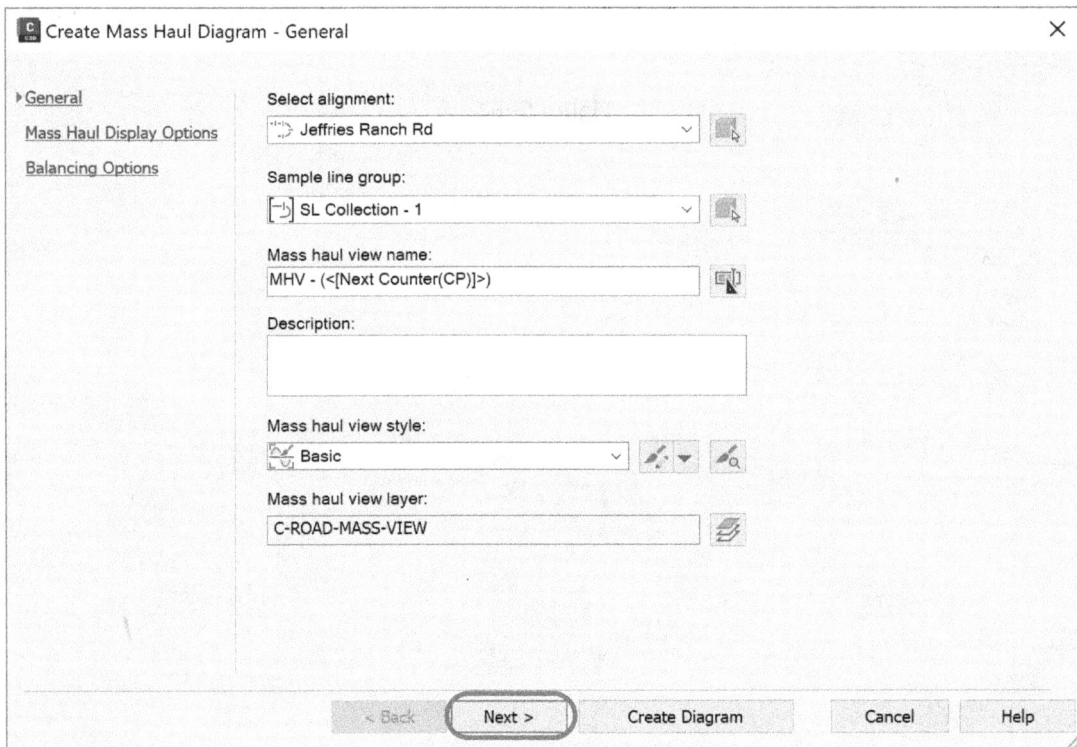

Figure 5–64

4. On the *Mass Haul Display Options* page, leave all the settings as their defaults and click **Next**, as shown in Figure 5–65.

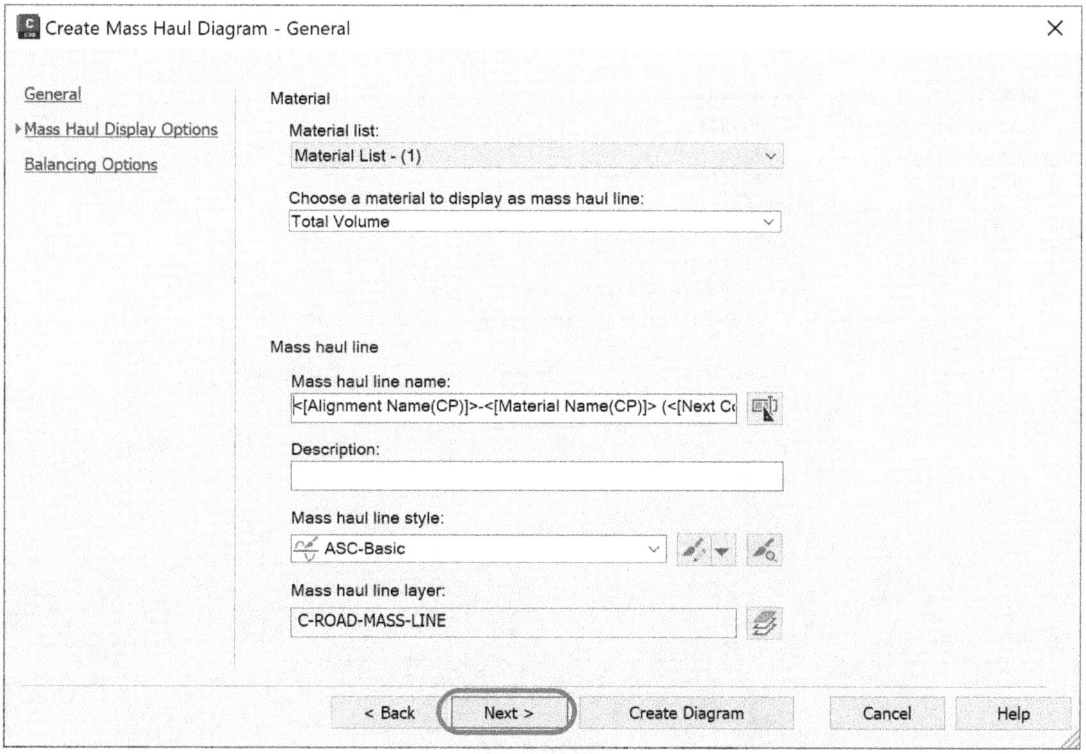

Figure 5–65

5. On the *Balancing Options* page, check the **Free haul distance** option and enter **500.0'**, as shown in Figure 5–66. Click **Create Diagram**.

Figure 5–66

6. You are prompted for a location. Select somewhere above the **Jeffries Ranch Road** profile view. The point you pick is the left-hand side of the datum axis.

7. The result is shown in Figure 5–67. There are no balancing options assigned. The *Free Haul Area* is assigned blue and the *Overhaul Area* is assigned salmon.

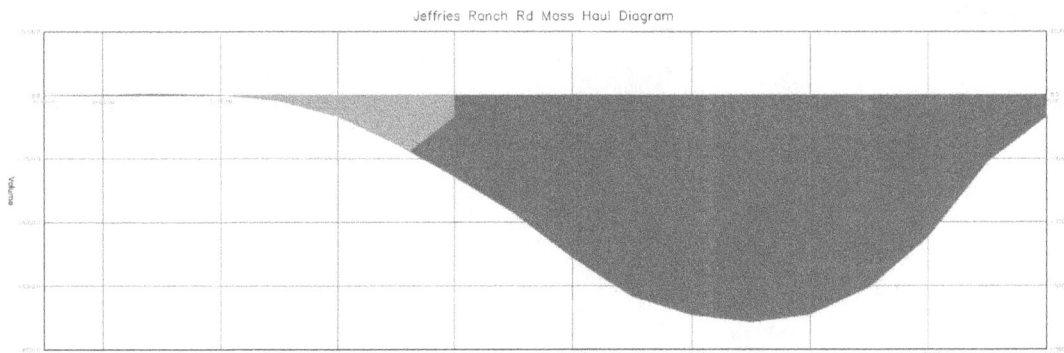

Figure 5–67

8. Select the mass haul view. In the contextual ribbon>*Modify* panel, select ⚖ (Balancing Options).

9. In the *Mass Haul Line Properties* dialog box, click **Add Borrow Pit** to add a borrow pit. For the values, enter **5+00.00** for the *Station* and **2000.00** for the *Capacity*, as shown in Figure 5–68.

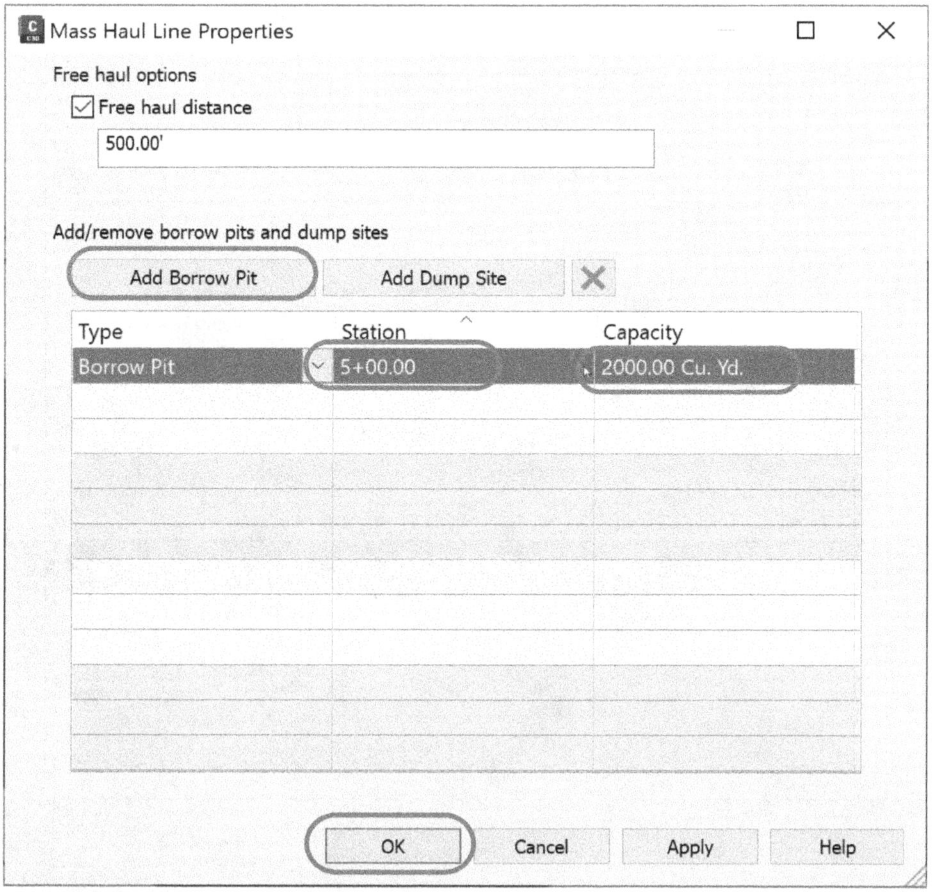

Figure 5–68

10. Click **OK** to close the *Mass Haul Line Properties* dialog box. Review the results on screen.

11. Repeat the procedure to add the following:

Type	Station	Capacity
Borrow Pit	6+00.00	3000.00 Cu. Yd.
Dump Site	9+50.00	2000.00 Cu. Yd.

12. When finished, click **OK** to close the *Mass Haul Line Properties* dialog box. The result is shown in Figure 5–69.

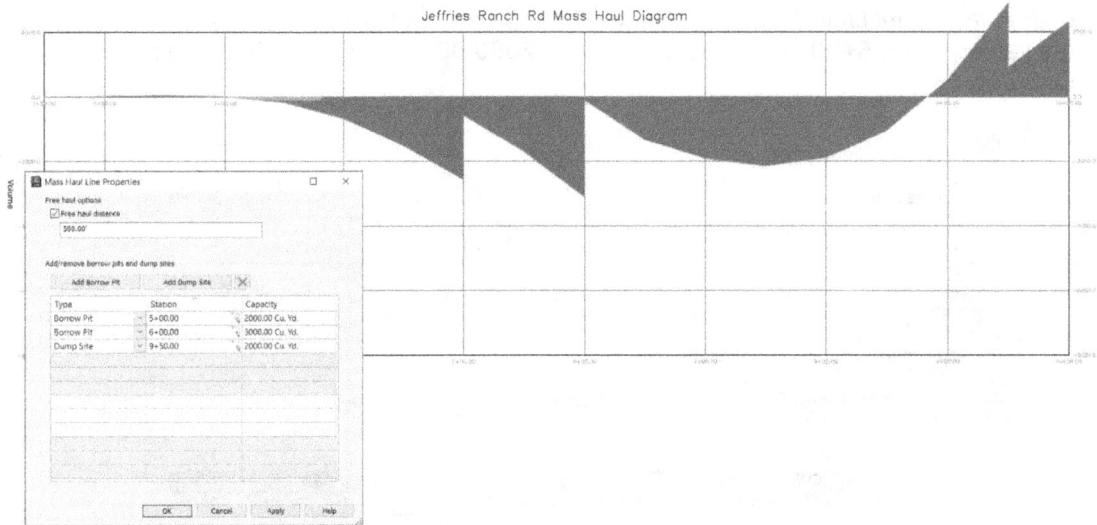

Figure 5–69

13. Save and close the drawing.

End of practice

5.9 Code Set Styles

Code set styles are assigned to corridors, sections, and assemblies. They control how these objects are displayed. Since code set styles influence multiple types of Civil 3D objects, code sets and each of these styles are all configured under the *Multipurpose Styles* collection in the *TOOLSPACE>Settings* tab, as shown in Figure 5–70.

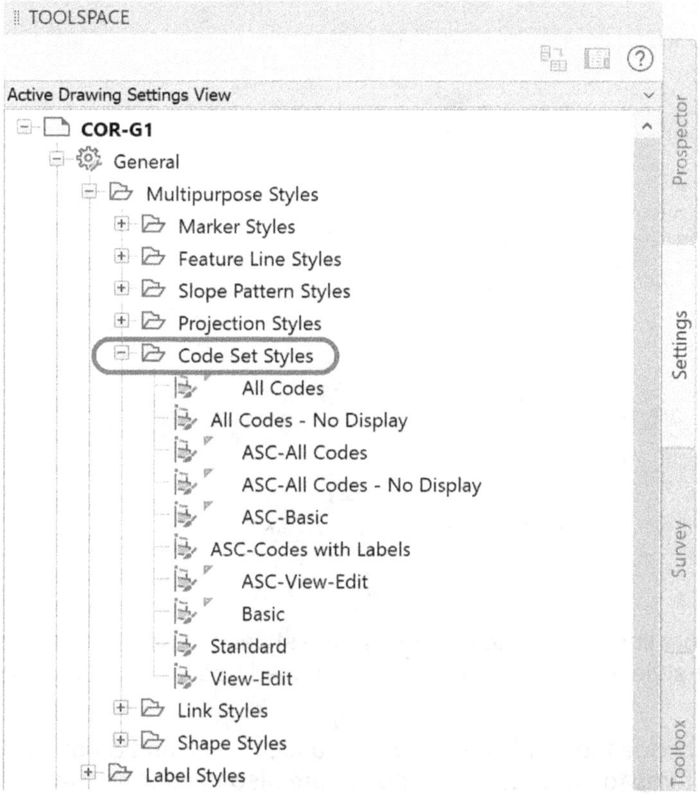

Figure 5–70

Code sets gather styles for links, shapes, and markers for the specific Civil 3D object (corridors, sections, and assemblies). These link, shape, and marker styles are also listed under the *Multipurpose Styles* collection.

For corridors, the *Codes* tab in the *Corridor Properties* dialog box lists all of the codes that are available in the corridor based on the subassemblies in the assembly, as shown in Figure 5–71. These codes are combined into code set styles. They control the appearance of the corridor (as well as cross sections and assemblies) by applying styles to each of the subassemblies.

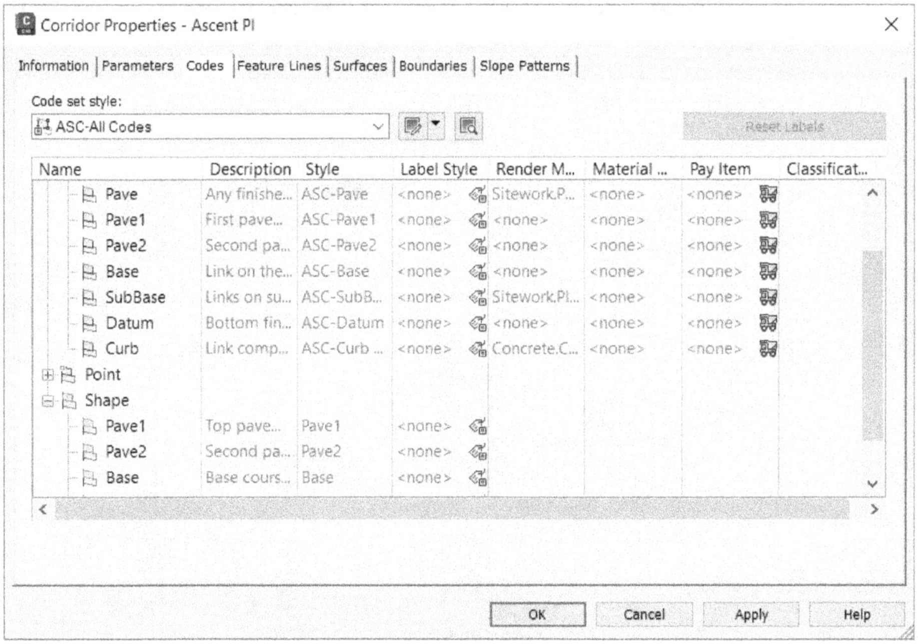

Figure 5–71

Marker styles, feature line styles, and link and shape styles are all assigned based on a code set style. The code set style assigns the styles to be applied based on the codes assigned to these objects.

These codes can change the display of corridors, assemblies, and cross-sections from solid colors to hatch patterns to none, etc. Such codes are also used to set section labels and for quantity takeoff. For example, they can specify which labels display in a section view.

- All link styles annotate a grade or slope.

- All point styles annotate an offset and elevation.

Other code set styles are available (or can be created or modified by the BIM manager) for specific purposes, such as:

- Plotting with or without hatching

- Design development

- No display

- Visualization

Practice 5h
Change Code Set Styles

Practice Objectives

- Change the display of the corridors using code set styles.
- Change the display of the assemblies using code set styles.

The corridors are now designed and ready to be shared with the rest of the design team. Before you share the corridors, you need to make some changes to their display so as not to show the assemblies. You can also change the display of the assemblies. This is done with the appropriate code set styles.

1. Continue with the previous drawing or open **COR-H.dwg** from the *C:\Civil 3D Beyond\ Working\Corridors* folder.

2. Select all four corridors in the project.

3. In the *Properties* palette, under *Data*, expand the drop-down list for *Code Set Style* and select **ASC-All Codes - No Display**, as shown in Figure 5–72.

Figure 5–72

4. Note the changes in how the corridors are displayed, as shown in Figure 5–73.

Figure 5–73

5. Select the preset view **Assem-Residential**.

6. Select any one of the assemblies and in the right-click menu, select **Select Similar** (at the bottom of the list). This selects all assemblies in your drawing.

7. As you did above, change the *Code Set Style* using the *Properties* palette. Experiment with the different styles, then set the style to **ASC-View-Edit**, as shown in Figure 5–74.

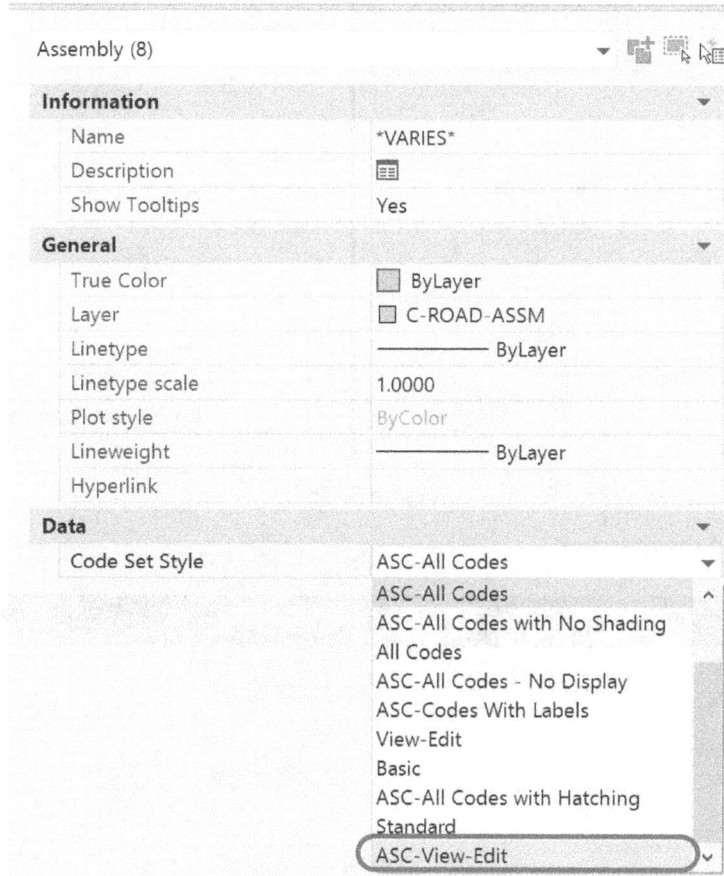

Figure 5–74

8. Note the changes in how the assemblies are displayed, as shown in Figure 5–75.

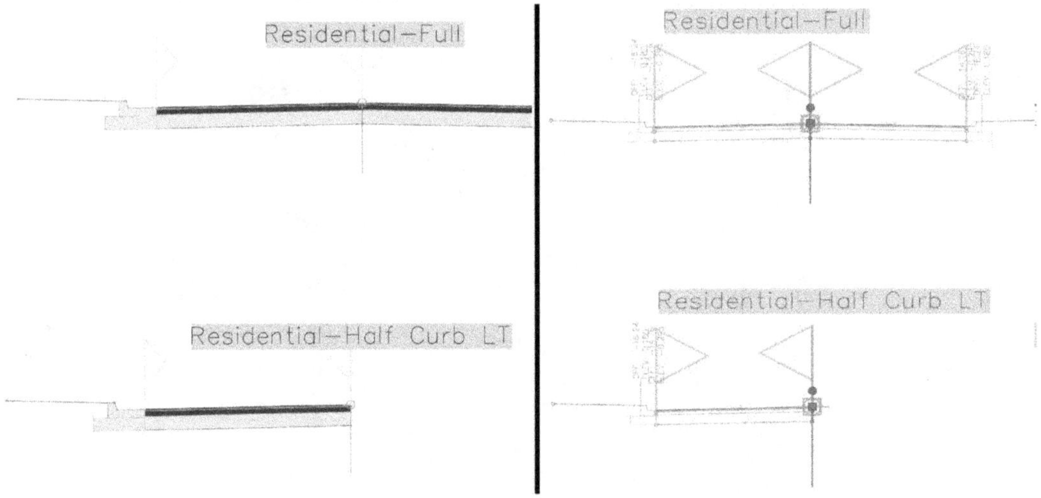

Figure 5–75

9. Save and close the drawing.

End of practice

Chapter Review Questions

1. How do you change the width of a lane in the corridor model? (Select all that apply.)
   a. Advanced Properties
   b. Assembly Properties
   c. Subassembly Properties
   d. Corridor Properties

2. How do you insert an assembly into the drawing? (Select all that apply.)
   a. Insert as a block
   b. Through a tool palette
   c. By right-clicking in the *TOOLSPACE>Prospector* tab
   d. Drag and drop from the Design Center

3. How do you insert an assembly into a tool palette?
   a. Right-click in the tool palette
   b. Drag and drop from Model Space
   c. By right-clicking in the *TOOLSPACE>Prospector* tab
   d. You cannot place assemblies in a tool palette

4. Which of the following are NOT required to generate a roundabout? (Select all that apply.)
   a. Civil 3D existing and final surfaces (optional)
   b. Point groups
   c. Alignments
   d. Profiles (optional)
   e. Feature lines

5. What does the *Corridor Section Editor* enable you to do?

   a. Review and edit each parameter of a subassembly.

   b. Adjust the existing ground grade at a specific station.

   c. Change the assembly being used at a specific station.

   d. Change the grid displayed behind a cross-section.

6. What does a mass haul diagram represent?

   a. The total cut and fill materials for a project site.

   b. The total weight of a corridor mass.

   c. The total weight that can be hauled on a corridor model.

   d. The cumulative cut and fill material volumes along a corridor.

Command Summary

Button	Command	Location
	Balancing Options	• **Contextual Ribbon:** *Mass Haul* tab>*Modify Subassembly* panel • **Command Prompt:** EditBalancingOptions
	Corridor Properties	• **Contextual Ribbon:** *Corridor* tab>*Modify Corridor* panel • **Command Prompt:** editcorridorproperties
	Corridor Section Editor	• **Contextual Ribbon:** *Corridor* tab>*Modify Corridor Sections* panel • **Command Prompt:** vieweditcorridorsection
	Creating Roundabouts	• **Ribbon:** *Home* tab>*Create Design* panel • **Command Prompt:** createcorridor
	Assembly Properties	• **Contextual Ribbon:** *Assembly* tab>*Modify Assembly* panel • **Command Prompt:** editassemblyproperties
	Copy Subassembly	• **Contextual Ribbon:** *Assembly* tab>*Modify Subassembly* panel • **Command Prompt:** copysubassemblyto
	Field	• **Ribbon:** *Insert* tab>*Data* panel **Command Prompt:** Field
	Mass Haul Diagram	• **Ribbon:** *Analyze* tab>*Volumes and Materials* panel • **Command Prompt:** CreateMassHaulDiagram
	Mirror Subassembly	• **Contextual Ribbon:** *Assembly* tab>*Modify Subassembly* panel • **Command Prompt:** mirrorsubassembly
	Move Subassembly	• **Contextual Ribbon:** *Assembly* tab>*Modify Subassembly* panel • **Command Prompt:** movesubassembly
	New View	• **Ribbon:** *View* tab>*Named View* panel • **Command Prompt:** View
	Subassembly Properties	• **Contextual Ribbon:** *Assembly* tab>*Modify Subassembly* panel • **Command Prompt:** editsubassemblyproperties
	Select Similar Subassemblies	• **Contextual Ribbon:** *Assembly* tab>*Modify Subassembly* panel • **Command Prompt:** selectsimilarSA

Button	Command	Location
	Tool Palettes	• **Ribbon:** *Home* tab>*Palettes* panel • **Shortcut:** <Ctrl>+<3>

Pipes - Beyond the Basics

In this chapter, you will learn how to configure parts lists for the pipe and pressure pipe networks for your Civil 3D project. You will make adjustments to a pressure pipe network and add appurtenances to water mains.

Learning Objectives

- Configure pipe network and pressure pipe network parts lists.
- Fine tune pipe settings.
- Add parts to a pressure network.

6.1 Pipes Configuration

The *TOOLSPACE>Settings* tab contains values and styles affecting pipe networks. The *Parts Lists* and *Pipe Rules* are the most important settings. Parts lists contain typical pipes, fittings, appurtenances, and structures for a utility. Pipe rules trigger error alerts if pipes/structures are not created in accordance with predefined constraints, such as the minimum or maximum pipe length or slope.

Edit Drawing Settings

The *Edit Drawing Settings* dialog box contains values affecting the pipe layout layers (e.g., pipe networks, fittings, profiles, and section views).

Pipe Network Feature Settings

The *Edit Feature Settings - Pipe Network* dialog box (shown in Figure 6−1) contains values that assign styles, set the pipe network naming convention, set the default pipe and structure rules, and set the default location for pipe and structure labels. To open the *Edit Feature Settings* dialog box, right-click on **Settings** in the *Pipe Network* collection and select **Edit Feature Settings**.

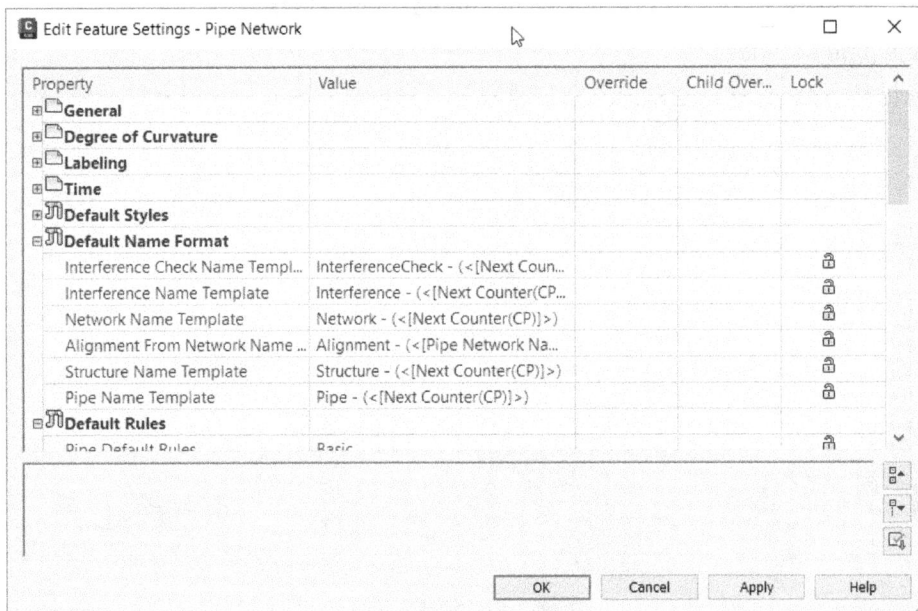

Figure 6−1

Pipe Catalog

The Autodesk Civil 3D software includes standard catalogs in both imperial and metric units. Catalog specifications define the size and shape of the underground structures and pipes for sanitary or storm gravity systems.

- The *Imperial Pipes* folder contains **Imperial Pipes.htm**, which displays the components of the Pipe catalog.

- The Pipe catalog includes circular, egg, elliptical, and rectangular shapes. For each pipe shape, the catalog includes inner and outer pipe diameters and wall thicknesses.

Pipe catalog components can be edited by selecting **Modify>Pipe network>Parts List>Part Builder**.

Structure Catalog

The Structure catalog includes specifications for inlets, junction structures (circular, rectangular, or eccentric) with or without frames, and simple junction shapes (rectangular or circular). Additional structures can be created by using the Infrastructure Parts Editor. This is a separate program that runs outside of Civil 3D. The Structure catalog consists of tables and lists that define allowable sizes, thicknesses, and heights.

Pressure Pipe Catalog

The Pressure Pipe catalog contains configuration files for many different types of pressure pipes, materials, fittings, and appurtenances. Furthermore, additional parts can be created by using the Infrastructure Parts Editor. This is a separate program that runs outside of Civil 3D.

Pipe Network Parts Lists

While the catalogs are shared between multiple projects (and multiple users), each Autodesk Civil 3D drawing can contain any number of parts lists that are specific to that drawing.

Parts lists are populated with pipes and structures from the catalog and are organized for a specific task (such as sanitary sewer and drain).

- Parts lists are found in the *TOOLSPACE>Settings* tab under the *Pipe Network* and *Pressure Network* collections, as shown in Figure 6–2.

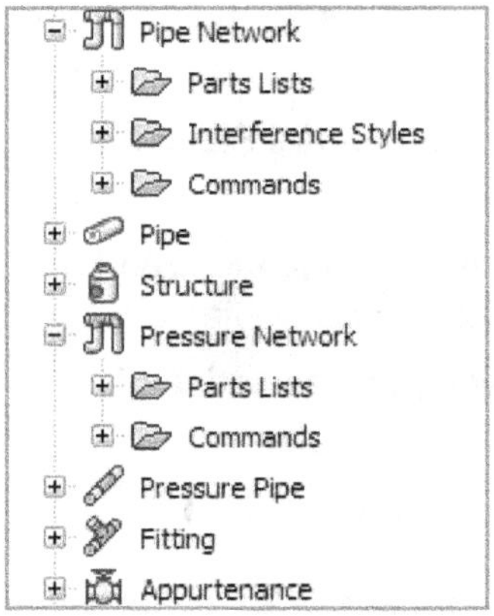

Figure 6–2

- To display a parts list, right-click on its name and select **Edit**.

The *Network Parts List* dialog box has typical pipe sizes in the *Pipes* tab and typical structures in the *Structures* tab, as shown in Figure 6–3. If required, you can change a pipe or structure size list, or add a new part type.

An important setting for each tab is *Rules*. This is discussed in greater detail later in this chapter.

The *Render Material* affects how the pipes and structures display in 3D.

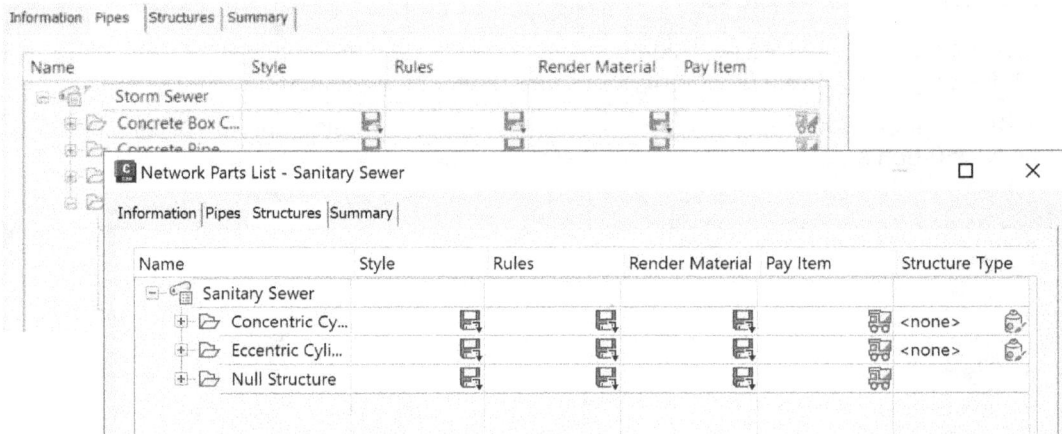

Figure 6–3

- To add a pipe size or structure size, select the part type heading, right-click, and select **Add a part size**. In the *Part Size Creator* dialog box, select a new part size from the size list, as shown in Figure 6–4.

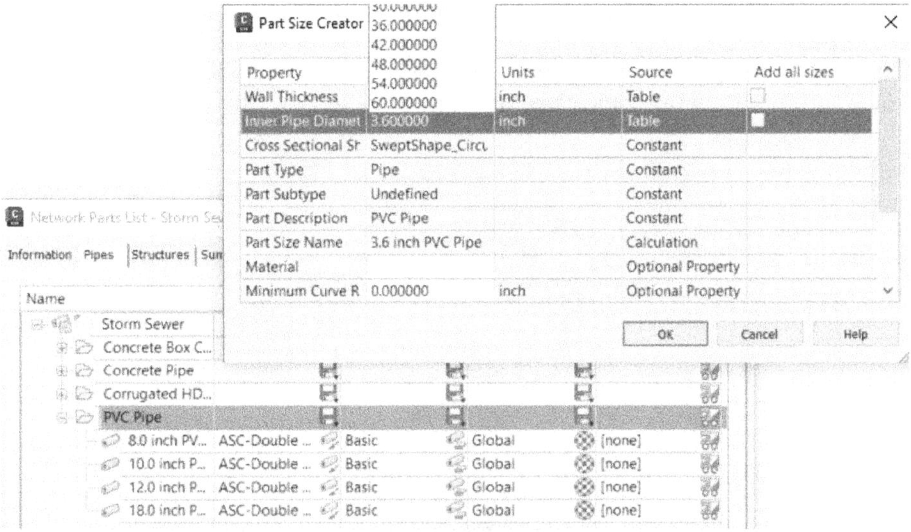

Figure 6-4

- To add a new part family (e.g., concrete pipes for a sanitary system), select the name of the part list, right-click, and select **Add a part family**. In the *Part Catalog* dialog box, select a new part family from the list of available parts in the catalog, as shown in Figure 6-5.

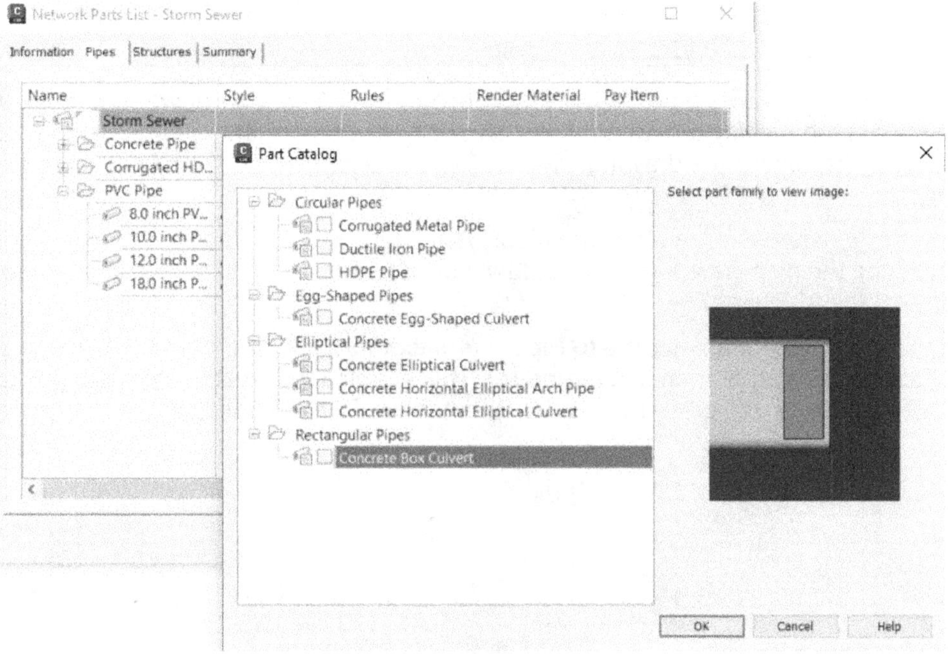

Figure 6-5

The *Pressure Network Parts List* dialog box has typical pipe sizes in the *Pressure Pipes* tab, typical fitting sizes in the *Fittings* tab, and typical appurtenance sizes in the *Appurtenances* tab, as shown in Figure 6–6. If required, you can change any of the size lists or add a new part type. *Render Material* affects how the various parts display in 3D.

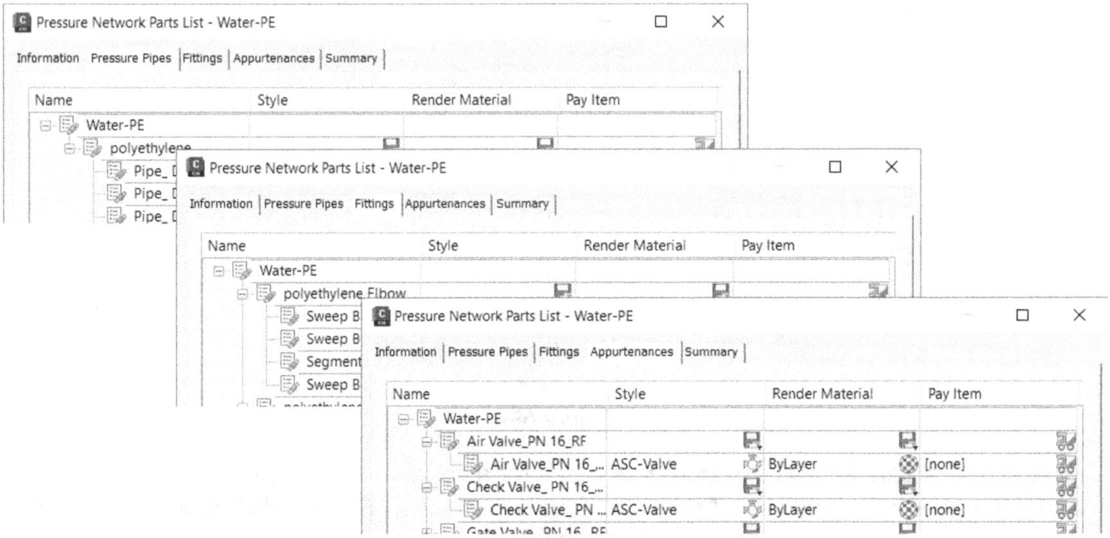

Figure 6–6

Pipe and Structure Styles

The pipe style defines how a pipe displays in plan, profile, and section views. The most used tab of a pipe style is the *Display* tab. By toggling on or off the component display, a style affects how a network displays in the drawing window (e.g., as a single or double line), its layer name, and color.

A structure style defines how a structure displays in plan, profile and section views. The plan settings include the plan view symbol and how a structure displays in profile and section views (the outline of the 3D shape).

Pipe styles include the **Clean up Pipe to Pipe Intersections** option for networks, where one pipe connects to another (rather than to a structure). This enables the pipes to seem to join together. For this option to work, the pipes must be connected with a *null* structure.

Pipe and Structure Rules

Since pipes and structures often need more than one rule applied to them, individual rules are organized into collections called **rule sets**. The rules are then prioritized from most important to least important by organizing the order in which they display in the list. You can have different sets for different types of pipe, sizes, and/or systems.

- Pipe rules define minimum/maximum slopes, cover, minimum/maximum pipe segment length, how pipes of different sizes align, and how they are truncated when attached to a structure.

- Pipe rule sets are located in the *TOOLSPACE>Settings* tab, in the *Pipe Rule Set* collection, as shown in Figure 6−7. To display or edit a rule set, right-click on it and select **Edit**.

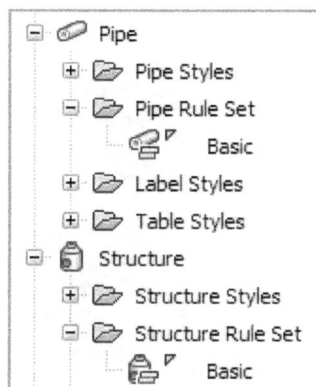

Figure 6−7

- Structure rules define the across structure drop's default value, maximum value, maximum pipe size, and sump depth.

- Structure rule sets are located in the *TOOLSPACE>Settings* tab, under the *Structure Rule Set* collection.

  Note: Pressure networks do not use rules. They have other means of checking for conformity to design conditions.

Some pipe and structure rules directly control the layout of new pipes and structures, such as minimum and maximum slope. Some rules are checks that are made after creation, such as maximum pipe length. Rules such as maximum pipe length, for example, do not prevent you from creating a pipe that is over the maximum length. However, if a pipe is over the maximum length, you are prompted with a warning in the *TOOLSPACE>Prospector* tab and in the *Pipe Network* vista, as shown in Figure 6−8.

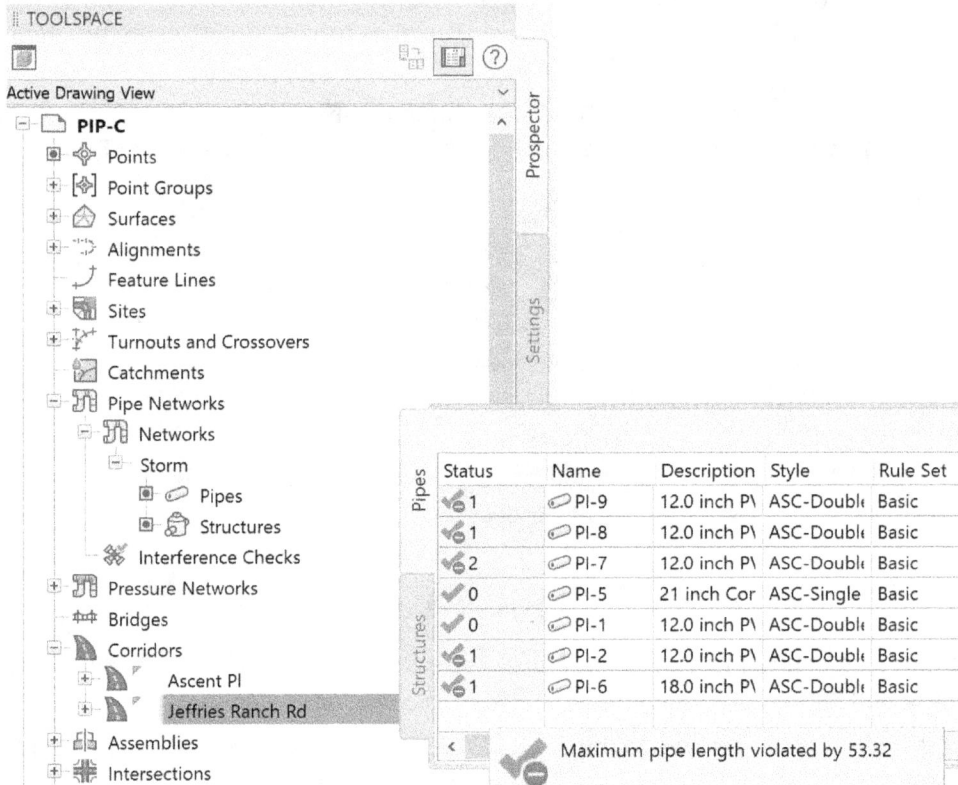

Figure 6−8

Reapplying Pipe Rules

Structure Invert Out elevations are automatically calculated based on the given rules when the structure is first created. Therefore, if new connecting pipes are added to a structure below the lowest invert, the outlet is not automatically lowered until you click ⬚ (Apply Rules) in the *Modify* tab>*Pipe Network*>*Modify* panel. An example is shown in Figure 6–9.

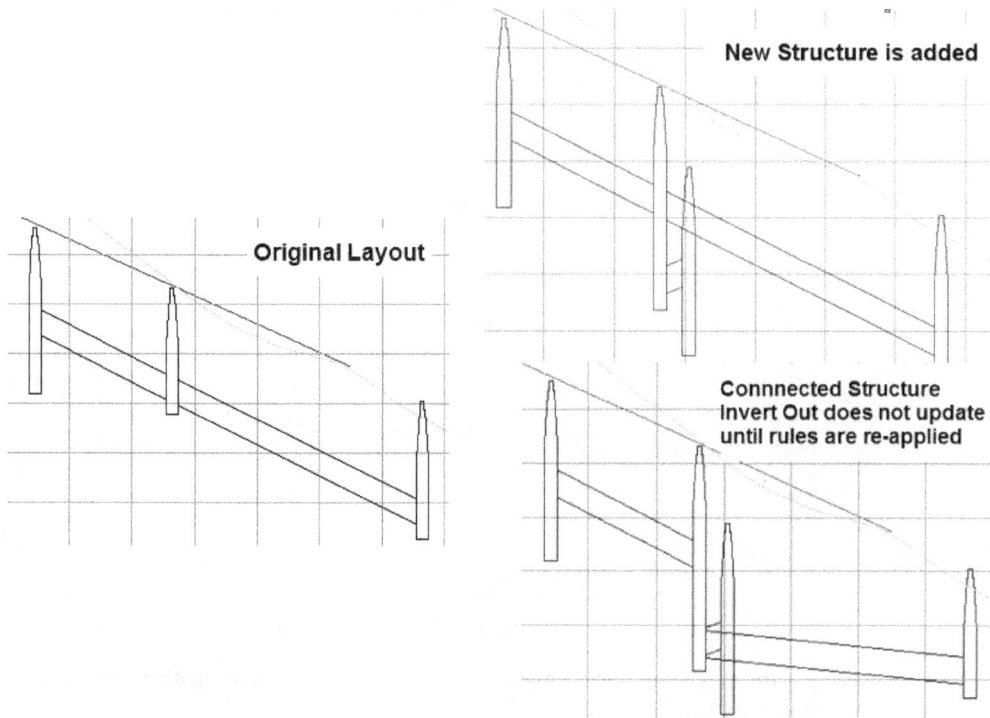

New Structure is added

Original Layout

Connnected Structure Invert Out does not update until rules are re-applied

Figure 6–9

Pipe Layers

Unlike most Autodesk Civil 3D objects, pipe network layers typically need to be manually reassigned when a pipe network is created. Layers need to be assigned for pipes and structures in plan, profile, and section views. For example, the default Autodesk Civil 3D templates automatically map to layers appropriate for storm drainage structures when using the *Pipe Network Creation Tools* and water structures when using the *Pressure Pipe Creation Tools*. The respective *Pipe Network Layers* dialog boxes are shown in Figure 6–10.

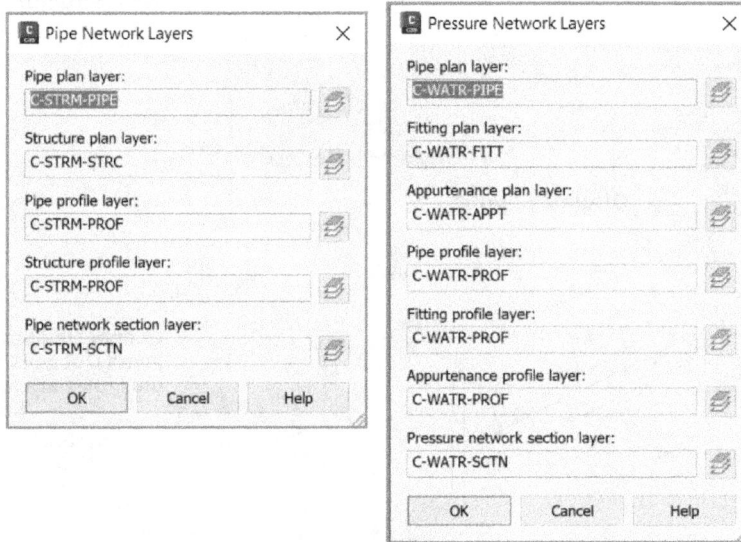

Figure 6–10

If creating a sanitary sewer line, each one needs to be remapped to layers specific to sanitary sewer utilities, such as the example shown in Figure 6–11.

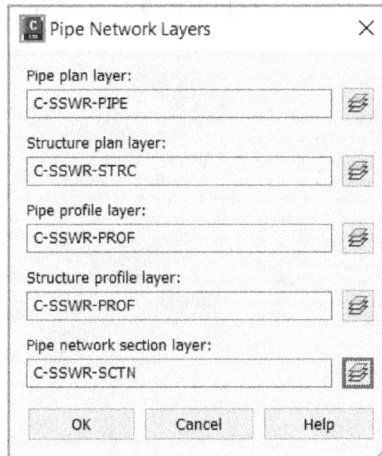

Figure 6–11

Pressure Pipe Parts Lists

As with the *Pipe* and *Structure* catalogs, pressure pipes can be shared among multiple projects (and multiple users). They can contain any number of *Pressure Network Parts Lists* that are specific to that drawing.

Each *Pressure Network Parts List* can contain multiple catalogs for different materials, allowing for one pressure network to have a combination of parts with different materials, as shown in Figure 6-12.

When parts of a catalog are used within a network, the *Status* states it is **In Use** and there is a lock symbol. If no parts are used, the *Status* states it is **Loaded** with a green checkmark. This means it can be unloaded at any time.

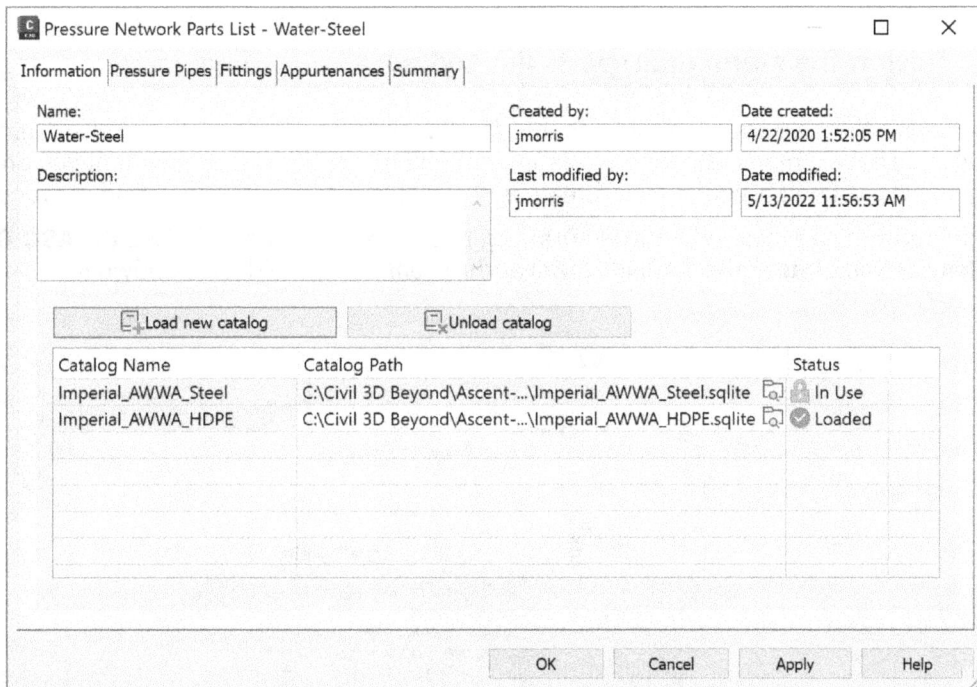

Figure 6-12

Practice 6a
Configure Pipe Networks

Practice Objective

- Create a new reference template for pipe networks with settings for your organization.

Hint: Software Configuration

For the practices in this chapter to work properly, the configuration changes as noted in the preface of this course must be made.

Task 1: Review the storm drain parts list and rules.

Before creating a network, you should become familiar with the configuration you are about to use. While you have already attached a reference template for the styles, now that you are working on pipe networks, you need to create and attach another reference template for pipes.

1. In the *Application Menu*, select **New>Drawing** to create a new drawing. Use the **ASC-Base-Styles.dwt template** in the *C:\Civil 3D Beyond\Ascent-Config* folder, as shown in Figure 6–13.

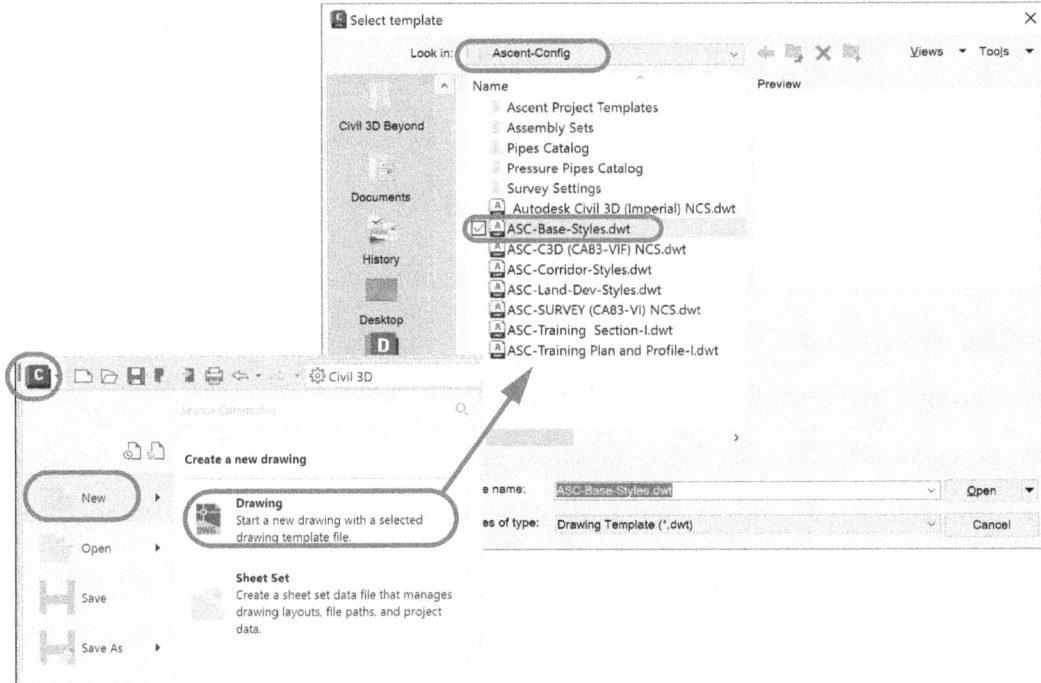

Figure 6–13

2. Save the file as **XXX-Pipe-Styles.dwg** (substitute your initials for XXX) in the *C:\Civil 3D Beyond\Ascent-Config* folder.

3. In the *TOOLSPACE>Settings* tab, expand the *Pipe Network* collection, expand the *Parts Lists* collection, right-click on the **Storm Sewer** part list, and select **Edit...**.

4. In the *Network Parts List* dialog box, in the *Pipes* tab, the parts list currently contains a large number of concrete pipes. They are all assigned to use the **Basic** rule set and a pipe style that displays double lines in plan view, as shown in Figure 6-14.

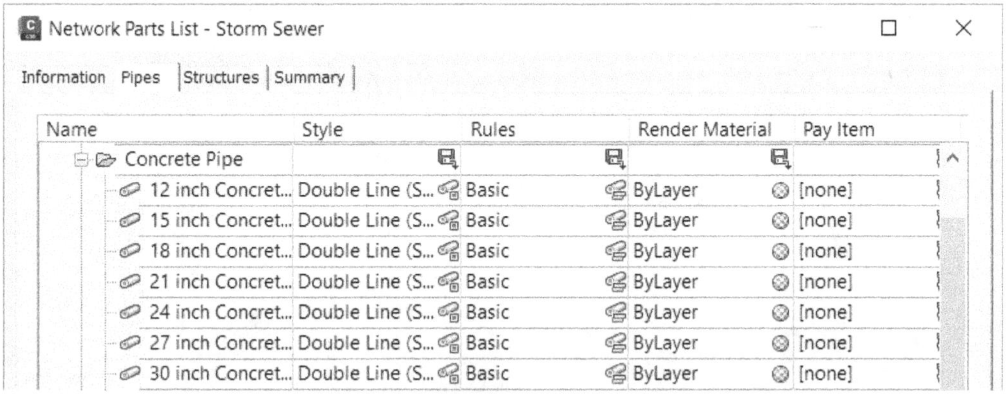

Figure 6-14

5. You do not need all these sizes. Click on the ones you want to remove, right-click, and select **Delete**, as shown in Figure 6-15 (note that you can only do this one at a time). Ensure that you keep the 12", 15", 21", 30", and 60" parts.

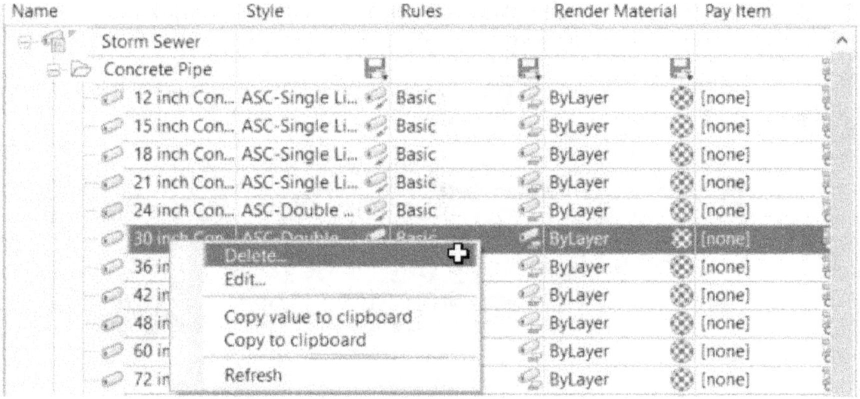

Figure 6-15

6. To change the *Style* of the smaller diameter pipes to be single lines, select the pipes up to size 21", select ✏️ (Pipe Style), and select **ASC-Single Line (Storm)** from the list, as shown in Figure 6–16. (Note: You can only select one size at a time.)

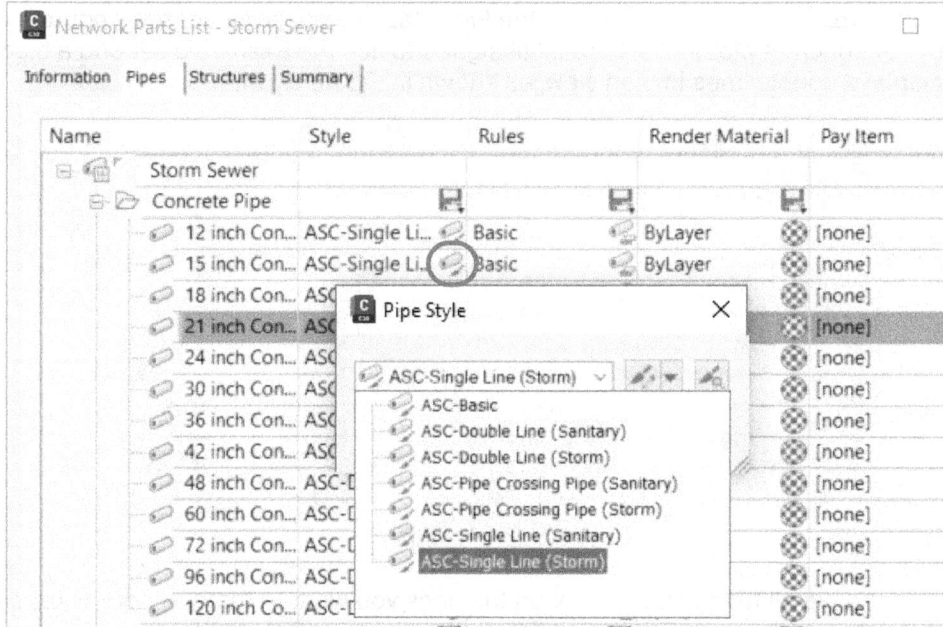

Figure 6–16

7. Delete the **Concrete Elliptical Culvert** type (if present) by right-clicking on it and selecting **Delete...**. Confirm that you want to delete this pipe type.

8. To add another pipe type, right-click on **Storm Sewer** and select **Add part family...**, as shown in Figure 6–17.

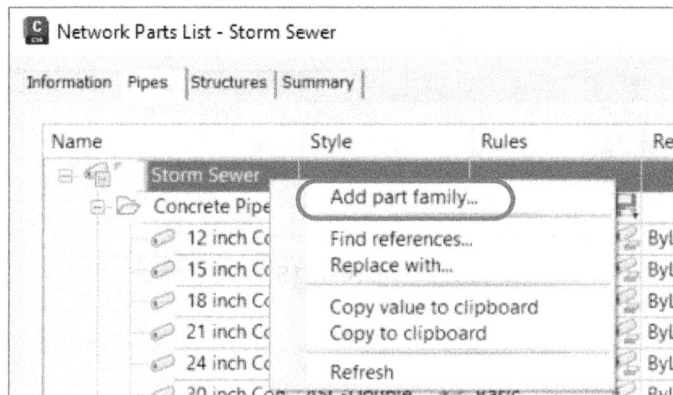

Figure 6–17

9. In the *Part Catalog* dialog box, select **PVC Pipe**, as shown in Figure 6–18, and click **OK**. Note that the pipe parts that are already in your parts list do not show in this list.

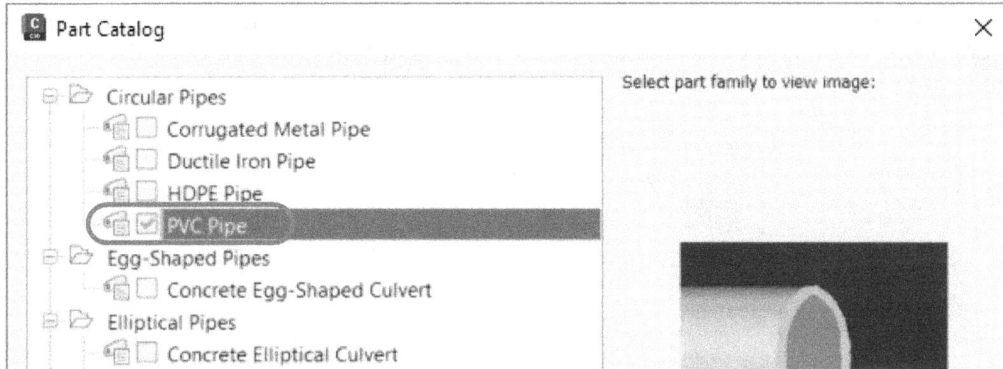

Figure 6–18

10. To add sizes to the part family, select **PVC Pipe**, right-click, and select **Add part size...**, as shown in Figure 6–19.

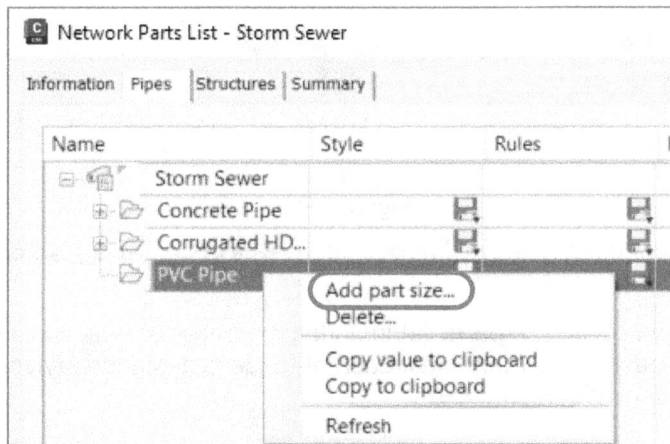

Figure 6–19

11. In the *Part Size Creator* dialog box, select and add the pipe sizes **8, 10, 12,** and **18.** Note that you cannot select all four of these sizes at once. You will need to add each one separately. To add a part size, select the individual size in the *Value* drop-down list (or you can select the checkbox in the *Add all sizes* column to add all of the available sizes), as shown in Figure 6–20. Change the part *Material* to **PVC if it is not already set.** Click **OK** to add each one.

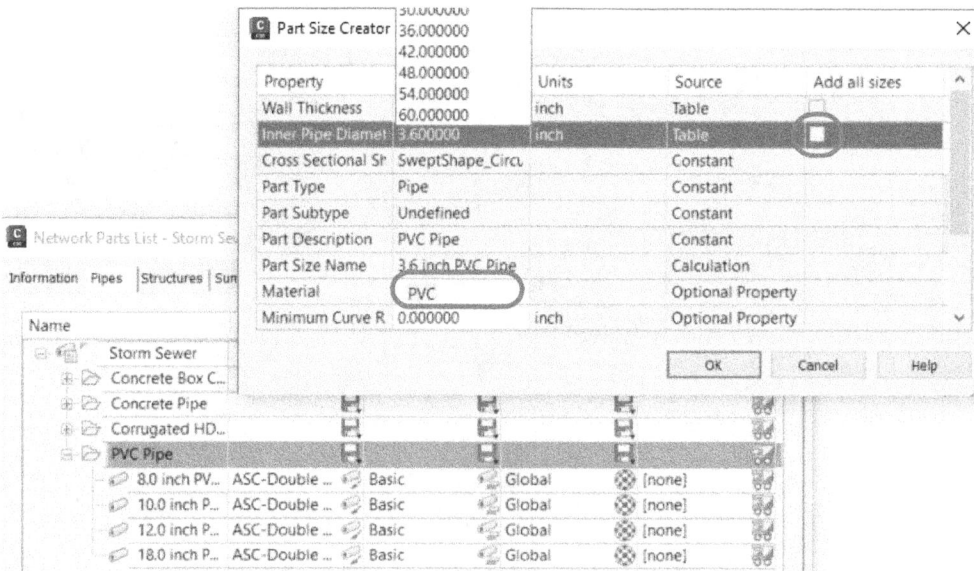

Figure 6–20

12. Change the *Style* of the 8.0" and 10.0" PVC pipes to **ASC-Single Line (Storm)** as you had done previously.

13. Select the *Structures* tab. The parts list includes a number of headwalls of different sizes, as well as catch basins and manholes. Each of these is assigned styles and rules specific to each type, as shown in Figure 6–21.

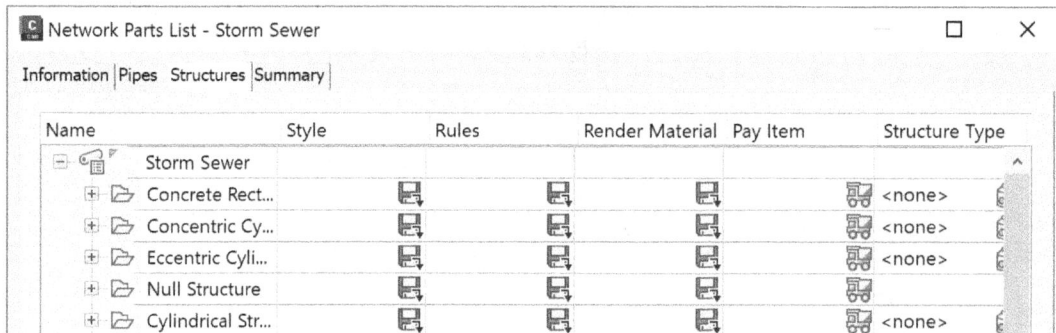

Figure 6–21

14. As you did with the pipes, add a structure part family by right-clicking on **Storm Sewer** and selecting the **Concrete Flared End Section**, as shown in Figure 6–22.

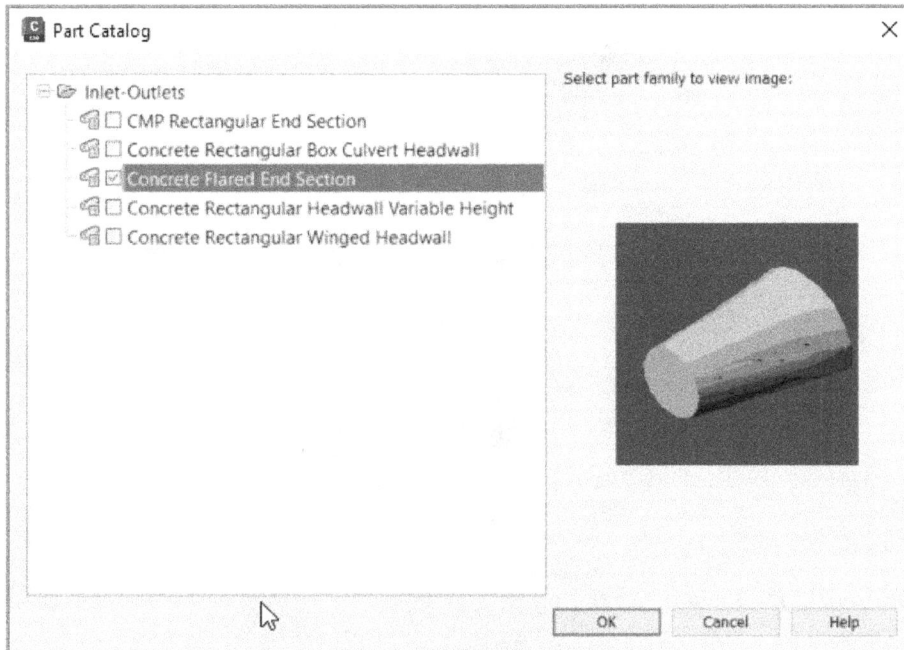

Figure 6–22

15. Add **12"** as the part size and click **OK** to exit the *Part Catalog*.

16. Click **OK** to close the *Network Parts List* dialog box.

17. In the *TOOLSPACE>Settings* tab, expand the *Structure* collection, expand the *Structure Rule Set* collection, right-click on the **ASC-Basic** rule set, and select **Edit...**, as shown in Figure 6–23.

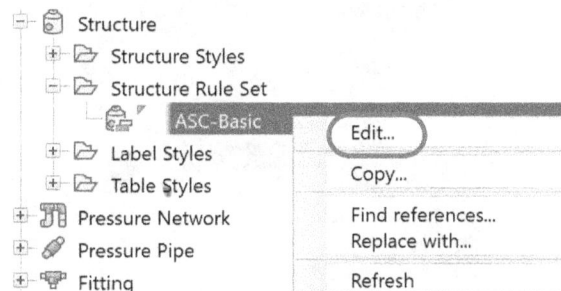

Figure 6–23

18. In the *Structure Rule Set* dialog box, in the **Maximum pipe size check** rule, set the *Maximum pipe diameter or width* to **4'**. In the **Pipe Drop Across Structure** rule, set the elevations based on **Invert** and a drop across the manhole to **0.10'** with a **3'** maximum interior drop, as shown in Figure 6–24.

Figure 6–24

Note: The arrows available on the right side of the Rules tab enable you to prioritize the rules. The rules are processed sequentially from bottom to top. Therefore, place the most important rule at the top of the list.

19. Click **OK** to exit and save these changes.

Task 2: Review and append pressure network parts list.

1. Continue working with the drawing from the previous task or open **ASC-Pipe-Styles-1.dwg** from the *C:\Civil 3D Beyond\ Ascent-Config* folder.

2. In the *TOOLSPACE>Settings* tab, expand the *Pressure Network* collection, expand the *Parts Lists* collection, right-click on the **Water-Steel** parts list, and select **Edit...**, as shown in Figure 6–25.

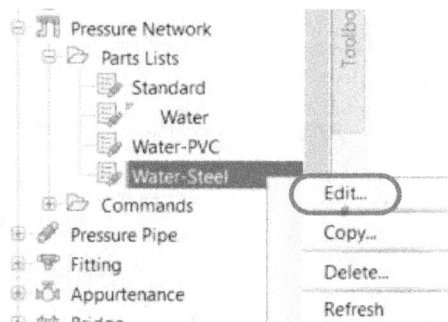

Figure 6–25

Note: If you get an error about a missing catalog, consult the Configuration Changes section in the Preface for proper configuration.

3. In the *Pressure Network Parts List* dialog box, in the *Pressure Pipes* tab, review the available pipe sizes. To the right of the steel family, select the diskette icon to change all of the styles to **ASC-Double Line (Water)** if not already set, as shown in Figure 6-26.

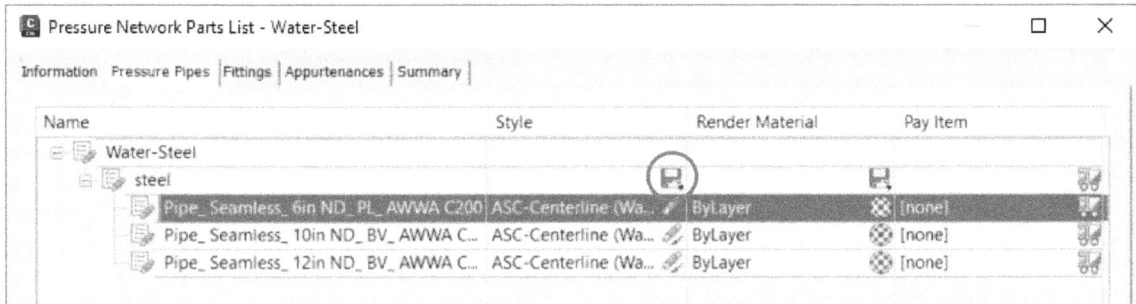

Figure 6-26

4. In the *Fittings* tab, review the available fittings. To the right of each family, select the diskette icon to change all of the styles to **ASC-Fitting** if not already set, as shown in Figure 6-27.

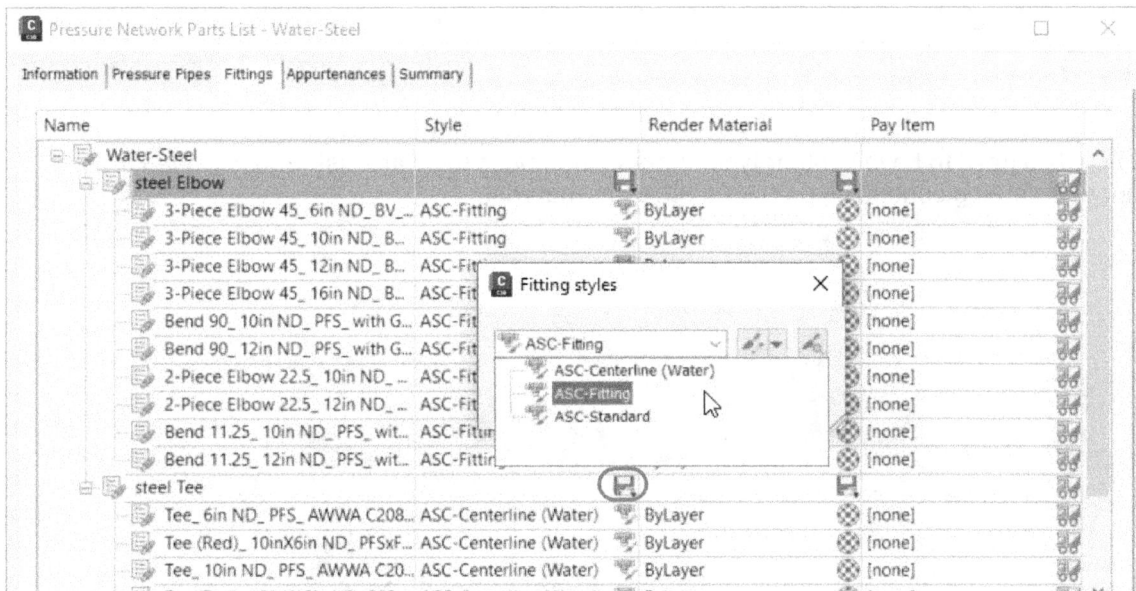

Figure 6-27

5. In the *Appurtenances* tab, review the available valves. To the right of each family, select the diskette icon to set the style to **ASC-Valve** if not already set, as shown in Figure 6−28.

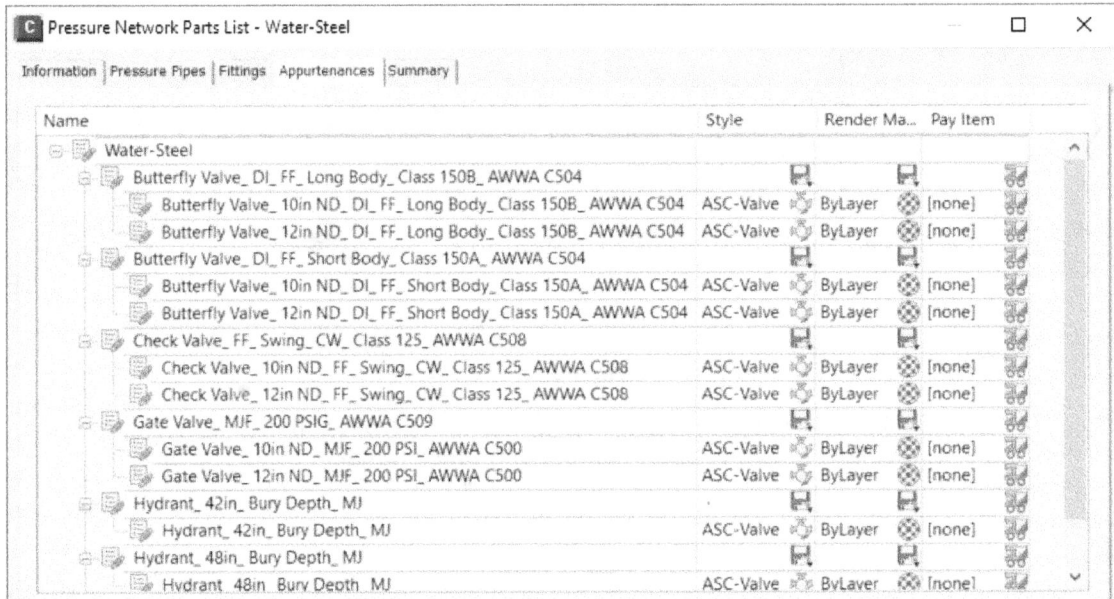

Figure 6−28

There is a need to have another type of pressure pipe in this parts list. You will need to load another catalog containing parts of a different material.

6. Go to the *Information* tab and click **Load new catalog**, as shown in Figure 6–29.

7. Browse to the *C:\Civil 3D Beyond\Ascent-Config\Pressure Pipes Catalog*Imperial folder, select the **Imperial_AWWA_HDPE.sqlite** catalog (as shown in Figure 6–29) and click **Open**.

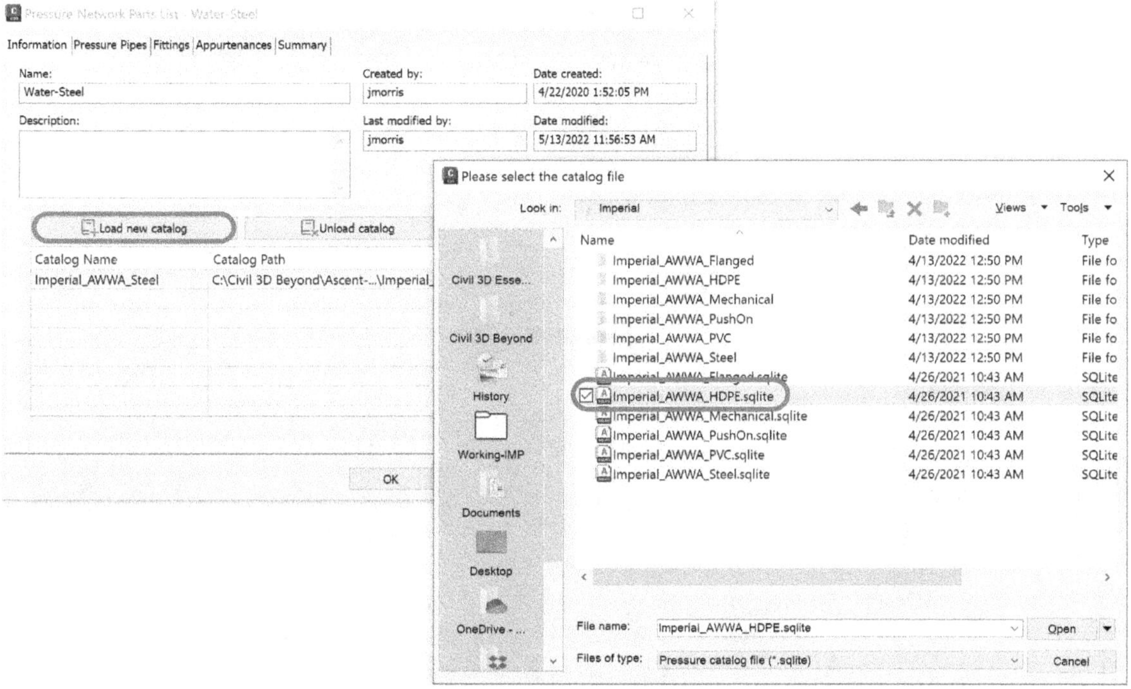

Figure 6–29

- Note that the existing catalog is in use and cannot be unloaded, since the parts list contains parts of this catalog. The newly loaded catalog has a **Loaded** status and can be unloaded, since no parts from this catalog are used, as shown in Figure 6−30.

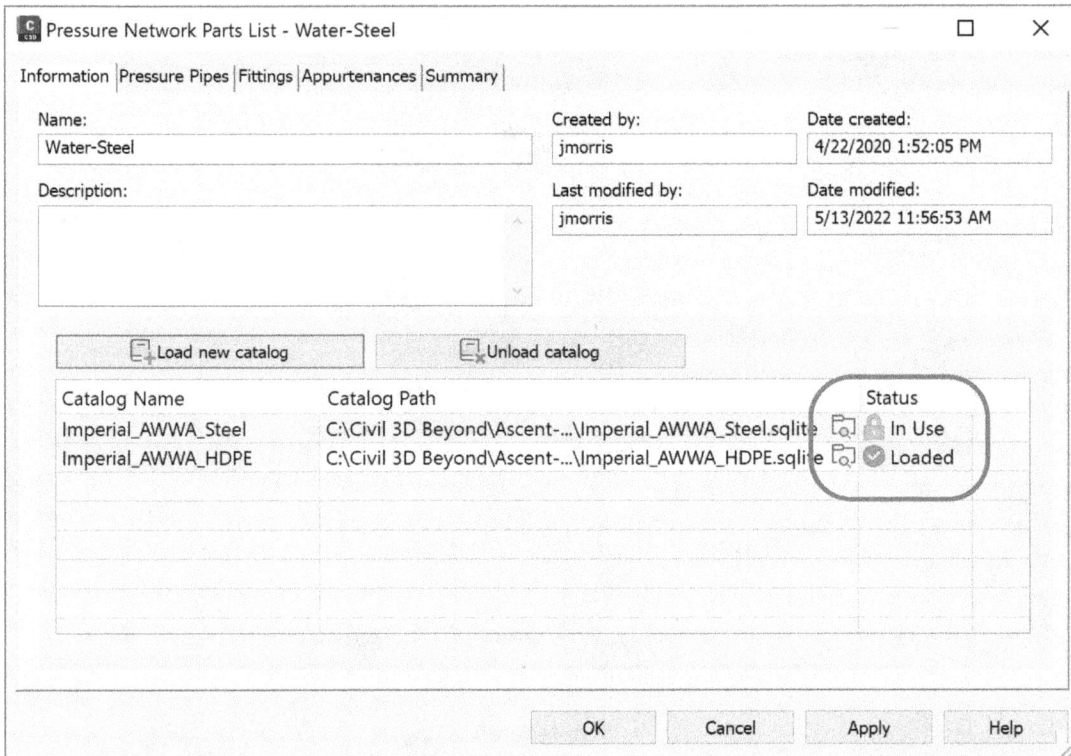

Figure 6−30

8. To load pressure pipe parts from the newly loaded catalog, go to the *Pressure Pipes* tab, right-click on Water-Steel, and select **Add Material**.

9. In the *Pressure Network Catalog* dialog box, use the drop-down menu to select the **Imperial_AWWA_HDPE.sqlite** catalog. Once selected, check the box next to the **High Density Polyethylene (HDPE)** listing to load this material, then click **OK**, as shown in Figure 6–31.

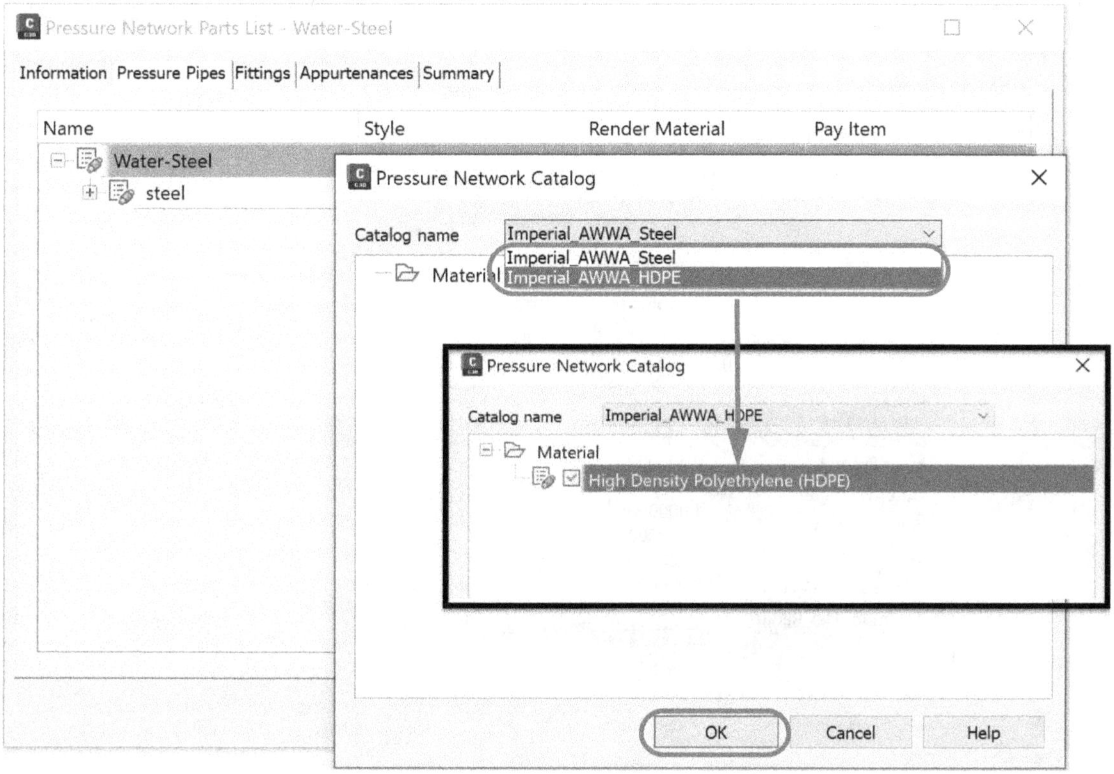

Figure 6–31

10. Now you can load different sizes of pipes as you did earlier. Right-click on **High Density Polyethylene (HDPE)** and select **Add Size...**, then in the *Add Pressure Pipe Sizes* dialog box, select **3.000** from the drop-down list for *Nominal Diameter*, as shown in Figure 6−32.

Figure 6−32

11. Click **OK** to close the *Add Pressure Pipe Sizes* dialog box. The newly added pipe is listed under its material, as shown in Figure 6–33.

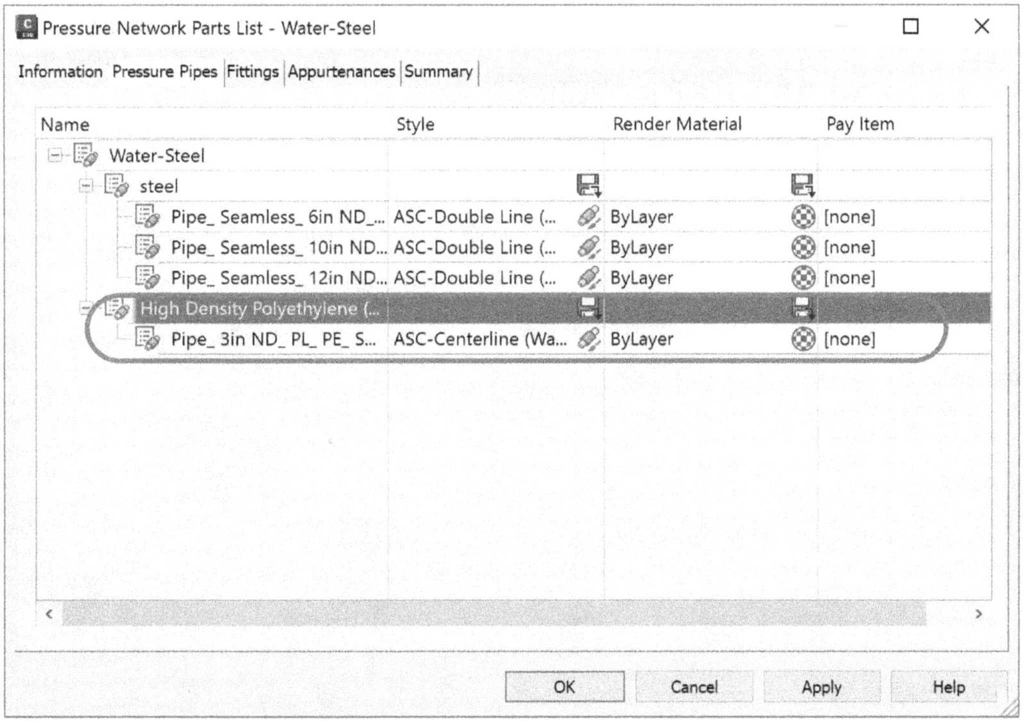

Figure 6–33

12. Click **OK**.

13. If time permits, you can add other sizes in a similar manner, or add other appurtenances and fittings.

14. Click **OK** to close the *Pressure Network Parts List* dialog box.

15. Save and close the drawing.

End of practice

6.2 Pressure Pipes

When pipes of different pipe runs intersect, there is a ⚓ (Branch Fitting) tool to connect them. If the appropriate fitting (such as a tee fitting) is found within the parts list, it will connect the pipes appropriately. If there is no proper part in the parts list, Civil 3D will get as close as it can with the parts available.

Appurtenances

Appurtenances are valves, which can be added in the same manner as fittings. Click 🛢 (Add Appurtenance) in the *Pressure Network Plan Layout* tab>*Insert* panel.

Included in the Pressure Pipes catalogs are the following appurtenances:

- Gate valves

- Butterfly valves

- Air valves

- Hydrants (above and below ground)

- Shut-off valves

- Check valves

- Globe valves

Appurtenances are attached to existing pipes. Hydrants can only be connected at the end of a pipe with a free connection. As the insertion point nears the end of a pipe, the Connect Pipe glyph (⊐) appears, which suggests the potential to connect to the pipe. When accepted by picking the point, the connection is created.

Other appurtenances can be inserted either at the end of a pipe or anywhere along a pipe. When placed along a pipe, the *Broken Pipe* glyph (⊐ ⊏) indicates that the existing pipe will be broken and another pipe is created beyond the inserted appurtenance.

Pressure Pipe Styles

In the fitting and appurtenance styles, you can choose to display the parts as boundaries, catalog-defined blocks, or user-defined blocks. For parts drawn in profile views, you can add masks to hide underlying geometry, you can add hatching to the parts, and you can crop the pipes at the extent of the profile view.

Swap Pressure Parts

Similar to gravity-fed pipe networks, pressure pipe networks have the option to exchange one part for another, but in a different type, part family, or size. To start the command, select the

part, right-click, and select **Swap Pressure Part**, or click    (Swap Pressure Part) in the contextual tab. The *Swap Pressure Network Parts* dialog box displays, as shown in Figure 6–34.

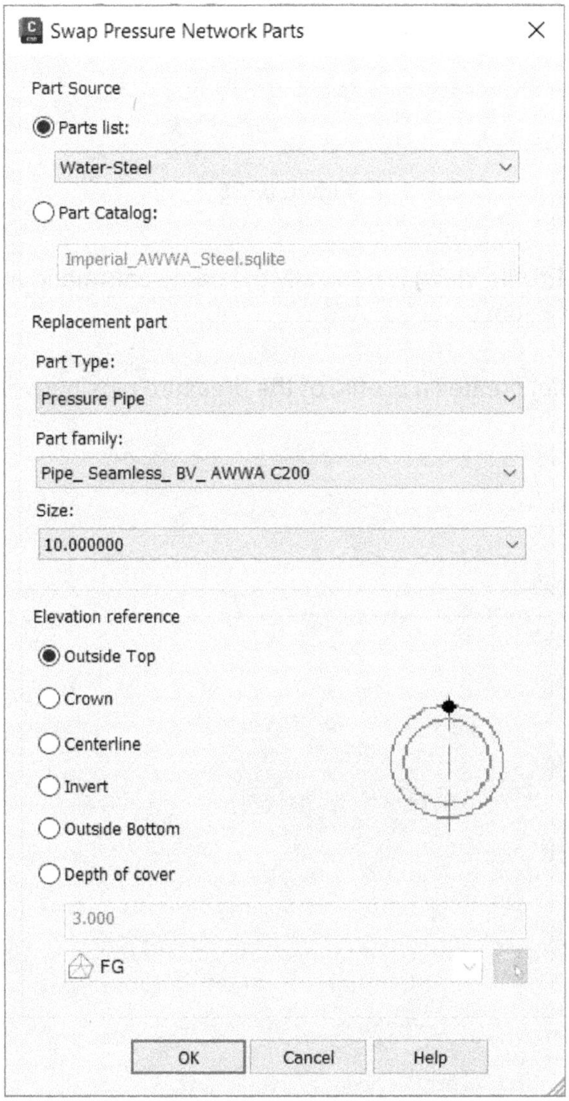

Figure 6–34

Pressure Pipes in profile views

As with Gravity pipe networks, parts of pressure pipes can be added to profile views. There are two options. These commands are available through the *Pressure Network Plan Layout:Water* contextual tab>*Profile* panel, or through the **Modify** Tab, *Pressure Pipe Network* section (available on the *Design panel* drop-down list)s, as shown in Figure 6–35.

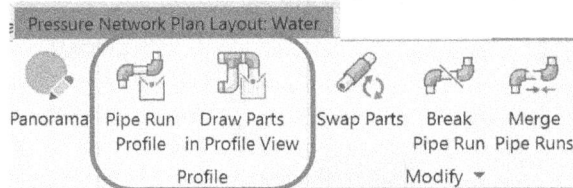

Figure 6–35

The [icon] (Draw Parts in Profile View) is basically the same command and options as for adding gravity networks to profile views.

The [icon] (Pipe Run Profile) creates a profile of the pressure pipe network in the selected profile view.

In the *Pipe Run Profile Settings* dialog box>*General* tab, the following can be set (as shown in Figure 6–36):

- *Offset Style:* **Cut Length** or **Offset at Bends**
- *Reference Profile:* Select the surface for Reference Profile to follow.
- *Offset Distance:* the distance between the Offset Style location and the pipe run Reference Profile.
- *Draw Profile in:* Select a new profile view, an existing profile view, or updating a profile (without prompting).

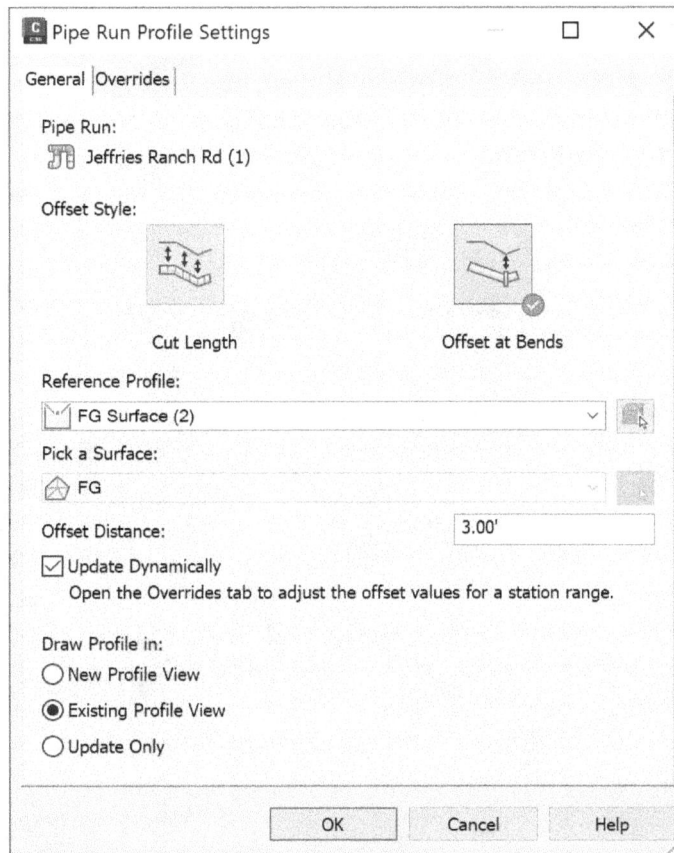

Figure 6–36

In the *Pipe Run Profile Settings* dialog box, the *Overrides* tab is for overriding the pipe profile at specific station ranges. The following can be set (as shown in Figure 6–37):

- *Add Station Range override*
- *Delete Station Range override*
- *Specify for each station range override:*
  - *Starting Station*
  - *Ending Station*
  - *Reference Profile* (select from drop-down list)
  - Distance of offset
  - Offset style (select from drop-down list)
- *Clean up PVIs checkbox: removes PVIs from overridden station ranges that are static and that do not contain vertical bends.*

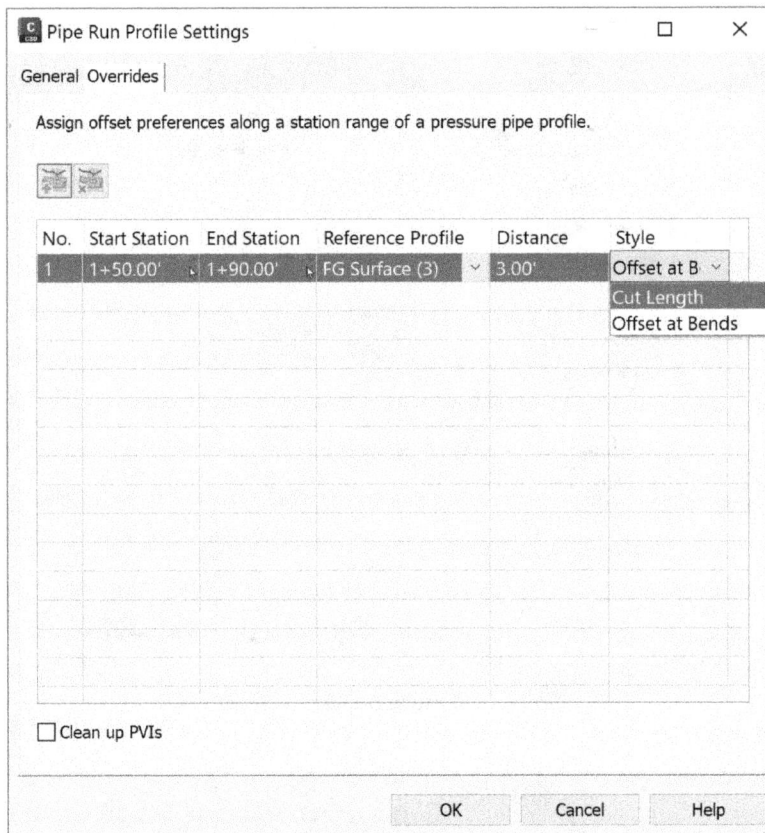

Figure 6–37

Practice 6b
Pressure Pipes

Practice Objectives

- Create pipe runs for hydrants.
- Notice error messages in pipe runs.
- Add appurtenances to a pressure pipe network.
- Add a pressure pipe network to a profile view.
- Adjust pressure pipes in a profile view.

Task 1: Add pipe runs for hydrants and add appurtenances.

In this task, you will create a water network branch for a fire hydrant.

1. Open **PIP-A.dwg** from the *C:\Civil 3D Beyond\Working\ PipeNetworks* folder.

2. Select the preset view **Pipe-Intersection**.

3. Select any pressure pipe object in the drawing. In the *Pressure Network Plan Layout:Water* contextual tab>*Pipe Run* panel, expand the *Add New Pipe Run* drop-down list and select **Create Pipe Run from Object**, as shown in Figure 6–38.

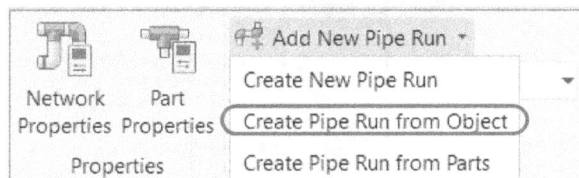

Figure 6–38

4. Type **X** to be able to pick the line that is part of the XREF.

5. Select the short blue line running between the hydrant symbol and the water main in the western portion of the intersection. Ensure that the direction arrow is pointing northward (as shown in Figure 6–39); if needed, type **R** to reverse the direction.

6. In the *Create Pipe Run from Objects* dialog box, set the following (as shown in Figure 6–39), then click **OK**:

   - *Pipe Run name:* **Hydrant - (<[Next Counter(CP)]>)** (Simply replace the text "Pipe Run" with "Hydrant")

   - *Pipe size:* **Pipe_ Seamless_ 6in ND_ BV_ AWWA C200**

   - *Reference surface:* **FG**

   - Uncheck **Create surface profile to follow***Reference alignment:* Can leave the default since you are not following a surface profile

   - *Horizontal offset distance:* **0.000**

   - *Cover:* **3.00'**

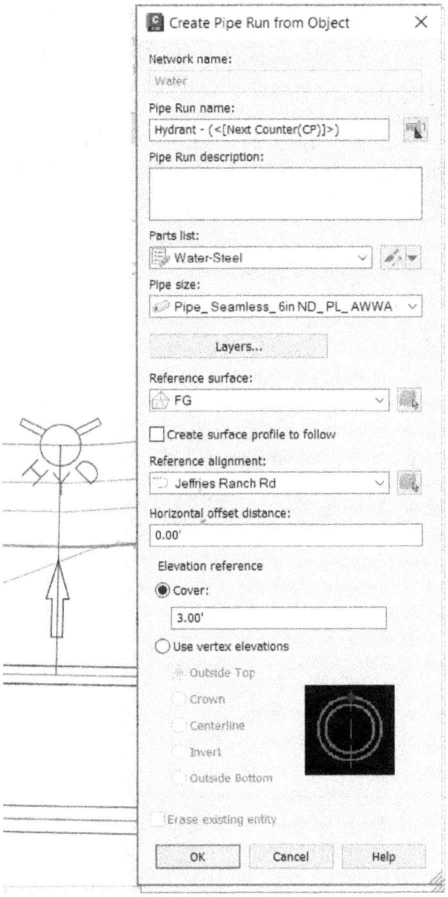

Figure 6–39

7. The connection to the water main is incomplete. To rectify this, select the hydrant waterline. Use the triangular grip at the bottom and pull it upward until it reaches the upper edge of the water pipe and you see the *Connect Pipe* glyph (——⊡—). Release the water main and the fitting is made, as shown in Figure 6–40.

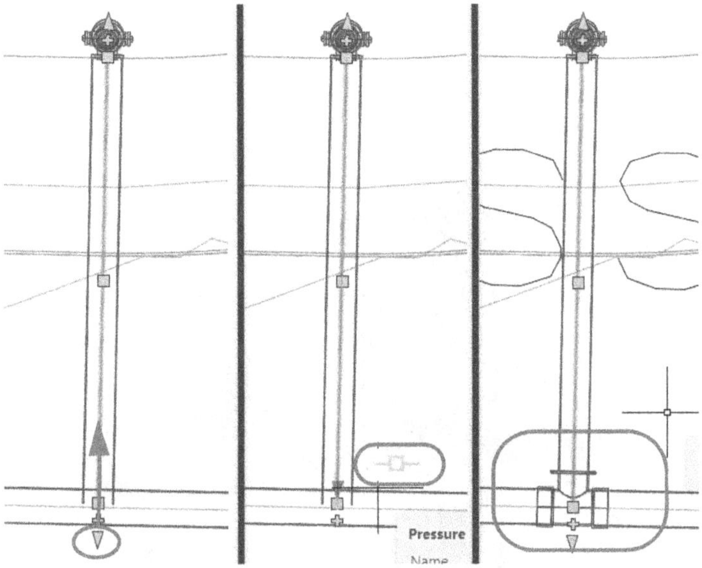

Figure 6–40

8. Press <Esc> to clear the selection.

9. In the *Pressure Network Plan Layout:Water* contextual tab>*Layout* panel, select **Hydrant_42in_ Bury Depth_ MJ** from the *Appurtenance* drop-down list, as shown in Figure 6–41.

10. Click 🛢 (Add Appurtenance), as shown in Figure 6–41.

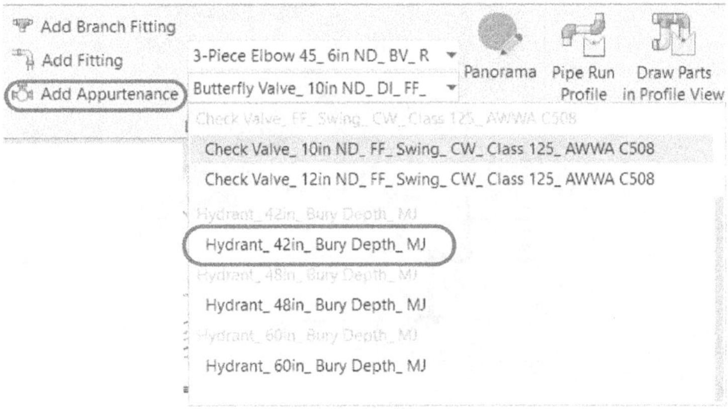

Figure 6–41

11. Select the northern endpoint of the water line you just created, make sure you get the

    Connect Pipe glyph (   ), and press <Enter> to finish. Do not select the blue XREF line, but the end of the pipe.

12. Use the AutoCAD window selection to select the pipe run. Right-click and select **Object Viewer**, as shown in Figure 6–42.

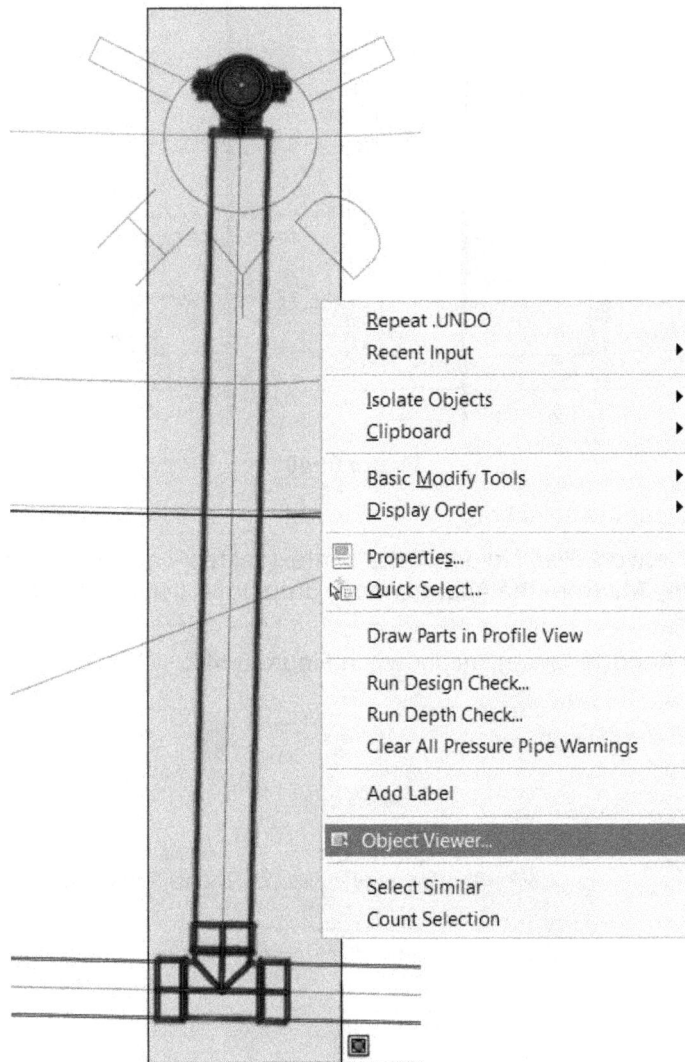

Figure 6–42

13. In *Object Viewer*, click and drag the view, as shown in Figure 6–43, to rotate the 3D view to study the connections. Change the visual style to **Conceptual** using the drop-down list in the top left corner.

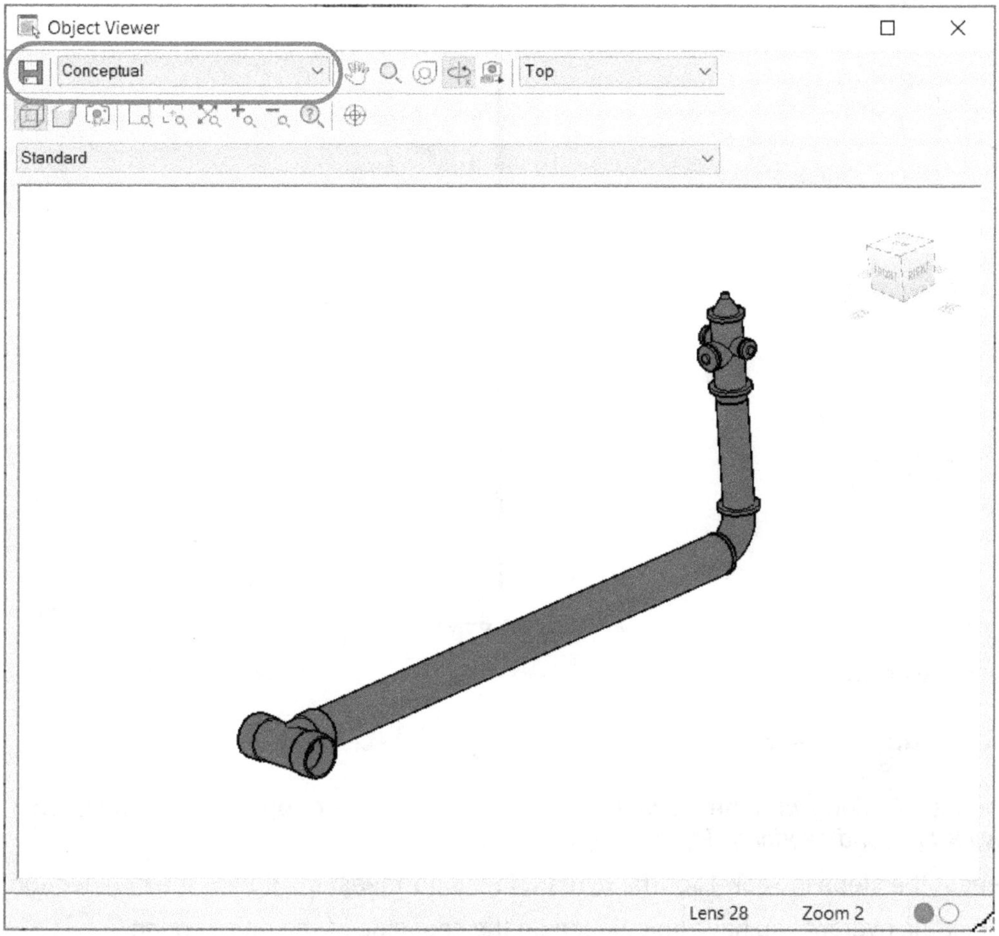

Figure 6–43

14. Close the *Object Viewer* by clicking the **X** in the top right corner of the dialog box.

15. In 3D view, the hydrant looks good; however, in plan view, the hydrant does not line up with the x-referenced hydrant symbol, as shown on the left in Figure 6−44. Select the hydrant and drag the square cyan grip down, as shown on the right, so it is better aligned with the hydrant symbol from the base drawing.

Figure 6−44

16. Save the drawing.

Task 2:   Add more appurtenances.

1. Continue working with the drawing from the previous task or open **PIP-B.dwg** from the *C:\ Civil 3D Beyond\Working\ PipeNetworks* folder.

2. Repeat the steps in Task 1 for the hydrant in the northeast portion of the intersection.

3. Select the hydrant you have just placed on the east side of the intersection.

4. In the *Pressure Network Plan Layout:Water* contextual tab>*Modify* panel, click (Swap Parts).

5. You may have to select the hydrant again, then press <Enter> to finish the selection.

6. In the *Swap Pressure Network Parts* dialog box, select **Hydrant_48in Bury Depth_MJ**, as shown in Figure 6−45.

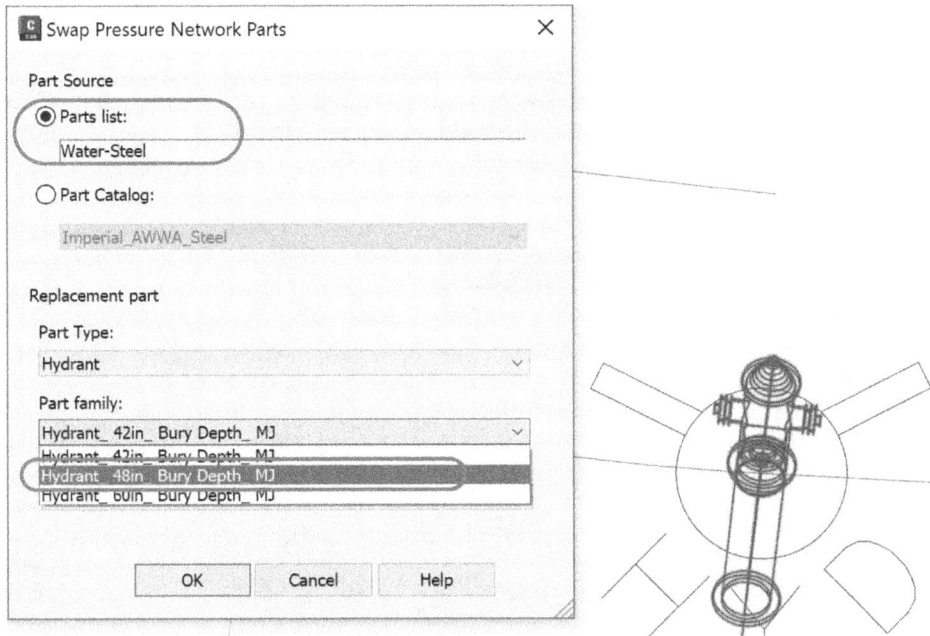

Figure 6-45

7. Click **OK** to close the *Swap Pressure Network Parts* dialog box.

8. Note that there is now a yellow triangle indicating something is amiss at the connection of the hydrant to the water main. When you hover over the symbol, a tooltip explains that the diameters between the water pipe and the hydrant are not equal, as shown in Figure 6-46.

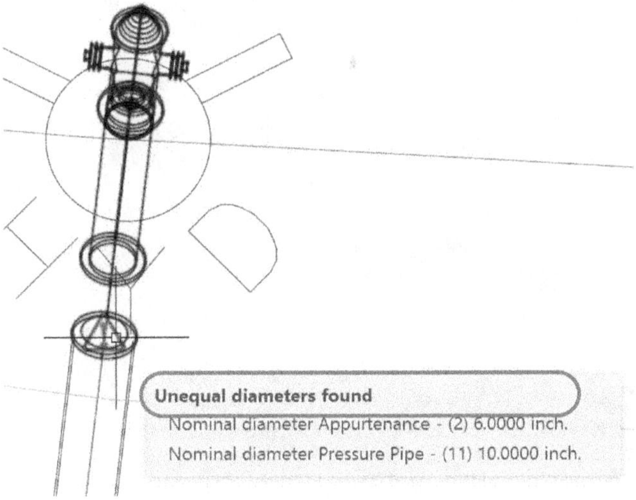

Figure 6-46

9. You can ignore this for now. Press <Esc> to clear the selection.

10. Select the preset view **Pipe-Valves**.

11. In the *Pressure Network Plan Layout:Water* contextual tab>*Layout* panel, select **Gate Valve_ 10in ND_ MJF_ 200 PSI_ AWWA C500** from the *Appurtenance* drop-down list, then click (Add Appurtenance), as shown in Figure 6–47.

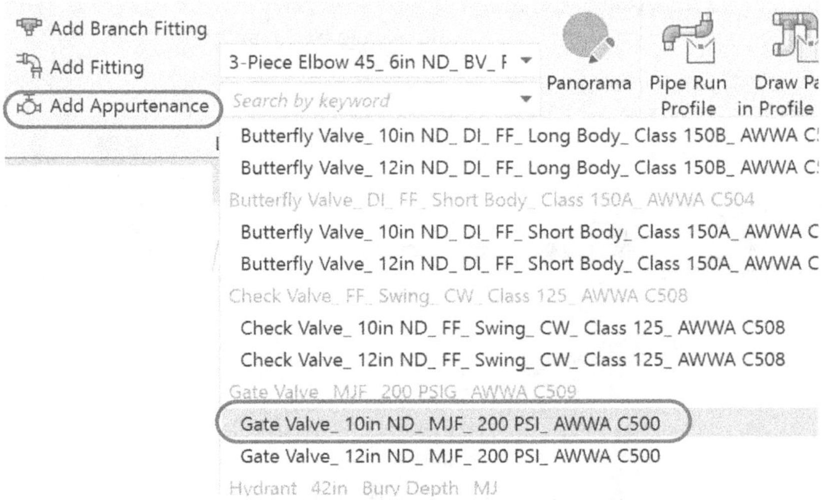

Figure 6–47

12. Place the gate valve near the WV (water valve) symbol along **Jeffries Ranch Road** and move it as required. Ensure your Osnap is disabled and you see the *Broken Pipe* glyph (⊣▢ ▢⊢).

13. Press <Esc> to clear the selection.

14. If you need to reposition the valve, you will need to select it twice slowly until the diamond-shape grips appear, as shown in Figure 6–48. Then, you can slide the valve along using the diamond grips. (The first time you select the valve, you are selecting the entire pipe run alignment.)

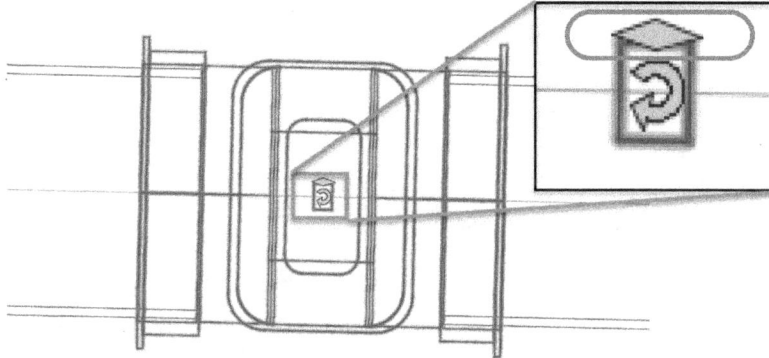

Figure 6–48

15. In a similar manner, place a **Check Valve_ 10in ND_ FF_ Swing_ CW_ Class 125_ AWWA C508** check valve near the WSO (water shutoff valve) symbol along Ascent Place.

16. Press <Esc> to clear the selection.

17. Freeze the **Base-Proposed Engineering|C-WATR** layer.

18. Save the drawing.

Task 3: Draw pressure pipes in the profile view.

1. Continue working with the drawing from the previous task or open **PIP-C.dwg** from the *C:\ Civil 3D Beyond\Working\ PipeNetworks* folder.

2. Select the water line running along **Jeffries Ranch Rd**. In the *Pressure Network Plan Layout:Water* contextual tab>*Profile* panel, click (Pipe Run Profile).

3. In the *Pipe Run Profile Settings* dialog box, set the following (as shown in Figure 6–49):

   - *Offset Style:* **Offset at Bends**
   - *Reference Profile:* **FG Surface (2)** (The Reference Profile might be FG Surface (1)).
   - *Offset Distance:* **3.00'**
   - *Draw Profile in:* **Existing Profile View**

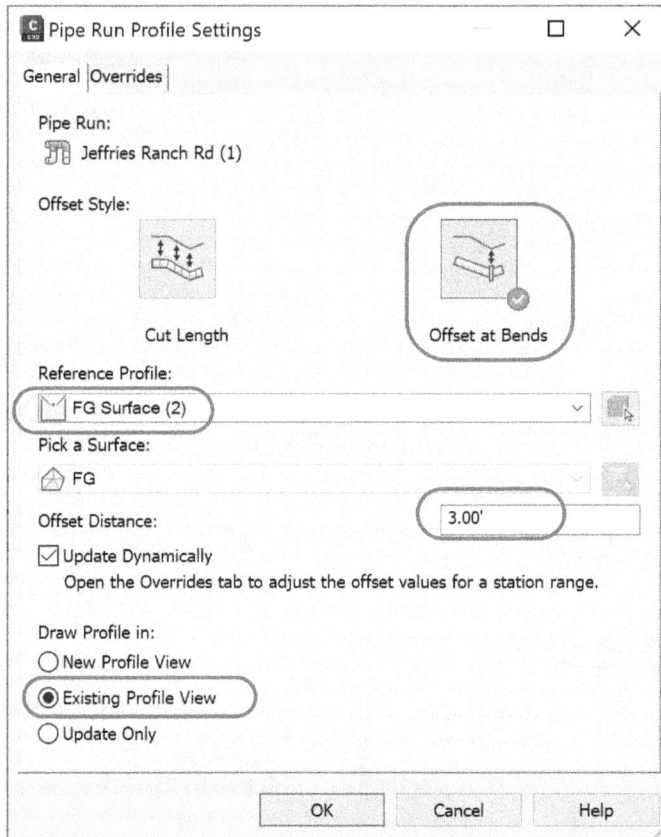

Figure 6–49

4. Click **OK**.

5. When prompted, select the **Jeffries Ranch Rd** profile view.

6. In the **Jeffries Ranch Rd** profile view, select **Pressure Pipe (1)**, as shown in Figure 6–50.

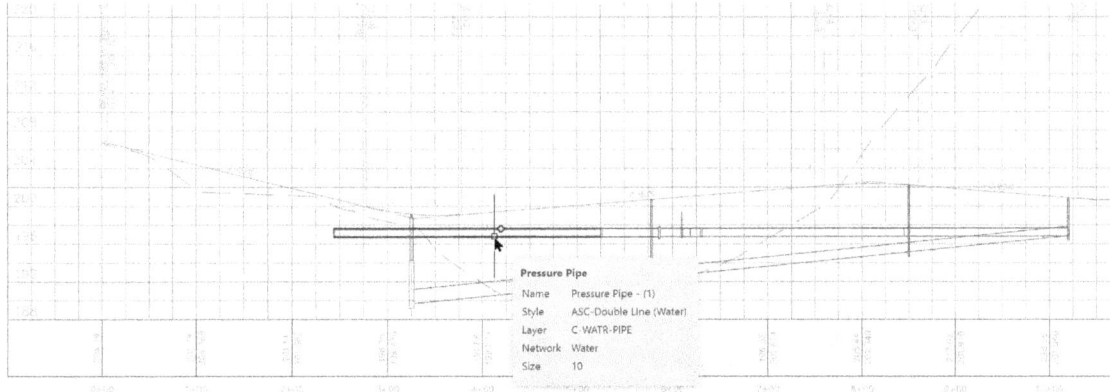

Figure 6–50

7. Click on the round grip in the center of the pipe and pull it downward to put a downward bend in the pipe, as shown in Figure 6–51.

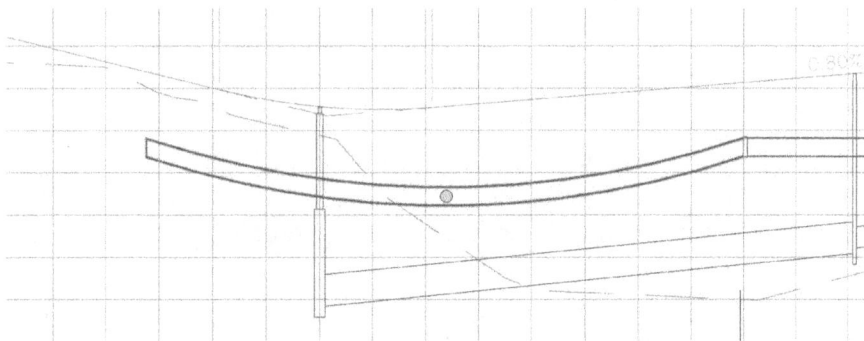

Figure 6–51

8. Press <Esc> to finish.

9. Undo the bending of the pipe to straighten it again.

10. The pipe run is quite straight in profile, even with the bend. That is because you selected **Offset at Bends** for the *Offset Style*. This meant that at every bend the pipe had a cover of **3.00'**. The result isn't very appropriate.

11. Once again, select the water line running along **Jeffries Ranch Rd**. In the *Pressure Network Plan Layout:Water* contextual tab>*Profile* panel, click 🖈 (Pipe Run Profile).

12. This time in the *Pipe Run Profile Settings* dialog box, set the *Offset Style* to **Cut Length** and to set the *Draw Profile in* option to **Update Only** (as shown in Figure 6−52).

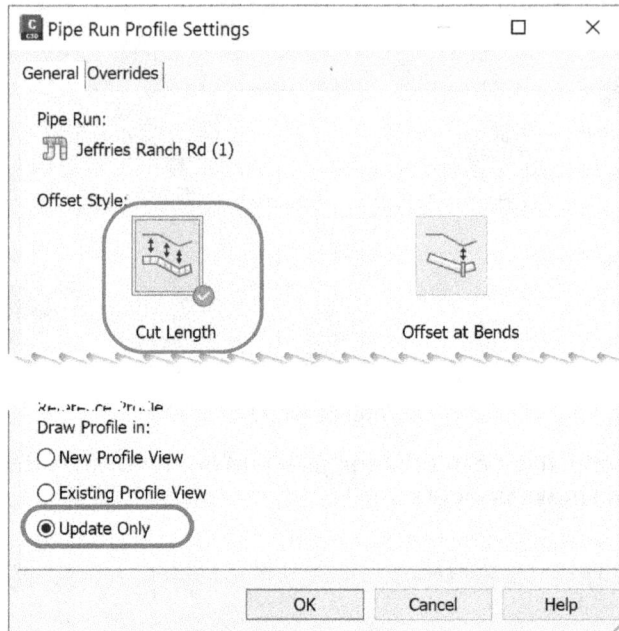

Figure 6−52

13. Click **OK**.

14. Select the **Jeffries Ranch Rd** profile view to update the profile, as shown in Figure 6−50.

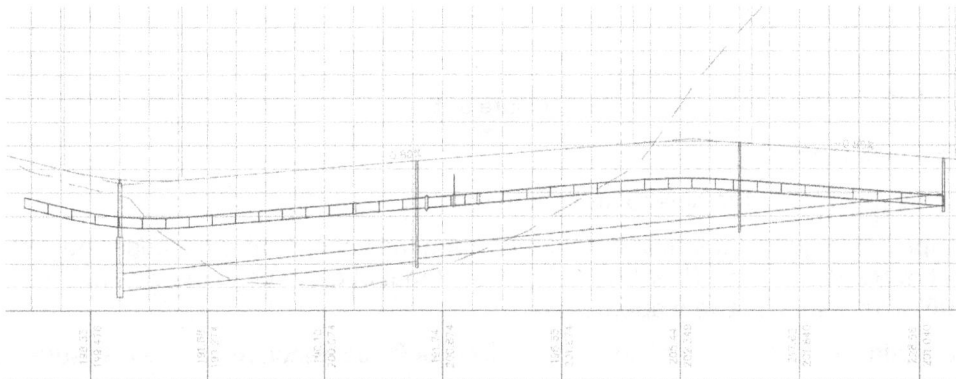

Figure 6−53

15. Save and close the drawing.

End of practice

Chapter Review Questions

1. How do you add another type of structure to the drawing?

    a. Insert the structure as a block.

    b. Add a different reference template.

    c. Update the Pipe Network Parts List.

    d. Draw it with AutoCAD.

2. Which of the following are valid rule sets for Civil 3D pipe networks? (Select all that apply.)

    a. Appurtenances

    b. Pipes

    c. Pressure Pipes

    d. Structures

    e. Fittings

3. Can a Pressure Network Parts List contain multiple catalogs for different materials?

    a. Yes

    b. No

4. Which of the following is NOT a pressure pipe appurtenance?

    a. Hydrant

    b. Gate valve

    c. Check valve

    d. Sprinkler

Command Summary

Button	Command	Location
	Add Appurtenance	• **Contextual Ribbon:** *Pressure Network* tab>*Layout* panel • **Command Prompt:** AddAppurtenance
	Apply Rules	• **Right-click menu**
	Branch Fitting Tool	• **Contextual Ribbon:** *Pressure Network* tab>*Layout* panel • **Command Prompt:** AddFittings
	Network Parts List	• **Toolspace>***Settings* **Tab:** *Pipe Network* branch
	Pipe Run Profile	• **Contextual Ribbon:** *Pressure Network* tab>*Profile* panel • **Command Prompt:** EditPipeRunProfile
	Pressure Network Parts List	• **Toolspace>***Settings* **Tab:** *Pressure Network* branch
	Swap Pressure Parts	• **Contextual Ribbon:** *Pressure Network* tab>*Modify* panel • **Command Prompt:** SwapPressureNetworkParts

Sheet Set Manager

In this chapter, you will modify the sheet set properties and title block to make the project information automatically display on every sheet.

Learning Objectives

- Edit sheet and sheet set properties to make annotating sheets easier.
- Create a sheet list.
- Add a page to the drawing set as a sheet index.

7.1 Sheet Sets

The sheet set is not exclusive to the Autodesk Civil 3D software, but is used in all AEC products. A sheet set is a collection of sheets that are created from a combination of several different drawings. Sheets listed in the Sheet Set Manger file (.DST) refer to layouts in a drawing file. The sheet set can reference any number of layouts from any number of drawings.

For example, you might be working on a commercial site plan or a highway project drawing. Using the Sheet Set Manager, you can create a construction set or tender documents by compiling a sheet set that lists all of the required sheets from the existing conditions plans and a variety of design models. Additionally, if the project is a multi-disciplined project that includes structural engineers and architects, you can compile a list of sheets from those sources as well. Figure 7−1 outlines the structure of sheet sets in a project.

1   **2**   **3**

1. Drawings residing in various folders from various disciplines

2. Layouts in those drawings organized into sheet sets

3. Final documents

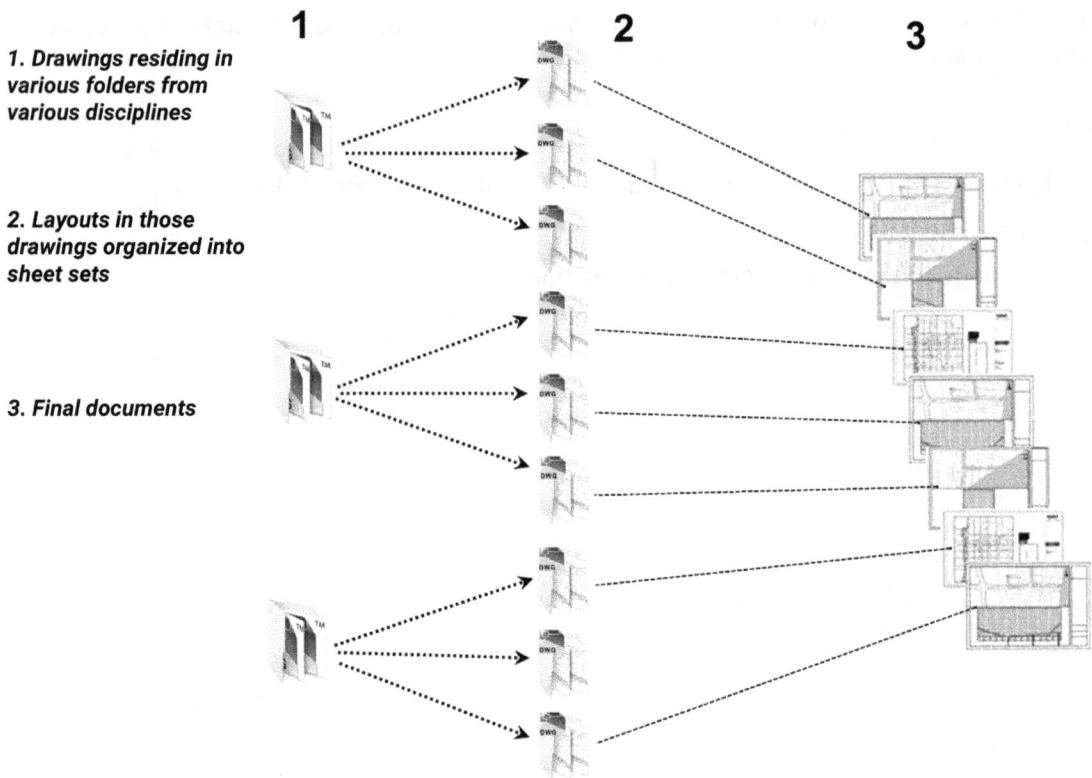

Figure 7−1

Sheet Set Manager

All tools required for managing sheet sets are available through the *Sheet Set Manager*, which is accessible though the *View* tab>*Palettes* panel. Expand the panel and click ⬙ (Sheet Set Manager), as shown in Figure 7–2.

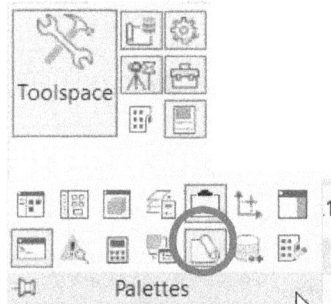

Figure 7–2

- The <Ctrl>+<4> keyboard shortcut also invokes the Sheet Set Manager.

You can also access sheet sets from the *Start* tab of Civil 3D, as shown in Figure 7–3.

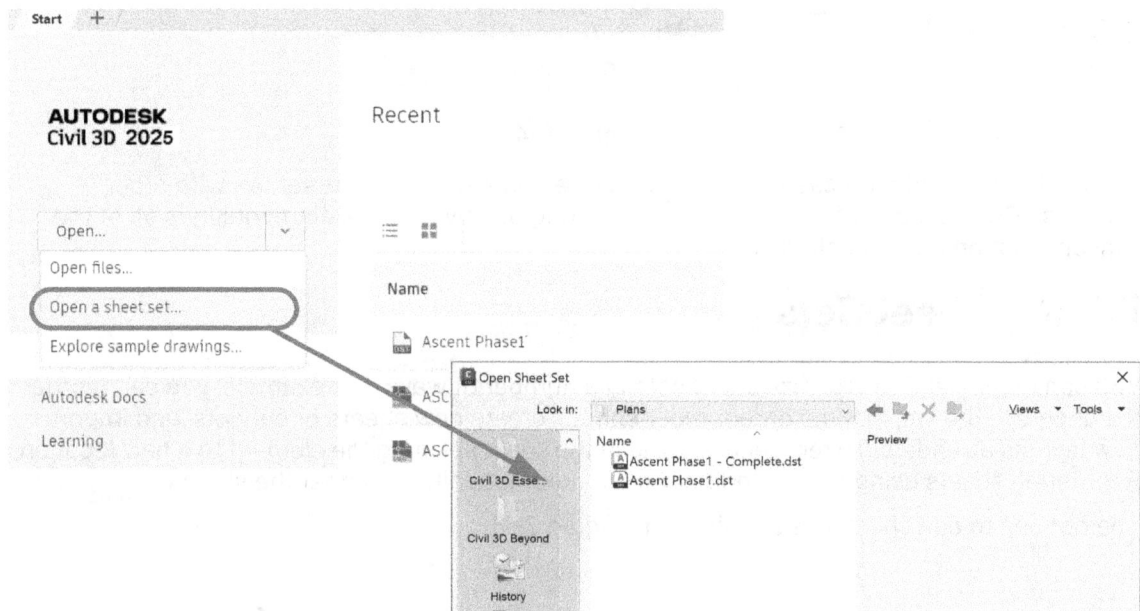

Figure 7–3

Structuring Sheet Sets

Figure 7–4 displays a typical hierarchical structure of the sheet set elements.

- The *Sheet Set Name* (1) identifies the sheet set (i.e., the DST file). This file can reside anywhere on your server.

- The *Sheet* subset (2) is used to organize sheets in a logical manner (e.g., plan profiles, structural, electrical, etc.).

- The *Individual Sheets* (3) are layouts from drawings imported into the sheet set.

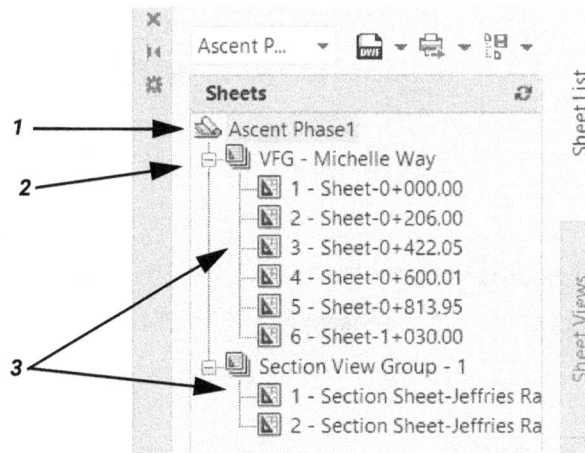

Figure 7–4

Each of the elements represents a core component in a typical sheet set. As with other Autodesk Civil 3D object functionality, right-clicking on any of these elements lists all of the available options for that element.

Editing Sheet Sets

You can modify and re-organize sheet sets in a number of ways. For example, you can reorder the sheets in the set, rename or renumber sheets, create new sheets or subsets, and import new layouts as sheets. To reorder elements in the sheet set, drag the element to a new location. Reordering sheets using this method does not automatically renumber the sheets.

The options to edit sheet sets are shown in Figure 7–5.

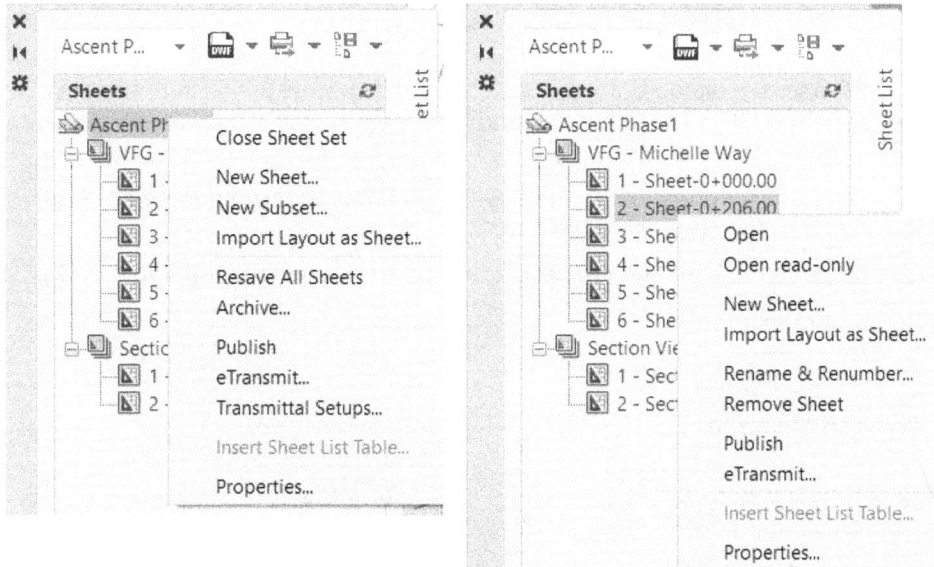

Figure 7–5

To rename and renumber sheets automatically, enter a *Number* and *Sheet title* in the *Rename & Renumber Sheet* dialog box. To change the associated filename, type a new *File name*. You can also have the associated filename change when you rename the sheet. To enable this feature, select the **Sheet title** option to rename the drawing file to match the sheet title, as shown in Figure 7–6.

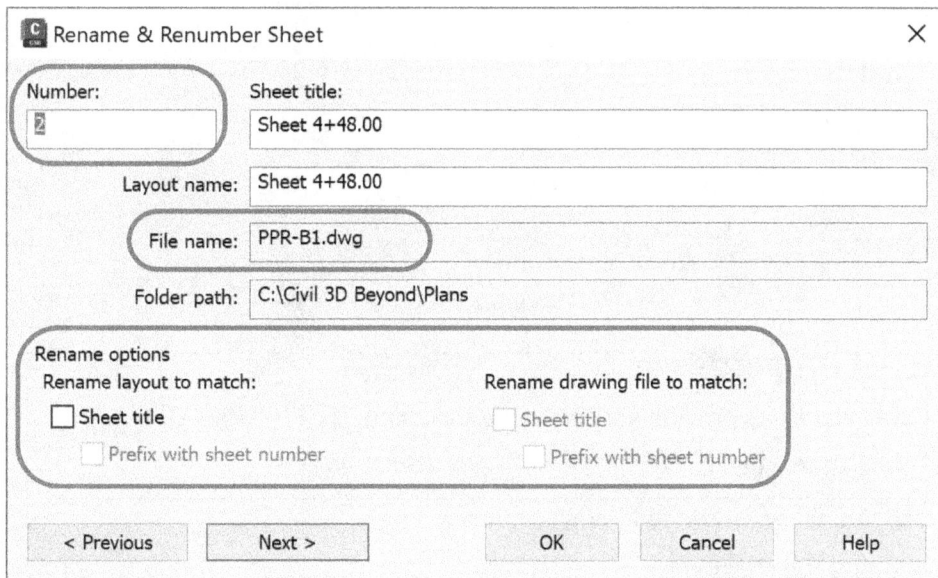

Figure 7–6

Sheet Set Manager Properties

In the *Sheet Set Properties* dialog box, you can change the name, the path of the drawing files or the template associated with the sheet set, and any custom properties associated with the sheet set.

To access the properties, right-click on the *Sheet Set Manager* name and select **Properties**. Information specific to the sheet set displays.

The *Sheet Set Properties* dialog box contains the following, as shown in Figure 7–7:

*   **Sheet Set** properties (1)
*   **Project Control** properties (2)
*   **Sheet Creation** properties (3)

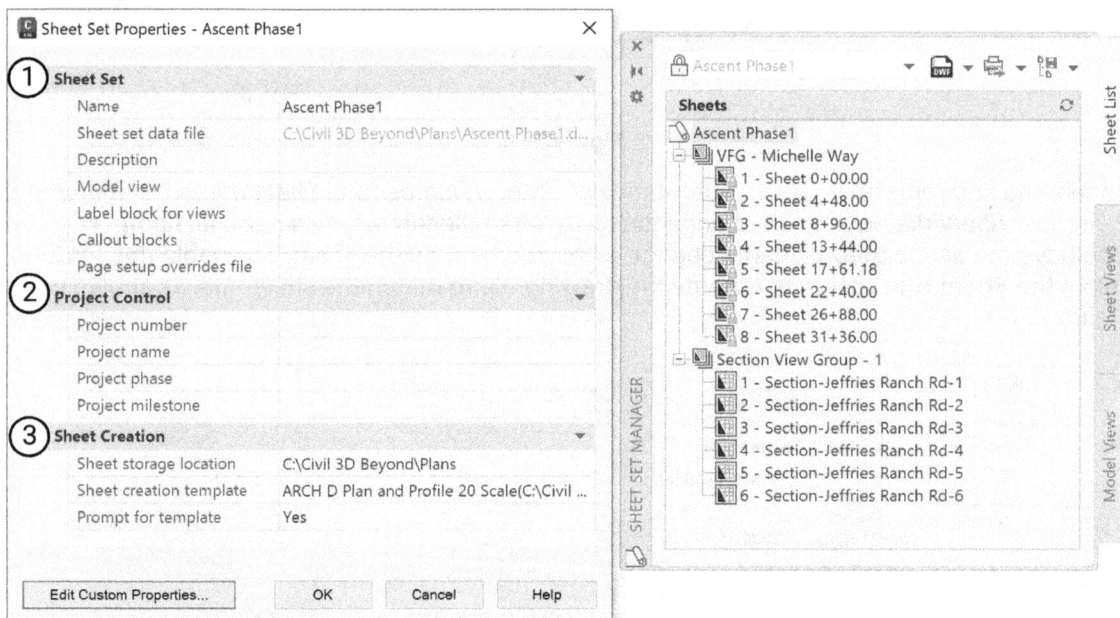

Figure 7–7

1. Sheet Set Properties

The **Sheet Set Properties** provide access to the following:

*   Name of the sheet set.
*   Sheet set data file location (read-only).
*   Description for the sheet set.
*   Model view drawing location (the location of the resource drawings).

- Label block for views (the location of the drawing and blocks that contain the block, which can be used for the views).

- Callout blocks (a list of blocks that can be used for callouts), which ensures that drawing references in the various callouts (such as details) are always up to date.

- Page setup override file (a drawing template that contains the page setup overrides for the sheet set). The page setup override enables you to override existing page setups for individual drawings in the sheet set.

2. Project Control Properties

You can use four preset **Project Control Properties**: *Project number, name, phase,* and *milestone*. These properties can also be displayed on the individual sheets. In addition to these four properties, you can create custom properties. There are two types of properties:

- *Sheet Set* properties are applied to all of the sheets in the set.

- *Sheet* properties are only applied to a single sheet.

3. Sheet Creation Properties

In the **Sheet Creation Properties**, you can access the location of the folder to store your sheets and the default template that is used when creating a new sheet. The *Sheet storage location* is where the new drawing sheet that is created is stored. The *Sheet creation template* is the template that is used when creating the new sheet.

Sheet Set Manager for Web

When Civil 3D projects are stored in the Autodesk cloud platform, the sheet sets can also be stored there. The **Sheet Set Manager for Web** is a lighter version of the desktop *Sheet Set Manager* that is optimized for performance in the cloud.

Opening sheet sets on the web is efficient and safe. The Autodesk Desktop Connector handles all the reference files and connections.

The **Sheet Set Manager for Web** enables users to:

- Create and remove sheets and subsets.

- Define sheet set properties, including sheets and subsets.

- Publish sheet sets to PDF.

- Transmit sheet sets.

  Note: *Using the Autodesk cloud platform is beyond the scope of this guide.*

Practice 7a
Sheet Sets

Practice Objective

- Edit sheet and sheet set properties to make annotating sheets easier.

Task 1: Define the Sheet Set Manager properties.

1. Close any drawings you may have open so that only the *Start* tab is open in Civil 3D.

2. In the *Start* tab, use the *Open...* drop-down list to select **Open a sheet set...**, then browse to the *C:\Civil 3D Beyond\Plans* folder. Select **Ascent Phase1.dst** and click **Open**, as shown in Figure 7–8.

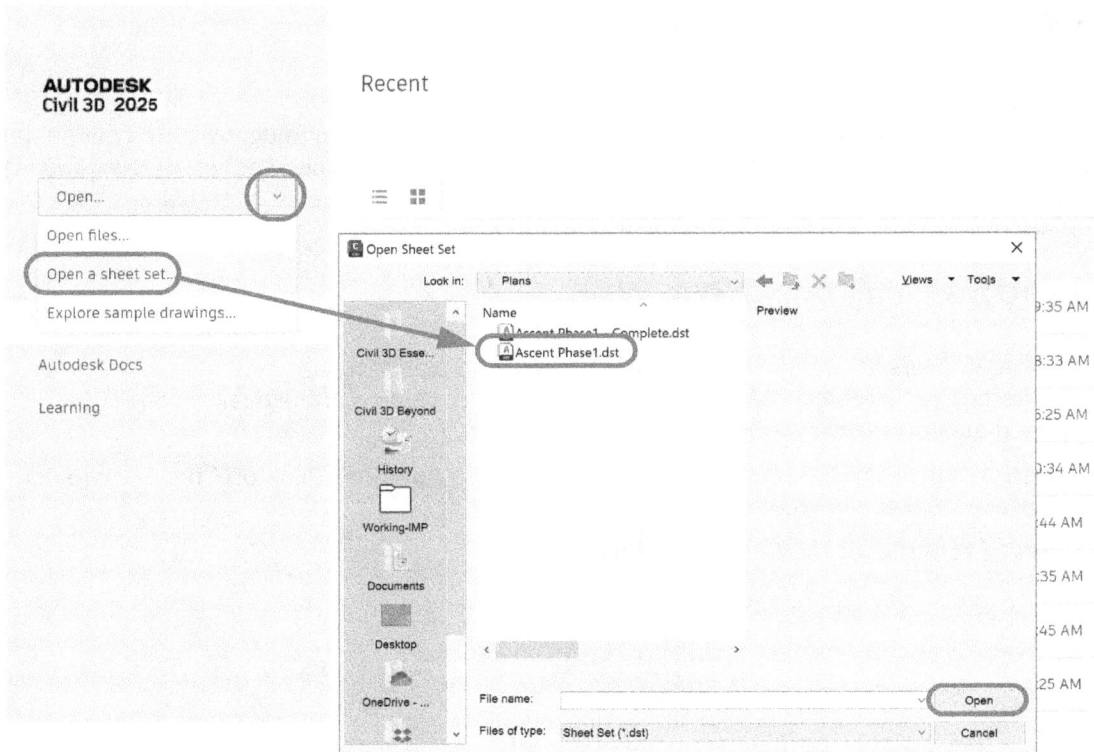

Figure 7–8

3. In the *Sheet Set Manager,* double-click on the first sheet listed, as shown in Figure 7–9. Note that the drawing name opens to the *Sheet-0+000.00* layout tab, just as it is listed in the *Sheet Set Manager*.

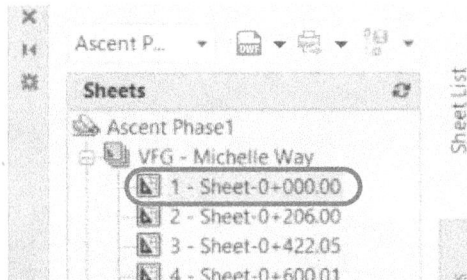

Figure 7–9

4. In the *Sheet Set Manager,* select **VFG - Michelle Way**, right-click, and select **Rename Subset...**, as shown on the left in Figure 7–10. In the *Subset Properties* dialog box, for the *Subset Name*, type **Plan-Profile - Michelle Way**, as shown on the right. Click **OK** to close the dialog box.

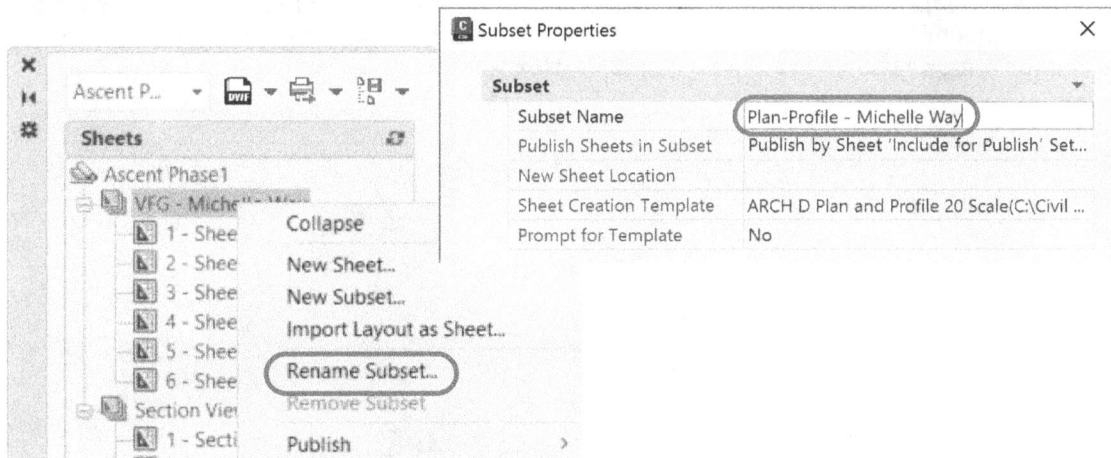

Figure 7–10

5. In the *Plan-Profile - Michelle Way* collection, select **1 - Sheet 0+00.00**, right-click, and select **Rename & Renumber**, as shown in Figure 7−11.

Figure 7−11

6. In the *Rename & Renumber Sheet* dialog box, change the *Number* to **3** to make room to add a title sheet and overall plan sheet later, and select **Sheet title** in the *Rename layout to match* area, as shown in Figure 7−12. Click **Next>**.

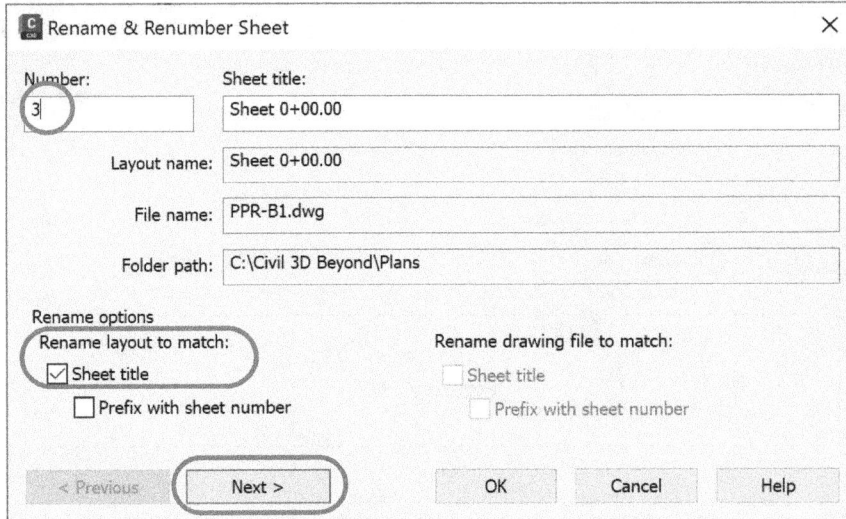

Figure 7−12

7. Change the next sheet number to **4**, and continue to click **Next>** to continue increasing the page number for each sheet until all of the sheets are renumbered, as shown in Figure 7−13. Note the changes to the sheet names. Click **OK** to accept the changes and close the dialog box.

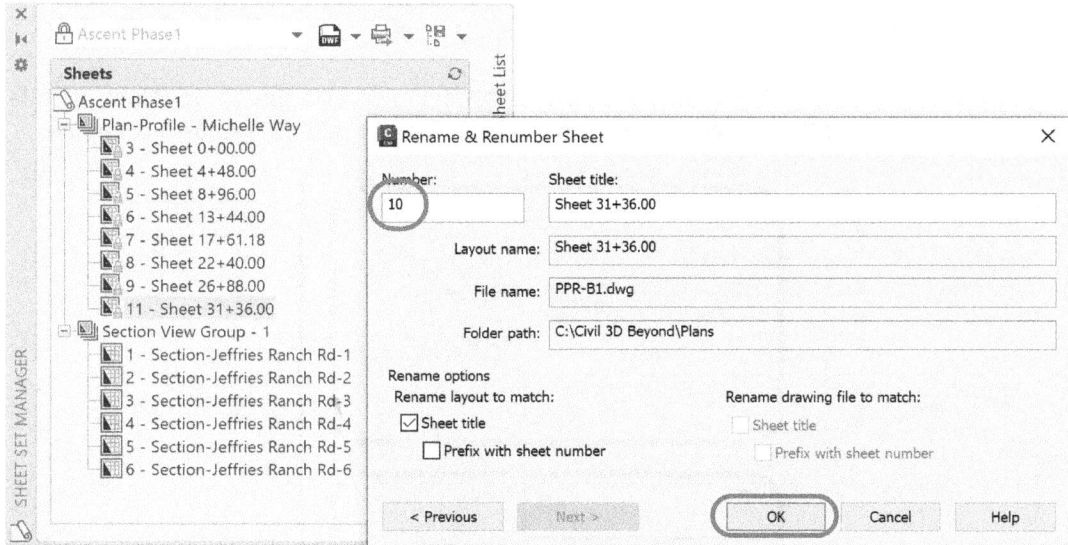

Figure 7–13

8. Repeat the same procedure for the *Section View Group - 1* subset, as follows:

   • Rename the subset to **Sections - Jeffries Ranch**.

   • Renumber the six sheets **11** through **16** respectively.

   • Select **Sheet title** in the *Rename layout to match* area.

9. In the *Sheet Set Manager,* right-click on the **Ascent Phase1** sheet set name and select **Resave All Sheets**, as shown in Figure 7–14.

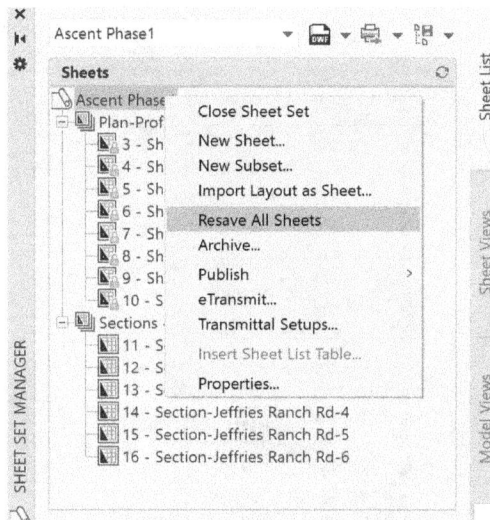

Figure 7–14

Task 2: Define the sheet set properties.

1. Zoom in to the lower right corner of the drawing, as shown in Figure 7–15. Note the title block. The fields for the **Project Name** and **Project Number** do not display any values.

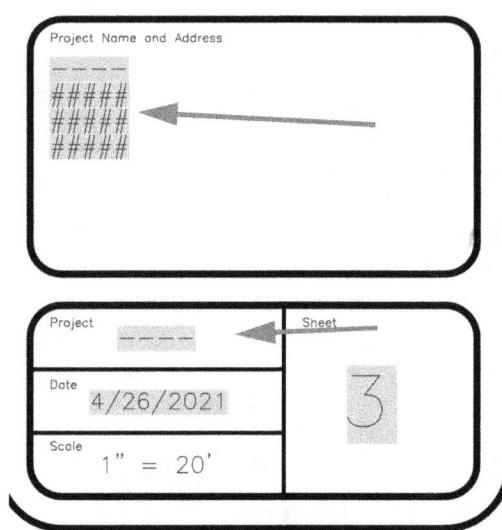

Figure 7–15

2. In the *Sheet Set Manager* for *Ascent Phase1*, select the **Ascent Phase1** sheet set name, right-click, and select **Properties...**, as shown in Figure 7–16.

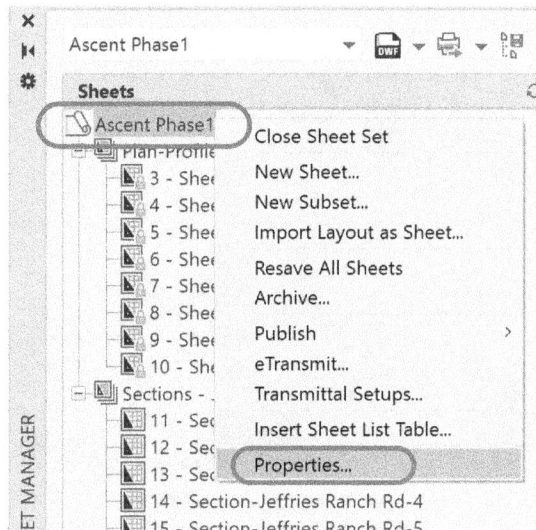

Figure 7–16

3. In the *Sheet Set Properties - Ascent Phase1* dialog box, enter the following (as shown in Figure 7–17):

   * *Project number:* **30042020**
   * *Project name:* **ASCENT C3D TRAINING**
   * *Project phase:* **PRE-TENDER**
   * *Project milestone:* **66%**

4. Click **Edit Custom Properties...**.

5. In the *Custom Properties* dialog box, click **Add...**.

6. In the *Add Custom Property* dialog box, set the following (as shown in Figure 7–17):

   * *Name:* **CIVIC ID**
   * *Default value:* **Z-1234**
   * *Owner:* **Sheet Set**

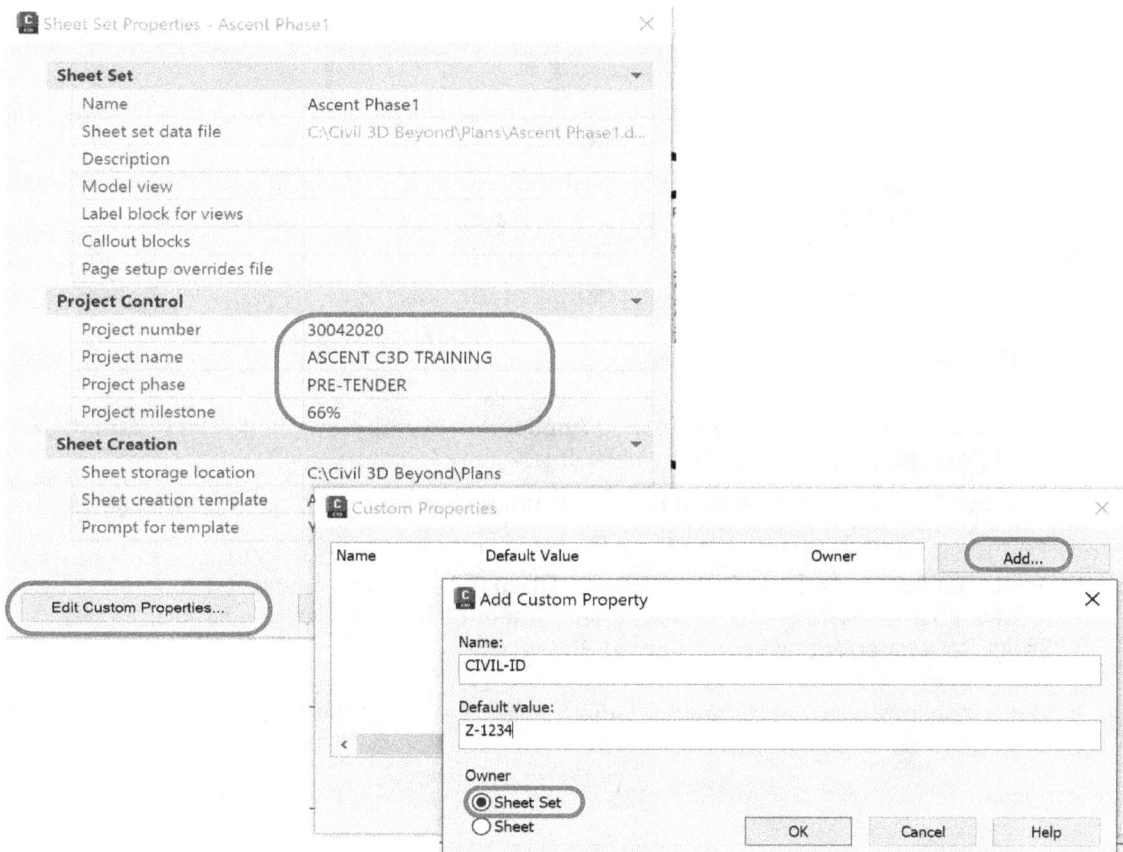

Figure 7–17

7. Click **OK** three times to complete the procedure. You will need to type **regen** and press <Enter> in the Command Line to display the updated fields. The values in your drawing title sheet should now be displayed, as shown in Figure 7−18.

Figure 7−18

8. For the custom properties (such as *CIVIC ID*), the *Project milestone,* and the *Project phase* to appear in the title block, special attributes need to be added. Your CAD manager is responsible for configuring this.

9. Resave all sheets as you did earlier and exit all of the drawings.

Task 3: Define sheet set properties.

1. Open a new drawing session by selecting **Application Menu>New**, then select **_Autodesk Civil 3D (Imperial) NCS.dwt** from the default template location.

2. If the *Sheet Set Manager* for *Ascent Phase 1* is not active, you can open the sheet set.dst file using one of the following methods:

   • Select the Autodesk Civil 3D file and click **Open**. Either select **Sheet Set**, browse to the C:*Civil 3D Beyond\Plans* folder, and select **Ascent Phase1A.dst**, or select **Open the Sheet Set Manager** and select **Ascent Phase 1** in the drop-down list.

   • In the *View* tab>expanded *Palettes* panel, click ⬒ (Sheet Set Manager).

3. In the *Sheet Set Manager*, select the **Ascent Phase1** sheet set, right-click, and select **New Subset...**, as shown on the left in Figure 7–19. In the *Subset Properties* dialog box, type **Baseplan** for the *Subset Name*, as shown on the right. Set the *Prompt for Template* to **No** so that all new sheets use the preset template. Click **OK** to close the dialog box.

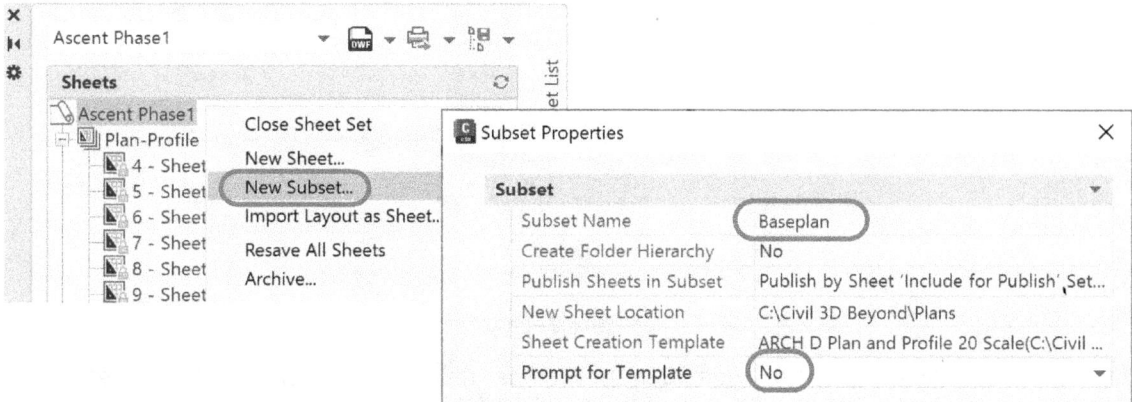

Figure 7–19

4. In the *Sheet Set Manager*, select the **Baseplan** subset and drag it to the top, as shown in Figure 7–20.

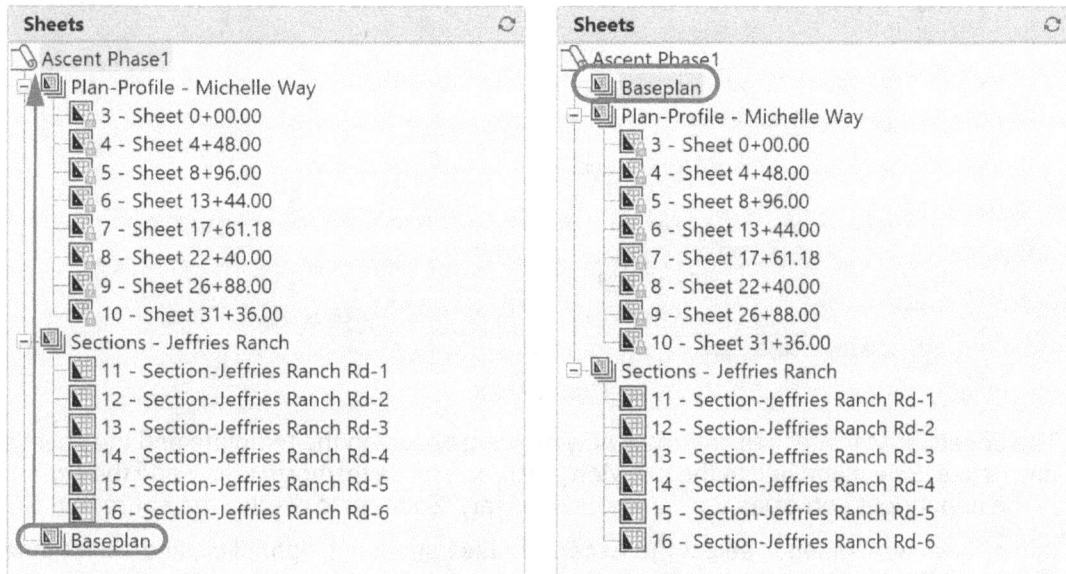

Figure 7–20

5. To create a new sheet, select the **Baseplan** subset, right-click, and select **New Sheet...**, as shown in Figure 7–21.

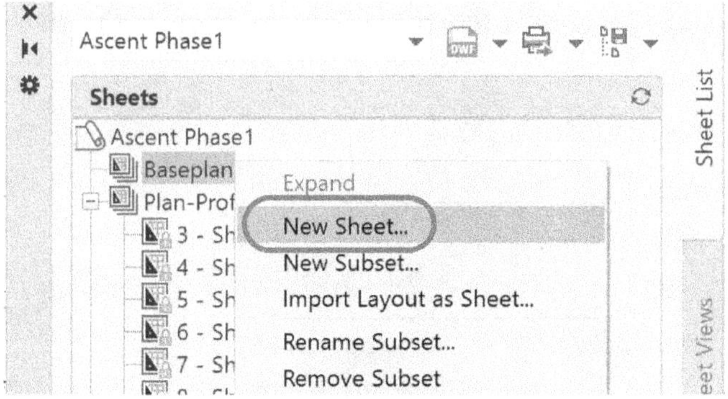

Figure 7–21

6. In the *New Sheet* dialog box, type **00** in the *Number* field, and type **Index** in the *Sheet title* field, as shown in Figure 7–22. Select the **Open in drawing editor** option to open the drawing when done and click **OK**. The *Sheet Set Manager* will create a drawing named **00 Index.dwg**.

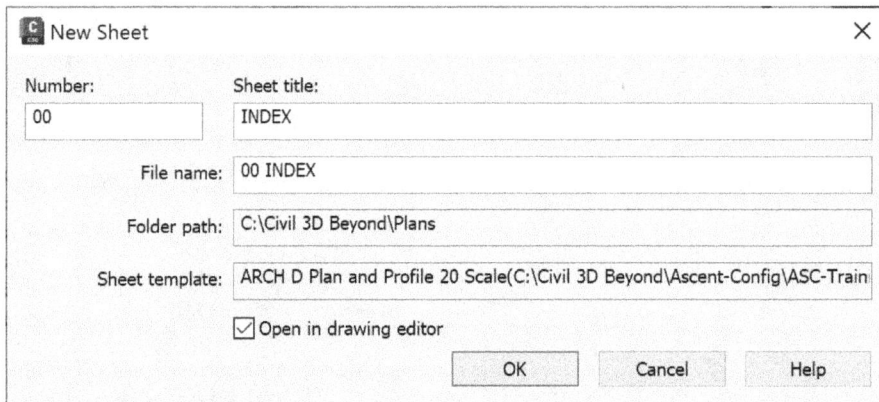

Figure 7–22

7. The *Sheet Set Manager* has created a new drawing based on the template and the sheet set properties. Select and delete the two viewports, as well as the north arrow and the scale bar in the upper right corner, as they are not necessary. Zoom in to display the entire title block.

8. In the *Sheet Set Manager*, select the **Ascent Phase1** sheet set, right-click, and select **Insert Sheet List Table...**, as shown in Figure 7–23.

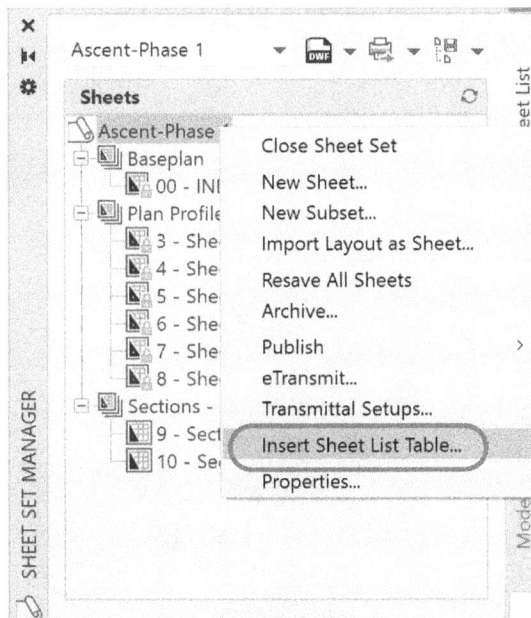

Figure 7–23

9. In the *Sheet List Table* dialog box, expand the *Table Style name* drop-down list and select **Legend**. Select the **Show Subheader** option and click **OK** to close the dialog box, as shown in Figure 7–24.

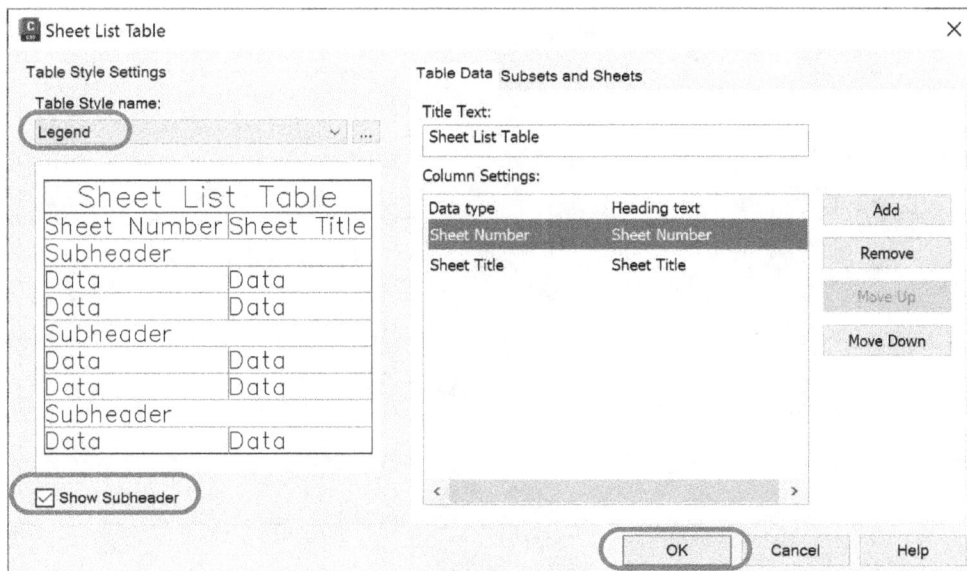

Figure 7–24

10. When prompted for the location of the table, select a point in the middle of the title block, as shown in Figure 7–25.

Sheet List Table	
Sheet Number	Sheet Title
Baseplan	
00	INDEX
Plan–Profile — Michelle Way	
3	Sheet 0+00.00
4	Sheet 4+48.00
5	Sheet 8+96.00
6	Sheet 13+44.00
7	Sheet 17+61.18
8	Sheet 22+40.00
9	Sheet 26+88.00
10	Sheet 31+36.00
Sections — Jeffries Ranch	
11	Section–Jeffries Ranch Rd–1
12	Section–Jeffries Ranch Rd–2
13	Section–Jeffries Ranch Rd–3
14	Section–Jeffries Ranch Rd–4
15	Section–Jeffries Ranch Rd–5
16	Section–Jeffries Ranch Rd–6

Figure 7–25

11. Save and close the drawing.

End of practice

Chapter Review Questions

1. How do you ensure that the project name and number display on every sheet automatically?

   a. This cannot be automated.

   b. Set up the sheet template with project name and number fields, and then set the project name and number in the **Sheet Set Manager>Sheet Set Properties**.

   c. Set up the sheet template with project name and number fields, and then set the project name and number during the *View Frame Creation* process.

   d. When generating the sheets, select the option to add the project name and number to the sheets.

2. After creating the plan and profile sheets, you can easily create additional sheets using the Sheet Set Manager.

   a. True

   b. False

Command Summary

Button	Command	Location
	Sheet Set Manager	• **Ribbon:** *View* tab>expanded *Palettes* panel • **Command Prompt:** Sheetsets

Quantity Takeoff and Visualization

In this chapter, you will inspect your Civil 3D project, both visually and quantitatively. You will add content to the model to give it more realism so observers can gain a sense of scale and familiarity. You will also calculate miscellaneous quantities on non-Civil 3D objects, such as the items you have added, to assist in estimating. Finally, you will navigate around the model and save some vantage points.

Learning Objectives

- Insert Civil 3D multi-view blocks.
- Examine the 3D model from various vantage points.
- Calculate the cost of design by assigning pay items to specific objects.
- Navigate through the model and "drive" along a corridor.

8.1 Civil 3D Multi-view Blocks

Autodesk Civil 3D multi-view blocks are a collection of special blocks that can add a greater degree of detail to your drawing for reference and a sense of familiarity. There are a variety of predefined blocks representing items, including the following:

- **Highways**: road signs, lighting columns, railings, vehicles, etc.

- **Landscape**: trees and shrubs, for rendering purposes, for annotation purposes

- **External Works**: amenity lighting, playground, fencing, people, etc.

- **Building Footprints**: apartments, row housing, single family dwellings, sheds, etc.

Multi-view Blocks

Multi-view blocks are a type of special AutoCAD block that has separate embedded blocks for different view directions. You can create your own multi-view blocks from AutoCAD blocks that represent the different views of the item you want to display.

There are a good collection of multi-view blocks representing different types of objects in Autodesk Civil 3D. For example, the top view of a multi-view block representing a building shows only the building footprint as would be seen in a plan view. There are representations for left, right, front, and back views, which are your standard architectural elevation views. Additionally, in 3D you get a three-dimensional representation that can be rendered or viewed in wireframe mode, as shown in Figure 8–1.

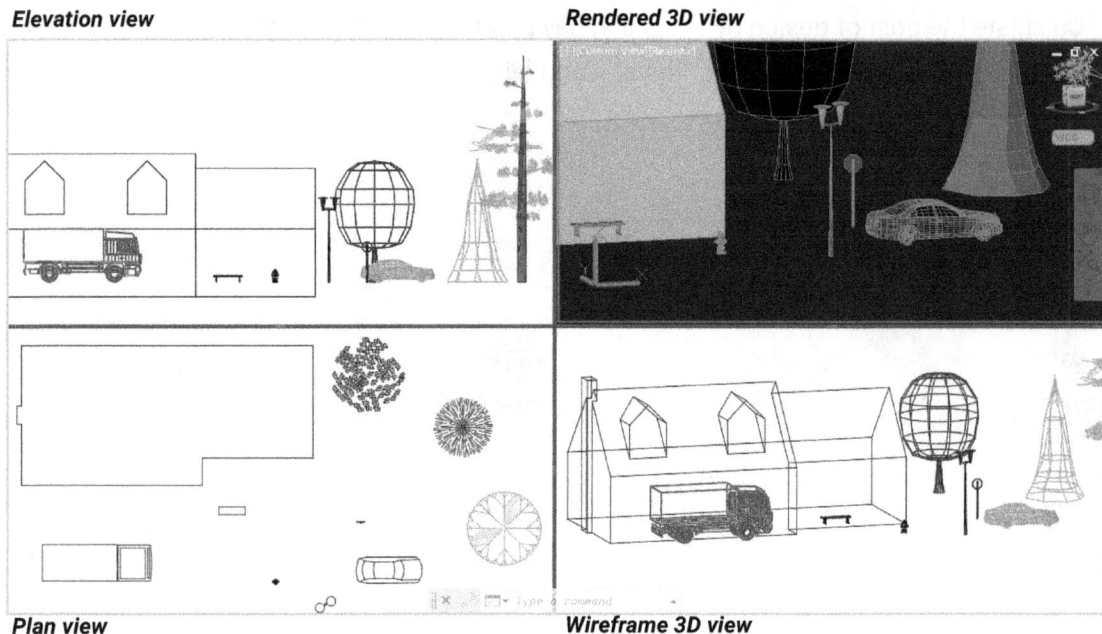

Elevation view

Rendered 3D view

Plan view

Wireframe 3D view

Figure 8–1

Tool Palettes

The easiest way to add an Autodesk Civil 3D subassembly to an assembly is using the *Tool Palettes*. You can open the *Tool Palettes* by clicking 🖻 in the *Home* tab>*Palettes* panel (as shown in Figure 8–2) or in the *View* tab>*Palettes* panel. You can also use <Ctrl>+<3>.

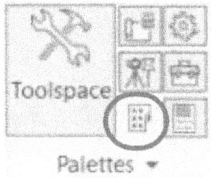

Figure 8–2

The Autodesk Civil 3D software provides a number of stock multi-view blocks divided into different tabs of the *Civil Multiview Blocks* tool palette, as shown in Figure 8–3.

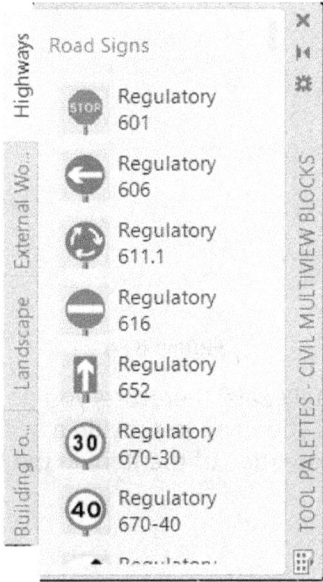

Figure 8–3

To select the correct palette, right-click on the *TOOL PALETTES* band and select the **Civil Multiview Blocks** tool palette.

You can customize various properties of the block to be inserted, such as its layer, color, and linetype, by right-clicking on the block name and selecting **Properties**, as shown in Figure 8−4.

Figure 8−4

Most of the blocks are created at full scale; therefore, you do not need to adjust their size. However, for the landscape blocks, you need to provide a scale after you insert them. You can pre-define the scale through the properties of the item in the tool palette, as shown in Figure 8−5.

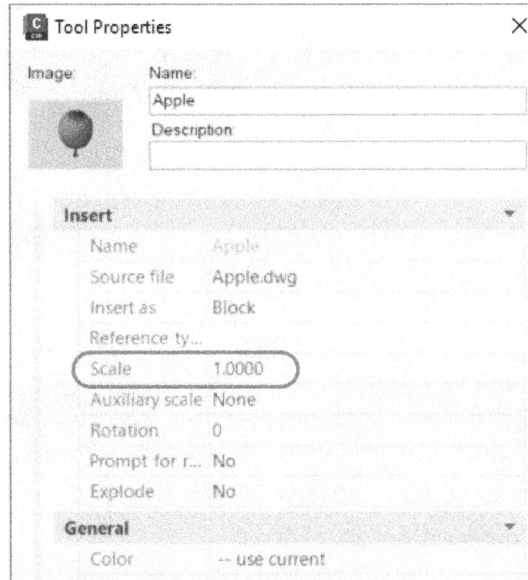

Figure 8–5

Once the landscape block is inserted, you can change the X, Y, and Z scale of the block. If you want a taller, more slender tree, increase the Z scale. Conversely, for a shorter, broader tree, either increase the X and Y scales, or decrease the Z scale.

To insert a block, click on the block name and select the insertion point on-screen. Do not click and drag – you need to "click and click". Once you select the insertion point, you will set the rotation angle, depending on the type of block.

Do not worry about the elevation value of the insertion point of the inserted blocks. Once all the blocks are inserted, there is a routine in the Surface textual ribbon to move blocks to the surface. You select the blocks from a list (as shown in Figure 8–6), and the routine adjusts the Z value of the insertion point of the block to the surface elevation.

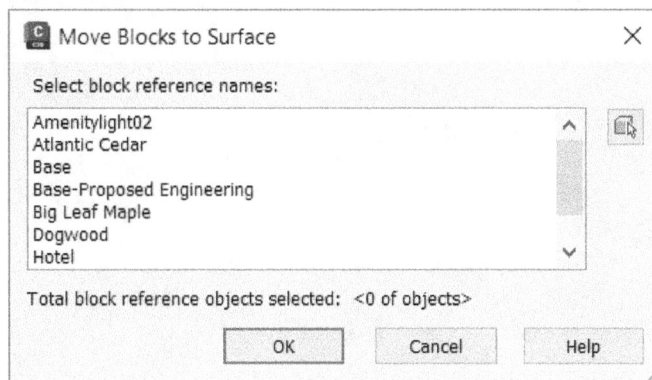

Figure 8–6

Practice 8a
Add Detail to Drawings

Practice Objective

- Populate the drawing with objects to add contextual references.

Task 1: Insert Civil 3D multi-view blocks.

For this drawing, a variety of multi-view blocks have already been inserted in the northern portion of the site. You will add some more detail near the **Jeffries Ranch Road** and **Ascent Place** intersection. The XREF models of the hotel, school, and office building have been swapped from 2D building footprint drawings to 3D models.

1. Open **QTO-A1.dwg** from the *C:\Civil 3D Beyond\Working\QTO-Viz* folder.

2. Select the preset view **Intersection-2D**.

3. Open the *Tool Palettes* by clicking 📋 in the *Home* tab>*Palettes* panel, as shown in Figure 8–7, or using the <Ctrl>+<3> keyboard shortcut.

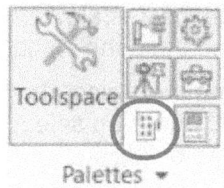

Figure 8–7

4. Right-click on the *TOOL PALETTES* band and select the **Civil Multiview Blocks** tool palette, as shown in Figure 8–8.

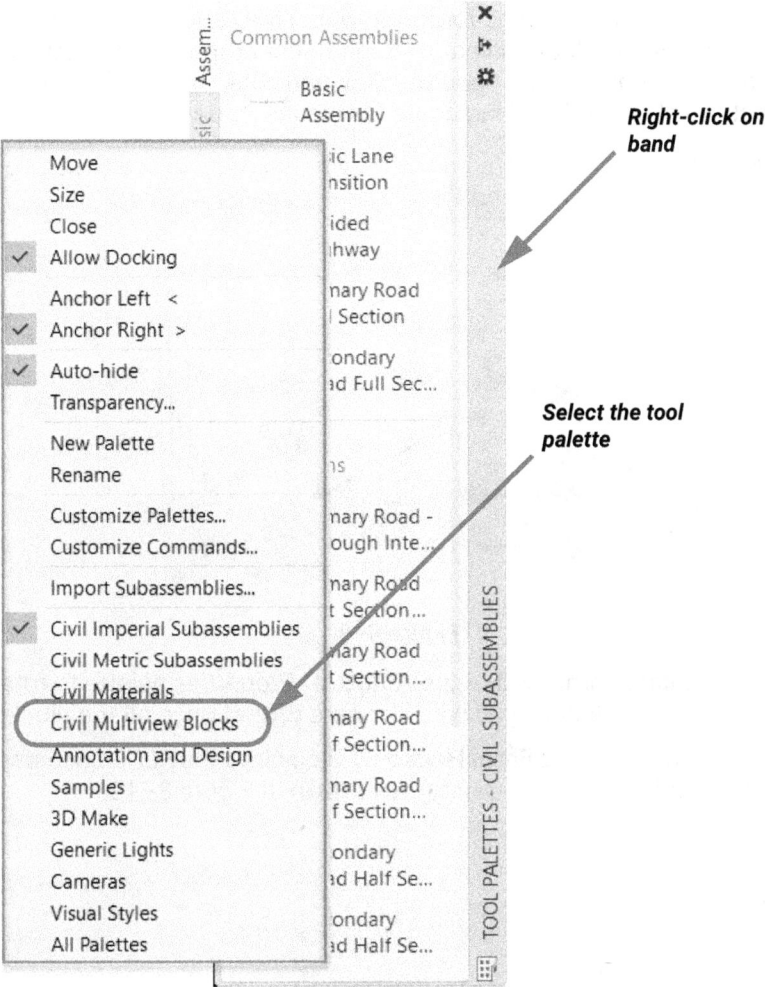

Figure 8–8

5. In the *Civil Multiview Blocks* tool palette, click on the *Building Footprints* tab and select **Colonial 01C**, as shown in Figure 8–9. (Note: It may take a short while for the block to be loaded into the drawing.) Move your cursor into the drawing area into the *BLK1-Lot 1* parcel. You will see a preview of the building footprint, which may appear to be oversized. Once you pick an insertion point, the block will adjust itself to the proper units (metric or imperial). Do not click and drag; instead you will need to "click and click" by releasing the mouse button after you select the block and clicking again for the insertion point.

Note: *If the block does not resize itself properly, you will need to scale it using the AutoCAD Properties palette by setting the X, Y, and Z scale to 0.3048.*

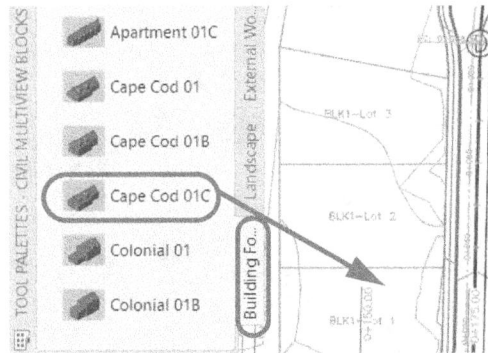

Figure 8–9

6. Use the AutoCAD **Rotate** command or the AutoCAD *Properties* palette to rotate the block. Do not worry about the elevation; you will take care of that once all the blocks are inserted.

7. Repeat the process to insert the **Farm House 01** block into the *BLK2-Lot 6* parcel and adjust its rotation angle (and scale, if necessary), as shown in Figure 8–10.

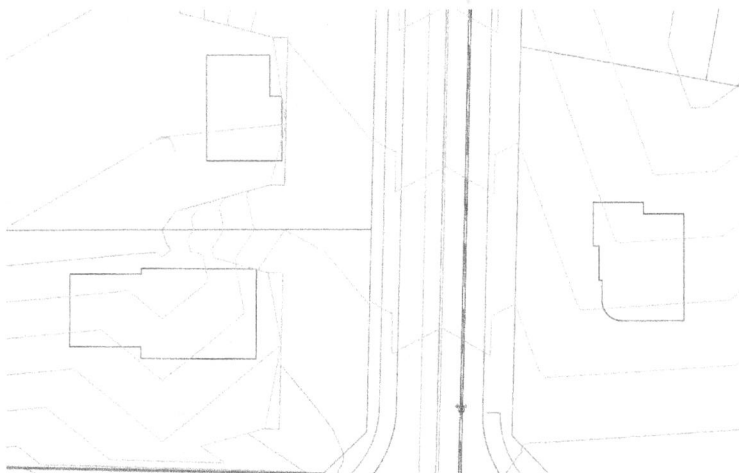

Figure 8–10

8. In the tool palette, select the *Landscaping* tab and scroll down to the *LandScape MV Blocks* section. Select the **Apple** tree and insert it into the *BLK1-Lot 1* parcel.

9. Select the block in the drawing and go to the AutoCAD *Properties* (either using the contextual ribbon, the right-click menu, or the <Ctrl>+<1> keyboard shortcut).

10. Adjust the *Scale X*, *Scale Y*, and *Scale Z* factors by setting them all to **5**, as shown in Figure 8–11. If you want the tree a bit taller, you can increase the *Scale Z* value.

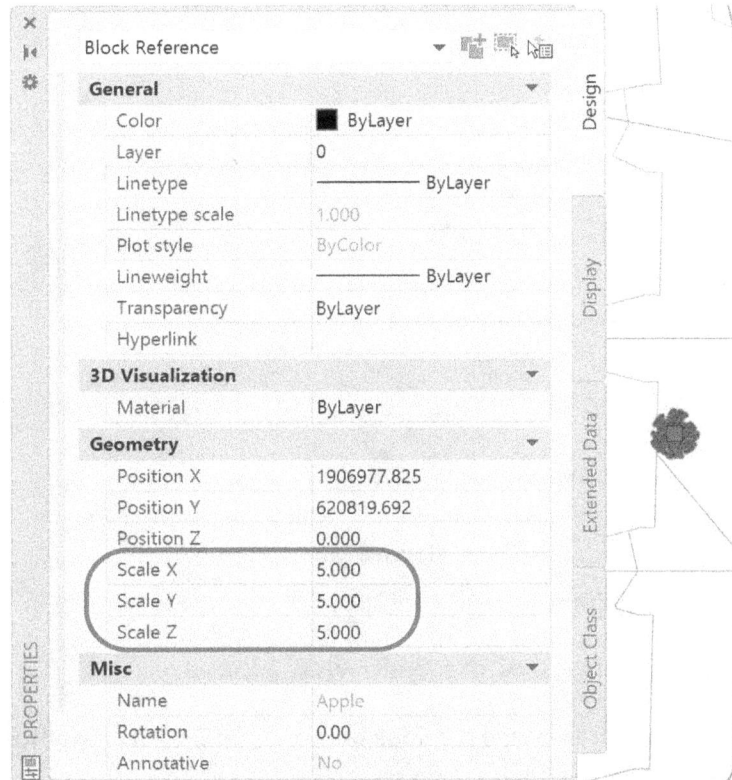

Figure 8–11

11. Insert some more trees around the two lots and adjust their scales. Experiment with providing a different *Scale Z*.

12. In the tool palette, select the *Highways* tab and pick the **Stop sign** at the top of the list. Select a point at the intersection of the two corridors for the insertion. When you set the rotation angle, ensure it is parallel to the curb.

13. Continue to populate the area with a variety of multi-view blocks, adjusting their scales and rotation angles as required. A finished example is shown in Figure 8–12.

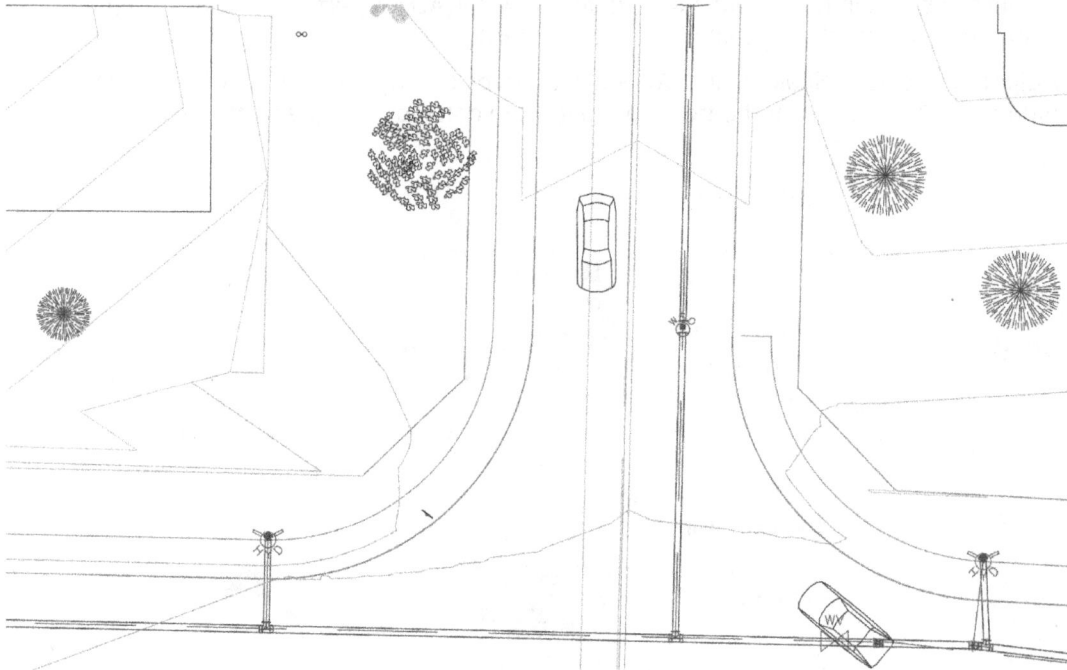

Figure 8–12

14. When finished, save the drawing.

Task 2: Adjust the elevations of the multi-view blocks.

1. Continue with the drawing from the previous task or open **QTO-A2.dwg** from the *C:\Civil 3D Beyond\Working\QTO-Viz* folder.

2. Select the **Final** surface in the drawing (select one of the contour lines).

3. In the *Final surface* contextual tab>*Surface Tools* panel, expand **Move to Surface** and select

   ◻ (Move Blocks to Surface), as shown in Figure 8–13.

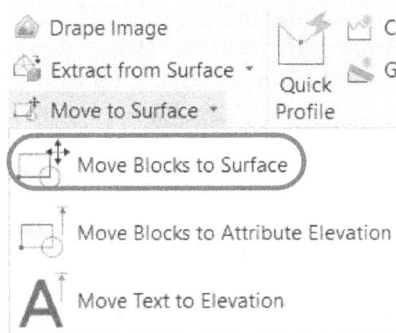

Figure 8–13

Note: Select the first item and hold <Shift> when selecting the last item, then hold <Ctrl> and deselect the blocks you do not want.

4. In the *Move Blocks to Surface* selecting window, select all multi-view blocks you had previously inserted. Do NOT select the following (they are the existing XREFs):

   * Base
   * Base-Proposed Engineering
   * Hotel
   * Office
   * School
   * Residential

5. Click **OK** when done. The multi-view blocks are adjusted so the Z value of the insertion point matches the elevation of the surface.

6. Select the preset view **Intersection-3D** to ensure the blocks have moved properly. (Later, you will learn how to change the visual style of this view.)

7. Select the preset view **Intersection-2D**.

8. Save the drawing.

End of practice

8.2 Pay Items

An important element in any design is the cost of the design. The cost of a design can be determined by putting a price on a specific unit of work. To do this in the Autodesk Civil 3D software, you assign a pay item to specific objects. Using the QTO Manager helps to automate this task, which can reduce errors and eliminate disputes with contractors.

There are three commonly used pay item properties:

- **Item number:** A unique number for each item in a plan.

- **Specification:** Determines how the work is measured and paid for, the material to use, and the method for incorporating the material.

- **Cost estimate:** Ensures that the design falls in the available project budget.

Pay Item File

Civil 3D ships with a default Pay Item file in a comma delimited text file **Payitems-BidItems.csv**. It can be copied into your organization's standards folder, opened up in MS Excel, and edited to suit your standards. It has the following columns:

- Name
- Item Description
- Units
- Bid Description
- Pay Item Type
- Year
- Date added/modified
- Division
- Comments

Assigning Pay Items

Pay items can be manually assigned to any of the following items once they have been created in the drawing file: AutoCAD lines, polylines, and blocks, and Autodesk Civil 3D entities. They can be assigned to individual items or linear objects, or within enclosed areas.

You can also assign pay items to Autodesk Civil 3D code set styles, pipe network parts lists, and pressure pipe network parts lists so that corridor objects and pipes/structures are automatically tagged with the correct pay items, as shown in Figure 8-14.

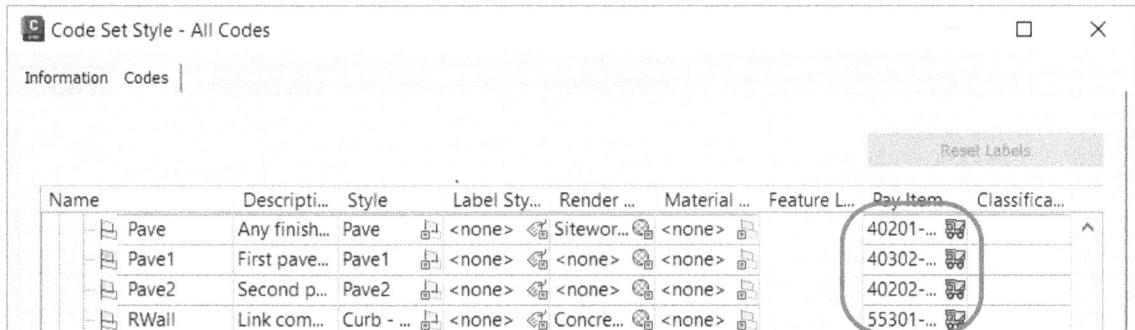

Figure 8-14

How To: Assign a Pay Item

1. In the *Analyze* tab>*QTO* panel, click 🚚 (QTO Manager).

2. Open the pay item file required for the project.

3. Assign a pay item to an object, such as:
   - Individual items, such as blocks
   - Linear objects, such as lines and plines
   - Areas

4. Run a report. The report can be limited to an alignment, and it is for this reason that you can associate a pipe-run to an alignment.

Practice 8b
Integrated Quantity Takeoff

Practice Objective

* Calculate the cost of design by assigning pay items to specific objects and then running a report.

Task 1: Assign pay item IDs.

A tool available in the Autodesk Civil 3D software enables you to automate the process of quantity takeoff. The traditional method involves a manual process of counting pay items (e.g., street lights) individually or performing linear measurements to obtain quantities of items (e.g., curbs and gutters).

1. Open **QTO-B1.dwg** from the *C:\Civil 3D Beyond\Working\ QTO-Viz* folder.

2. Select the preset view **Trees-2D**.

3. In the *Analyze* tab>*QTO* panel, click 🛒 (QTO Manager), as shown in Figure 8–15.

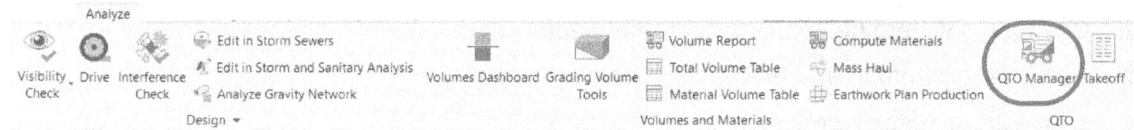

Figure 8–15

4. In the Panorama, expand 📂▾ and select **Open pay item file**, as shown in Figure 8–16.

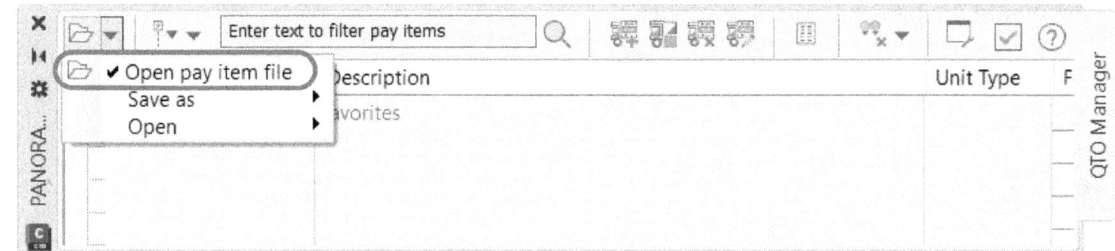

Figure 8–16

5. In the *Open Pay Item File* dialog box, do the following (as shown in Figure 8–17):

    • In the *Pay item file format* drop-down list, select **CSV (Comma delimited)**.

    • Next to the *Pay item file* field, click 📂. Browse to the *C:\Civil 3D Beyond\Ascent-Config* folder and select **ASC-Payitems-BidItems.csv**.

    • Click **OK** to accept the changes and close the dialog box.

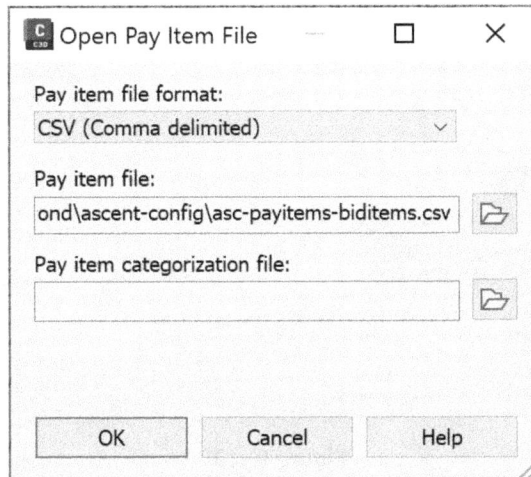

Figure 8–17

6. The *Pay Item ID* list will be populated with pay item numbers from the .CSV file. To display only the required pay items, type **shrubs** in the *Filter* field at the top and press <Enter>. Only the shrubs pay items will be listed.

7. Right-click on an ID number in the *Pay Item ID* column and select **Add to favorites list**, as shown in Figure 8–18, so you can find it more easily next time you need it. It will now be part of your *Favorites*.

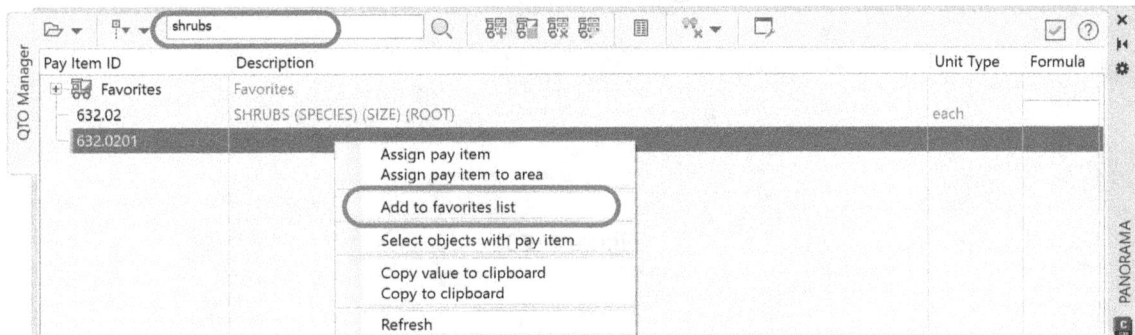

Figure 8–18

8. To assign a pay item ID to the object in the drawing, in Model Space, select a shrub, right-click, and select **Select Similar**, as shown in Figure 8–19.

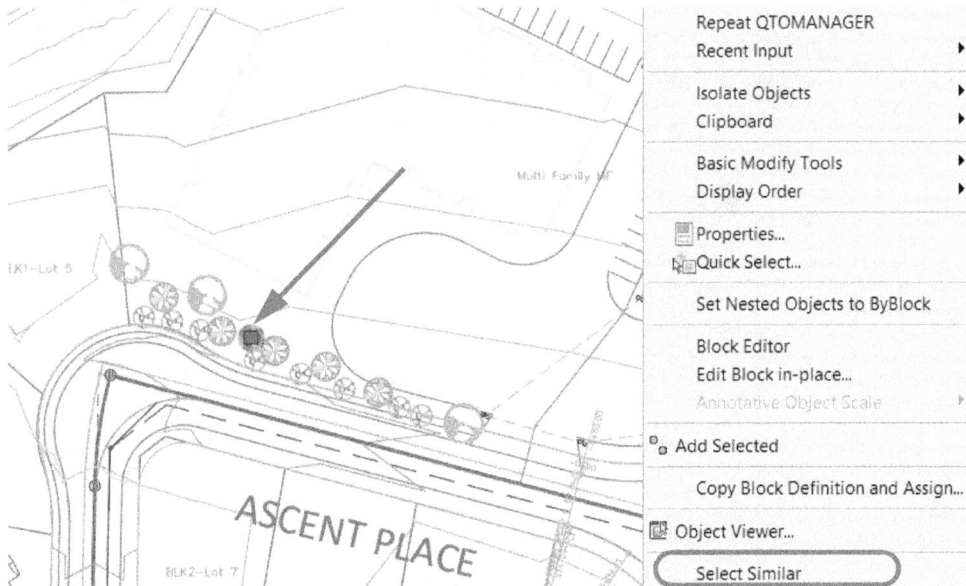

Figure 8–19

9. With all similar objects selected, select pay item **632.02** in the Panorama, right-click, and select **Assign pay item**, as shown in Figure 8–20. Press <Esc> to clear the current selection. At the Command Line, a message prompts you that pay items are assigned to objects.

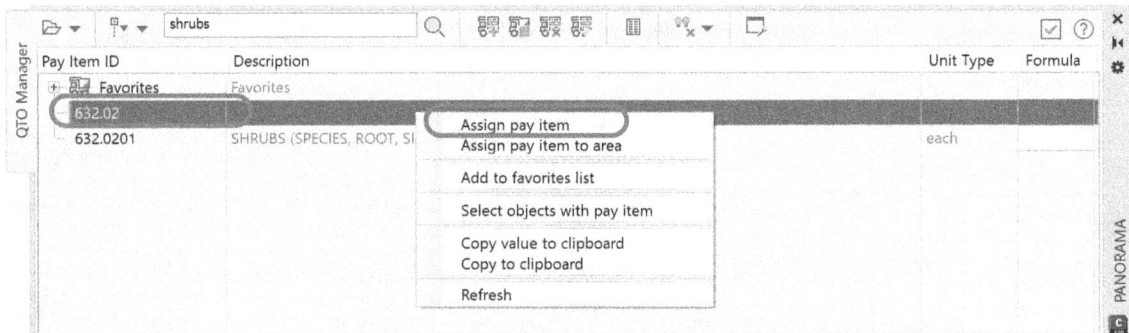

Figure 8–20

10. To apply pay items to street light objects, type **light** in the *Filter* field at the top of the Panorama and press <Enter>. Only pay items with the word *light* will be listed, as shown in Figure 8–21.

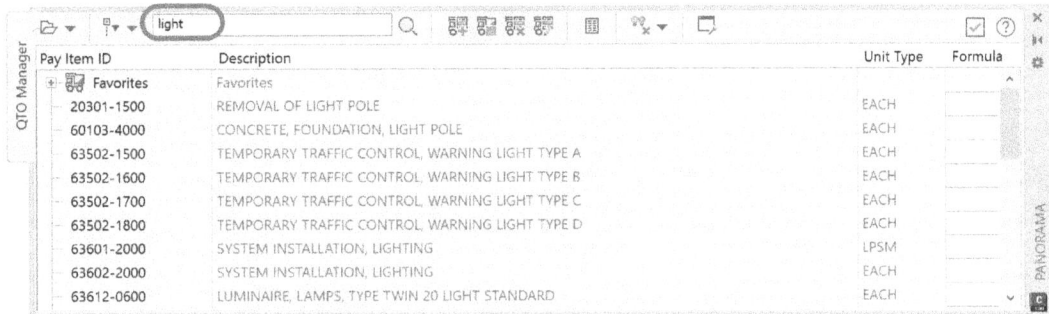

Figure 8–21

11. To assign a pay item ID to the object in the drawing, ensure that the previous selection set has been cleared by pressing <Esc>. In Model Space, select a street light (as shown in Figure 8–22), right-click, and select **Select Similar**.

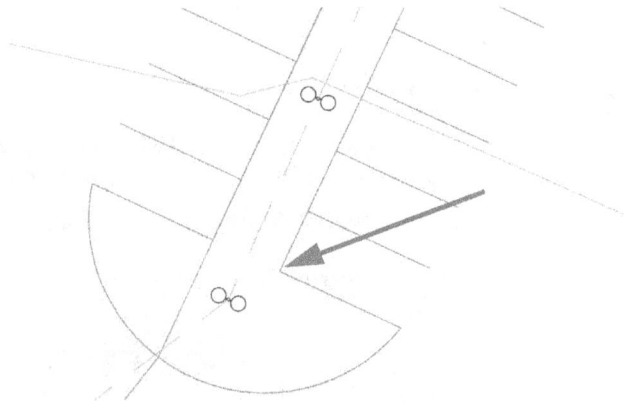

Figure 8–22

12. With all similar objects selected, select pay item **60103-4000 CONCRETE, FOUNDATION, LIGHT POLE** in the Panorama, as shown in Figure 8–23. Right-click and select **Assign pay item**. In the Command Line, a message prompts you that pay items have been assigned to objects. Press <Esc> to clear the current object selection.

Figure 8–23

13. As these objects are now linked to QTO pay items, using the AutoCAD **Copy** command will also copy the reference to the pay item list. Press <Esc> to clear the selection set. Launch the AutoCAD **Copy** command, select any of the street lights, and copy them to the far west end of the parking lot, as shown in Figure 8–24.

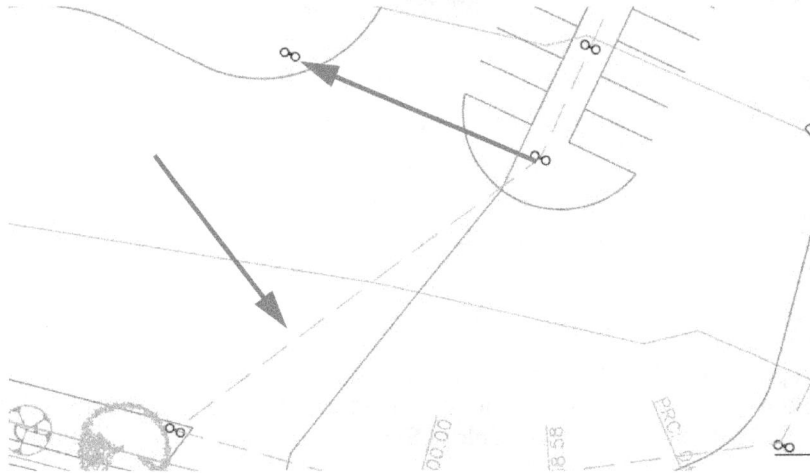

Figure 8–24

14. In the Panorama, search for **Conduit**, select **63610-0500 Conduit, 1 INCH, RIGID GALVANIZED STEEL**, and add it to your *Favorites* list, then assign it to the orange dashed pline, as shown above in Figure 8–24. Also assign **655.061 ELECTRICAL WIRE LIGHTING 12 AWG** to the same pline. (Search for **Wire**.) Add it to your *Favorites* list.

15. Search for **Sod** and select **62701-0000 SOD, SOLID**. Add it to your *Favorites* list, then either

    right-click on the item and select **Assign pay item to area** or click 🔲 (Assign pay item(s) to a closed area), as shown in Figure 8–25.

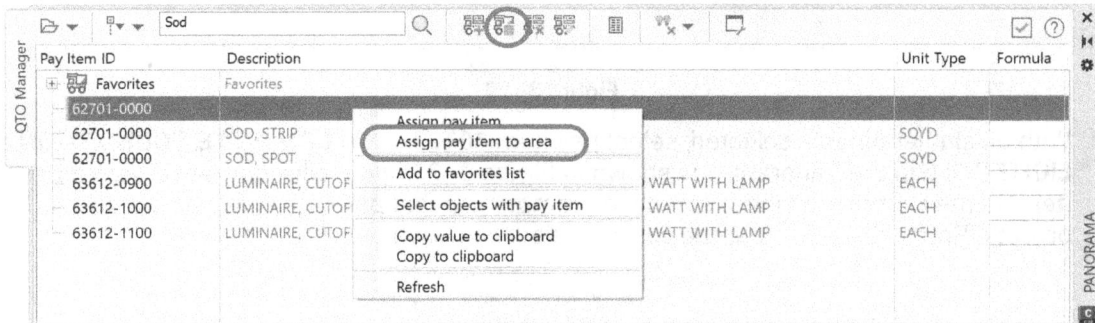

Figure 8–25

16. Type *O* for **[select Object]** and then select the two green plines, as shown in Figure 8–26. When you pick them, they turn black. This is because QTO adds a hatch pattern, by default solid, on the current layer. Press <Esc>.

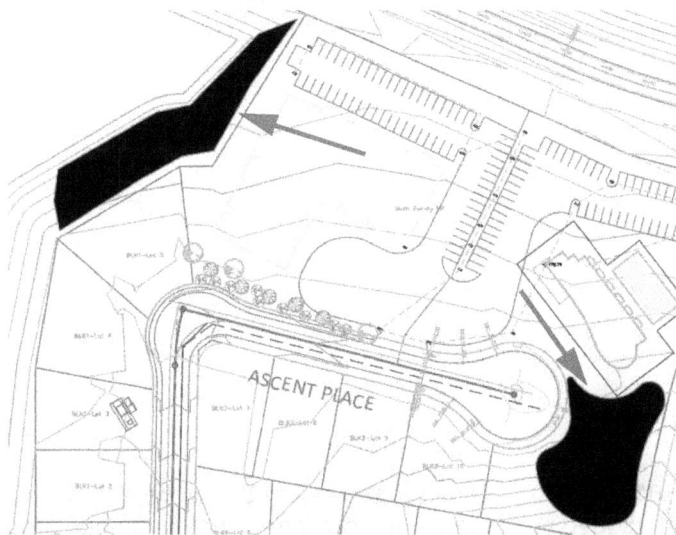

Figure 8–26

17. Select the two hatches created. In the *Hatch Editor* contextual ribbon, select the **GRASS** pattern and set the scale to **12.0**, as shown in Figure 8–27. Also, change the layer to **L-PLNT-TURF** and the color to **BYLAYER** (through the AutoCAD *Properties* palette).

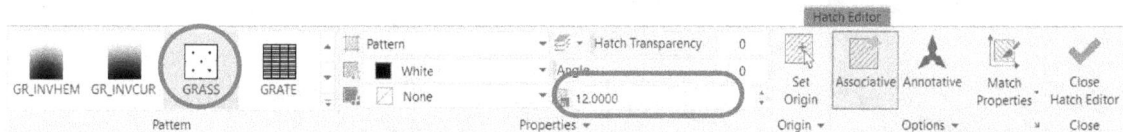

Figure 8–27

18. (Optional) Add another conduit line to the new (copied) light and assign the proper pay items. (That is why you added them to the *Favorites* list.) Add your choice of pay items to the remaining trees (two types).

19. Save the drawing.

Task 2: Compute quantity takeoff.

Once pay items have been assigned to Autodesk Civil 3D or AutoCAD objects in the model, you will be able to compute quantities and generate a report.

1. Continue working with the drawing from the previous task or open **QTO-B2.dwg** from the *C:\Civil 3D Beyond\Working\ QTO-Viz* folder.

2. View the objects that have been tagged with pay item IDs. In the *Analyze* tab>*QTO* panel, click 🚚 (QTO Manager).

3. In the Panorama, type **light** in the *Filter* field at the top and press <Enter>. Only the lighting pay items will be listed, as shown in Figure 8–28.

Pay Item ID	Description	Unit Type	Formula
⊞ 🚚 Favorites	Favorites		
20301-1500	REMOVAL OF LIGHT POLE	EACH	
60103-4000	CONCRETE, FOUNDATION, LIGHT POLE	EACH	
63502-1500	TEMPORARY TRAFFIC CONTROL, WARNING LIGHT TYPE A	EACH	
63502-1600	TEMPORARY TRAFFIC CONTROL, WARNING LIGHT TYPE B	EACH	
63502-1700	TEMPORARY TRAFFIC CONTROL, WARNING LIGHT TYPE C	EACH	
63502-1800	TEMPORARY TRAFFIC CONTROL, WARNING LIGHT TYPE D	EACH	
63601-2000	SYSTEM INSTALLATION, LIGHTING	LPSM	
63602-2000	SYSTEM INSTALLATION, LIGHTING	EACH	
63612-0600	LUMINAIRE, LAMPS, TYPE TWIN 20 LIGHT STANDARD	EACH	

Figure 8–28

4. Select pay item **60103-4000**, right-click, and select **Select objects with pay item**, as shown in Figure 8–29. All tagged pay items in the drawing with this unique pay item ID will be highlighted. Review your selection, then press <Esc> to clear the current object selection.

Figure 8–29

5. To generate a quantity takeoff report, in the *Analyze* tab>*QTO* panel, click ⬚ (Takeoff), as shown in Figure 8-30.

Figure 8-30

6. In the *Compute Quantity Takeoff* dialog box, do the following (as shown in Figure 8-31):

- In the *Report type* area, select **Summary**.
- In the *Report extents* area, select **Drawing** from the drop-down list.
- Accept all other default values.
- Click **Compute** to accept the changes and calculate the quantities.

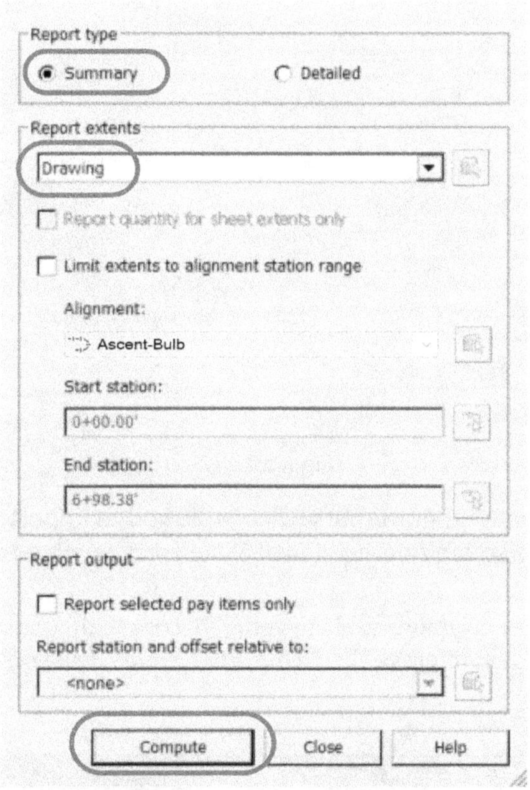

Figure 8-31

7. In the *Quantity Takeoff Report* dialog box, select **Summary (HTML).xsl** as the output type, as shown in Figure 8-32.

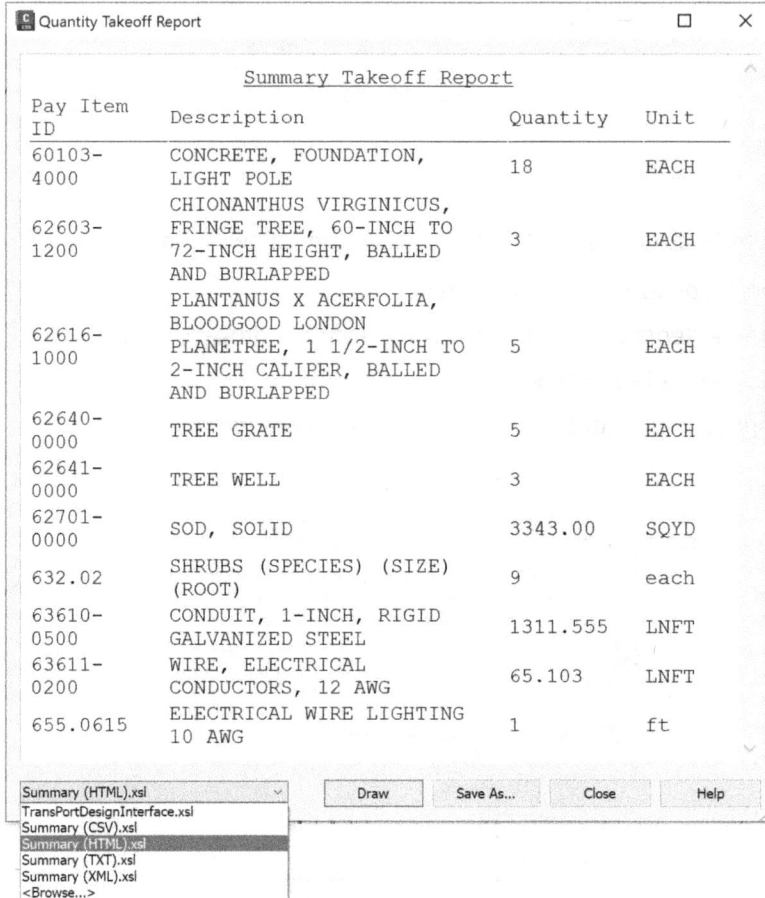

Quantity Takeoff Report

Summary Takeoff Report

Pay Item ID	Description	Quantity	Unit
60103-4000	CONCRETE, FOUNDATION, LIGHT POLE	18	EACH
62603-1200	CHIONANTHUS VIRGINICUS, FRINGE TREE, 60-INCH TO 72-INCH HEIGHT, BALLED AND BURLAPPED	3	EACH
62616-1000	PLANTANUS X ACERFOLIA, BLOODGOOD LONDON PLANETREE, 1 1/2-INCH TO 2-INCH CALIPER, BALLED AND BURLAPPED	5	EACH
62640-0000	TREE GRATE	5	EACH
62641-0000	TREE WELL	3	EACH
62701-0000	SOD, SOLID	3343.00	SQYD
632.02	SHRUBS (SPECIES) (SIZE) (ROOT)	9	each
63610-0500	CONDUIT, 1-INCH, RIGID GALVANIZED STEEL	1311.555	LNFT
63611-0200	WIRE, ELECTRICAL CONDUCTORS, 12 AWG	65.103	LNFT
655.0615	ELECTRICAL WIRE LIGHTING 10 AWG	1	ft

Summary (HTML).xsl
TransPortDesignInterface.xsl
Summary (CSV).xsl
Summary (HTML).xsl
Summary (TXT).xsl
Summary (XML).xsl
<Browse...>

Draw   Save As...   Close   Help

Figure 8-32

- A number of different output formats will enable you to import the results into other software. You can also tag Autodesk Civil 3D objects (such as corridor materials with pay item ID).

8. You can save this report or draw a table in your CAD drawing. Click **Close** to close the dialog box, and click **Close** again to close the *Compute Quantity Take off* dialog box.

9. Save the drawing.

End of practice

8.3 Visualization

For this phase, more data shortcuts are being used. The storm pipe network and corridors (and their surfaces) have been referenced, while the grading surfaces have been combined into a final grade/ground (FG) surface and referenced as well.

From the architect, both 2D and 3D drawings were received and have been incorporated. Some landscaping features (vegetation, sod, lighting, and wiring) have been added, as shown in Figure 8–33.

Figure 8–33

Some tricks have been used to easily move from 2D to 3D elements, such as using provided multi-view blocks from the *Tool Palettes* and switching 2D and 3D drawings through the *Xref Manager*, as shown in Figure 8–34.

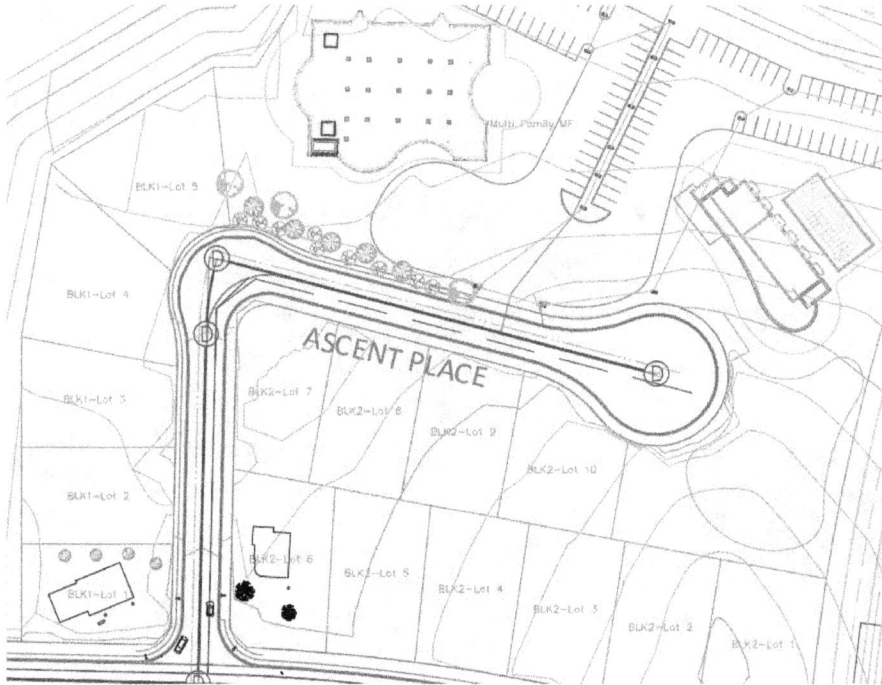

Figure 8–34

8.4 3D Navigation Tools

The AutoCAD software includes two additional tools to help you navigate 3D drawings: the ViewCube and the SteeringWheel (located in the *Navigation Bar*), as shown in Figure 8–35.

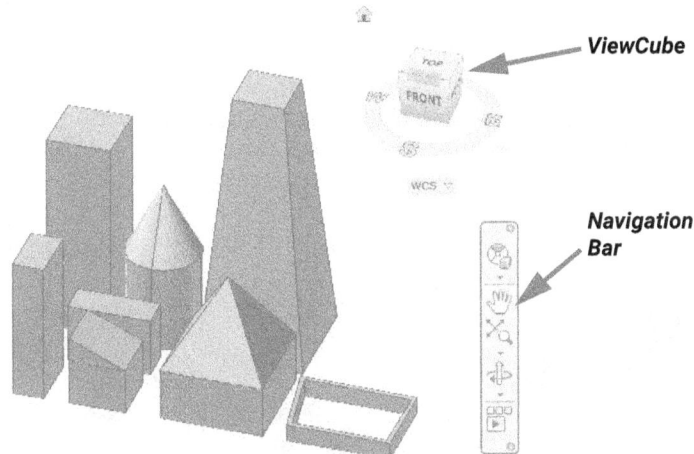

Figure 8–35

ViewCube

The ViewCube provides visual clues as to where you are in a 3D drawing and makes it easier to navigate to standard views, such as top, front, right, corner, and directional views. Move the cursor over one of the highlighted options and select it. You can also click and drag on the *ViewCube* to rotate the box, which rotates the model. The ViewCube is shown in Figure 8–36.

Figure 8–36

- 🏠 (Home) displays when you move the cursor over the ViewCube. Click it to return to the view defined as **Home**.To change the *Home* view, set the view you want, right-click on the *ViewCube* and select **Set Current View as Home**.

- To toggle the ViewCube on and off, expand ⬚ (User Interface) in the *View* tab>*User Interface* panel and select **ViewCube**.

💡 Hint: Parallel and Perspective Views

Traditional 2D drawings display objects in orthographic (parallel) views, where parallel edges on the object seem to be parallel in the drawing. Perspective views display as the eye sees and parallel edges seem to converge at a vanishing point on the horizon. You can view the model in either parallel or perspective projection, as shown in Figure 8–37.

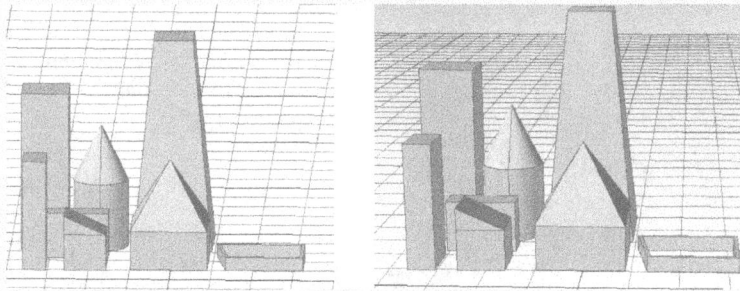

Figure 8–37

A parallel view helps you to evaluate the object's shape and size proportions without any distortion, while a perspective view gives you a better sense of space and depth, especially with large objects (such as buildings).

- You can draw, select, and modify objects while you are in a perspective view.
- You can switch between **Parallel**, **Perspective**, and **Perspective with Ortho Faces** when you right-click on the ViewCube or while you are in a **3D Orbit** command.
- You can also switch between **Parallel** and **Perspective** in the **View Controls** label list of the drawing window.
- Perspective mode is not available in the 2D wireframe visual style.

If you save a drawing as a version earlier than AutoCAD 2007, the perspective view is automatically toggled off.

ViewCube Settings

ViewCube settings control the display of the ViewCube, how it works when you are dragging or clicking, and several other settings. Right-click on the *ViewCube* and select **ViewCube Settings...** to open the *ViewCube Settings* dialog box, as shown in Figure 8–38.

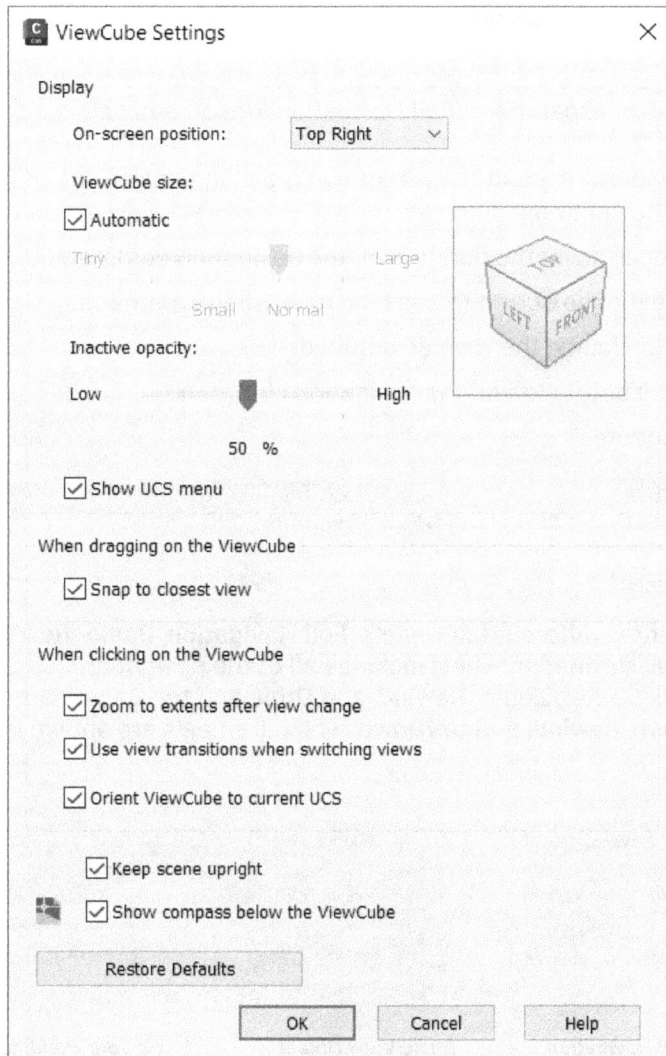

Figure 8–38

Steering Wheel

The SteeringWheel provides access to navigation commands such as **Zoom**, **Pan**, **Orbit**, and **Rewind**. The **Rewind** command navigates through all previous views of the model.

How To: Use the SteeringWheel

1. In the *Navigation Bar*, expand ⊚ (Full Navigation Wheel) and select a SteeringWheel.

   - Alternatively, you can expand ⊚ (Steering Wheel) in the *Navigation Bar* or type **navswheel** in the command line.

2. In the SteeringWheel, hover the cursor over the navigation command that you want to use.

3. Click and hold the mouse button to start the navigation command.

4. Move the cursor to change the view as required.

5. Release the mouse button to end the navigation command.

6. Close the SteeringWheel.

   Note: The SteeringWheel follows the cursor in the drawing window. Verify that the cursor is positioned correctly before launching a navigation command.

Full SteeringWheels

You can select from three different full wheels: **Full Navigation**, **Basic View Object**, and **Basic Tour Building**. The Full Navigation wheel includes all of the navigation tools; the Basic View Object wheel contains **Center**, **Zoom**, **Rewind**, and **Orbit**; and the Basic Tour Building wheel contains **Forward**, **Look**, **Rewind**, and **Up/Down**. The full wheels are shown in Figure 8–39.

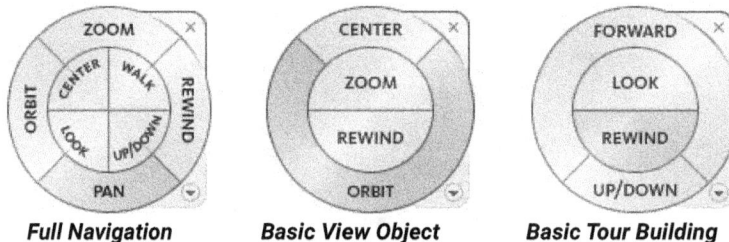

Full Navigation *Basic View Object* *Basic Tour Building*

Figure 8–39

To close the SteeringWheel, press <Esc> or <Enter> or click the **X** in the SteeringWheel.

Rewind Command

Use the **Rewind** command to navigate to previously displayed views of the model, as shown in Figure 8−40.

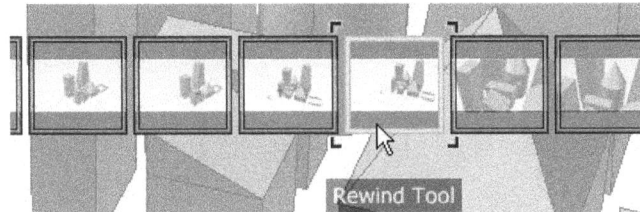

Figure 8−40

How To: Use the Rewind Command

1. Start the **SteeringWheel** command.
2. Hover the cursor over the **Rewind** option.
3. Click and hold the mouse button to start the **Rewind** command. A series of thumbnails displays.
4. Move the cursor over the thumbnails to navigate to the highlighted view. The model updates as you move over the thumbnails.
5. Release the mouse button to make the highlighted view active.

SteeringWheel Settings

The *SteeringWheels Settings* dialog box (shown in Figure 8–41) controls the appearance of the SteeringWheels. With a SteeringWheel active, right-click and select **SteeringWheels Settings...** to open the dialog box.

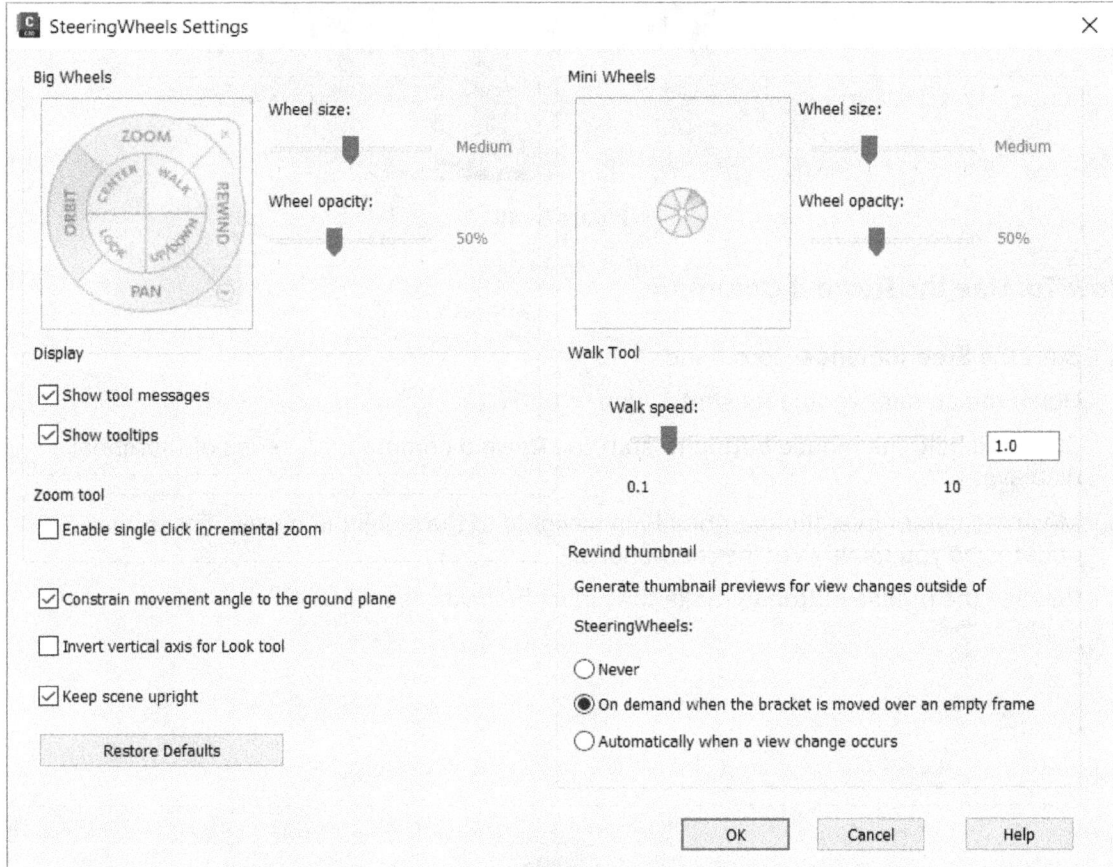

Figure 8–41

8.5 Managing Views in 3D

Named views capture your current vantage point of a drawing under specified names that can easily be restored in the drawing window.

Existing named views are available in the *View* tab>*Named Views* panel, or through the *Viewport Control* in the top left corner of your drawing area, as shown in Figure 8–42.

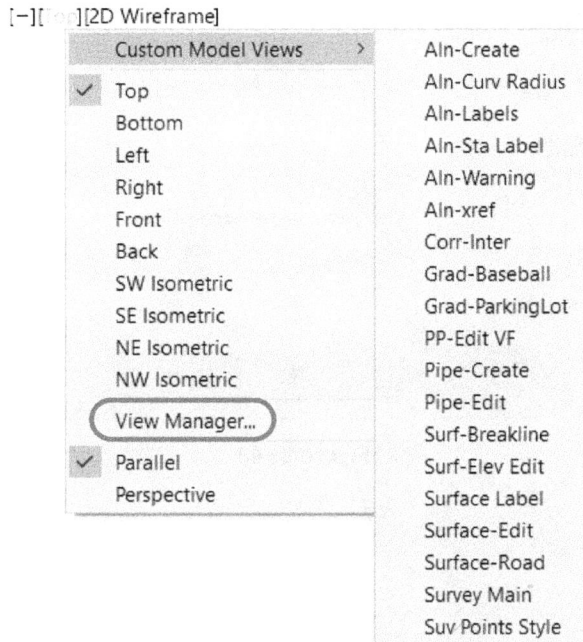

[−][ ][2D Wireframe]

Custom Model Views >	Aln-Create
✓ Top	Aln-Curv Radius
Bottom	Aln-Labels
Left	Aln-Sta Label
Right	Aln-Warning
Front	Aln-xref
Back	Corr-Inter
SW Isometric	Grad-Baseball
SE Isometric	Grad-ParkingLot
NE Isometric	PP-Edit VF
NW Isometric	Pipe-Create
View Manager...	Pipe-Edit
✓ Parallel	Surf-Breakline
Perspective	Surf-Elev Edit
	Surface Label
	Surface-Edit
	Surface-Road
	Survey Main
	Suv Points Style

Figure 8–42

- Named views can be used in Model Space or in an active layout viewport.

- The *View Manager* dialog box sets, creates, deletes, modifies, and renames named views. It also manages model views, layout views, preset views, and camera views. You can select a named view and click **Set Current** to make it the current view.

- To open the *View Manager* dialog box, click ⬚ (View Manager) in the *Visualize* tab>*Named Views* panel or through the *Viewport Control* (as shown above in Figure 8–42).

How To: Create a New Named View

1. Set up the view as you want it to be saved.

2. In the *Home* tab>*View* panel, expand the *3D Navigation Control* and select **View Manager...**.

3. In the *View Manager* dialog box, click **New**, as shown in Figure 8–43.

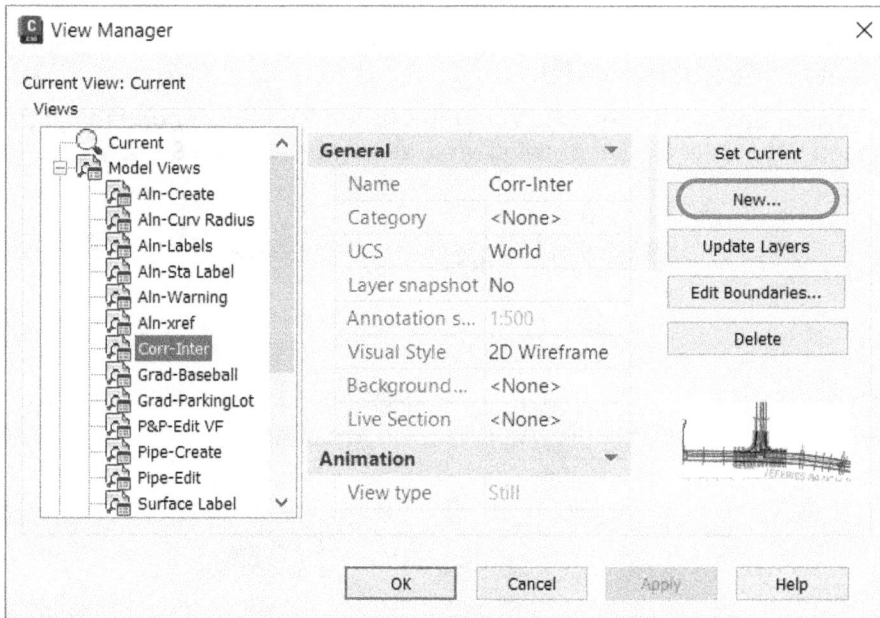

Figure 8–43

4. Fill out the *New View/Shot Properties* dialog box, as shown in Figure 8–44, including the *View name*, *Boundary*, *Settings*, and *Background* areas.

*Note: The **View category** option refers to views that are used in sheet sets, such as plans and elevations. The categories are created in the Sheet Set Manager.*

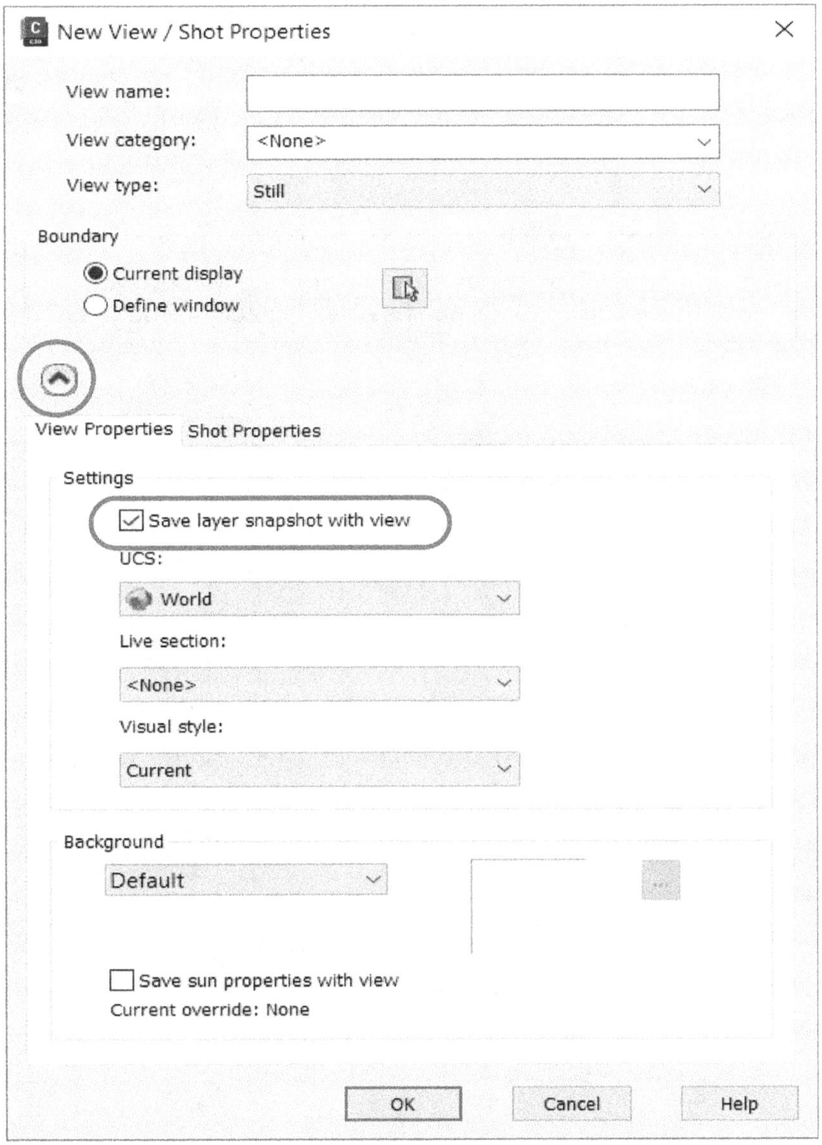

Figure 8–44

5. Click **OK**.

New View Options

Save layer snapshot with view	Enables the view to retain the layer states that are set when the view is saved. Use this with caution because it may change your layers whenever you restore a view.
UCS	Sets a UCS to be saved with the view.
Live section	Enables you to activate a section plane, if one is available in the drawing. Once a live section is on, it stays on until you deactivate it through the **Section Plane** shortcut menu option.
Visual style	Sets a visual style to be saved with the view.

Adding Backgrounds to Views

To add more realism or to highlight your design in the drawing window, you can add backgrounds to views. These backgrounds can be a solid, gradient, image, or Sun & Sky, as shown in Figure 8–45.

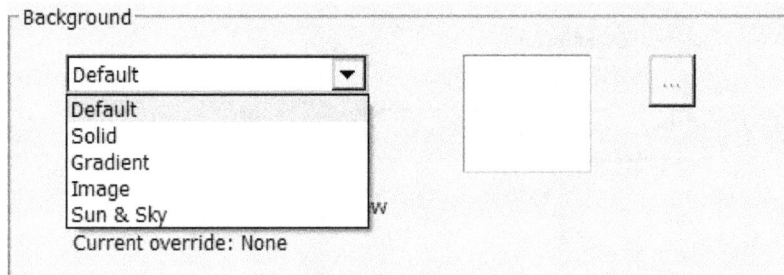

Figure 8–45

* Solid backgrounds can be any single color, while gradient backgrounds can be a mix of two or three colors.

- Images can be any of the standard image files that the Civil 3D software can view. In the *Background* dialog box (shown in Figure 8–46), click **Browse** to select an image and then click **Adjust Image...** to modify the image as required.

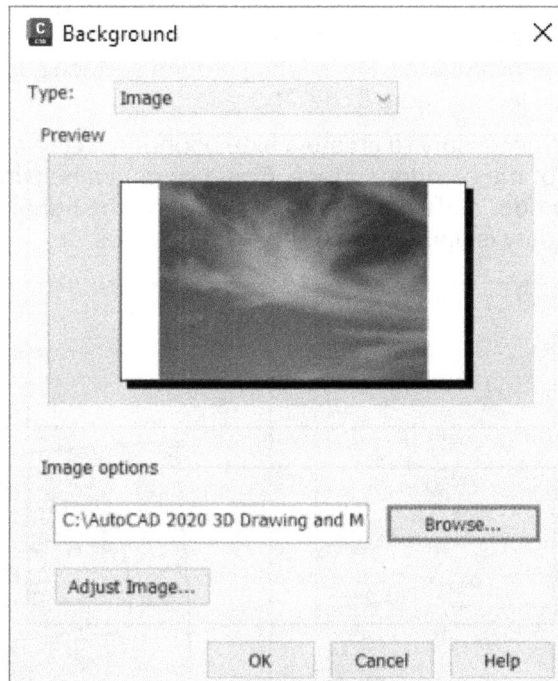

Figure 8–46

- The Sun & Sky setting mimics the effects of sunlight in your drawing. The position of the sun is determined by the geographic location and the time settings. To remove a background, select a view in which a background has not been set. Preset views do not remove a background.

8.6 Corridor Visualization

Visualizing corridors in a 3D view can be very helpful to ensure that the true design intent has been followed. Displaying the corridor along with the existing ground surface around it also helps to ensure that there are good sight distances as you drive down the corridor. Unfortunately, if there is a large cut area, the existing ground surface might obstruct the corridor from view, as shown on the left in Figure 8–47.

In these cases, it might be necessary to create a hide boundary in the existing ground surface using the outer boundary of the corridor surface. Doing so cuts a hole in the existing ground surface only where the corridor surface resides, as shown on the right in Figure 8–47. In addition, the interior boundary is updated if the corridor changes.

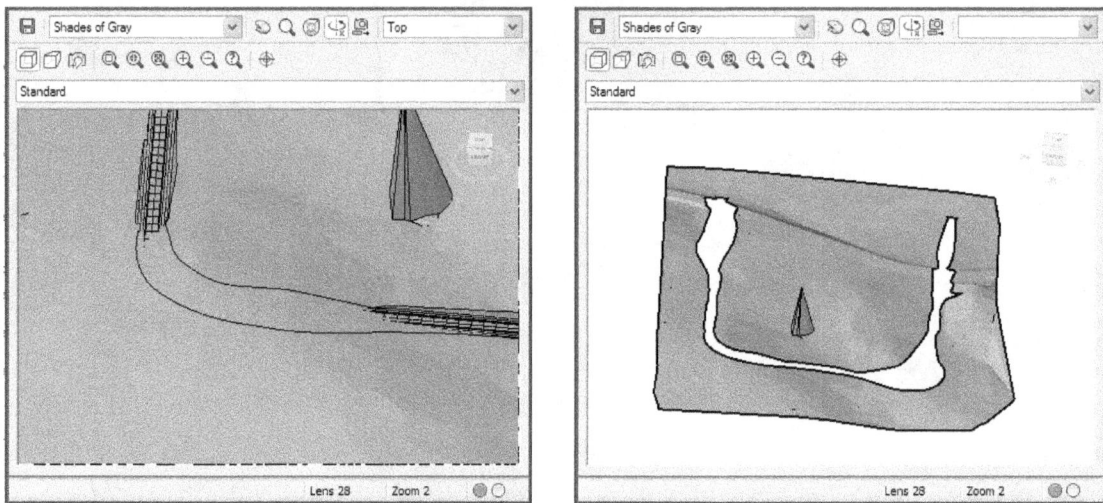

Figure 8–47

To make this work correctly, you need to copy the existing ground surface before adding the corridor surface as a hide boundary. This is because the corridor daylight lines reference the existing ground. If a hide boundary is then created from a surface that is referencing the surface into which it is being placed, a circular reference is created. To avoid this, create a new surface, paste the existing ground surface into it, and then create the hide boundary for the existing ground from the corridor surface. This ensures that the boundary is updated as the corridor changes without creating a circular reference.

Once the circular reference issue has been corrected, you can use ⚫ (Drive) in the *Alignment*

tab>*Analyze* panel. You can then click ▷❙❙ (play/pause) in the *Drive* contextual tab to preview the finished design in relation to the existing ground surface as you drive down the corridor, as shown in Figure 8–48. While in the **Drive** command, you can change the drive path to another linear object if you have a network of road alignments, such as a subdivision, that you want to simulate driving through.

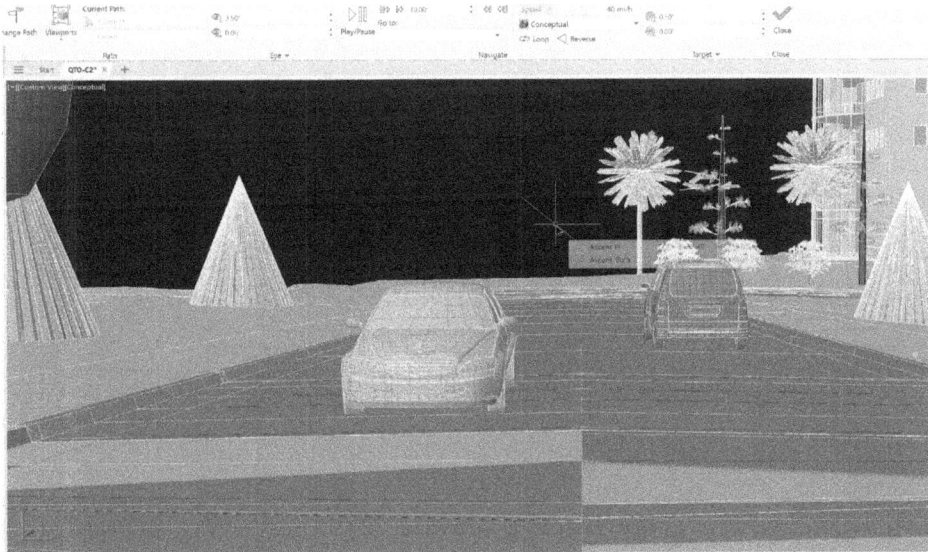

Figure 8–48

Line of Sight Analysis

The sight distances along a roadway can be calculated using the 🔍 (Sight Distance) command found in the *Corridor* contextual tab>*Analysis* panel. This enables you to ensure that the design meets the minimum sight distances at specified intervals along a corridor. You can set the minimum sight distance.

How To: Check Sight Distance Along a Roadway

1. In the *Corridor* contextual tab>*Analyze* panel, click ⊕ (Sight Distance).

2. In the *Sight Distance Check* wizard, on the *General* page, select the *Alignment* and *Profile* to analyze. Set the *From station*, *To station*, *Check interval*, and *Select surface to check against* fields, as shown in Figure 8–49. Click **Next>**.

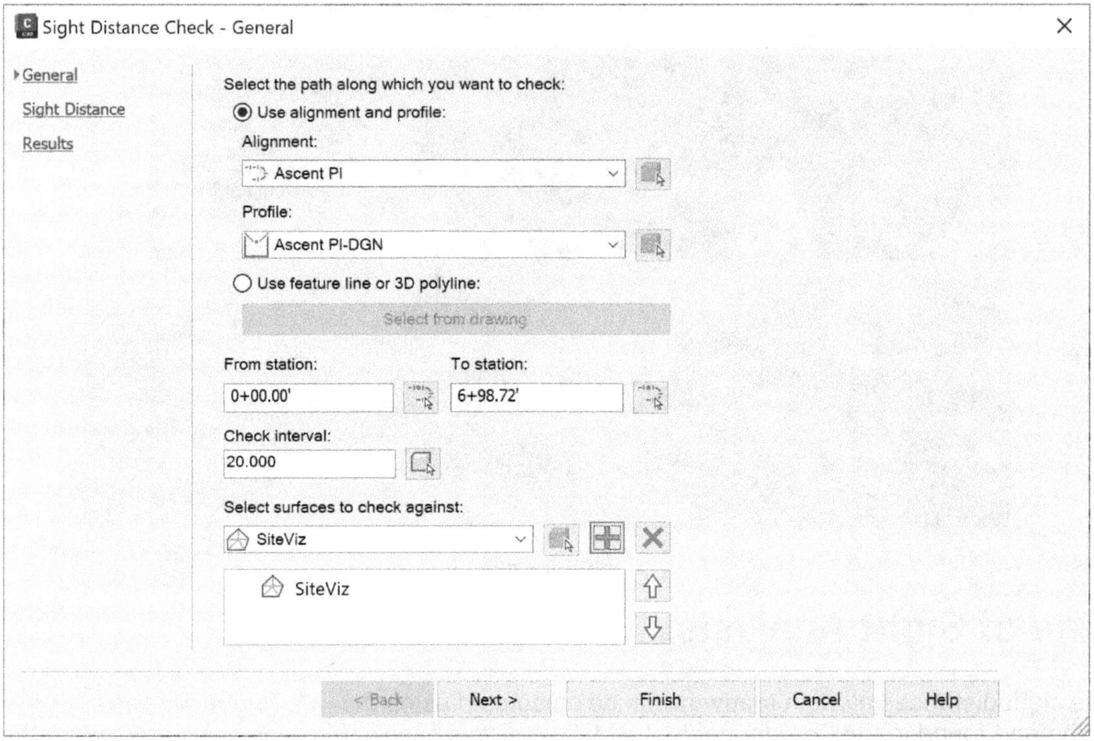

Figure 8–49

3. On the *Sight Distance* page, set the *Minimum sight distance, Eye height, Eye Offset, Target height,* and *Target offset,* as shown in Figure 8−50. Click **Next>**.

Figure 8−50

4. On the *Results* page, select the components to display in the model. If you want to follow the National CAD Standards Layers, you can set them as shown in Figure 8–51. These layers are not included in the Autodesk Civil 3D templates, so you will have to create them.

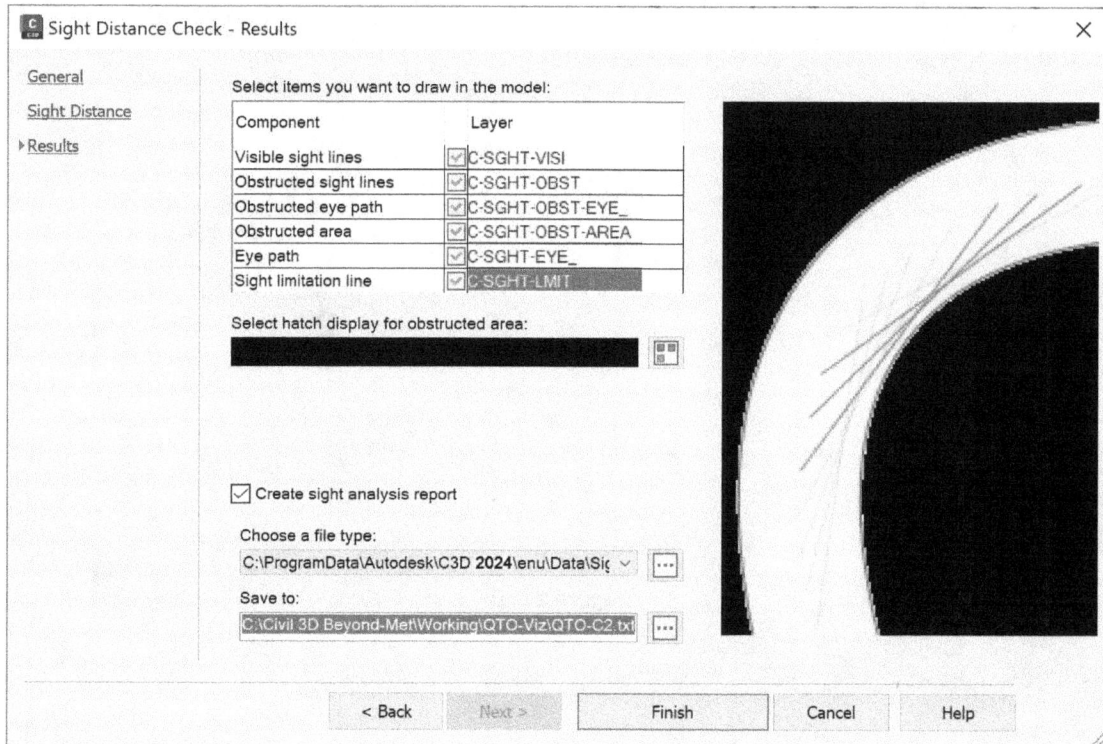

Figure 8–51

5. Set the *Select hatch display for obstructed area* pattern and select the file format and save location for the report.

6. Click **Finish**.

Practice 8c
Visualize Corridors

Practice Objective

* Display the corridor in 3D along with the existing ground surface to visualize what it is like to drive on the road.

Task 1: Analyze the site visually using the Drive command.

In this task, you will create a copy of the corridor surface to avoid possible circular references when you use the corridor surface as a hide boundary inside the existing site surface.

1. Open **QTO-C1.dwg** from the *C:\Civil 3D Beyond\Working\QTO-Viz* folder. Do not continue from the last drawing.

2. In the *Home* tab>*Create Ground Data* panel, click ✍ (Create Surface). In the *Create Surface* dialog box, do the following:

    * Type **SiteViz** for the name.
    * For the description, type **Existing & Road Surface for visualization purposes.**
    * Select **ASC-Contours 2' and 10' (Design)** for the style.
    * Select **Sitework.Planting.Grass.Thick** for the render material.
    * Click **OK**.

3. In *TOOLSPACE>Prospector* tab, expand the definition of the new **SiteViz** surface. Right-click on **Edits** and select **Paste Surface**. Select **Existing-Site** and click **OK**.

4. Right-click on **Boundaries** and select **Add**.

5. In the *Add Boundaries* dialog box, name it **Ascent Pl** and select **Hide** in the list of boundary types. Verify that **Non-destructive breakline** is selected and click **OK**, as shown in Figure 8–52.

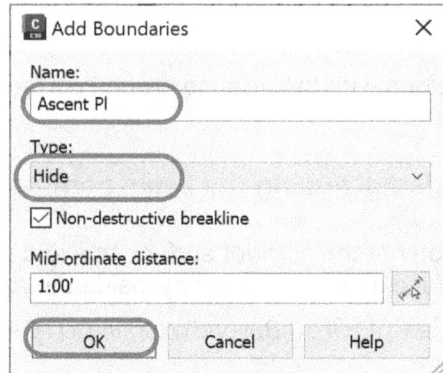

Figure 8–52

6. Type **S** for surface (as shown in Figure 8–53), select the **Ascent Pl Top** surface, and press <Enter>.

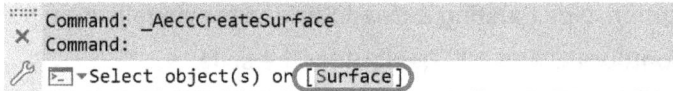

Figure 8–53

7. In the *Modify* tab, select **Alignments**. In the *Alignments* contextual tab>*Analyze* panel, click

    (Drive). When prompted to select an alignment, press <Enter> to select **Ascent Pl** from the alignment list and **Ascent Pl-DGN** from the profile list, as shown in Figure 8–54.

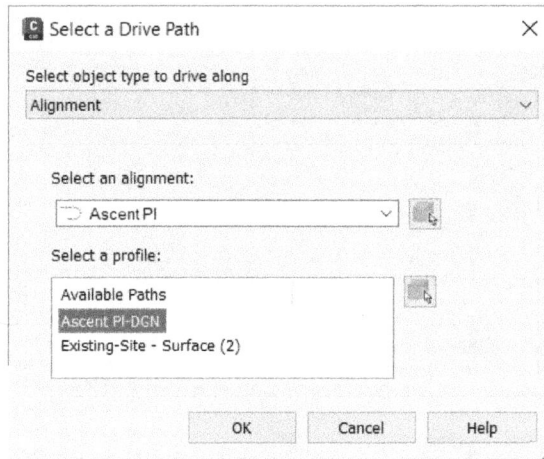

Figure 8–54

8. Click **OK**.

9. In the *Drive* contextual tab, click ▷❚❚ (Play/Pause).

10. When you have arrived at the end, in the *Navigate* panel, use the *Go to:* drop-down list and select station **3+34.98**.

    Note: If the Navigation Bar is not visible on the screen, go to the View tab>Viewport Tools panel to display it.

11. Click and drag on the ViewCube to orbit around the drawing.

12. From the *Navigation Bar*, invoke the **Full Navigation Wheel**.

13. Experiment with the **Walk, Look, Orbit, Up/Down,** and **Rewind** buttons.

14. When you have an interesting vantage point you want to save, close the *Navigation Wheel* by clicking the **X** in the upper right corner.

15. Go to *View Manager* and click **New...** to save this view. Give it a meaningful name.

16. Select the blue *Drive* contextual tab and click ✔ (Close) to close it.

Task 2: Analyze the sight distance.

In this task, you will use the **Sight Distance** command to ensure that the design meets the minimum required sight distances.

1. Continue working in the same file from the last task, or open **QTO-C2.dwg** from the *C:\Civil 3D Beyond\Working\QTO-Viz* folder.

2. In the *Modify* tab>*Design* panel, click ▨ (Corridor).

3. In the *Corridor* contextual tab>*Analyze* panel, click 👁 (Sight Distance).

4. In the *Sight Distance Check* wizard, on the *General* page, do the following (as shown in Figure 8–55):

- Select **Use alignment and profile**.
- For *Alignment*, select **Ascent PI**.
- For *Profile*, select **Ascent PI-DGN**.
- In the *To station* field, type **550**.
- In the *Select surfaces to check against* field, select **SiteViz** and the **+** icon.
- Click **Next>**.

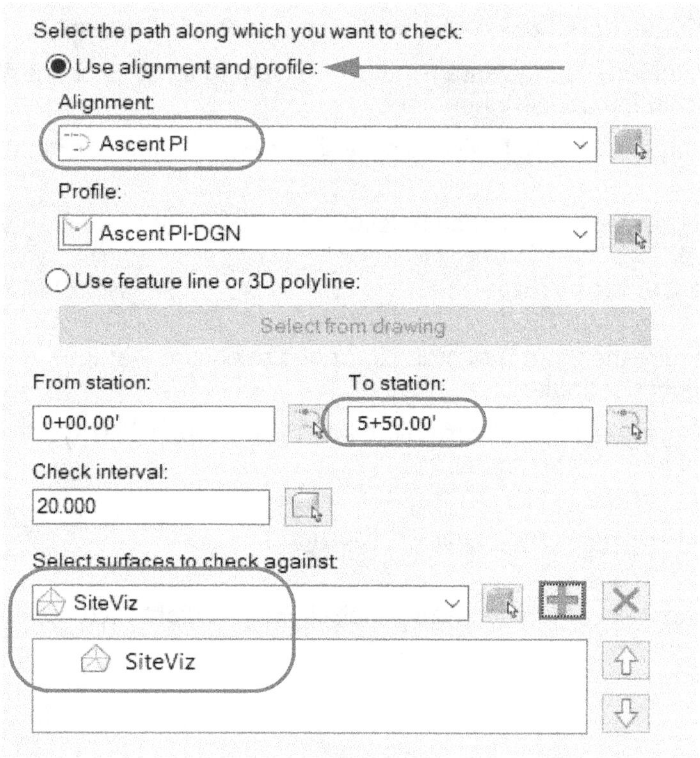

Figure 8–55

5. On the *Sight Distance* page, do the following (as shown in Figure 8–56):

   - In the *Minimum sight distance* field, type **100**.
   - If need be, set the other values as shown.
   - Click **Next>**.

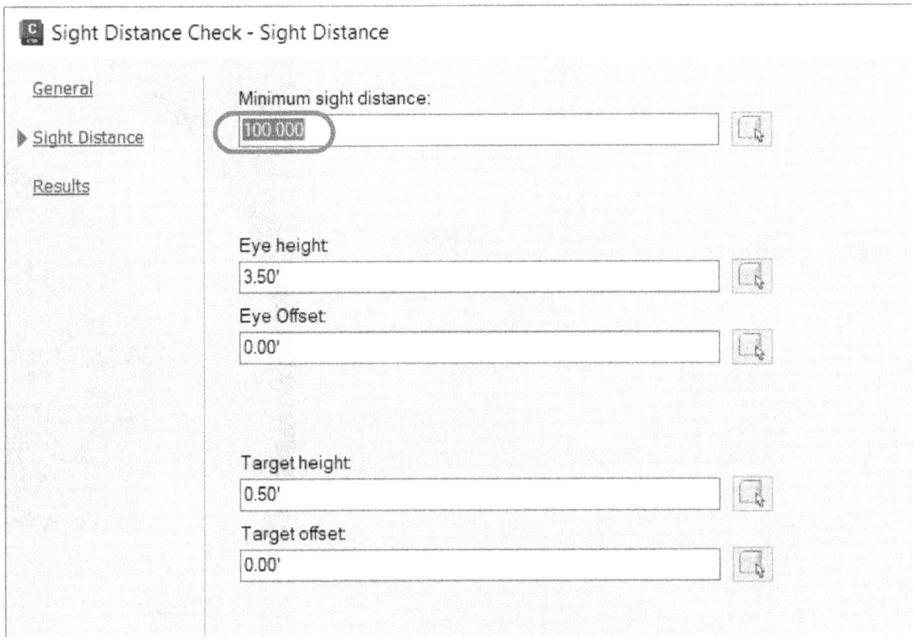

Figure 8–56

6. On the *Results* page, leave all the layers set to layer 0.

7. If you want to follow the National CAD Standards Layers, you can set them as shown in Figure 8–57. These layers are not included in the Autodesk Civil 3D templates, so you will have to create them.

Component		Layer
Visible sight lines	☑	C-SGHT-VISI
Obstructed sight lines	☑	C-SGHT-OBST
Obstructed eye path	☑	C-SGHT-OBST-EYE_
Obstructed area	☑	C-SGHT-OBST-AREA
Eye path	☑	C-SGHT-EYE_
Sight limitation line	☑	C-SGHT-LMIT

Figure 8–57

8. On the *Results* page, note how the image on the right of the wizard updates as you hover over each component, as shown in Figure 8–58.

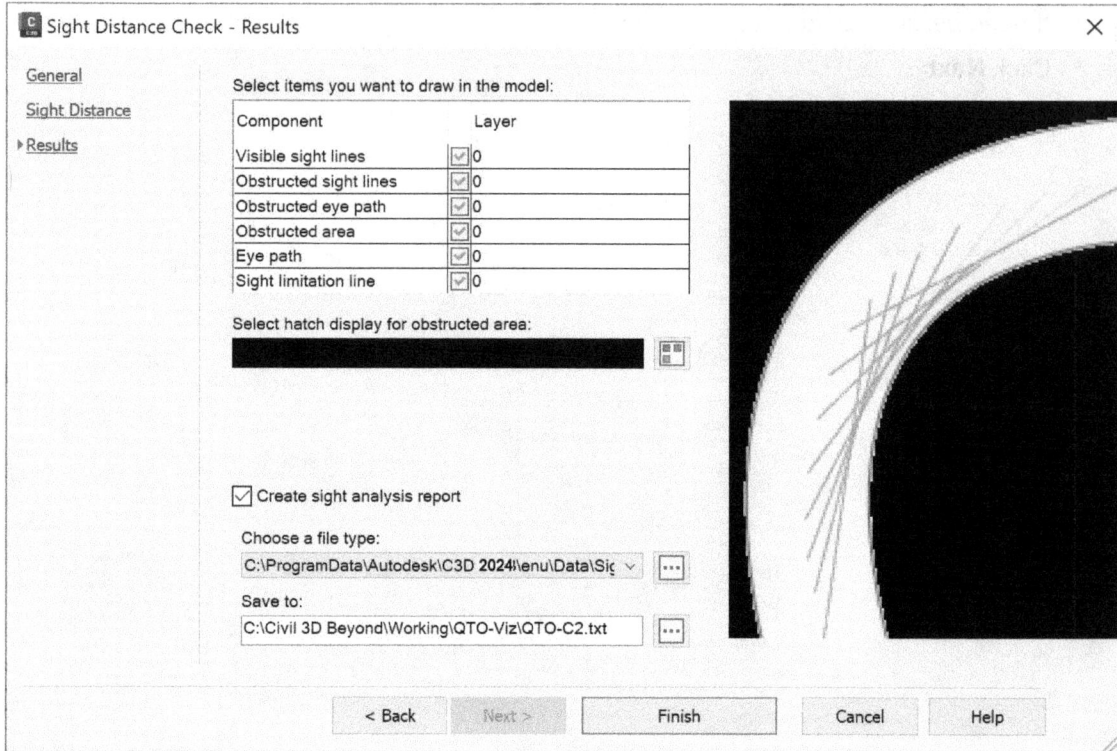

Figure 8–58

9. Click **Finish**.

10. In the model, note that the obstruction lines go right to the South-Eastern property line, as shown in Figure 8−59.

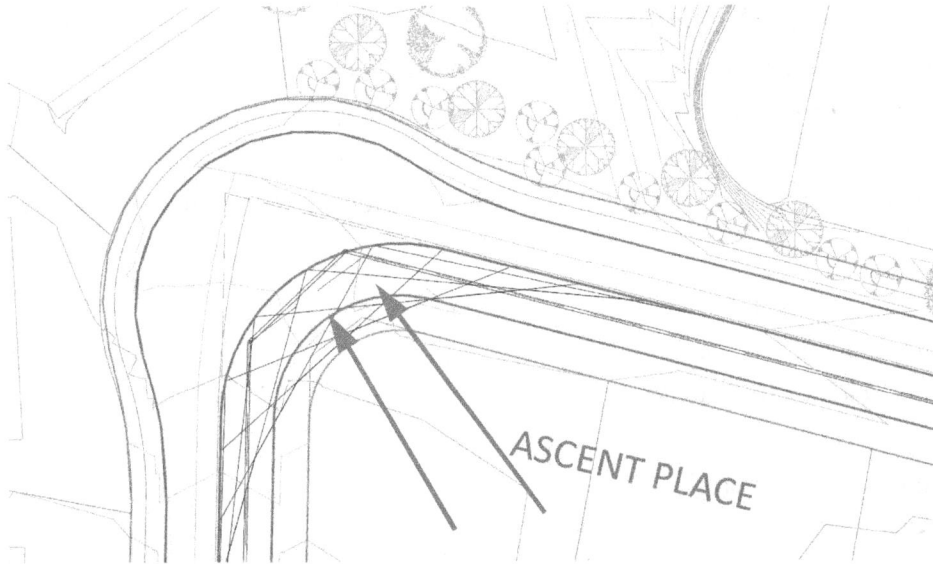

Figure 8−59

11. Save and close the drawing.

End of practice

Chapter Review Questions

1. What does the *View Manager* dialog box do?

    a. Creates a Model Space viewport for viewing sections.

    b. Captures the current vantage point of a drawing under a specified name.

    c. Creates a Paper Space viewport for viewing sections.

    d. Enables you to review and edit sections interactively using the appropriate panels.

2. Where do you assign pay items?

    a. In the Grading Volume Tools.

    b. In the Volumes Dashboard.

    c. In the QTO Manager.

    d. In the Volume Reports.

3. What is the most efficient way to assign elevations to multi-view blocks?

    a. You switch to a side view and move the blocks up.

    b. You find the elevation of the surface and change the block's Z value in the *Properties* palette.

    c. You use the **Move Blocks to Surface** routine.

    d. Multi-view blocks are automatically inserted at the proper elevation.

Command Summary

Button	Command	Location
	Full Navigation Wheel	• Navigation Sidebar • Command Prompt: Navswheel
	Move Blocks to Surface	• **Ribbon:** *Surface Textual* tab>*Surface Tools* panel • **Command:** AeccMoveBlocksToSurface:
	QTO Manager	• **Ribbon:** *Analyze* tab>*QTO* panel • **Command Prompt:** QTOManager
	Takeoff	• **Ribbon:** *Analyze* tab>*QTO* panel • **Command Prompt:** Takeoff
	Play/Pause Drive	• **Contextual Ribbon:** *Drive* tab> Navigate panel
	Sight Distance	• **Contextual Ribbon:** *Alignment* tab>*Analyze* panel • **Contextual Ribbon:** *Corridor* tab>*Analyze* panel • **Contextual Ribbon:** *Profile* tab>*Analyze* panel • **Command Prompt:** SightDistanceCheck
	ViewCube	• Upper right corner of drawing area.
	View Manager	• **Ribbon:** *View* tab>*Named Views* • View Control bar • **Command Prompt:** View

Index

www.ingramcontent.com/pod-product-compliance
Lightning Source LLC
Chambersburg PA
CBHW080133220326
41598CB00032B/5047